Writing Against Hitler

George L. Mosse Series in the History of European Culture, Sexuality, and Ideas

WRITING AGAINST HITLER

*Hermann Budzislawski and the Making of
Twentieth-Century Socialism*

Daniel Siemens

Translated by Ben Fowkes

THE UNIVERSITY OF WISCONSIN PRESS

Publication of this book has been made possible, in part, through support from the George L. Mosse Program in History at the University of Wisconsin–Madison and the Hebrew University of Jerusalem.

GEORGE L.
MOSSE
PROGRAM IN HISTORY

The University of Wisconsin Press
728 State Street, Suite 443
Madison, Wisconsin 53706
uwpress.wisc.edu

Originally published in German as *Hinter der "Weltbühne": Hermann Budzislawski und das 20. Jahrhundert*, copyright © 2022 Aufbau Verlage GmbH & Co. KG, Berlin
Translation copyright © 2025 by the Board of Regents of the University of Wisconsin System

Printed in the United States of America
This book may be available in a digital edition.

Library of Congress Cataloging-in-Publication Data

Names: Siemens, Daniel, author. | Fowkes, Ben, translator.
Title: Writing against Hitler : Hermann Budzislawski and the making
of twentieth-century socialism / Daniel Siemens ; translated by Ben Fowkes.
Other titles: Hinter der Weltbühne. English | George L. Mosse series in the history
of European culture, sexuality, and ideas.
Description: Madison, Wisconsin : The University of Wisconsin Press, 2025. |
Series: George L. Mosse series in the history of European culture, sexuality, and ideas |
Originally published in German as Hinter der Weltbühne: Hermann Budzislawski
und das 20 Jahrhudert, ©2022 Aufbau Verlage GmgH & Co. KG, Berlin. |
Includes bibliographical references and index.
Identifiers: LCCN 2024021697 | ISBN 9780299351304 (hardback)
Subjects: LCSH: Budzislawski, Hermann, 1901–1978. | Journalists—Germany—
Biography. | German periodicals—History—20th century.
Classification: LCC PN5213.B83 S5413 2025 | DDC 070.4/44092 [B]—
dc23/eng/20241030
LC record available at https://lccn.loc.gov/2024021697

For Emilia, Jan, and Magdalena

Contents

Illustrations

Acknowledgments

It took several years before I was able to write this story. It then became a surprisingly personal book. I am very grateful to Ben Fowkes for agreeing to translate it from the German original. He is not only an excellent translator but also an expert in the history of the European Left in the early twentieth century. Thank you, Ben, for taking on this task!

A project of this kind could not have become a reality without the support of numerous colleagues, archivists, experts, contemporary witnesses, and good friends. I should like to thank Gleb J. Albert, Marina Astakhova, Bernhard H. Bayerlein, Klaus Bellin, Giles Bennett, Gunnar Berg, Rosina Berger, Rüdiger Bergien, Ulf Bischof, Matthias Biskupek (†), Verena Blaum, Michal Bodemann, Hans Bohrmann, Christian Booß, Jan Brandt, Gottfried Braun, Chad Bryant, Helen Camarade, Christoph Classen, Marcus Dahmker, Rob Dale, Sabine Deckwerth, Janet Dilger, Jürgen Dinkel, Susanne Doetz, various members of the Eckert family, Alfred Eichhorn, Wolfram Eilenberger, Regina Elzner, Dirk Engel, Susanne Erdmann, Stefan Fink, Karl-Ulrich Gelberg, Jay Geller, Cornelia Gisevius, Katharina Guttenbrunner, Gregor Gysi, Hermann Haarmann, Frank-Burkhard Habel, Anna Hájková, Levke Harders, Wolfgang Hempel, Violetta Hionidou, Petra Höhenberger, Barbara Honigmann, Klaus Höpcke (†), Andreas Horn, Rebecca Jewett, Andreas Juhnke, Jan Kahuda, Gabriele Kaiser, André Keil, Mario Keßler, Tim Kirk, Christian Klein, Ilko-Sascha Kowalczuk, Thomas Kuczynski (†), Emanuel La Roche, Mark Lehmstedt, Stefan Lehr, Vera Lengsfeld, Philipp Lenhard, Marcel Lepper, Charlotte Lerg, Paul Liss, Siegfried Lokatis, Birgit Lulay, Bernd F. Lunkewitz, Bernhard Malkmus, Melissa McMullen, Maryas Mervay, Patrick Merziger, Michael Meyen, Christina Möller, Marcel Neudeck, Robin Ostow, Alexandra Otten, Katharina Prager, Bernhard Praschl, Gabriele Radecke, Katharina Rauschenberger, Jörn Retterath, Karl-Heinz Röhr, Irene Runge, Thomas Rütten, Axel Rütters, Klaus G. Saur, Joanne Sayner, Martin Schaad, Johanna Schall, Katharina Schlieper, Dieter Schmidt, Sven Schneidereit, Anett Schubotz, Kerstin Schulte, Felix Robin Schulz, Michal Schvarc, Lisa Städtler, Bettina Theek, Johannes Wagemann, Alexander Walther, Angela Wandelt, Matthias Wedel, Markus Wegewitz, Annette Weinke, Thomas Welskopp (†), Bianca Welzing-Bräutigam, Navena Widulin, Michael Wildt, Ursula Winnington, Sabine Wolf, Larry Wolff, Teo Zagar, Ulrike Zecher, Michael Zingler, Stefan Zollhauser, and many others.

For their comments on earlier versions of the German manuscript, their time, and their attention to detail, my particular thanks go to Hanna Erl, Wolfgang Hardtwig, Magali Karee, Thomas Karlauf, Stefan Laffin, Christoph Links, Christoph Luther, Christoph Nußbaumeder, Magdalena Ptaszyńska, Christian Schemmert, Kay Schiller, Jens Thiel, and Karina von Tippelskirch. Particularly during the uneasy time of the pandemic, when this book reached its final stages, their involvement went beyond what one might have a right to expect from friends or colleagues. I am very appreciative of their efforts!

Benjamin C. Hett and Ofer Askenazy recommended that this book be translated and published in the George L. Mosse Series in the History of European Culture, Sexuality, and Ideas—many thanks to you both!

Thanks are also due to the Fritz Thyssen Stiftung; the Leibniz-Zentrum für Zeithistorische Forschung, Potsdam; the Centre for Holocaust Studies at the Institut für Zeitgeschichte in Munich; the Historische Kolleg, Munich; Syracuse University; and the School of History, Classics and Archaeology of Newcastle University for their material and intellectual promotion of this project. After the German edition of this book was published, I presented this story at the University of Oxford, the University of Cambridge, and the Hebrew University of Jerusalem. For these kind invitations I am very grateful to the convenors of the Modern History Seminar at the University of Oxford in 2022–23: Tom Buchanan, Patricia Clavin, Martin Conway, and Nick Stargardt. At the University of Cambridge, I thank in particular Bianca Gaudenzi and the Humanities Society at Wolfson College. At the Richard Koebner Minerva Center for German History in Jerusalem my thanks go to Ofer Askenazi and Matthias Schmidt.

I also thank the Aufbau Verlag in Berlin under the former literary direction of Constanze Neumann; its chief nonfiction editor, Christian Koth; and Andrea Doberenz and Inka Ihmels. Thanks also go to my readers Ditta Ahmadi and Nora Samhouri and to my colleague and agent Thomas Karlauf for placing their confidence in this biography of a largely forgotten individual.

Finally, I am very grateful to my American copyeditor Mary Hill and to Nathan MacBrien, Skye Doney, and Sheila McMahon of the University of Wisconsin Press as well as the entire team in Madison for making this English-language edition of the book possible and for thereby bringing the project to a successful conclusion.

WRITING AGAINST HITLER

Prologue

It didn't happen the way one can tell it; but if one can tell it as it was, then one wasn't in on it, or it all happened so long ago that candor comes too easily.
—CHRISTA WOLF

I N TWENTIETH-CENTURY GERMANY, the name of the Left-liberal magazine *Die Weltbühne* had a near mythical sound that still resonated with me when I was a history student in Berlin around 2000. There were still good reasons to be fascinated by what was perhaps the most significant politico-cultural journal issued in the Weimar Republic whose title literally translated as "The World Stage." It was evident that the journalism of *Die Weltbühne* was inspired by the tempo and rhythm of Berlin, a city that in the 1920s was both a laboratory of modernity and the locus of intense social and political antagonisms.[1] My Berlin of the postunification years was, of course, very different from the metropolis of the interwar period. It was again a city full of contrasts, yet it struggled to reconcile the ghosts of the past with the opportunities of the present. It was still very much a city divided in two. The biggest difference was not between the East and the West, with their distinct Cold War mentalities and different accents (the typical Berliner dialect was more frequent in the East), but between those who lived for decades in their respective neighborhoods, or "Kieze," and those who, like me, had only recently moved to Berlin.

We young people were attracted by the excitement and promises of the big city that was once again the capital of Germany but in many ways an unusual place with lots of space, creative people of all nationalities, and cheap rents. And it was full of history. One could not fail to notice when walking through the city center where the bullet holes of the 1945 fighting were still visible and where the former Berlin Wall still separated the city, no longer as a concrete

3

barrier but more as a shadow that impacted the mindset of Berliners. Local politics were philistine, and the struggles of the day in any case were less grandiose than in the early twentieth century, when the *Weltgeist* had taken headquarters on the river Spree for a few years, or so it seemed to a young history student eager to explore the new environment in the present and in the past.

One of my ways to learn more about the past was the 1978 reprint edition of *Die Weltbühne*. The magazines, with their unmistakable red covers, were still a source of fascination, even if, in the end and despite all the brilliance, these writers and journalists had "achieved almost nothing," as István Deák had put it in his seminal study *Weimar Germany's Left-Wing Intellectuals.*[2] At a time when I longed to find my place in society and certainly had no impact whatsoever, the alleged lack of success probably even increased my sympathy for the magazine's writers. In any case, I became an avid reader. What tremendous acerbity, humor, and passion the writers put into fighting their battles in *Die Weltbühne* in those days! I was still impressed, decades later, by the way in which they regarded themselves as spreaders of enlightenment who were convinced that the truth had to be told whatever obstacle stood in the way. Naive and presumptuous as this might sound today, I regarded these journalists as my guides both politically and in my first attempts to write, which were still very clumsy. To a certain extent, this was a natural path of development for a young man from provincial eastern Westphalia for whom the big city of Berlin had been a place of longing ever since I read Erich Kästner's popular children's book *Emil and the Detectives.* It was a feeling that continued even after I had long taken up residence in the city.

Several years had to elapse before it dawned on me that *Die Weltbühne* did not cease publication with the establishment of the National Socialist dictatorship, as was suggested by the date range of 1918 to 1933 covered by the reprint. On the contrary, the journal continued to appear in exile for several years—first in Vienna, then in Prague, and finally in Paris—and after the war gained a new lease on life in the German Democratic Republic (GDR, East Germany) until finally it fell silent in 1993. The central figure of *Die Weltbühne* in exile, which then operated under the name *Die neue Weltbühne*, was Hermann Budzislawski. Born in Berlin in 1901, he was editor in chief of the journal from 1934 onward and soon afterward also its proprietor. Later, in the GDR, he functioned as professor and dean of the Faculty of Journalism at the Karl Marx University in Leipzig. The journalism faculty was commonly known as the "Red monastery" on account of its strict adherence to the party line of the ruling Socialist Unity Party (SED). Other editors and editors in chief of *Die Weltbühne*—such as the theater critic Siegfried Jacobsohn; the widely read essayist, poet, and satirist Kurt Tucholsky; the political commentator and recipient of the Nobel Peace Prize Carl von Ossietzky; and, to a lesser extent, the journalist and later fierce anti-Communist Wilhelm (later William) S. Schlamm—are still much talked about even today. By contrast, Budzislawski is pretty well unknown.

This book is dedicated to presenting his life story for the first time as well as depicting the multitude of networks within which this unusual journalist and propagandist was successively embedded, a task that involves tracing the history of *Die Weltbühne* since the 1930s. Budzislawski was a "public intellectual" in Ralf Dahrendorf's sense in that he saw it as his task "to take part in the dominant discourses of the epoch, indeed even to determine their themes and mold their direction."[3] While still a schoolboy he had already read texts by Karl Marx, learning from him that—to paraphrase the latter's famous dictum—the point is not just to interpret the world but to change it. Throughout his life, as an attentive observer of his environment and of world events, Budzislawski always chose sides. He repeatedly had to assimilate himself into new political systems and adapt the course of his political life to changed circumstances. When he was an old man, he avoided committing his life story to paper. This was not least a result of his repeated need to harmonize his political trajectory with new situations, though it also stemmed from late modernity's often bemoaned crisis of linear autobiographical narration. It also mattered that, in the "actually existing Socialism" of the GDR, there was no official demand for the autobiographies of complex, contradictory intellectuals who existed in the contested gray zone between Social Democracy and dogmatic party-line Communism. The SED had no interest in exploring ruptures in the overall Marxist narrative of progress; hence, the printed biographies of its cadres display a curious uniformity. The party's "ahistorical leadership dogma" excluded "authentic life stories."[4] Late in life, SED member Budzislawski complied with these overall requirements, paying for this with a loss of "narrative identity," but he may also simply have found it impossible to write a book.[5] After all, he had already made repeated attempts to do so when in exile in the United States in the 1940s, but to no avail.

Hence, the ten chapters of this book narrate a story Budzislawski was himself neither willing nor able to tell. Its central theme is the life and forms of self-presentation of an individual just outside the top rank who experienced the catastrophes and upheavals of his epoch at close range but who was only able to deal with them politically and therefore to a certain extent abstractly. He was a man who fell between all stools. Like many members of his generation, he lived through four political regimes, and he survived all of them. He successively made his appearance as a leftist Social Democrat, an anti-Fascist, a Western liberal, and last of all a hard-nosed Communist, according to the requirements of need and opportunity, without ever being an opportunist in the narrow sense. With astonishing flexibility, he succeeded again and again not only in overcoming direct threats to his personal existence but also in creating for himself new sources of journalistic and political influence.

Nevertheless, even to his intimate friends he appeared as an "impersonal personality."[6] Early in life he had acquired a kind of character armor with which he consistently sealed off his innermost being from other people and probably from himself too. He thereby did much to make things difficult for prospective later biographers who are traditionally interested in the individual or, better still, the singular experiences of their subject. Right up to the present, popular history writing has not always been able to resist the temptation to search out the fundamental character of a past epoch by examining the life of an outstanding individual. This book, however, chooses a different approach: taking up the insights of biographers of historical migrations, it combines the lives of transnational and transcultural individuals with developments in local and global history, bringing them into a reciprocal relationship with each other.[7] The butcher's shop of Budzislawski's father in Berlin and the critical food situation in Leipzig during the first years after the Second World War will therefore concern us just as much as the anticolonialist networks of the interwar period and the plans of the early 1940s for the establishment of a worldwide peace order.

The original title of this book translates as "Behind the World Stage" and was a play on words. It referred to the way Budzislawski's life was closely involved with the fate of *Die Weltbühne* for four decades, beginning in the early 1930s, but it should also be taken literally, because the story that will be told is in fact a story of transnational significance—he was not *on* the world stage but *behind* it. The title of this American edition, by contrast, stresses another key feature of Budzislawski: his lifelong engagement against Nazism and Fascism more broadly and his contribution to a socialist renewal after the Second World War. In the 1930s and 1940s he was one of the most important anti-Fascist intellectuals in Europe and the United States, albeit little known to the public. He involved himself in the campaign to secure the Nobel Peace Prize for Carl von Ossietzky, who had been imprisoned by the Nazis in 1933 and severely mistreated in a concentration camp. Ossietzky was finally released in 1936, but he died two years later of the long-term effects of the Nazi torture. Budzislawski also worked closely with the writer Heinrich Mann, he researched and wrote as the trusted friend of the stellar US journalist Dorothy Thompson, and after the end of the Second World War he rehearsed with playwright and lyricist Bertolt Brecht the latter's appearance before the House Un-American Activities Committee of the US Congress. Later, in the GDR, he molded a whole generation of "Socialist journalists," and he also cut a good figure for the GDR on the international stage. Despite having led this exciting life, Budzislawski is nearly completely forgotten. Part of the explanation is related to Germany's reunification in 1990. Since the end of the GDR, hardly anyone has displayed any interest in the life and the journalistic activity of this political professor and propagandist, who died in 1978 after receiving many state decorations.[8] In the Federal Republic, Budzislawski has been regarded as a "mediocre careerist in bondage to Ulbricht," the First Secretary of the SED until 1971, and as the assassin of the "real" *Weltbühne* from the years of the Weimar Republic, in the words of the writer and political commentator Kurt Hiller, who had been at daggers drawn with him since the mid-1930s.[9] While vilifying the former editor in chief, Budzislawski, Hiller, and many other leftist intellectuals in the second half of the twentieth century glorified *Die Weltbühne* of the Weimar years as a model of polemical pugnacity, independence, and "fairness." Not the least of the traditions these writers ought to have continued was the "complete lack of respect for official values," as the writer Erich Mühsam had put it in 1930, which was cultivated by the periodical back then and lacking in the Federal Republic, they thought.[10]

The later *Weltbühne*, which reappeared in East Berlin from 1946 onward and in which Budzislawski held the position of editor in chief again between 1967 and 1971, was no longer able to lay claim to Mühsam's earlier accolades. It followed the line of the ruling party, the SED, on which it was also financially dependent, and it avoided any confrontation with the holders of political power. On 12 April 1990 its publisher, the Weltbühne GmbH, was saved from bankruptcy for the last time by a decision of the GDR minister of culture that injected a million marks from the state budget into the business.[11] Yet three years later, its new owner, the publisher Bernd F. Lunkewitz, who had become wealthy through investments in real estate, decided to discontinue the highly indebted periodical when a dispute over title rights began to escalate—a situation that had already occurred several times in its previous history. This time there was no one left to save the magazine.

There were also pragmatic reasons why it was difficult to write a biography of Budzislawski. A family quarrel over his intellectual and material inheritance had the result that his extensive personal archive remained in private ownership until recently and was therefore either completely inaccessible to journalists and scholars or only accessible in part. The same applies to the former editorial archives of *Die neue Weltbühne*. Today both of these archival holdings, if we leave aside a few remnants stored today in the Moscow "Special Archive," are designated as part of the data bank of protected cultural assets of the Federal Republic of Germany and can be consulted in the Literature

Archive of the Berlin Akademie der Künste (Academy of the Arts). My book is primarily based on this literary heritage, but it also makes use of archival holdings in several European states and in the United States. It tells the story of a Prussian Jew who through hard work, ability, and ruthlessness rose to the top of *Die Weltbühne* and continued to influence and shape German-language political journalism for decades. At the same time, it addresses the question of how a person could maintain his political convictions in the face of the challenges of the modern era—and the price that had to be paid for doing so.

In addition to examining the life story of one individual and the intellectual constellations he was involved in, the book also highlights some of the central features of the history of the twentieth century by welding together biography, social history, and the history of ideas. First, the example of Budzislawski demonstrates an important line of political continuity in the German Left, starting from the extreme left wing of Social Democracy in the 1920s, passing through anti-Fascist engagement in exile, and extending to the construction and consolidation of the GDR after the end of the Second World War as a supposedly better Germany. Second, Budzislawski's life and the significance of the networks in which he moved constitute a prime example of the way different histories have been transnationally intertwined in the twentieth century. This is not just because of the successive stages of exile he passed through, taking in Switzerland, Czechoslovakia, France, and the United States, but also on account of his early involvement in anticolonial movements starting in the mid-1920s.[12] Third, his career represents a model of life one might describe as bourgeois Socialism—not so much in relation to his family background but because of the well-groomed appearance he retained whatever country he was in.[13] Fourth, this story makes a contribution to the cultural history of inheritance in the modern era: it exemplifies its function not only in the directly material sense but also more generally because it offers the possibility of universalizing an intellectual heritage and transmitting it posthumously to children and grandchildren.[14] Finally, the case of Budzislawski illustrates how the political influence of the Cold War, above all the "West German claim to sole representation," has continued to have an impact, long after 1990, among both journalists and historians.[15]

This book is therefore also an intervention into the German politics of the past. It is intended to contribute to a more nuanced understanding of the history of the GDR through observing a middle-level participant who eludes overhasty categorization. In the 1990s and the early 2000s the center of public discussion in Germany was occupied by the unmasking of the SED dictatorship and the struggles between "victims" and "perpetrators," who were supposedly clearly distinguishable from one another. Against the background of the now defunct GDR, the star of the Federal Republic, as a bastion of democracy and the rule of law, shone even more brightly. These battles over the political past, which were often conducted with sword thrusts and sledgehammer blows, have now come to an end, but their consequences continue to reverberate. The fact that even experienced and highly astute individuals opted to live in the GDR after the Second World War appears to be a source of amazement today, especially among the young. This book aims to adopt a more nuanced approach and to treat the participants' self-presentations with as much skepticism as the political metanarratives. This will make it possible to comprehend the complexity of the decisions taken and the life courses pursued in the GDR with reference to a concrete example. I hope that international readers will find it a stimulating read, too, and that the book helps to spotlight the passions and troubles of the complex history of Central Europe and its transnational entanglements in the twentieth century.

This book is unusual even for a German audience, for which it was originally written. The lives of intellectuals in the early GDR who were members of the SED or simply close to the party have hardly received much attention until very recently, unless they were authors whose works had already found readers in the Federal Republic before 1989 or unique figures such as Victor Klemperer, the professor of Romance languages who became internationally known through the publication of his diaries, in which he chronicled his life as a German Jew in the Third Reich. Following the views of the influential German sociologist Mario Rainer Lepsius, some scholars argue even today that the concept of "an intellectual" cannot usefully be applied in relation to the GDR. This line of argument is, however, derived from normative premises that fail to address the realities of life for the East German intelligentsia. Moreover, it appears more than questionable in view of the outstanding significance of intellectuals in the neighboring countries of Poland and Czechoslovakia from the 1960s to the 1980s.[16] Yet even so, contemporary historians have predominantly regarded biographical studies of East German intellectuals as exemplifying failure and defeat, consciously or unconsciously projecting the collapse of the GDR onto the life of the individual who is being portrayed. Studies of the young Socialists of the interwar period, dealing with their struggle against National Socialism and their later life in the GDR, therefore generally refer, at best, to misguided idealism followed by political domestication.

My intention is to take a more open-minded approach to such biographies. The story of Hermann Budzislawski and his fight for *Die Weltbühne* is ultimately a variant of the fundamental tension (and often mismatch) between political power and intellectual possibilities. Budzislawski embodied an extreme, politics-oriented position in this field of force, whereas the former

Weltbühne star writer Kurt Tucholsky opted to do the opposite and stood aside from party-political controversies. He had already withdrawn from the day-to-day political struggle before Hitler became German chancellor, and in his Swedish exile in the early 1930s he maintained an eloquent silence. Shortly before his death in December 1935, Tucholsky expressed the depth of his disappointment in a letter to his fellow writer Arnold Zweig in which he claimed that he would have nothing more to do with Germany, "that country whose language I speak as little as possible," adding, "Let it perish; let it conquer Russia. I am finished with it in any case."[17] Budzislawski was very different. It was only in exile that he discovered his mission, and from then on he never ceased to come forward as a kind of left-wing *praeceptor germaniae* (teacher of Germany)—a self-proclaimed schoolmaster of a country that had first to be liberated from the Nazis and then to undergo a fundamental transformation. He sent a letter to Tucholsky at the beginning of 1934 in which he formulated what he regarded as a realistic political program: "The new approach consists in an abandonment of dogmatic positions, in an undogmatic analysis of the situation, and in fresh—but not foolish—attempts to overcome this situation. In an unacademic attitude toward politics. But not in waiting for 'original' truth to manifest itself. If anyone has this, well and good. But to wait for it to emerge would be terrible."[18]

From the late 1920s onward, Budzislawski lived from and for politics. One might even say that he defined himself from first to last through his position in the fields of journalism and politics. Again and again, therefore, he made a fresh start in different countries and under different political regimes. Giving up was not an option. This book deals with this continued urge to press on, with its reasons and its consequences. It thereby tells the story of the hopes and disillusionments of the twentieth century, condensed into a single example.

Jew, Socialist, Eugenicist

Early Influences

I T IS THE beginning of February 1901. Anticlerical students are demonstrating in Madrid. They throw stones at Jesuit dignitaries; they set off an explosion in a bookshop. In South Africa the English colonial authorities are fighting the Boers. Cuba is heavily in debt. Romania is undergoing a government crisis. In Berlin, meanwhile, there is renewed controversy over the behavior of the kaiser. On a visit to London, Wilhelm II has spoken out in favor of a rapprochement between the two Great Powers. Some of the kaiser's subjects are unhappy with his conciliatory language toward England, the German Empire's political and economic rival: the British Empire had dominated the world during the nineteenth century, but in Berlin they were convinced that the future belonged to the rising power of Germany under Prussian leadership.[1]

It was into this atmosphere of national anticipation that Hermann Budzislawski was born in Berlin on Monday, 11 February 1901. He was the third child of the thirty-six-year-old master butcher and merchant Isidor Budzislawski, who originated from Bromberg, now the Polish city of Bydgoszcz, and his wife, Jenny. They already had two children: Leo, who came into the world on New Year's Day 1895, and Martin, who followed him a year later. The 1901 address book for Berlin and its suburbs gave the place of residence of the family as Reinickendorfer Straße 8a, a street located between the district of Wedding and the Brunnenviertel in Berlin Mitte, but they must have moved house before Hermann was born, because his birthplace was registered by the Royal-Prussian Registry Office in Berlin-Gesundbrunnen as Gerichtsstraße 29. Presumably the city's annually updated telephone book was already out of date again at the start of 1901, because the family's address changed nearly every year. What remained constant despite their repeated moves was the father's business address: the kosher butcher's stall of Isidor Budzislawski was always

Hermann Budzislawski and his two brothers,
Leo and Martin (*from right to left*), 1906.

located in the Central Market Hall of Berlin, on the Alexanderplatz, where it occupied stands 64 and 65.[2]

The Budzislawskis were a family of Prussian Jews with Polish roots. Hermann's parents had left their Pomeranian homeland in the late 1880s, intending to make their fortune in the booming capital of the new German Reich.[3] Berlin had at that time some 1.5 million inhabitants, a third of whom had first moved into the city during the last ten years. The new residents originated for the most part either from the country's less industrialized eastern provinces or from the Habsburg crownland of Galicia. The city was bursting at the seams, and many of the newcomers had to make do with damp, dark, and gloomy slum dwellings, despite the brisk pace at which houses were being built. Jews made up a not inconsiderable proportion of the new Berliners, so there was a rapid increase in the demand for kosher meat. Two decades later, a third of the Jewish population of the Reich resided in the capital city: in absolute numbers this amounted to over one hundred thousand people.

For a few years, Isidor Budzislawski ran another branch of his butchery business at Beuthstraße 17, in addition to his stall in Berlin's Central Market Hall.[4] The family was modestly prosperous; at any rate, they lived in conditions of material security. Budzislawski's parents placed considerable value on providing their children with a good education. According to his youngest son, Isidor was an "educated artisan" who spent his evenings carefully perusing the newspapers, studied books "with great seriousness, and also went twice a month to the theater." He regarded himself as a Jewish Prussian who was educating his children to "do their jobs well, behave perfectly, and be absolutely punctual." Hermann noted that he became grumpy on Sundays because he did not know what to do with his free time: "The little word 'duty' was printed in bold in his vocabulary, and in compensation for this the word 'leisure' was completely struck out."[5] The writer Henry Jacoby (actually Heinrich Jacobi), one of Hermann's former fellow students, has given a vivid description in his memoirs of the Jewish middle-class milieu in Berlin at the beginning of the twentieth century:

> Generally speaking, we lived like other families of the lower and middle bourgeoisie, perhaps with fewer alcoholic drinks, better food, and more books in the house. It went without saying that we belonged to the German nation. Everyone had passed through the German educational system and shared the opinions and prejudices of their social stratum, albeit with a number of nuances. There was a greater tendency toward cosmopolitanism and a more liberal attitude in the political sphere. . . . But however German we felt, social interaction took place largely—if with significant exceptions—between Jewish families, and marriages with a non-Jewish partner were rare.[6]

Hermann Budzislawski's mother, Jenny, whose maiden name was Lewin, was a year younger than her husband. She came from the town of Tempelberg, in Pomerania, which is today the Polish town of Czaplinek. Her youngest son informs us that she was an "ordinary woman. From early in the morning, she was involved in the small-scale business operations of a butcher's shop, and she did her housework late at night. Father was the boss, and he visibly enjoyed watching us tremble. Mother held the family together. She was very shrewd." These comments offer a rare glimpse into the emotional world of the son, who throughout his life said very little about his family or himself. Budzislawski's father appears in his recollections as a respected but authoritarian figure, his mother as an overworked, kindhearted woman who was ready to lend an ear, who sympathized with the tribulations of her fellow human beings, and who "avoided giving offense" even in situations of conflict. When he was an old man, Budzislawski indicated that he had been particularly close to his mother, who died in 1937, but he had nothing to say about his relationship with his father.[7] The two busy parents could only devote a limited amount of time to their children: "Father let his duties swallow him up completely. They gave him the feeling that his life had some meaning. . . . He took the view that the purpose of his existence was limited to feeding his family and doing his duty to them without bothering about the rest of humanity." There is an unmistakably critical tone to these remarks by Hermann Budzislawski, made a quarter of a century after his father's death.[8] He was the youngest son, and at five feet, four inches he was physically on the small side. From an early age he was obliged to become financially independent.[9] Like many young men of his generation whose puberty coincided with the First World War, he was alert to current events and had an interest in politics. He was not particularly attracted to either the trade of a butcher or the lower-middle-class milieu of his parents. He was captivated instead by the books through which he discovered new worlds beyond his own.

Between 1907 and 1911 Hermann attended the boys' school of the Jewish community in Berlin, which now bears the name Jüdisches Gymnasium Moses Mendelssohn. When Budzislawski joined it, this school, which saw

The Central Market Hall on Alexanderplatz, where Isidor Budzislawski sold his kosher meat products, ca. 1920.

itself as the successor institution to the Jüdische Freischule, founded in 1778 by David Friedländer, had only just moved into new premises at Große Hamburgerstraße 27 the previous year.[10] At the beginning of the twentieth century it was a place that combined modernity with an awareness of Jewish tradition; parents who applied for their children to go there were also consciously committing themselves to their Jewish roots. After a few years of elementary school, the boy was transferred to the Leibniz-Oberrealschule in Charlottenburg, a town that was then still administratively separate from the city of Berlin. *Oberrealschulen* (secondary high schools) had been introduced into Prussia at the end of the nineteenth century. They were an alternative to the humanist schools with their concentration on classical antiquity and ancient languages. The *Oberrealschulen* centered their teaching on the natural sciences; apart from that they offered an education in the modern foreign languages of French and English. Parents who sent their children to an *Oberrealschule* wanted them to receive the best possible training for modern industrial life. Practical abilities that would stand them in good stead in the future were seen as of greater value than immersion in the nineteenth-century idealist traditions of the educated bourgeoisie (*Bildungsbürgertum*). Budzislawski passed his final high school examination (the *Abitur*) in September 1919. In the subject of German, candidates could choose to answer one of these two questions: "With what justification was King Frederick II of Prussia described as 'Frederick the Great'?" and, for more creatively inclined students, "What entices and drives human beings to travel to distant lands?" In the French examination, the student had to describe in detail the events of the Seven Years' War. The educational system was strongly influenced by an attitude of Prussian patriotism, especially during the war years. Budzislawski's results in his final year as a student were consistently rated "good" or "satisfactory," except for his written English, which was rated "unsatisfactory." Apart from that, he was one of the best students of his year.[11]

The Leibniz-Oberrealschule at Schillerstraße 125–27 was attended by many Jewish pupils who lived in the middle-class western districts of the city. Even so, most of Budzislawski's classmates were Protestant by religion, and their fathers were businessmen, state officials, architects, factory owners, men of private means, or parliamentary deputies.[12] In order to bring their son into contact with the right social circles, Budzislawski's parents were evidently prepared to tolerate the relatively long journey to the school—at least until 1914, when the family moved into a house in Charlottenburg at Sybelstraße 5, from which Hermann could reach the school on foot.[13] After school, when he was between the ages of nine and thirteen, young Hermann had to help his parents run their stall in the Central Market Hall.[14] One of his former classmates, the writer Hans Sahl, remembered him as a precocious, impressively serious teenager who was deeply involved in his studies:

> Budzislawski wore a pair of rimless spectacles which gave him the look of an academic. He occasionally looked over them as if to say he didn't need them any longer as he already knew everything. He was what we used to call a "swot." He was always the first to raise his hand, and he read books we did not know about, for example, by Marx and Engels, whose names meant nothing to us. But the way he raised his index finger when he spoke caused us to sit up and take notice. I liked Budzislawski; he already gave the impression of being an old man who had stayed young through some oversight, and he displayed a precocious superiority, especially toward his teachers, which impressed me.[15]

Very little is known in detail about the life of the student Hermann Budzislawski before 1918. He was due to celebrate his Bar Mitzvah in 1913, but the relevant documentation from the Jewish community of Berlin has not survived.[16] He was unable to raise any enthusiasm for the First World War, which had caused waves of nationalist propaganda to sweep over many Prussian gymnasiums and high schools and had led to repeated "victory celebrations" in the hall of the school in the Schillerstraße. In an autobiographical sketch written in 1941 or 1942 Budzislawski recalled his *Oberrealschule* as having been a "strict Prussian school" where he was drilled by teachers "who regarded us as military recruits and themselves as army officers." The war put its stamp on the life of the school in every area. By January 1917 seven teachers, half of the staff, had died "a hero's death."[17] These were years when prisoners of war, mainly of Eastern European origin, were made to clear the snow from the streets and the paths of the Berlin schools. The Leibniz-Oberrealschule in the Schillerstraße was sometimes closed for weeks owing to an acute shortage of coal.[18]

The death of the young schoolboy's brother Leo, who had been expected by his parents to become a rabbi and who was declared missing in action during the battle for Verdun on 10 August 1916, was a "rupture of experience" that transformed Budzislawski's state of mind. The news meant that from one day to the next, Hermann ceased to be a child. As he wrote later, at the age of fifteen he became a "rebel against the kaiser's war," "stubbornly and mutinously" rejecting "the harsh discipline of his militarized school."[19] He claims to have distributed antiwar leaflets in the Berlin military hospitals and to have been reprimanded for his propaganda against the war, particularly by the school's principal, who was a German nationalist.[20] Since 1915, more and more schoolchildren had worn black armbands to indicate that a father or a brother

Thirteen-year-old Hermann Budzislawski (*on the right*), his brother Leo, and a friend named Henry Hiller, taken in July 1914 during a summer holiday in Bad Neuenahr. The First World War began a few days later.

had fallen in battle, but until the outbreak of the November Revolution in 1918 almost no one wanted to draw any political conclusion from this. For a long time, the pacifist Budzislawski was an isolated figure in the schoolyard. It was not until the autumn of 1918, recalls Jacoby, that there was any discussion in the Leibniz-Oberrealschule in the Schillerstraße of the political changes that were on the horizon and would soon become a dramatic reality. The student body now began to divide into two halves: the supporters of Kaiser Wilhelm and the republicans. According to Jacoby, "Opinion in both camps largely reflected parental views. The exceptions to this were in the republican camp, which was dominated largely by the Jewish students; the opinions advocated there were often more radical than those held by the parents. Young people had the feeling that the powers that had prevented their full integration into the surrounding world had been defeated."[21]

Seventeen-year-old Budzislawski was gripped by the revolutionary emotions of the epoch, which threw many young intellectuals on the political Left into a short-lived but intensely felt state of intoxication. For example, the pacifist writer Armin T. Wegner published no fewer than twenty-five manifestos between November 1918 and May 1919. They had dramatic titles such as "I

The Leibniz-Oberrealschule in the Schillerstraße, Charlottenburg. Budzislawski
passed his *Abitur* there in 1919.

separate myself from all of you," "A call for civil war," and "What should we
believe?"[22] It is not at all clear whether Budzislawski ever read any texts of this
kind. He wanted to take an active part in the revolutionary upheavals, although
in view of his youth his involvement did him little harm. His former classmate
Hans Suhl, writing as an old man, recalled this period with gentle and indulgent
irony: "It was the time of the workers' and soldiers' councils. We set up a school
students' council, and Hermann took a leading part in it, as he was someone
who knew what it was about. The job of the school students' council was essentially to tell the teachers what we thought of them and to forbid the school
principal from entering the classroom while our meetings were in session."[23]
The same events, when recorded by Budzislawski's later assistant Siegfried
Schmidt, who became acquainted with him in Leipzig in the 1950s, sounded
much more significant but at the same time more artificial, because Schmidt
adapted his protagonist's life story to the requirements of Marxist historiography. According to him, Budzislawski "expressed his solidarity with the striking
Berlin munitions workers" in the last year of the war, much to the annoyance
of the school principal. In addition to that, he declared his support for the Russian October Revolution. In November 1918 he was elected chair of the students' council of his school, and after that he even took over the leadership of
the central school students' council for the whole of Berlin.[24]

Budzislawski was at that time a member of the Uncompromising Youth, a left-wing offshoot of the Free German Youth, an organization whose leading prewar figure was the reforming educationalist Gustav Wyneken. Budzislawski published his first pieces of journalism in the periodical *Der neue Anfang* (The new beginning), which was closely associated with the Uncompromising Youth.[25] Using emotive language typical of the time, this periodical called in its first issue for a "class struggle by youth" in which the word "class" did not refer to a particular social stratum but rather to a noble attitude of mind.[26] The journal's tone was set by its contributors, among them Ernst Toller and Kurt Hiller, who were Left-inclined teenagers and youthful adults of middle-class origin. They remained an isolated group despite all the supraclass emotionalism of their proclamations. None of the articles in the journal bears Budzislawski's full name; many of them appeared anonymously or were identified only with initials. There were at times some contributions signed N.B., one of which bore the place-name Munich, although the editors, who were located in Munich, may have assigned an incorrect place of origin to the article.[27]

Independently of details of this kind, one can assume that at least the tendency of the articles in *Der neue Anfang* was in line with the objectives of school student representative Budzislawski.[28] The authors who wrote for this periodical called for a "school revolution" and demanded the introduction of school student councils all over the country, for regular discussions between teachers and students in the school community, and for the introduction of working groups whose purpose would be to conduct regular mental and physical training. Sex education was also intended to become a permanent part of the curriculum. The Free School Student Body of Berlin even organized a working group on sexology, which was located at the Dorotheenstädtisches Gymnasium.[29] In terms of politics, many of these young people favored an ethically based form of Socialism.

A new generation of young men and women who saw each other as comrades and to some extent as the national leaders of the coming epoch aspired to overcome what they saw as a decadent and utterly exhausted bourgeois society.[30] They had already held these views as members of the Wandervogel movement before the war. Now, in the upheavals of the months that immediately followed its end, the same views were put forward as the "education of middle-class youth toward Socialism." But this did not increase their impact.[31] Although its name pointed forward to the future, *Der neue Anfang* lasted only three months.

Despite this disillusioning initial experience, the November Revolution made a deep and lasting impact on the young Budzislawski. As a member of the school students' council, he encountered both Erwin Marcusson, a physician who was to become the assistant minister of health in the GDR, and Helmut Liebknecht, one of the sons of Karl Liebknecht, the Socialist, Communist, and founder member of the Communist Party of Germany (KPD) who was murdered on 15 January 1919 along with his colleague Rosa Luxemburg.[32] The *Gymnasium* students were so politicized at that time that the classmates of Helmut Liebknecht's older brother Wilhelm, who attended the middle-class Steglitz *Gymnasium*, refused to sit on the same bench as the son of the dead Communist leader. It required the intervention of the new Prussian minister of culture and education, Konrad Haenisch of the Social Democratic Party (SPD), to bring a temporary calm to the wave of indignation. Budzislawski's teachers observed the leftward evolution of their gifted sixth former with concern. In the spring of 1919, they reported as follows: "He has displayed a keen interest in his courses to the extent that his intellectual preconceptions have not hindered this. He puts forward extreme views and seeks to spread them within the student body as far as he can. He is inclined to excessively critical thinking, and he is not without arrogance."[33] Freely translated, this meant that he possessed a Berlin snout and a sense of mission.

The immense impact of the political and social upheavals of the immediate postwar period on the teenagers and young adults who came to maturity in the heart of Berlin at that time has been depicted extensively by contemporary witnesses who were politically as far apart as the journalist Sebastian Haffner and the pastor's son and National Socialist Horst Wessel.[34] The intelligentsia of the "wartime youth generation" sympathized with radical positions, not least because of an antibourgeois feeling directed against their parents' generation. The writer Otto Flake had already concluded in a clear-sighted pamphlet published in 1920 that "everyone who is young, lively, does not wish to be a bourgeois, and finds restrictions intolerable is going over to Communism with all flags flying. But what does Communism mean today? It is identical with Bolshevism or Marxism and no longer has anything in common with the old concept of Communism in the sense of individualism."[35] Twenty years after Flake, Budzislawski was forced to note that the line of development had proceeded since then toward an entirely different outcome. As he wrote in retrospect, displaying a trace of self-criticism that was not entirely free of homophobia:

> I belonged to that curious German youth movement that soon degenerated completely, and the emergence of the secret orders of the movement, the *Männerbünde* [men's associations], was something I was able to see at close quarters. Their erotic abnormality later led, to our horror, to the formation of the Nazi

Group photograph taken at a soirée in Berlin on 22 February 1920. Hermann Budzislawski is seated in the first row at the far right. His brother Martin is third from the right.

"elite," the SS. The "führer principle" and the "cult of the führer" developed in these young men's clubs, and the false worship of heroes spread from there into the mass movement of sects and the esoteric secret societies of the revolutionary period. It was the beginning of Fascist ideology, but we did not know this.[36]

In the summer of 1919, after Budzislawski had obtained his *Abitur*, the path to university entrance lay open. He enrolled for the winter semester at the Friedrich Wilhelms University in Berlin. The subjects he took were jurisprudence and economics. A career in the higher ranks of the civil service or in industry would have been possible options after this course, but this must remain a matter of speculation, as we have no reliable statements from Budzislawski about his career goals at that time. Soon afterward he decided to take a semester at the Julius Maximilians University in Würzburg and then to return to Berlin. After that, he went on to study political science and economics at the Eberhard Karls University in Tübingen.[37] There were not just academic reasons for these repeated changes in his place of study. He recorded in a fragmentary autobiography dating from the early 1940s that he had participated actively in the resistance against the Kapp Putsch of 13 March 1920. His father reacted to this news by sending him to southern Germany to continue his studies in order to wean him off political activities in dangerous places.[38]

The plan had a successful outcome. Budzislawski ceased to be politically active, and he pursued his studies purposefully until he had completed all his courses.[39] He had already gained his doctorate in the spring of 1923. His student file at the University of Tübingen contains information about the lecture courses he attended. In those days, unlike now, one could choose one's professors. There was relative freedom of choice over the length of the course and who the teacher would be, as long as the money was there and the eventual goal of completing the course was not lost from view. The professors who taught him came from a broad spectrum of opinion. In the summer semester of 1921, he mainly attended lectures and tutorials on law, supplemented by a series of lectures on general economic theory given by the progressive Robert Wilbrandt (1875–1954). Budzislawski also attended a political economy seminar entitled Philosophy of Economics. A year later, he was present at lectures on economic policy and socialization as well as in a seminar run by Wilbrandt on Socialism and socialization. There were also tutorials in public law with Carl Sartorius (1865–1945), a member of the German Democratic Party (DDP), and a series of lectures, along with appropriate tutorials, from the upper-middle-class progressive Herbert von Beckerath (1886–1966), later an opponent of Hitler and an exile from Nazi Germany. Finally, during the winter semester of 1922–23, Budzislawski took part in a seminar on Marx run by Wilbrandt, attended further tutorials with Sartorius, and went to tutorials in administrative law with Ludwig von Köhler (1868–1953), who was the last minister of the interior of the Kingdom of Württemberg. Köhler went on to be a professor of public law and social science during the Weimar Republic, and he was also rector of the University of Tübingen for a short period during the academic year 1925–26.[40]

Budzislawski had presumably become aware of Wilbrandt, who was later to supervise his doctoral dissertation, through his books on Karl Marx (1918) and on current problems of Socialism (1919).[41] Wilbrandt advocated an undogmatic form of Socialism, and he formulated a program that many who worked for *Die Weltbühne* would follow in later years:

> Only someone who is not a Marxist can be a Socialist. We must free ourselves from the whole theory of waiting on events, letting things ripen, and prophesying. We must also extricate ourselves from the idea that Socialism is to be equated with state enterprise, socialization, and nationalization. We must look the present in the eye and in accordance with it shape a practical system that can remedy the misery suffered by present-day society as a whole and above all by

the working class but is also able to take the sting out of the hardships experienced every day.[42]

On 2 March 1923 Budzislawski received the degree of doctor rerum politicarum, or doctor of political science. This was the prescribed title for a degree in political and social sciences. The title of his dissertation was "Eugenik: Ein Beitrag zur Ökonomie der menschlichen Erbanlagen" (Eugenics: A contribution to the economic analysis of hereditary factors in human beings).[43] It is not clear why, as a Socialist, Budzislawski chose precisely this subject. His doctoral dissertation was almost 250 pages long, an unusually extensive and independent piece of work. In it he attempted from a Socialist perspective to determine the economic utility of the measures of racial hygiene that were under intense discussion among specialists at that time.[44] Arguing on the basis of the current assumptions about genetics, the young Socialist Budzislawski discussed the possible forms of "positive" and "negative" eugenics and the consequences of their implementation. Positive eugenics referred to education and improvements in hygiene, while negative eugenics involved "eradicating" genetically inferior individuals and deliberately excluding the genetically inferior from the chance of procreation. It was important for him to stress in this context that this exclusion must not apply to all "degenerates," because many "physically inferior" families would nevertheless pass on "intellectual qualities" to their descendants. To advocate a political utopia in which only "humans in perfect physical health" would be allowed to procreate would from an economic angle be to overstep the mark.[45] Budzislawski's Jewish origins may have contributed to this cautious attitude, yet he did not explicitly refer in his dissertation to the debates during the late Wilhelmine Reich and the early Weimar Republic around "the strengthening of the Jewish body."[46]

Budzislawski had no pity to spare for "unfruitful degenerates," nor had he any use for them. They were good for nothing economically, and they were nothing but a costly burden on society.[47] Three years earlier, Karl Binding, professor of law at Leipzig, together with the Freiburg psychiatrist Alfred Hoche, had coined the expression "superfluous existences" for this group.[48] Their comments were evidently unknown to Budzislawski, but his views were similar. The economist, he said, had the task of "adopting the measures necessary . . . to make sure that no one inherits a defect."[49] There were two possible ways of achieving this goal: either to breed as many "nonneedy individuals" as possible—which he regarded as unacceptable because it was a retrogressive step—or to change "the structure of the racial [völkisch] inheritance," in other words, the inherited genetic quality of an ethnic group (Volksgruppe) in such a way as to minimize the danger of defects for this group. Inherited defects became a real danger if the required "hygienic protection" became disproportionately costly and the productivity of the whole society was lessened by the need for everyone to bear these costs. In other words, as an economist, Budzislawski thought that negative eugenic measures were advisable, at least in theory. Inherited features that supposedly underlay "psychopathic illnesses" and "had no creative effect," such as idiocy and mental subnormality, should ideally be removed through selection, or "bred out." Individuals with these defects could not take part in economic production, or they could only do so to a very limited extent. To safeguard the "life of the people [*Volk*]" in the long term, it was permissible to select out these supposed degenerates.[50]

Budzislawski admittedly placed some limits on these far-reaching proposals in a later passage of his dissertation, where he pointed out that not everything economically rational was also philosophically or politically advisable. Even so, in view of the actual development of human labor, which had led to ever greater differentiation mainly as a result of the discoveries of the American engineer Frederick W. Taylor, the logic of exploiting human labor power was inescapable.[51] Taylorism and eugenics had to go hand in hand. Budzis-lawski's argument here tellingly highlights the way scientific discoveries had served to legitimize economic optimization already at the start of the twentieth century and, conversely, how capitalist interests were reflected in the advancement of scientific research.[52] According to Budzislawski, the task of the eugenically informed economist in a modern society was no longer to create the "full human being" with a broad education and a range of abilities but "to produce a single set of skills" and to remove supposed degenerates by a process of selection.[53]

Weeding out degenerates, in other words, artificially preventing the reproduction of the hereditarily feebleminded, could be achieved in various ways, he argued. The concrete examples he examined were infanticide, abortion, prevention of conception (using either contraceptive devices or "compulsory confinement in asylums," hence long-term detention), and, lastly, sexual abstinence.[54] All these methods, however, were problematic for various reasons. He regarded compulsory sterilization as the ideal route toward economically effective selection; this would lessen the allegedly undesirable effects of the social state that had been built up since the end of the nineteenth century. Budzislawski thought that with compulsory sterilization it would be possible in the near future to decimate the "lumpenproletariat," people who constituted the "dregs of human society," living often from the time of their birth in places where "feebleminded" criminals and prostitutes cavorted merrily.[55] He regarded the existence of this "hereditary lumpenproletariat" as a proven fact, demonstrated by the relevant international studies conducted in the United

States, Sweden, Switzerland, and Germany. Not least, a "constantly growing" and parasitic population group would profit from improvements in hygiene and benefits for the poor, and the cost of this would be a burden on the whole society. Eugenicist economics had to work against this. Even so, the sterilization of "certain criminals and feebleminded individuals" had to be handled carefully so as not to introduce a new kind of "inquisition" by a roundabout route.[56] In general, the state of knowledge was as yet so inadequate that "it must be regarded as premature to express any desire for measures of racial hygiene or eugenic economic policy that go beyond weeding out the most valueless individuals." Budzislawski deliberately avoided dealing with ethical issues in order to prevent his dissertation from being understood as a direct recommendation for political action.[57]

Despite these important reservations, the course taken by the argument of Budzislawski's doctoral dissertation shows that it was by no means only nationalist advocates of racial hygiene who put forward eugenicist ideas on the alleged connection between inherited ailments, economics, and criminality at the beginning of the Weimar Republic and who were made able to put their proposals into practice a decade and a half later by the National Socialist regime. At the start of the 1920s, young Socialists like Budzislawski placed the modern logic of the exploitation of human labor power above everything else, deriving very far-reaching eugenic proposals from this presupposition. If we leave aside the antisemitic element, the measures of racial hygiene introduced by the National Socialist state before the beginning of the Second World War were in line with the proposals twenty-two-year-old Budzislawski had already formulated in 1923: "A policy directed at raising the quality of the production of inherited dispositions will have to protest against rearing feeble children and artificially keeping alive feeble adults as long as no precautions have been taken against the further multiplication of their numbers."[58]

Budzislawski's dissertation met with few objections from his examiners. His work was awarded the classification *summa cum laude*—"with highest praise." Before giving the dissertation the highest grade, Wilbrandt had secured the backing of his colleague from the Faculty of Medicine, the psychiatrist Robert Gaupp. The latter was clearly better acquainted with the subject of the dissertation than its actual supervisor, and he praised the "diligent, well-written and instructive presentation of the problems of Eugenics," noting with a twinkle in his eye that the work gratifyingly stood out from "the frequently insubstantial dissertations of our medical students." However, he also noted that the statistics presented by Budzislawski on the inherited burden of mental illness were "of no value" because most of what the medical press wrote on the subject "was based on an incorrect methodology." Even so, this should not be counted against the candidate, who was "a well-informed person, capable of reaching his own judgement." Gaupp asked for a copy of the dissertation for his own library, as he was giving lectures on degeneration.[59] Two years later, in 1925, Gaupp's lecture course was printed under the title *Die Unfruchtbarmachung geistig und sittlich Kranker und Minderwertiger* (The sterilization of mentally and morally sick and inferior persons). Like Budzislawski, Gaupp advocated for the compulsory sterilization of supposedly inferior human beings: "The burden imposed on the German Reich by the mentally and morally inferior of all classes is immense, and in view of our poverty and our severe economic difficulties it is a wretched burden."[60] Let it be mentioned in passing that Gaupp did not utter a single word in this book about the work of the Jewish doctoral candidate Hermann Budzislawski.[61]

Budzislawski's dissertation was never printed. The problems he faced in 1923 were of an entirely different character. "I went hungry as a student" and "I ate in mass eating halls," he wrote later, a comment that was clearly a reference to the local soup kitchens rather than the student canteen.[62] Generalizing his own personal fate, he went on to say, using the sociological jargon of the era, "It was the terrible time of the inflation, when the wealth of our fathers was melting away. The middle classes were becoming economically proletarianized, but they retained their pride and haughtiness, and were unable to come to terms with their plight."[63] In the face of these circumstances, Budzislawski appears not to have considered pursuing an academic career, although his Tübingen supervisor allegedly offered him a position as assistant professor with the possibility of gaining a postdoctoral lecturer's qualification (*Habilitation*).[64] It is no longer possible to determine whether the marginalization of Jewish scholars in previous decades played a part in his decision. In most cases, German Jewish academics could expect to lead a precarious existence as nonsalaried private teachers, because they were regularly passed over when professorial appointments were made. On the other hand, perhaps Budzislawski simply had different expectations of his future life.[65] All that can be said with certainty is that he never spoke about the subject of his dissertation in later years, with one exception. That was in 1966, when he allowed himself to be quoted in the GDR *Weltbühne*: "From the point of view of present-day Marxism" his dissertation had been "a comical affair, and as far as I can recall this forgotten piece of work, it would hardly be possible to defend it."[66] However, he also maintained that his dissertation had been "highly regarded" then. That was a daring assertion to make in view of the absence of any response to his work in either the public or the scientific literature of the time. Moreover, the call for the compulsory sterilization of supposedly inferior human beings was now less than ever a "comical business" after the euthanasia program of the

Nazis and the Holocaust, to which some of Budzislawski's own relatives had fallen victim. Although it was evidently painful to him to contemplate this early work, he avoided making any kind of self-critical analysis of it. The Nazis' crimes against humanity had laid bare, in an almost inconceivable fashion, the murderous depths plumbed by far-reaching sociotechnological utopias, but the ambivalence involved in the dream of creating a new Socialist human being remained a taboo subject for Budzislawski. He may have needed to repress any reflections of this kind to retain some hope for the future, but perhaps this was simply a case of intellectual self-righteousness.

Despite distancing himself half-heartedly from his doctoral dissertation on racial hygiene, Budzislawski continued for the rest of his life to regard his academic title as an important distinction. He continued to use it even after the University of Tübingen had withdrawn his degree on 29 September 1938 because, as the university put it in Nazi terminology, he had contravened "his duty of loyalty to the Reich and the Volk."[67] Wilhelm Merk, a professor in the university's Faculty of Law, was still defending this action in 1947, pointing out that in the 1930s it had been open to Budzislawski to appeal the decision if he did so within the prescribed one-month period. The decision could have been rescinded if there were "particular reasons of equity" to justify doing so.[68] Budzislawski was unaware of Merk's impudent remarks, which were typical of the immediate postwar period in their reversal of the burden of guilt and expected the expatriated and persecuted individual to have held strictly to the legal route in a state that was itself lawless. He had sent a letter from New York on 7 July 1947 to the University of Tübingen asking cunningly whether it could send him a copy of the 1938 decree that deprived him of his academic status and whether anything had happened in the meantime to "make reparation for an injustice committed during the Hitler era."[69] Eventually, the Ministry of Education in the French occupation zone took a hand in the matter, putting pressure on the university. In response, the Lesser Senate of the University of Tübingen resolved on 14 October 1947 "to regard as invalid the revocation of academic degrees for political reasons" during the period of National Socialist rule.[70] The moral theologian Theodor Steinbüchel, who was now the rector of the university, wrote to Budzislawski in New York on the same day, stating that he was pleased "to be permitted to reintroduce your name into the list of our doctors."[71] But he did not include an apology for the injustice Budzislawski had suffered.

On this occasion, no one seems to have even looked at the content of Budzislawski's doctoral dissertation. The fact that it had not been printed in 1923 turned out in retrospect to be a piece of good fortune for the author. According to the version of the story Budzislawski himself propagated for the rest of his life, he began his career as a professional journalist in Berlin, where he made his name as a *Weltbühne* author, before he took over the chief editorship of the journal in March 1934 and continued to edit it in the spirit of his renowned predecessor. But in actual fact, the story was somewhat more complicated.

First Steps as a Journalist

Navigating Berlin in the Weimar Republic

BEFORE HERMANN BUDZISLAWSKI could make a name for himself as a political journalist, he had first to pursue other forms of employment to earn his daily bread. His father had emerged from humble beginnings and established himself as a master butcher and shopowner in the Prussian capital. Despite his pride in his twenty-two-year-old son's hunger for education, he stood too firmly on the ground of economic reality to advise him to take up the precarious existence of an intellectual. This was particularly the case in 1923, the year of hyperinflation, when money finally became so worthless that it could only be used to makes fires with. In the autumn of that year, food shops in the poorer districts of Berlin were repeatedly plundered: once again the air started to smell of revolution.[1]

Hermann Budzislawski, the newly graduated doctor of political and social sciences, took his first steps in professional life as a salesman and metal dealer for the Berlin branch of the Frankfurt firm of Beer, Sondheimer & Co.[2] He started the job on 1 April 1923. According to his own declaration, he was at that time "deeply discouraged about developments in Germany" during what was a critical year for the young German Republic.[3] As the Reich had got into arrears with its reparation payments, French and Belgian troops had marched into the economically vital Ruhr district on 11 January, and the government in Berlin had replied by calling for passive resistance. The French occupiers then responded to German acts of sabotage with the harsh verdicts of martial law. As a result, at least ninety-two people were killed in the months that followed, and inflation rose sharply. For Budzislawski, this was a very difficult time, not least because he was obliged to put himself under the parental roof again after the relative freedom of his former life as a student. Despite his successful entry into professional life, he apparently felt so desperate in August 1923 that he decided to immigrate to the United States. He claimed later that he made his way to Hamburg without a penny in his pocket and that his aim was to be taken on as a seaman. Elements of truth and invention probably lie side by side in the following autobiographical notes:

> For some months I lived in the slums of St. Pauli. I got to know the underworld of a big port city. My experiences were both amusing and horrifying, and they aroused in me the envious desire for a life free of all ties. But I was soon brought back to the world of order and civilization. My parents came to Hamburg to bring me back home before I set sail for New York on the American steamer "Cleveland," on which I had been offered a position as assistant cook. They had secured for me an important commercial job in the Free City of Danzig. I became a dealer in wood, and I had to travel to Warsaw to buy Polish timber and then ship it on to England by boat. It was a time of reconstruction and incipient stability for Germany, for Europe as a whole, and for myself.[4]

All his life, Budzislawski only wrote down the details of this Hamburg episode once, in an exposé written for a book project when he was in exile in America. In that situation it was impossible for him to avoid exaggerating and dramatizing his own life story for marketing purposes. In reality, he was perhaps without any means of support in the autumn of 1923, but he did not lack connections, because he was traveling with a letter of recommendation from his previous employer in which he was described as a "reliable person" with a quick grasp of affairs. This letter, dated 30 August 1923, was addressed to a Mr. Weinberg, a representative of the International Minerals and Metals Corporation, a firm whose New York headquarters was 61 Broadway. The writer asked Mr. Weinberg to help the young man "to get over the first difficulties" of the job, adding that Budzislawski was the nephew of the Berlin banker Ernst Joachimssohn, who was apparently personally acquainted with the addressee of the letter.[5]

Given our knowledge of Budzislawski's good behavior as a student in previous years, it does not seem very likely that as the son of a merchant and the holder of a doctorate he really spent his nights in the bars and brothels of the Hanseatic city with such a letter of recommendation in his luggage. On the other hand, the steamer *Cleveland* did indeed resume its route between Hamburg and New York in 1923. The information he gives about his later activities in Danzig is also correct, as Budzislawski did work in both Danzig and Warsaw for some time as an export merchant for the German timber-trading firm of Weigel & Company.[6] But he soon returned to Germany. Later, he was very reluctant to recall his time in the Polish capital. It is not very clear whether what he found upsetting in Warsaw was the need to earn a living by engaging in commerce or the foreign environment, in which, as a young man, he perhaps found few friends.[7]

Once back in Berlin, he tells us, he realized what he actually wanted to become: a journalist and an author. According to his own assertions, his endeavors were dazzlingly successful: "My articles appeared in the big newspapers and journals, such as the *Berliner Tageblatt*, the *Vossische Zeitung*, and the *Magazin der Wirtschaft*. My book on eugenics attracted the attention of State Secretary Julius Hirsch, who was at that time professor at the Berlin School of Commerce. I was appointed his assistant."[8] There is a considerable degree of exaggeration in this reference to his early success as a journalist. By the mid-1920s, Budzislawski had at most been able to get a few short texts published in Berlin newspapers, and no one had taken any particular notice of them. Just a handful of articles appeared under his real name between 1924 and 1926. The most substantial one was printed in the *Magazin der Wirtschaft*, the journal published by Leopold Schwarzschild, who was at the time mainly known as one of the publishers of the left-wing democratic weekly *Das Tagebuch*. The article was an attack on the state investment program for German shipbuilding. Apart from that, Budzislawski was still completely unknown as an author in Germany.[9]

From 1925 onward he worked as an editor for the fortnightly English-language journal *Industrial and Trade Review for India: Indo-German Commercial Review*, which began to appear in February of that year but only survived until March 1926. Its editorial office was located in the Berlin district of Halensee. The publisher replaced the word "India" in the title with the more general term "Asia" a few months later after the British colonial government of India prohibited importation of the journal. The establishment of this journal was linked with the creation of the League against Colonial Oppression (later renamed the League against Imperialism), an organization set up by Willi Münzenberg, one of the leading German Communists who was, above all, a successful media entrepreneur in the service of the Communist International (Comintern). The league was intended to give a global impulse to the proletarian revolution by supporting anticolonial movements of liberation in Asia and Africa. The *Industrial and Trade Review* similarly advocated turning the political consciousness of the "workers and peasants" of Asia against the "imperialist enemy" and mobilizing them politically for the anticolonial liberation struggle.[10] From the mid-1920s onward the city of Berlin lay at the hub of these transnational activities.[11]

The *Industrial and Trade Review* was printed in Berlin-Charlottenburg and later in Kreuzberg, and it was exclusively destined to be circulated in India, where, if we can trust the editors, its articles were soon reprinted in numerous local newspapers. It was edited at first by two Indian residents of the Prussian capital, Arathil Chandeth Narayanan Nambiar, later Indian ambassador to the German Federal Republic, and Virendranath Chattopadhyaya, who was called Chatto for short by his friends. Born in 1880, Chatto came from a wealthy Bengali family who had sent him to study law at Oxford University at the age of twenty-two as preparation for a professional career in the Indian civil service. But while he was in England, Chatto encountered Indian revolutionary nationalists, and in 1909 he became editor of a short-lived anticolonialist periodical, *The Talvar*. In 1914 he moved to Germany, where, during the next three years and among other activities, he took part in the Indian Independence Committee, which had the aim of preparing a revolt against the British colonial power. From 1917 onward he lived in Sweden and Moscow, but he returned to Germany shortly after the war ended.

In the years that followed, Chattopadhyaya was one of the best-known anticolonial activists in Berlin. He founded the Indian News Service and Information Bureau, which rapidly became a favorite point of contact for the comparatively large number of Indian students in the city. He occasionally functioned as first secretary of the League against Imperialism, and he delivered reports to the intelligence service of the Red Army. He particularly emphasized the economic opportunities offered by closer cooperation between the Indian nationalists and a Germany that had in the meantime been forcibly deprived of its colonies.[12] This political objective was also served by the *Industrial and Trade Review*, which in December 1925 was transferred completely into German hands. The Zionist Alwin Loewenthal now stepped forward as publisher and editor in chief. Loewenthal had already founded the Jewish Welt-Verlag in 1918, yet he presented himself to the British authorities in India as the director of a European cargo and luggage insurance company.[13] It is unclear how far this was an attempt to disguise his identity to get around the threat of a renewed prohibition on the distribution of the journal in India, which appeared to be imminent at the beginning of 1926. In any case, there was no real change in the journal's political line. It folded in March 1926 after it was again prohibited by the British colonial government in India, despite all the publisher's efforts and the financial support offered by Münzenberg.[14] In Germany, too, the League against Colonial Oppression had been under police observation.[15] By 1926 at the latest, Budzislawski was describing himself as the "responsible editor" of the monthly. It seems that he came into contact with Indian revolutionaries through Chattopadhyaya's former partner, the American journalist Agnes Smedley.[16] She had moved to Berlin with him at the start of the 1920s, and she worked there among other things as a correspondent for the US journals *The Nation* and *New Masses*.[17]

Budzislawski, who had gained his doctorate two years earlier, was for several reasons a good choice to edit the *Industrial and Trade Review*: his understanding of economics, acquired during his studies; his practical experience as a businessman; his good command of English; and his pronounced sympathy toward Socialism. As an old man, he recalled his days in the largely Indian editorial office of the journal, where it was "almost like living in an English-speaking island in Berlin."[18] He continued in later years to keep in regular contact with anticolonial activists who spent time in Germany. Together, they developed an anti-imperialist vision of the world and attempted to overthrow the current system. Budzislawski drew for the rest of his life on the cultural capital he acquired at this time, not only when he produced his reflections on the international economy, published in leading articles in *Die neue Weltbühne* between 1934 and 1939, but also after the end of the Second World War, when anticolonialism became the GDR's official doctrine. In 1961 Budzislawski was even invited by Jawaharlal Nehru to make a semiofficial visit to India. Chattopadhyaya and Nehru had cooperated closely for a period during the 1920s. Budzislawski also remained in contact with Agnes Smedley for a long time, at least into the 1930s, because she was one of the few women authors who wrote for *Die neue Weltbühne* while he was the journal's editor.

Budzislawski's activity for the Communist-backed periodical *Industrial and Trade Review* was an involvement he prudently passed over in silence later on, when he was a political refugee in the United States. After the journal's involuntary cessation, he again left Berlin, spending the next few months in Fiesole, a small hill town overlooking the Tuscan capital city of Florence. Here he lived with the family of the sculptor professor Paul Peterich as the private tutor of Peterich's son Eckart. He later reinterpreted this sojourn as a period of political fact-finding, claiming that he had stayed in Italy for just under six months "in order to study the Fascism of that epoch in greater detail."[19] Anyone who had lived in Italy during that time could have said the same thing, of course, but studying Fascism sounded more exciting than home tutoring, obviously. Be that as it may, Budzislawski did travel through the country, and he learned the language well enough to be able to speak it "fluently" by the time he returned to Germany, according to his own assertion. Italian was his third modern foreign language, after English and French, the two languages of which he had a firm grasp both orally and in writing.

The fact that Budzislawski took a job as a home tutor indicates how difficult it was for him to find his feet in a profession.[20] Parental connections were initially helpful, but a network of friends and acquaintances on the political Left soon became more important to him than family ties. It is also very likely that he got to know his future wife in and through these circles. Her name was

Johanna "Hanna" Levy, and she was born on 12 June 1901. Definite information on the circumstances of their first meeting has not come down to us. Nor
do we know much about their married life. Personal, let alone intimate, letters
between the pair written during the 1920s are absent from the otherwise surprisingly extensive papers he left after his death. It is not clear whether such
letters, if they existed, have been lost permanently or were kept back by Budzislawski's heirs when they handed over the material to the archives. Later letters
between the two never refer, as far as we know, to the time of their first
acquaintance, and in general they hardly mention intimate feelings. The marriage, the birth of their only daughter, Beate, on 14 September 1929, and the
deaths of their parents and siblings are all depicted in a strangely lifeless manner; these events appear as the external stages of a life that was presented as
having been entirely devoted to journalism and politics.

One thing, at least, is certain: the marriage of Hermann and Hanna Budzislawski took place on 18 December 1926 in the registry office of Berlin-
Tiergarten.[21] Hanna was a good match from a mixed Christian-Jewish family,
and like her husband she was strong-willed and had a lust for life. Before her
marriage she had lived with her mother, Martha Levy, maiden name Wille, who
had converted from Protestantism to Judaism, in a house at Wikinger Ufer 1,
Moabit. Her younger brother, Fritz, born in 1903 and paraplegic from childhood, also lived in the house. He had spent many years in a home, and he was
later one of the founders of a self-help group of physically disabled Jews. Some
years later, in 1934, he was living independently, but he lost his job and started
to suffer from dilation of the heart muscles as well as from loneliness, which
was worsened by the exile of his sister and her young family. He died at age
thirty-two on 23 May 1935 as the result of an accident. He was praised by Jewish
friends in an obituary as "one of the best fighters for the improvement of living
conditions for the disabled." His life had been full of "bitterness and suffering,"
but he had in the main been able to disguise this behind the façade of "a mind
that was always wide awake" and replete with "admirable energy."[22]

But let us return to the year 1926. The house of the Levy family lay only two
streets away from the abode of Budzislawski's parents, which was Levetzow-
straße 119; hence the paths of the two young people who lived in the same
neighborhood might well have crossed.[23] They did not know each other from
school, because Hanna had attended the Simonsche Privatschule in Charlottenburg, going on after that to the Kleist-Lyceum in Moabit. She had then left
school at the early age of sixteen to work as an apprentice gardener in the
Berlin Schlossgarten Bellevue. It must remain an open question whether she
took this step because of bad school reports, early youthful independence, or
the worsening financial situation of her parents. In a later account of her life,

Hanna wrote that she had "been in opposition to her parents at a very early age" and had moved over into the "camp of revolution," the so-called Westend Circle, together with Alfred Kurella, who was a left-wing member of the Wandervogel, and joined the Free German Youth after the split of 1917. Like her husband, Hanna was politicized early on by the First World War. In 1918, in a protest action to show her rejection of the hated world of bourgeois conservatism, she and her friends carried out the symbolic hanging of a scarecrow meant to represent the right-wing nationalist youth group the Wandervogel.[24] After the war she lived for some time on an experimental farm in Möser near Magdeburg, which at the time belonged to William Friedrich Hahlo, Kurella's father-in-law. Self-sufficiency, vegetarian food, and "sexual liberation" were typical features of such life-reform-oriented Socialist land communes, which often consisted of nothing more than a farmhouse with a piece of land attached. There were over a hundred such communes in Germany.[25]

For Hanna, the new decade started with a shock. On 20 January 1920 her father, the writer, land reformer, and liberal economist Louis Levy, who was born on 17 March 1867, took his own life. His suicide at the age of fifty-two was presumably a result of the financial difficulties he had experienced after the collapse of the German Empire. His father, Alexander Levy, had founded a successful cotton mill in the North Hessian town of Eschwege during Germany's nineteenth-century period of industrialization, with the result that both his sons had grown up in relatively well-off circumstances.[26] As an adult, Louis Levy published his work under the pseudonym Ludwig Eschwege. He collaborated closely with the well-known life and land reformer Adolf Damaschke, and during the First World War he attracted public attention with his articles exposing dishonest real estate transactions. His books about land speculation and the problems of mining and metallurgy are forgotten today, but they were quoted by Lenin, among other people, a fact Hanna Budzislawski was keen to point out in her later years in the GDR.[27]

The death of her father forced Hanna to return to Berlin and start earning her living. Her first job was with the gramophone manufacturer Akkuston, located at Ritterstraße 21, in Kreuzberg. After the firm went bankrupt in 1924, she worked for three years as an office manager at the Berlin Court of Textile Arbitration, which dealt with disputes in the clothing industry. Six months after her marriage to Budzislawski she gave up this position, thereby losing the modest degree of financial independence she had hitherto possessed. This was a typical step for a member of the relatively new profession of female office employee. Most of these young women, while enjoying the freedom associated with an independently earned salary, wanted to realize the dreams of marriage, children, and a happy family life—a lifestyle that the films of the 1920s offered

Portrait of Louis Levy, Hanna Budzislawski's
father, in uniform. He took his own life in
1920.

for mass consumption.[28] Hanna would probably have found the modest aspirations of the "typing-pool mademoiselles" a source of amusement, but she
too was unable to escape the economic realities of the epoch. Contact with her
brother and her mother, who by 1930 at the latest was living with the wealthy
Berlin businessman Gerhard Hinsching, who was originally from Leipzig and
whom she married in 1939, seems to have been slight in the years that followed. Their relationship only revived after the birth of the Budzislawski
grandchildren in the 1950s.[29]

The friends and acquaintances of the two young people, some of whom
later became famous both at home and abroad, were more important to them
than their families. In addition to Chatto and Agnes Smedley, the young
Budzislawskis knew the translator Olga Katunal, who was originally from
Lithuania, and her friend, the Austrian Robert Gruenwald. Through them, in

turn, they were probably also in loose contact with the "philosophical group" that formed in Berlin around the Jewish philosophers of religion Oskar Goldberg and Erich Unger. This social circle also included Bertolt Brecht; Alfred Döblin; Gerhard Scholem, who later changed his first name into the Hebrew form Gershom; Simon Guttmann, one of the pioneers of press photography; and Walter Benjamin, whom the Budzislawskis later described as an "old friend."[30] If the pair were not out and about or receiving visitors, they enjoyed playing chess—a game from which they learned many lessons that could be applied to real life. At least, the later journalist and businessman Budzislawski was distinguished by his grasp of strategy and ability to anticipate events.[31]

The pair also had a close friendship with Helene and Herman Reichenbach, whom they already knew from their time spent together in the radical left wing of the youth movement. The two couples went on holiday together at the end of the 1920s. Herman Reichenbach, who was born in Hamburg in 1898 as the youngest of three highly gifted brothers, was one of the leading speakers among the Berlin Socialist student body during the 1918 November Revolution, while his older brother Hans was the editor of *Der neue Anfang*, the journal in which Budzislawski had published his first articles at the beginning of 1919. In 1922, after studying mathematics, physics, music, and the theory of composition at Freiburg University, Herman Reichenbach gained his doctorate under the supervision of Wilibald Gurlitt, who was one of the sons of the then influential art historian Cornelius Gurlitt. From 1925 until 1930 Reichenbach was the director of the City School of Folk Music in Berlin-Charlottenburg, of which he was a cofounder. After that, he ran the music department of the Central Institute for Training and Education in Berlin. At the end of the 1920s he joined the Social Democratic Party (SPD). In 1933 he was dismissed on the basis of the anti-Semitic Law for the Restoration of the Professional Civil Service.[32] He got to know his second wife, Helene "Lo" Reichenbach, in Berlin in 1918 while she was attending the Folk Music School. She was the daughter of a Chinese British commission agent and was born Helene Antoni Chai in the London borough of Lewisham on 18 December 1902.[33] Later, Helene was a member of the Free School Student Movement, and she subsequently recalled this period of her life as a "great emotional milestone." She remained particularly fond of Budzislawski even later on, when they were both in exile, although for most of the time they lived in different countries. In 1935 she became a partner in *Die neue Weltbühne*.[34]

There is a photograph of Hermann and Hanna Budzislawski that was taken sometime during the first two years of their marriage while they were on a holiday in Florence. It was shot on the Piazzale Michelangelo, the famous square that provides a panoramic view of the river Arno and the old city. The two young people from Berlin look self-confidently at the camera. Both are elegantly clothed—she with a cloche hat and a fashionable spring jacket that deliberately does not emphasize the waist, he with rimless spectacles, suit and tie, and a pocket watch. In the words of the well-known hit song created by Robert Gilbert and Werner Richard Heymann that was a fine expression of the liveliness of the 1920s:

> Here I come, here I come, here I come!
> Whoever tags along will get a treat.
> I'd like to grab a mouthful of the lovely, lovely world
> And live my life the way I want and never miss a beat

The Budzislawskis' holiday snap reflects this mood. The young couple also made two journeys to Paris, in 1927 and 1928.[35] In the late 1920s the Budzislawskis seemed to be well on the way to success, like the Weimar Republic itself. Private tragedies such as the death of Hermann's other brother, the businessman Martin Budzislawski, who died at the age of only thirty-four after an operation to deal with the aftereffects of being poisoned by gas during the First World War, seem hardly to have left any traces in the letters that have come down to us.[36] By now, their circle of acquaintances already extended beyond Europe—or, to be more precise, it also included intellectuals and political activists from America, Africa, and Asia who were living in the German capital. The papers of the Berlin journalist Walter Zadek, who as a sixth former in the Königsstädtisches Realgymnasium was also one of the "school revolutionaries" of 1918–19, contain one of Budzislawski's visiting cards, on which he put in a good word for Joseph Ekwe Bilé, a "negro from Cameroon, who has studied in Germany."[37] Zadek, who worked as an editor on the *Berliner Tageblatt* at the start of the 1930s, lived, like the Budzislawski couple, in the artists' colony at Laubenheimer Platz in Berlin-Wilmersdorf. Twice a month he organized so-called Jours there, events at which the capital's journalists and artists met informally.[38] Bilé, wrote Budzislawski to Zadek, had been very badly treated in Germany "on account of the color of his skin"; perhaps he could be helped?

The gentleman Budzislawski was referring to was born in 1892. He had studied architecture, but he initially earned his living as an actor in numerous variety theaters and in films. In addition, he was the secretary of the League for the Defense of the Negro Race, founded on 17 September 1929. This was an association of Africans from the former German colonies who were fighting against the discrimination they suffered in Europe and committed to supporting the anticolonial liberation struggle in Africa. Bilé was soon seen in Com-

Hanna and Hermann Budzislawski on a trip to Italy. Photograph taken in Florence in 1927 or 1928.

munist circles as a poster boy of anticolonialism. At the beginning of the 1930s he was arrested at least twice, and it is possible that Budzislawski's recommendation to Zadek was related to one of these arrests. Bilé's defense league was a Comintern-financed section of the League against Imperialism run by Münzenberg, which was the successor organization to the League against Colonial Oppression.[39] Although Bilé joined the Communist Party of Germany in 1930 and took part in the Fifth World Congress of the Red International of Labor Unions in Moscow, there were some doubts about his suitability as a Communist agitator. Chattopadhyaya, the former publisher of the anticolonial *Industrial and Trade Review*, had in the meantime begun to work for Münzenberg in the Comintern apparatus. One of his tasks was to supervise the League for the Defense of the Negro Race, and he was critical of Bilé's abilities.[40] The question of whether Budzislawski was a Communist who carried out instructions from 1934 onward to bring *Die neue Weltbühne* onto a Soviet course is still disputed to this day. Details of this kind do offer at least some suggestions of an answer. Since the mid-1920s Budzislawski had been acquainted with leading anticolonial activists in Germany; thus he was circulating in a political milieu that was essentially financed and increasingly directed by the Comintern.

In 1929 Budzislawski joined the German Writers' Defense Association, and in the years that followed he was a member of its executive, together with the Hungarian literary scholar Georg Lukács and his fellow countryman, the Communist exile Andor Gábor.[41] He also became a member of the SPD in 1929, allegedly on the advice of his Communist friends, in order to work as an "active Marxist" within that party. Between 1929 and 1933 Budzislawski and his wife belonged to Branch 72 of the SPD in Wilmersdorf. After the war they informed the SED that they had repeatedly been subjected to SPD party investigations on account of their "activities on the extreme Left." As Hanna wrote in 1950 in an autobiographical statement, "We took pains to remain in the SPD, but by 1932 we would have liked to leave it and join the KPD." But of course by then this was no longer a choice they could make as individuals. Andor Gábor discussed the case with Walter Ulbricht, the political director of the KPD district Berlin-Brandenburg-Lausitz-Grenzmark, and Ulbricht decided that Hermann Budzislawski should continue to be involved in "intellectual work" within the SPD.[42] It is not possible to decide whether this actually happened or whether the story was intended as a retrospective demonstration of their attachment to Communism, but it is noticeable that Hanna Budzislawski did not even mention the Socialist Workers' Party of Germany (SAP), which was founded in 1931. The Budzislawskis had direct contact with this splinter party, which emerged from the SPD, through the lawyer and Reichstag deputy Kurt Rosenfeld, who also represented Carl von Ossietzky before the court, among other things. They also remained in close touch later when they were in exile.

Hermann Budzislawski told Zürich police detectives in May 1933 that he had been part of a "Left opposition" within the SPD in previous years and among other activities had conducted "Marxist education courses."[43] He claimed in addition that in 1928 or 1929 he had spent a year as honorary secretary of the Society for the Promotion of Jewish Settlement in Birobidzhan in the Soviet Union. From the end of the 1920s, a Jewish Soviet Zion was supposed to be under construction around the town of Birobidzhan, which was located in eastern Siberia, close to the Soviet-Chinese border. Jewish farmers there were supposed to play their part in supplying the Soviet Union with provisions. In this context, Budzislawski claimed that he had been approached in his Berlin flat in the artists' colony by members of the Moscow State Jewish Theater, headed by the renowned Solomon Mikhoels. He had also discussed projects for Jewish settlement in the Soviet Union with Arnold Zweig in the latter's house in the neighboring locality of Eichkamp.[44] The Birobidzhan district was very thinly populated; even from the Soviet point of view it lay at the back of beyond, and despite propaganda to the contrary it was by no means a good substitute for the Crimea, the region initially considered for the project. The ground was rock hard with frost during the long and bitterly cold winter months. Then in late spring it turned into a gigantic swamp, and during the short summers it was plagued by mosquitoes, which made working in the fields very difficult. The cultural isolation of the area soon made it clear even to optimists that it was an extremely unsuitable place of settlement for Jews who came predominantly from the urban areas of the western Soviet Union.[45]

Budzislawski did not emerge as a political journalist in the narrower sense before 1932. Instead, he earned a living for himself and his young family as the editor of the Wissenschaftliche Korrespondenz, literally "Scientifique Correspondence." This was a press service called into being by Budzislawski himself that concentrated above all on natural scientific matters. He had no more than a handful of associates working with him but claimed to have supplied information to several hundred newspapers in Germany, Austria, and Switzerland. Budzislawski obtained an additional source of income from occasional lectures to secondary schools and from radio transmissions for Radio Hour Berlin (Funk-Stunde Berlin), a radio station that could be received all over Northern Germany and whose literary director was the journalist and writer Edlef Köppen. Some of Budzislawski's radio talks were directed explicitly at children. He stepped forward as an enlightener, a man who knew how to transmit scientific knowledge to specific target groups in a comprehensible manner. His twenty-to-thirty-minute broadcasts addressed topics such as "The East in Europe" and "The Menu of Mankind." During the Youth Hour he discussed "bacteria as friends and foes of humanity. . . . The lecturer took this opportunity to acquaint his young listeners with luminaries of scientific research such as Robert Koch and Louis Pasteur."[46] The world of science and developments in the world economy were the favorite themes treated by Budzislawski the radio journalist, who willingly accepted the radio station's occasional invitations, which provided him with an extra income. In 1930 he traveled to the Balkans at the invitation of the Yugoslav government, reporting subsequently on the Berlin radio station about the situation of the Bosnian Muslims. The year after that he went on a journey to Great Britain and Ireland, which provided useful material for further broadcasts. Radio continued to be his second favorite medium of communication in later decades.[47] Despite his appearances before the microphone, however, his name was known to only a few people during the Weimar Republic. When he later presented himself as a veteran contributor to *Die Weltbühne*, this was factually incorrect, at least for the period before 1933, because his first signed article in the well-known journal did not appear until 6 December 1932, only a few weeks before German democracy lay in ruins.

These final months of the Weimar Republic were a dangerous time for *Die Weltbühne*, which had been founded in 1906 as *Die Schaubühne* by the theater critic Siegfried Jacobsohn. Its editor in chief, Carl von Ossietzky, a man of absolute integrity who had a polite and reserved nature but who was inflexible on matters of real importance, had been sentenced in November 1931 by the Supreme Court in Leipzig to a term of eighteen months in prison for treason and the betrayal of military secrets. The occasion for this was an article that appeared on 12 March 1929 in *Die Weltbühne* under the title "Shady Doings in the German Air Force." It was a report on the secret reconstruction of the Luftwaffe by the Reichswehr, which was an obvious breach of the Versailles Treaty. Ossietzky started his prison term on 10 May 1932, and he was held in Tegel Prison until the "Christmas amnesty" of 22 December 1932. His supporters had vainly appealed to him to flee abroad, but he told them that he was not going to prison out of a sense of loyalty but rather because as a prisoner he could cause the greatest inconvenience to the government.

Friends and supporters of Carl von Ossietzky say goodbye to him on 10 May 1932 before he enters Tegel Prison in Berlin to begin his period of imprisonment. The writer Lion Feuchtwanger, the lawyer and journalist Rudolf Olden, and Ossietzky himself are in the first row, from left to right. Kurt Grossmann is standing in the row behind them. The writer Ernst Toller is facing Ossietzky, and Ossietzky's lawyer, Alfred Apfel, is behind Toller.

Ossietzky's predecessor as editor in chief, Kurt Tucholsky, had already lived abroad since 1929, near Gothenburg in Sweden, and from there he had observed developments in Germany with an increasing feeling of resignation. Long before Hitler became chancellor, Tucholsky had declared that he wanted to have nothing more to do with day-to-day political events in Germany. Although this meant that *Die Weltbühne* had lost its veteran star author, who on some occasions had simultaneously published articles under five pseudonyms, at the start of 1930 the journal was still a flagship for the leftist German intelligentsia, enjoying a wide reputation both at home and abroad. What was written there was of weighty public significance—to a greater extent than the modest print run of eight thousand to sixteen thousand copies a week might lead one to assume. *Die Weltbühne* stood for polemical and often witty attacks on contemporary abuses and an unconditional will to tell the truth without excessive deference. As Tucholsky put it in 1926, *Die Weltbühne*'s editorial board was "a center of ideas, radiating energy," denouncing errors, and "rubbing the noses of well-meaning people in what was really important."[48] In the eyes of the nationalist Right, however, the journal embodied everything they hated about the Weimar Republic. They saw Jewish exponents of "gutter literature" at work, people without a sense of honor or shame whose activities had to be stopped at the earliest possible opportunity. In short, *Die Weltbühne* was a particularly polarizing phenomenon in a situation that was already highly polarized, but even its opponents did not question its relevance. Berlin, a world metropolis, spoke in the journal's pages, though perhaps only for an increasingly marginalized public.[49]

Considering the dramatic circumstances of the time, Budzislawski made an unspectacular debut at *Die Weltbühne*. His first article was a sympathetic portrait of Ernst Wagemann, the business cycle researcher and president of the Imperial Statistical Office; it was also a kind of review of the latter's pamphlet *Was ist Geld?* (What is money?), which had appeared some months before. Another contribution, which was much more important, analyzed the illegal flight of capital from crisis-wracked Germany and the significance of these money transfers for the way the parties of the extreme Right were financed. Another article of his introduced to the reader Friedrich Syrup, the new minister of labor in the short-lived cabinet of Kurt von Schleicher.[50] Fewer than a dozen articles by Budzislawski appeared in *Die Weltbühne* until March 1933, when the journal was prohibited, and his articles alternated with those of the long-standing economics editor of the *Vossische Zeitung*, Richard Lewinsohn, who wrote under the alias Morus.

Budzislawski's articles were well informed, compared to other contributions, but they had neither literary pretensions nor a recognizable personal style. Some of them are simply boring when one reads them today—at least, they are when compared to the far more elegant and lively essays of the journal's most eloquent contributors, who are able to stir enthusiasm even today. But perhaps that is an unfair comparison. At any rate, Ossietzky did in fact praise his new contributor's first articles. He commented in February 1933 that they were "fresh, informative and written with great journalistic verve."[51] This may simply have been a case of politeness at a difficult time when he did not want to lose any colleagues, but it was certainly an accolade, if a rather restrained one. Budzislawski's last article was a preview of the court case brought against the Bremen entrepreneur Gustav Lahusen for delaying the bankruptcy declaration of the important textile firm Nordwolle, whose bankruptcy during the world economic crisis led to the collapse of a number of prominent banks. The article appeared on 7 March 1933 under the pseudonym Ulrich Schweitzer. For anyone in the know, this was a barely disguised reference to Budzislawski's possible future place of residence in Switzerland. After the Reichstag fire at the end of February his whereabouts were officially unknown.[52] The firm association with *Die Weltbühne* to which Budzislawski aspired did not materialize either under the chief editorship of Carl von Ossietzky or that of his interim replacement, Hellmuth von Gerlach.[53] It is therefore also very unlikely that the then proprietor of the journal, the publisher and translator Edith Jacobsohn, had already made Budzislawski its editor in chief in the summer of 1932, as he claimed in the 1960s.[54] After all, at that time he had not yet written a line for it.

Budzislawski was, nevertheless, personally acquainted with many of the artists, writers, and journalists who lived in the capital by the beginning of the 1930s. This was not so much on account of his journalism as because of his move to Bonner Straße 1, in Berlin-Wilmersdorf, which brought him into the heart of the artists' colony that had just been built. Since 1927 almost six hundred affordable dwellings had been constructed in the streets around Laubenheimer Platz on behalf of the Cooperative of German Theater Professionals and the German Writers' Defense Association. In his autobiography, one of the colony's former residents, the author Gustav Regler, described life there as having been not particularly glamorous: "We lived in a block of flats. It was cheap, but scarcely one of the occupants was able to pay his rent; neither the salaries nor the earnings of the so-called free professions were adequate. Many of the apartments contained no furniture other than a mattress on the floor. . . . But none starved, each man helped his fellow, and those in need went from one door to the next, knowing by instinct where someone had found work and there was a little bacon and cheese to be had."[55] By moving to the artists' colony, Hermann Budzislawski finally became a participant in an important center of Berlin's leftist intelligentsia, and the friendships he made there would turn out to be particularly helpful, one might even say lifesaving, when he was in exile a few years later. Seen from this perspective, the years spent in the artists' colony had a formative influence on the later life of the young couple, serving as an apprenticeship in both politics and communal living.

The results of the world economic crisis that began at the end of 1929 worsened the situation in the artists' colony, which had only just been set up. It was known in Berlin, not without reason, as the Hunger Fortress, or, on account of the political preferences of its inhabitants, as the Red Block. The political camps were becoming radicalized there, as they were everywhere else in Germany. The KPD gained ground among those intellectuals who demanded a fundamental transformation of the social order. Capitalism, they thought, had reached the end of its usefulness, as was shown with absolute clarity by the economic crisis, which had thrown millions of people into misery. The Weimar Republic was only "the Kaiserreich in disguise," a "nature conservation park for East Elbian Junkers", the Prussian landed aristocrats. The characteristic features of the epoch were secret rearmament and economic crisis, Budzislawski wrote later.[56] The ground-floor apartment of Alfred "Kanto" Kantorowicz was the Communists' stronghold in the artists' colony. Kantorowicz, two years older than the Budzislawskis, likewise came from a Jewish business family and had also worked as a journalist in Berlin since the mid-1920s. Fifteen to twenty party members and sympathizers regularly came to his flat to plan joint actions. They took the National Socialist threat extremely seriously, but they assumed that it was possible to defeat Fascism by putting up determined political resistance. In July 1932, in order to repel the Nazis, over a hundred of the colony's inhabitants finally set up the Anti-Fascist Defense League, which was headed by a committee of five, chaired by the young journalist Axel Eggebrecht. Other members included the anarchist Albert Arid, the Communists Max Schroeder and Kantorowicz himself, and Budzislawski, who later claimed that the "revolutionary block newspaper" of the artists' colony was put together in his apartment. Moreover, Hanna was an active member of the Workers' International Relief.[57]

On 30 January 1933 Budzislawski tells us that he was present at the press conference of the Reich government where it was announced that a new Reich chancellor, Adolf Hitler, had been appointed: "It was a dramatic moment. For me it was the end of my regular career. I knew that for us democrats the political struggle would henceforth take other forms." That is how Budzislawski portrayed both the historic occasion and his own attitude some years later.[58]

The "dramatic moment" occurred shortly before his thirty-second birthday, when his journalistic career as an author publishing under his own name in *Die Weltbühne* had hardly started. Four weeks later, the Reichstag was ablaze. The fire service was still extinguishing the flames when the National Socialists began to arrest thousands of actual or suspected opponents of the regime all over the country according to blacklists drawn up in advance. Ossietzky was taken from his bed on 29 February at 3:30 in the morning, again put in custody, and three weeks later incarcerated in Sonnenburg concentration camp, where he was severely mistreated.[59] Like him, many other *Weltbühne* authors were in great danger. The journal was prohibited on 13 March, and its editorial offices at Kantstraße 152 were searched by the police and sealed up. Two days later, the SA, together with regular police units, conducted an extensive raid around the Laubenheimer Platz. "'Artists' Colony' Südwestkorso Finally Rooted Out—Immense Stocks of Subversive Literature—Washbasins Full of Weapons"—that was the headline in the *Völkische Beobachter* the next morning. And *Der Angriff*, the newspaper set up some years before by the Berlin gauleiter Joseph Goebbels, announced triumphantly: "We can now say that with this action one of the worst Bolshevik plague boils in Berlin has been lanced."[60]

Notwithstanding such vainglorious propaganda, only a few of the political opponents of the National Socialists fell into their hands during this raid. Many residents of the artists' colony had escaped to safety in good time. Hermann Budzislawski too went underground. "I lived illegally for three weeks, and every night I slept in a different place, until I managed to escape to Switzerland."[61] His wife, who followed him some weeks later with their daughter, was "a secret reporter for the *Manchester Guardian*" during this time, according to Budzislawski, and she provided the outside world with "the first authentic information about the Nazi terror."[62] Further pieces of hot news reached Paris via Switzerland and were used in *The Brown Book of the Reichstag Fire and Hitler Terror*, which exposed the truth about early Nazi rule. It was published in several languages and achieved a great success.[63] Both the Berlin political police and the Ministry of Propaganda had files on Budzislawski, a fact he learned from a reliable source.[64] These claims can hardly be checked, especially as such information could only be passed on at very great risk, and people therefore avoided putting things down in writing. But they have an overall ring of plausibility.

However, the Budzislawskis were no longer living in the artists' colony at the beginning of 1933. To judge by the stationery used by Hermann Budzislawski in that year, the young family's Berlin address was actually Auerhahnbalz 21, a small terraced house in the Zehlendorf housing estate designed by

Bruno Taut and built between 1926 and 1932 that they had either bought or rented. The source of funds for this move is not clear. The Budzislawskis could hardly have been able to build up significant financial reserves from Hermann's income as a journalist, especially in the years of the world economic crisis. Since potential ownership of this piece of real estate is never mentioned in his papers, it is reasonable to assume that they had only rented the property. They would certainly have needed parental assistance to buy it. That a certain degree of financial support would have been possible was shown after 1933, when monthly transfers of money from Berlin to Zürich were vital to the survival of the exiled couple, at least for a limited period.

A good illustration of Hermann Budzislawski's upward social mobility until 1933 is provided by changes in his Berlin home address: he was born in the working-class district of Wedding and grew up in various dwellings in Mitte, Kreuzberg, and Charlottenburg; as a young man he initially lived with his parents and his brother Martin in Moabit before acquiring an apartment of his own for the first time, after his marriage to Hanna. After 1930 he could be found in the telephone book as "Dr. Budzislawski, Editor" at the address Bonner Straße 1, in other words, in the artists' colony, to which they had moved in 1929. The relocation to Zehlendorf three years later can now only be traced through the documents of the Swiss federal prosecutor's office and the SED's cadre files. One can clearly assume that after the war Budzislawski was happy to keep quiet about his final Berlin address so as to place greater emphasis on his services as a persecuted anti-Fascist from the artists' colony.[65] After the establishment of the National Socialist dictatorship it would be fifteen long years before he was again able to return to the city where he was born.

Writing Against Hitler

Budzislawski as an Anti-Fascist Journalist in Switzerland and Czechoslovakia

ERMANN BUDZISLAWSKI WAS one of over half a million people who emigrated from Germany, Austria, and the Sudeten German areas of Czechoslovakia between 1933 and 1939 as a result of the transfer of power to the National Socialists. Approximately thirty thousand of them can be counted as political exiles in the narrower sense, and within this group, sixteen hundred had previously been active as writers and journalists.[1] With one or two exceptions, they found it very difficult to make ends meet in a foreign country, and they were desperately dependent on the scanty remuneration offered by the exile presses and the anti-Fascist periodicals.

The rise and consolidation of Fascist regimes was a major feature of the European scene in the 1930s. Supporters of the political Left developed various strategies for dealing with this situation. While many adapted themselves to the new relationship of forces, some engaged in active resistance, and a small minority went underground. The leaders of the working-class parties were looking for opportunities to turn things to their advantage. This was not just true of the parties of the Communist International under Moscow's leadership. It also applied to European Social Democracy, a point that has occasionally been overlooked. The latter's representatives endeavored to reply to the existential threats they faced by building up a strong transnational network for the defense of democracy and social rights.[2] Budzislawski stood between the two camps of the Left, or, to put it more accurately, he stood with one leg in each and was always ready to shift his weight to one side or the other if necessary. The outer flexibility of the exiled Budzislawski, who between 1933 and 1948 lived successively in Switzerland, Czechoslovakia, France, and the United States, was paralleled by an inner agility that allowed him to avoid becoming dependent on a particular political party, despite placing himself unambiguously on the anti-Fascist Left. Nevertheless, it became increasingly clear between 1935 and 1938 that he was more inclined to support Communist positions than Social Democratic ones.

Budzislawski's first stopping point as a political exile was Switzerland. He entered the country via Basel on 23 March 1933, accompanied by the writer Moritz A. Loeb, who had been one of the contributors to the Big City documents series (Großstadtdokumente) issued by Hans Ostwald, a journalist and pioneer in the history of everyday life, at the beginning of the twentieth century.[3] Budzislawski settled first in Zürich at Hottingerstraße 67, in the elegant Seventh District, but he soon moved to Bäckerstraße 54, which was located in the city's working-class area. "For the moment this is not a flight but rather a business trip," he told the Swiss criminal police in May 1933, presumably on the assumption that this would improve his chances of obtaining a residence permit. The Swiss Federal Prosecutor's Office assumed in the summer of 1933 that Loeb was planning to open a "press bureau" and that he would employ Budzislawski as an editor. Shortly after his arrival in Zürich, Budzislawski was personally informed by a "trusted individual from Berlin" that he would "immediately be arrested and placed in a concentration camp" if he returned to Germany. From then on, he no doubt regarded himself as a political refugee, but he was concerned to stress that his presence in Switzerland should not be brought "in any way into connection with the persecution of the Jews" in Germany: "What is involved here is a purely political matter on which my freedom depends."[4]

Although his cause was advocated by his Zürich fellow writer Max Grünfeld and by the Swiss Social Democrat and National Council member Hans Oprecht, who was also the leader of the Swiss Union of Public Service Employees, the Swiss authorities were at first unwilling to recognize him as a political refugee.[5] The Swiss Federal Prosecutor's Office informed the Zürich cantonal police that Budzislawski was being pursued "largely as a result of the general measures taken against Israelite intellectuals." The explanation was formulated in such a way as to suggest that the persecution of the Jewish intelligentsia in Germany was legitimate.[6] The assertion that the action by the German police against the staff of *Die Weltbühne* could "be seen from the viewpoint of a measure of general cultural policy" also sounded problematic.[7] The Swiss authorities were clearly anxious to limit the number of victims of persecution arriving from Germany, and if possible they wanted to prevent the entry of Jews altogether. Because he was aware of this, Budzislawski insisted to the police on the distinction between political and racial persecution. He ascribed his political persecution to his activities in the German Writers' Defense Association, his anti-Fascist speeches for the SPD, his direct journalistic attacks on right-wing politicians, and his "articles on economic policy" in *Die Weltbühne*, in which he "analyzed the economic theories of the National Socialists." As we have seen, the last statement was an exaggeration. It was not false, but it lay right at the edge of what could be asserted with honesty.[8]

On 29 June Budzislawski finally received a permit to remain, initially limited to three months and conditional on his avoiding political activity of any kind in Switzerland. A bond of 4,000 Swiss francs was also demanded. The money was deposited by Otto Lang, who was a Social Democratic politician, lawyer, and chief justice, and by Ludwig Frank, a physician. But Budzislawski's application to be allowed to establish a press office was rejected. He said later that he had acted as the "disguised editor" of an anti-Fascist news service he created, the Neue Presse-Korrespondenz (New Press Correspondence, NPK).[9] Private letters indicate that he and his associates also considered "organizing a café in P"—presumably Paris, less likely Palestine or Poland—but it seems that this plan was quickly abandoned.[10] Unlike many other refugees, Budzislawski was not in a precarious financial situation in 1933. Every month he received 500 or 600 Swiss francs by bank transfer from his wife and later also from other family members who had remained in Berlin. "I shall at worst receive support from the Swiss refugee assistance organization, but this will hardly be necessary," he stated confidently. Where this money came from is not entirely clear. If the young couple's savings were insufficient, master butcher Isidor Budzislawski would probably have stepped in, as would Hanna's mother, who after the suicide of her first husband had lived since the end of the 1920s with a relatively wealthy man. In May 1933 Hanna followed her husband to Switzerland with their daughter, and the Budzislawskis moved into the Werkbund settlement of Neubühl, on the outskirts of Zürich. Many of the houses, which had only just been completed, stood empty at the time, with the result that, in addition to members of the cooperative, "mere tenants," whose residential status was precarious, such as the family from Berlin, could find a place to stay at a rent of 155 francs a month.[11]

On 6 October 1933 Hermann Budzislawski was finally granted the status of political refugee, although he was still prohibited from engaging in any form of political activity. He was expressly forbidden to publish reports on the National Socialist regime, which was currently establishing itself in Germany.[12] He responded by adopting the alias Nepomuk Frisch for correspondence of a political character, and he wanted his future articles in *Die neue Weltbühne* to be printed under the pseudonym Hermann Eschwege. That was an acknowledgment of his wife's deceased father, who had published his work under the name Ludwig Eschwege, alluding to his birthplace.[13] It was nevertheless clear to the exiled Budzislawski that he could not remain in Switzerland for long, and not just for legal reasons (it was not clear whether his "permit to remain," valid for three months, would be renewed). The group of Jewish emigrants in the Werkbund settlement was also subject to antisemitic hostility, which probably surfaced even before the start of 1934, when a veritable witch hunt broke out against the supposedly "Jewish settlement with Communist tendencies."[14] In view of these difficulties, Budzislawski finally decided to go to Prague. He wanted to continue his struggle against National Socialism as a journalist and propagandist from that city. Once again, he initially left his wife and child behind.

The writer Stefan Heym, who had also fled from Germany in 1933, recalled some decades later that the Prague of the era was "like a dream. The Golem was still there, supposedly lying in a secret chamber under the roof of the Altneuschul Synagogue. The fortune-tellers were still hanging around Alchemists' Alley on the Hradčany, . . . and there was still a hint of the Habsburg past in the wood-paneled cafés where elderly gentlemen would sit reading the newspapers for hour after hour with a bowl of black coffee and a glass of water."[15] Within a short time, the town on the Vltava with its rather tranquil atmosphere became one of the most important centers of German political emigration, side by side with Moscow, London, and Paris. The Social Democratic *Vorwärts* in exile appeared there between 1933 and 1938, as well as the Communist *Arbeiter-Illustrierte-Zeitung*, with its photo montages produced by John Heartfield, which are still famous today. Between 1933 and 1935 one could also read the *Neue Deutsche Blätter*, produced by Heartfield's brother Wieland Herzfelde, who had founded the Malik Verlag after the First World War and now worked as an editor along with the writers Anna Seghers and Oskar Maria Graf. Prague's geographical proximity to the German capital and the existence of reliable German Czech networks, which had already proved valuable during the Weimar Republic, rendered the city attractive to the exiles from Germany, as also did the fact that it cost less to live there than in the metropolitan centers of Western Europe.[16]

The German-speaking exiles had a particular liking for the Café Continental, Conti for short, on the first floor of the Kolowrat Palace "Am Graben," as well as the Café Central, which was not too far away. Newspapers from various European countries were displayed there, and the waiters allowed customers to remain at a table for the whole evening with just one cup of coffee. Exiled journalists, writers, artists, academics, and both Czech and German police spies followed hard on each other's heels in a quite literal sense. The search for kindred spirits was for many people a flight from loneliness and insignificance in a foreign country. The emigrant Karl Otto Paetel later recalled the atmosphere, though not uncritically: "One felt at home—if only in the empire of fiction, the land of plans and perspectives, where the word no one listened to any more in its home country could put forth a last quiet plea to be heard."[17] The German Communists and their friends had their own regular table in the front lounge of the Continental, where Gustav, the head waiter, allowed them credit up to the amount of twenty Czechoslovak crowns. Budzislawski too was soon a regular visitor there.[18]

Prague Conservation Park, a drawing by Wilhelm Schulz. This antisemitic caricature, denouncing an alleged alliance between Jewish exiles and underworld forces, was printed on 4 March 1934 in the Munich periodical *Simplicissimus*.

Die neue Weltbühne had been published in Prague since 20 April 1933 under the editorship of Wilhelm S. Schlamm. It was a continuation of the Vienna *Weltbühne*, which had appeared there since September 1932 as an offshoot of the Berlin *Weltbühne*. The Vienna *Weltbühne* took roughly half of its articles from the Berlin publication, and it was an attempt to be forearmed against the threat of prohibition in Germany, which became more likely after Franz von Papen's "Prussian coup" of 20 July 1932 that saw the legal government of the largest German state replaced and fundamental rights restricted.[19] In the spring of 1933, after *Die Weltbühne* was prohibited in Berlin, what was originally its offshoot became the main paper. *Die neue Weltbühne* had two shareholders with equal rights: Edith Jacobsohn (later Edith Forster-Jacobsohn), the widow of Siegfried Jacobsohn, the founder of *Die Schaubühne*, and the Viennese Hans Heller, one of the sons of the wealthy Jewish confectionary manufacturer Gustav Heller. Hans Heller was a friend of editor in chief Schlamm, and in 1932 he contributed fresh capital to the journal, money that was urgently needed to keep it running.[20] But at the end of March 1933 the situation in Austria under the rule of Austrofascism became too dangerous, so Schlamm, with the support of Egon Erwin Kisch, transferred the offices to Melantrichova 1, in the Czechoslovak capital.[21]

In terms of content, *Die neue Weltbühne* continued its Weimar tradition of independent criticism, but Schlamm also endeavored to cover a broad spectrum of opinions from independent liberals and the political Left and including Stalin's opponent, Leon Trotsky, as a regular contributor. He called on the political Left to react to the Nazi takeover of power with a self-critical discussion of the mistakes of the last few years. Later on in the GDR, when the line of the exiled Communist Party of Germany, formerly a subject of dispute, was officially described as correct, he was accused of having attempted to stab the "anti-Fascist forces" in the back during the period of illegality.[22] But in 1933 the journal faced difficulties of a different and more urgent nature. Schlamm, a brilliant journalist, paid comparatively little attention to the financial requirements for the periodical's continued existence, which he regarded as secure thanks to the involvement of Heller. This lack of concern became a problem owing to the exile situation and the breakdown of the main markets for *Die neue Weltbühne* in Germany and Austria. Schlamm therefore repeatedly came into conflict with Edith Jacobsohn. She had achieved great success in the 1920s by translating and publishing German editions of *Winnie the Pooh* and *The Story of Doctor Dolittle*, but now, apart from questions of content, she was worried about the journal's profitability. After the sale of her children's book-publishing firm, Williams & Company, in 1933, she had lived in exile with her underage son, Peter, almost exclusively from the profits of *Die neue Weltbühne*. She was entitled by contract to withdraw a sum of 500 Swiss francs every month from the journal's Zürich account, deducted from its net profit. But in 1933 the journal experienced losses rather than profits, and thus the deposits melted away as one month followed the next.[23]

This was Budzislawski's opportunity.[24] He had tried in 1933 to become a regular editor of *Die neue Weltbühne*, but under Schlamm he was unable to get his way, one reason being disagreements over content.[25] By December 1933 at the latest, he had managed to persuade Jacobsohn's widow, the half owner of the journal, that the survival of *Die neue Weltbühne* could only be secured under his editorship. The removal of its offices from Prague to Paris or Geneva was also considered.[26] The Budzislawskis were currently living in a two-and-a-half-room terraced house in the Zürich Werkbund estate at Westbühlstraße 53, which meant that they were Frau Jacobsohn's close neighbors. She lived a few doors farther on in a room at number 60, which was an otherwise empty two-room house. She was obliged to rent a bed, table, and writing desk and to store the car in a garage. Even so, she was soon in arrears with her rent—a clear indication of how precarious her financial position had already become. Her accommodation had probably been negotiated by her lawyer, Wladimir Rosenbaum, who was the first president of the Werkbund settlement and the Neubühl cooperative from 1929 to 1935, although Hans Oprecht, who belonged to the board as an external member, was perhaps involved as well.[27]

Edith Jacobsohn and Hermann Budzislawski quickly agreed on how the change at the top of *Die neue Weltbühne* could be successfully accomplished, if necessary even against the wishes of the other shareholder, Hans Heller. Frau Jacobsohn presented Schlamm with what he rightly regarded as an unacceptable ultimatum; he replied on 18 December 1933 with a threat of resignation, which she accepted at once, to his great surprise.[28] Immediately afterward, on 21 December, she confirmed in writing to Budzislawski that he could take over as editor in chief starting 7 January 1934. That very evening, the latter traveled to Paris, where he had a number of discussions with former *Weltbühne* authors and possible new ones and gathered information about the expected cost of producing the journal there.[29] It was perhaps not a coincidence that he stayed in the Hôtel des Grands Hommes opposite the Panthéon, because he enjoyed comparing himself with great men in the next few weeks, as when he wrote to his wife that he had so much work to do at present that he slept as little as Napoleon, who is supposed to have made do with four or five hours' sleep a night.[30] Schlamm knew nothing about these maneuvers but instead proceeded on the assumption that he would continue to cooperate well with Budzislawski in the coming years, as the latter had indeed assured him in a friendly letter sent on 23 October 1933.[31]

After returning from Paris, Budzislawski started to prepare for the takeover. A letter to his wife before he left for Prague indicates his determination: "There will certainly be a battle."[32] In the Czech capital he took up his quarters in the Pension Arosa and conducted the fight for the editorship of the journal with all the legal and financial means he could muster. He was so preoccupied with the matter that it didn't just fill his thoughts during the day; he dreamed about it at night.[33] There was no plan B. He had to succeed!

On 8 January 1934 he introduced himself to Schlamm as the trustee and authorized representative of Edith Jacobsohn, demanding that he hand over the post of editor in chief immediately.[34] But Schlamm refused to clear his desk and said that he had retracted his resignation in the correct form. They almost came to blows. Both parties thereupon submitted their disagreement to an unofficial court of arbitration, as had been envisaged in the partnership contract concluded between Jacobsohn and Heller in 1932. However, before this court was able to give its verdict, the February 1934 uprising against the autocratic measures of the ruling Austrian chancellor, Engelbert Dollfuß, took place in Vienna, following which the Social Democratic Party of Austria was banned, and many participants were severely punished. To give any kind of support to leftist parties and movements in this tense atmosphere was a dangerous undertaking, perhaps even a life-threatening one. Budzislawski exploited the situation by threatening to sue the other partner, Heller, for libel before a Viennese court.[35] That Budzislawski would probably have lost the case was not important to him, because he speculated that Heller would not want to step forward publicly as the supporter and financial backer of *Die neue Weltbühne*.

The plan worked out well. Heller withdrew his accusation, and on the basis of an out-of-court agreement concluded on 8 March 1934, he was promised the sum of 15,000 Austrian schillings, which Edith Jacobsohn had to pay by installments until August of that year. He also agreed to give up all "material and nonmaterial rights" in *Die neue Weltbühne* and to confirm in writing to Edith Jacobsohn that she was the sole proprietor from that moment on.[36] On the very same day, Budzislawski took over Schlamm's position on the editorial board. The new editor in chief wrote to his wife that, even so, there had still been "a big row," and Schlamm had behaved like a "wild boar." All the readers of the journal learned about these events from the next issue was this: "Willi Schlamm has withdrawn from the editorial board of *Die neue Weltbühne*, and his involvement in the journal has ceased." The coup had succeeded. At the age of only thirty-three, Hermann Budzislawski, a journalist still unknown to the wider public, had taken over the editorship of what was, second only to

Das neue Tage-Buch, the most important German-language political and cultural periodical in exile.[37]

The new editor in chief was not particularly inclined at first to move the journal closer to Marxist positions, but he did not exclude this possibility for the future. At least, that is what he wrote to the proprietor: "For the present, I do not believe either in slaying that ambiguous beast called Marxism—which would be to Hitler's taste—or in setting it to drive our cart. The dragon is in a state of catalepsy. One can only talk about its usefulness if one is able to breathe fresh life into it."[38] In the meantime, one must become active oneself and create the world one wants to live in by one's own efforts: "We the Left must also *live our* reality (which we first only imagine), and indeed not wait until the design is complete, but advance by easy stages—something the Nazis also did. We must start with an incomplete design (but a forward-looking perspective) and settle in straight away. We must not wait, therefore, until a state permits us to adopt particular forms of communal life but go ahead immediately and firmly implement them."[39]

He had already sketched out his program in a similar fashion in a letter sent on 14 January 1934 to Kurt Tucholsky. To the extent that Marxism was "a struggle for the line, for the doctrine, for the initiated," Budzislawski would leave this to the "academics of the proletariat." A more promising approach, in contrast, would be "to use economic levers to drive narrow-minded, indebted peasants, careworn artisans, superfluous intellectuals thrown off their career course, and helpless shopkeepers who can no longer pay the rent to rise in revolt together with exhausted proletarians and the loitering unemployed and to liberate people from the dreariness of their existence through this redemptive process of rebellion." Ultimately, he added, arguments presented exclusively on paper had been unable to do anything to prevent the rise of Fascism. The Fascists had shown that people had already been able to adjust themselves to "Fascist forms of life" before they had gained power in the state. Why shouldn't that also apply to "rational, humane, positive, let us say Socialist forms of life? We would not yet be in power, of course, and so this would all be incomplete. But we should then have a claim to power, so this is how we want to do it."[40]

The earlier youth movement's aspiration for Socialism as a form of life and its belief in its power to shape events resounded in these programmatic declarations. At the same time, Budzislawski's comments in his letters to Jacobsohn and Tucholsky make it clear that he by no means positioned himself as a Communist. Indeed, he even wrote to his wife, Hanna, that the Communists he met in Prague were "insincere, self-important, and when it came to their literature disgusting." He added that he had also distanced himself somewhat from his fellow exiles, who engaged in an "unbelievable amount of gossip."[41] In the months that followed, Budzislawski endeavored to promote an optimistic left-wing policy of fierce opposition to National Socialism, but with whom could this best be conducted? That was a question he initially left open.[42] His modes of thought and action were politically astute and pragmatic, as is evident from the first leading article he wrote after taking over as editor in chief: "We should draw more closely together, not in an apocalyptic mood . . . but by going on the offensive." Internal power struggles on the left, which would inevitably result in the formation of sects, would only damage the common cause: "Sects may be in the right. But they never gain power."[43] In writing to his wife, however, he expressed himself far less optimistically. Indeed, after his first few weeks as editor his fury and disappointment appeared to be unbounded: "What a rubbishy enterprise! And there is no money! Many enemies! And bad authors! This is a very serious matter, and I'm heartily sick of Prague. But it's no use."[44] Meanwhile, Hanna was sitting in Zürich with suitcases packed, fearing she would receive a deportation order from the Swiss Federal Prosecutor's Office at any moment. She and her young daughter finally arrived in Prague in May 1934.[45]

The change in the ownership of *Die neue Weltbühne* involved a complicated series of financial transactions. The previous coproprietor, Heller, was bought out by Edith Jacobsohn, in line with the agreed contract. But she was unable to produce the money for the first installment from her own resources. Instead, she borrowed it from two of Budzislawski's friends, the lawyer and journalist Hans Nathan (1900–1971), who originally came from Görlitz and now lived in Prague, and his wife, Marianne. They personally handed over a "loan" of 89,617.50 Czech crowns in cash to Frau Jacobsohn on 23 March 1934.[46] The exchange rate of the crown to the reichsmark stood at roughly ten to one at that time, and the loan was therefore equivalent to approximately 8,900 marks, or 50,000 US dollars in present-day purchasing power. The Nathans had been able to transfer some of their wealth out of Germany, and Hans used it, among other things, to publish the satirical periodical *Simplicus* (later *Simpl*) in Prague. This was intended to be an uncensored exile version of the original *Simplicissimus*, which was now toeing the Nazi line at home.[47] The Budzislawskis said later that they had paid back the amount advanced by the Nathans in installments. They were in any case by no means hard up or reliant on financing from external donors; if they made use of this source of money, then it was for political reasons. As stated in October 1934 in a formal declaration by Budzislawski's Prague lawyer, they were "Reichsdeutsche" who had "saved a certain amount of assets" and therefore had not come to Czechoslovakia "without means." The Budzislawskis therefore borrowed the money not because they did not have it but because they were cautious. For Hans Nathan and his wife, the risk was also manageable, since they knew that their debtors were solvent. According to the lawyer, the Budzislawskis did not want to come out publicly as co-owners, because close relatives had remained in Germany, and the Budzislawskis wanted to avoid subjecting them to reprisals from the German authorities. They also sent private correspondence to family members who were still in Germany via Warsaw, not directly from Prague. With the exception of a two-day visit to the Czechoslovak capital by Hermann's parents in the summer of 1934, there were no further meetings with his mother before her death in 1937.[48]

At first, therefore, the Budzislawskis thought they would acquire Heller's share (under a disguise) and own the *Blättchen* (literally "little paper," the *Weltbühne*'s nickname) jointly with Edith Jacobsohn. But the new editor in chief was surprised to learn that Edith had already started to consider selling her share a few weeks after Heller's involuntary departure, in May 1934, because she did not want to remain in Prague at any price.[49] She explained her decision to Budzislawski on 6 May in a resigned but friendly letter as follows: "I have inherited the W[elt]b[ühne], and have always regarded it as my honorable obligation to preserve this inheritance in as good and pure a form as I can. . . . In the meantime the world has collapsed in ruins, and the same has almost happened to me. I feel as if I've received a blow to the head, and I am no longer as strong-willed as I used to be." She hoped that Budzislawski would not see her as a "skunk and a deserter," but she pointed out that she was "someone who still wants to try to live a life of her own for a little longer."[50] For the moment, however, it was impossible to move the journal away from Prague. For Budzislawski and his wife, this new situation represented both a risk and an opportunity. Since they were apparently not sufficiently wealthy to purchase the periodical completely or were unable to do so because of the reasons for concealment mentioned earlier, they absolutely had to find a buyer for *Die neue Weltbühne* with whom they could reach an agreement or, better still, whose actions they could influence. Only then could Hermann Budzislawski, after the departure of Jacobsohn, be sure of the position of editor in chief, which he had just acquired.

Behind the scenes, therefore, the Budzislawskis searched feverishly for interested individuals, and they managed to find a few. Starting 1 July 1934, *Die neue Weltbühne* had three new owners. Alongside the Nathans, who obtained a share of 31 percent, there were two others: the twenty-eight-year-old German Jewish physician Hans Albrecht Stein, who also came from Görlitz and who changed his name in exile to Seidler or Seidler-Stein in order to hide his true identity, acquired 60 percent; and the writer and long-standing

Isidor and Jenny Budzislawski in the summer of 1937 on the balcony of their apartment on Sybelstraße, in Berlin-Charlottenburg, together with Erna Budzislawski, the widow of their son Martin, who died in 1930. Erna was later Heinrich Mann's secretary in the United States. Jenny Budzislawski died some weeks after this photograph was taken. Her husband moved to live with Hermann in Prague, and from there Isidor traveled with Hermann's family to Paris and finally to New York, where he died in 1943.

Weltbühne author Heinz Pol was allotted the remaining 9 percent.[51] In the 1930s Stein practiced as a doctor, first in Dresden and later in Prague. He had come into a certain amount of wealth through his marriage to Susanne Bertha Stein, born Cohn, who was the daughter of the Görlitz hosiery manufacturer Ludwig Philipp Cohn, and he now wanted to keep his money out of the grasp of the Nazis. The Nathans had presumably told him about the opportunity offered by *Die neue Weltbühne*. Stein's involvement, therefore, was not necessarily political, but it was certainly a financial opportunity, if a highly risky one.[52] Finally, the thirty-three-year-old Heinz Pol, whose name was actually Heinz Pollack, had migrated to *Die Weltbühne* in the 1920s from the *Vossische Zeitung*, and he was particularly well known for his film criticism, although he had also gleefully torn apart Goebbels's novel *Michael*. In 1934 he was working as editor in chief of Nathan's *Simplicus*.[53] The three new proprietors were all in or around their thirties, they were very closely connected either personally or professionally, and, like the Budzislawskis, they all originated from the milieu of the German Jewish middle class. In this respect at least, continuity with *Die Weltbühne* of the Weimar era was maintained.[54]

There was no shortage of incredulous sarcasm and personal abuse from other exile journalists when they heard about Budzislawski's surprising take-over of the editorship of the famous periodical. As late as 1962, the permanently combative Kurt Hiller still became extremely angry when he thought of "Budzislawski's *Machtergreifung*," as he put it, an expression that implied that Budzislawski was a megalomaniac similar to Joseph Goebbels. According to Hiller, Budzislawski was known in 1934 only to a few insiders who could still remember his "deadly boring economic commentaries" in the very last issues of the Berlin *Weltbühne*. "A nobody who had hardly emerged from nothingness, without a trace of philosophical, political, or literary achievement, interesting neither from the scientific, nor the artistic, nor the martyro-logical angle, a scribbler of rock-bottom quality" had suddenly arrived at one of the most important positions of exile journalism "with the aid of dark forces."[55] The new editor knew that his appointment had provoked amazement and incredulity and from some people even hostility, but he did not let himself be put off by this. He immediately set to work to "cleanse" *Die Welt-bühne*, or "to pull it out of the mire," as he liked to describe his task. This meant two things: changing the journal's content to distance it from the allegedly indecisive positions of his predecessor and making it profitable again.

In order to place the newly acquired journal on a financially healthy basis in Prague, it was necessary first to increase its distribution and reduce its printing costs. It proved exceedingly difficult to produce an edition of thirty to thirty-two pages every week with the help of only a handful of employees. For obvious reasons, there could be no thought of an orderly transfer of editorial functions; there was simply no settling-in time available. The paramount task of the new editor in chief lay in maintaining contact with the long-standing authors, who had now been scattered to the four winds, and winning over new contributors. It was to Budzislawski's advantage that he had already started to build up an extensive network of journalists, writers, and artists in Berlin during the 1920s. Many of these acquaintances had gone into exile in the meantime. They not only had been robbed of their previous influence but also often struggeled for survival under financial conditions that had deteriorated considerably. For Budzislawski himself, this was only partially true. The new editor arranged for *Die neue Weltbühne* publishing house to pay him a fixed fee of 4,000 crowns a month.[56] This amount was enough to cover the rent of a house for his family, their living costs, and the wages of a housemaid.

One of Budzislawski's Berlin acquaintances was the journalist and author Gabriele Tergit (real name Elise Reifenberg), who after studying history and gaining her doctorate under Friedrich Meinecke in the second half of the 1920s had become well known as a court reporter for the highly influential paper the *Berliner Tageblatt* and for the *Berliner Börsenkurier*. She was now living in exile in Jerusalem. Tergit's articles, which stood out from the largely male-dominated journalism of the time, particularly for their close observation of the living conditions of women in the interwar period, were also occasionally printed in *Die Weltbühne*.[57] On 25 May 1934 Budzislawski invited her to contribute to *Die neue Weltbühne*: "There is not much in *Die neue Weltbühne* from the feminine angle, and in addition I am getting very little material from Palestine. If you can also give me the addresses of other authors there who might come into consideration for *Die Weltbühne*, I should certainly be very grateful. The female emigrant in Palestine—that would be a definite theme for us. The difficulties of reorientation, the illusions with which one arrives, and the reality of what actually occurs. The article would not have to be long. I should be happy to receive even a short commentary."[58] It is not known whether Tergit replied to this letter and, if so, what kind of reply she made. The friendly but also condescending tone and the stereotypical reference to "the feminine angle" probably left a nasty taste. In any case, she did not write for *Die neue Weltbühne* in the years that followed. The situation in Palestine remained a marginal theme for the journal, as did the woman question, although an analysis of this would have thrown "an intense spotlight upon the ideology (and the demagogy) of the Nazis," as was argued by one woman who sent in an article from France in the spring of 1934. The new editor in chief rejected her contribution as "unsuitable" without further explanation.[59]

Tergit was by no means alone in her apparently skeptical attitude toward *Die neue Weltbühne*. Many of the prominent authors who had written for the Berlin *Weltbühne* could not be induced to contribute to the new version, even after receiving persistent invitations from the editor. Tucholsky too had no interest in writing for German-language exile publications. He noted in his diary in September 1934 that periodicals such as *Die neue Weltbühne* could offer no credible approach to a political solution, and they would therefore be unable to mobilize anyone in Germany: "Almost all of them prophesy the end of the world, without noticing that the world they are talking about already perished long ago, not to put too fine a point on it. These are the voices of the dead—and they don't even notice it."[60]

Siegfried Kracauer, the sociologist who formerly edited the Berlin culture section of the *Frankfurter Zeitung*, also kept his distance. Three extremely polite letters sent from his Paris exile, postponing a decision but in practice rejecting Budzislawski's requests, have come down to us. They must have been a blow to the new editor in chief, made worse by the fact that the two men had already reached an agreement over possible themes for Kracauer's articles in a personal conversation in December 1933, when Budzislawski, then a refugee still living in Switzerland, was sounding out the possibility of moving the journal to Paris. At that meeting, Kracauer had proposed a sociology of migration that Budzislawski found "extraordinarily important." He accordingly pressed him to start writing.[61] But Kracauer's attitude changed after the power struggle over the editorship of *Die neue Weltbühne*. Now he repeatedly referred to his need to work on his biographical study of "Jacques Offenbach and the society of the Second Empire," pleading that he was in an extremely precarious financial situation. In the last of his letters, sent in April 1935, he said that his situation had become "completely desperate." That was not a very convincing argument, as reliable remuneration from *Die neue Weltbühne* would have alleviated rather than worsened his acute financial crisis, especially as it can be assumed that the virtuoso columnist and an experienced newspaperman Kracauer would have rapidly produced the work Budzislawski wanted.[62] But he kept his distance not only from *Die neue Weltbühne* but also from the German Left in general. He explained his aversion in blunt language to the Communist publisher Wieland Herzfelde: "One really does not live in Paris in order to meet up again with the old German literary rabble and their . . . problems. They will not be able to last out the atmosphere here, thank God."[63]

Budzislawski did not allow himself to be discouraged by these disappointments. For him, *Die neue Weltbühne* was both a means of survival and a career opportunity. He was firmly resolved to use the possibilities offered by exile for the struggle against National Socialism. The journal functioned under his direction as an extended family firm with clearly demarcated spheres of responsibility: Hermann was the editor in chief, writer of leading articles, negotiating partner with the authors, and representative of *Die neue Weltbühne* abroad, while his wife, Hanna, did the bookkeeping, typed the articles and letters, and attended to all the practical details on the spot, although she was also advisor and in-house critic, and at least in the early period she had a hand in every article printed in the journal.[64] With the Budzislawskis, as with many other political exiles, the female contribution to the struggle against Fascism was publicly invisible. Despite all the rhetoric about Socialist comradeship, exile aggravated the inequalities in the relationship between the sexes.[65] Whereas Hermann was able to build up cultural capital, which he was still able to draw on decades later owing to the international visibility of his accomplishments as a journalist, Hanna was honored at best for giving energetic

Hanna Budzislawski as a young woman.

support to her husband's work. Despite all her efforts for the anti-Fascist cause, she remained a woman whose voice was not perceived by the public.

It is not known whether this inequality in the relationship led to tensions. In the 1930s at least, the couple lived together in a symbiotic relationship, both domestically and professionally. They could also call on support from several reliable colleagues who were able to understand the value of Hanna's work, as is apparent from a multitude of letters. The writer and journalist Maximilian Scheer, who lived in exile in Paris, made himself particularly useful. He not only delivered articles regularly but also became a reliable source of information about the exile scene in the French capital. He undertook laborious and unexciting missions in person, and he did not think it was beneath his dignity to do market research. For example, the Budzislawskis asked him to report back on which Paris newspaper kiosks displayed *Die neue Weltbühne*, whether it sold well, and the day of the week on which the next issue became available.[66] Conversely, for exiles such as Scheer, *Die neue Weltbühne* was more than a periodical that informed them in their mother tongue about political and cultural developments in Europe. It was also a community project by middle-class German leftists of the generation born around 1900. It fostered a sense of belonging and created a sphere of communication in which representatives of the German-language exile community could exchange views and talk about each other.

Hermann Budzislawski lived with his family in a villa in Smichov, a suburb of Prague that lay to the west of the river Vltava. He operated there under the name of Herbert Beyer with the knowledge and agreement of the Czechoslovak authorities.[67] The deception was necessary because he feared he might be murdered by contract killers acting for the National Socialists. These concerns took on an acute form on 23 January 1935, when Rudolf Formis, a technician who had previously worked for Stuttgart Radio, was murdered on the orders of Reinhard Heydrich's Security Service (SD).[68] Formis had previously been a member of the SA, but in 1933 he had joined Otto Strasser's Black Front, a group of disappointed National Socialists from the socially revolutionary wing of the National Socialist German Workers' Party (NSDAP). Strasser and Formis had been sending broadcasts that were critical of Hitler and other supposedly "reactionary" National Socialists since 10 September 1934 from a self-built radio station in the Czech capital. The broadcasts could be received in Germany.[69] Budzislawski, who was combating the Nazis with the printed word, now feared for his life. Two days after the political contract killing of Formis, he approached the Prague police, claiming that two days before the murder two unknown men had come to his villa and waited for him there for some time. According to the live-in caretaker's account, one man was from Northern Germany, the other was a Sudeten German. "They had behaved very impudently, pushing the caretaker aside and going immediately into the garden. One posted himself at the entrance, and the other, who evidently knew the area, went through the garden to the rear of the house in order to see whether I was working in a room at the back." Budzislawski declared that he had only escaped the suspected contract killers because he had come home later than usual in a taxi.[70] After that, with the permission of the police, he obtained a 6.35 mm Walther pocket pistol, which he always carried around with him over the next few years.[71]

On 11 June 1935 Budzislawski was deprived of his German citizenship as a traitor to the country on account of his series of "inflammatory articles."[72]

After that he repeatedly attempted to secure Czechoslovak citizenship. This was not granted, however, until the end of 1940 or the beginning of 1941, and then only through the intercession of the Czechoslovak consul general in the United States—at a time, therefore, when Czechoslovakia had already been "destroyed" by the National Socialists and its territory partially occupied.[73] The removal of his German citizenship in the summer of 1935, a few weeks before the publication of the Nuremberg Race Laws, was a blow that struck Budzislawski at the most unfavorable moment that could be imagined. In 1933 and 1934 many exiles had at first been fairly optimistic that the Hitler regime would rapidly collapse, but from 1935 onward it became increasingly clear that they could not count on an end to the Third Reich and an early return to their country anytime soon.

But even such a gloomy prognosis was unable to sap Budzislawski's energy. He succeeded in converting *Die neue Weltbühne* "from an organ for a now only imaginary reading public," which under Schlamm had been "brilliant linguistically and stylistically but aloof in content and intellectually abstract," into one of the most important discussion forums for all those exiles who dreamed of a united Left front against the National Socialists and did not categorically exclude Communist participation.[74] This success owed less to the total of 281 leading articles he wrote until the prohibition of the journal in the summer of 1939 than to the fact that the new editor in chief was able to win over the internationally renowned writer Heinrich Mann, who actually also wrote for Leopold Schwarzschild's periodical, *Das neue Tagebuch*, as a regular contributor, "despite not inconsiderable initial differences of opinion." Between 1934 and 1939 eighty texts by Mann appeared in *Die neue Weltbühne*.[75] Budzislawski later frankly admitted that without Heinrich Mann's authority as a writer and shortly afterward as the honorary chairman of the Paris Action Committee of German Oppositionists, he could hardly have been able to make his journal a "rallying point for writers who were anti-Fascists but not yet always Socialists." It was not least thanks to Mann's spotless image and later his energetic advocacy that Budzislawski was able to print contributions from literary heavyweights such as Arnold Zweig, Lion Feuchtwanger, and Bertolt Brecht.[76] Admittedly, Budzislawski did not always have a good eye for quality. In the summer of 1936, he rejected a request from twenty-nine-year-old Hannah Arendt, then still largely unknown, who would have liked to write a piece on the Jewish World Congress for *Die neue Weltbühne*, mainly because she had indicated in her letter that she might also place it in *Das neue Tagebuch*, the rival journal.[77]

A further circumstance that contributed to the survival of *Die neue Weltbühne* between 1934 and 1938 was the goodwill and perhaps also the financial support of the Czechoslovak authorities. At least this is what the German lawyer Robert M. W. Kempner, who was later assistant chief prosecutor at the Nuremberg war crimes tribunal, told a member of the American Secret Services in 1943. Budzislawski, he said, had received money from the Czechoslovak government during the first few years after he had taken over the editorship of *Die neue Weltbühne*.[78] The various Czechoslovak aid committees did in fact distribute a total of 1.8 million crowns of government money to political refugees who had come from Germany between 1933 and 1938, out of which 700,000 crowns were expended solely on supporting the German-language exile press.[79] It is likely that Budzislawski received a large piece of this cake. He is said to have been regarded by Czechoslovak military intelligence as the "most reliable" of all the emigrants from Germany. He was therefore particularly worthy of support.[80]

According to Budzislawski, this favorable view related to an event in September 1935, which he described some years later when he was in exile in New York. He was arrested one day in his house by the head of the Prague immigration police, Ladislav Sapara. Another emigrant had accused him of heading a "murder club of Prague emigrants," but a confrontation between the two quickly showed that the alleged emigrant was a Nazi agent provocateur. This confrontation not only resulted in his exoneration from all such accusations but also won him credibility among the Czechoslovaks as the presumed target of National Socialist attacks. In the years that followed, the Prague police repeatedly asked for his views as an "expert on Gestapo matters"; they also put a round-the-clock watch on his house.[81] There are no concrete proofs of Czech support payments in *Die neue Weltbühne* archive, but that is only to be expected in the circumstances. Budzislawski was grateful to the end of his life to the authorities of his host country—among other things because, unlike the Swiss immigration police, they did not take offense at his activities as a political journalist in Prague, carried on in defiance of legal limitations, until the beginning of 1938. We can assume that in return for this benevolence he coordinated the political course of *Die neue Weltbühne* with Czechoslovak government officials, or at least took care not to alienate the people who were guaranteeing his security.[82]

Behind the scenes, though, all was not tranquil at *Die neue Weltbühne*, although less for political than for business reasons. The journal changed ownership three times between July 1935 and February 1936.[83] On 1 July 1935 the Nathans sold their share to Helene Reichenbach, Budzislawski's long-standing friend who had moved to London in the meantime and whose money was handled by Budzislawski, acting as a trustee. For her, involvement in the journal was probably not just a favor for a friend but also an opportunity to rescue at least part of her substantial wealth from the German treasury. The Law Changing the Regulations Covering the Reich Flight Tax, issued on 18 May 1934, had reduced the minimum level at which the wealth of German citizens who left the country became taxable from the original figure of 200,000 reichsmarks to 50,000. The practical effect of this change was that the National Socialist state could place an even heavier tax burden on persecuted Jews whose wealth reached that level if they emigrated.

Budzislawski raised the money to pay the agreed purchase price of 60,000 crowns on behalf of Helene Reichenbach at the beginning of July 1935 by selling on the London stock exchange some Japanese government bonds issued in 1907, which were deposited under his name at the Swiss Volksbank.[84] From the proceeds, the agreed amount was to be either paid by check to the Budzislawskis or transferred directly to the account of Edith Jacobsohn at the Böhmische Union Bank in Prague—evidently, the Budzislawskis still had debts to her. In addition, Budzislawski and his wife instructed their Swiss bank to send 400 Swiss francs "in small French notes" to Herman Reichenbach's private address in Moscow.[85] Reichenbach was at that time the director of the Moscow Conservatory. On 10 July 1935 Budzislawski altered his instructions once again, and on 15 July, in line with the new instructions, the Swiss Volksbank sold Japanese government bonds to the value of £800 and credited the Budzislawski account in Prague with the proceeds. In addition to this, the bank sent a check for $2,425.20 to Herbert Bobreker in New York. Bobreker, born in Berlin and forty-seven years old, was presumably a friend of Helene Reichenbach.[86] Soon afterward, she also moved from London to New York. Herman Reichenbach in Moscow now received not 400 but 2,000 Swiss francs, paid out in banknotes.[87] The fact that he and Budzislawski were personally at loggerheads during this period did not hinder their joint business dealings.[88] Reichenbach left the Soviet Union at the end of 1937 in order to escape Stalin's purges. He went to the United States, where he found a job as a music lecturer at Mary Washington College in Fredericksburg, Virginia.

On 30 November 1935 the partner with a 9 percent share in *Die neue Weltbühne*, Heinz Pol, also withdrew from the enterprise. The money he had contributed was returned to him in installments.[89] His private affairs, he wrote to Budzislawski a few weeks earlier, had reached such a critical point that he was in urgent need of cash, not least because he had to bring his father and his wife out of Germany and into safety.[90] From this time onward, Stein had a two-thirds share in the journal, and the Reichenbachs (with the Budzislawskis standing behind them) had a third. But even then the situation had not been entirely stabilized. In the early summer of 1935 Nathan's *Simpl* folded, and Heinz Pol, who was now in desperate straits financially, had to look around for

a new editorial post in exile journalism. At the turn of 1935 and 1936 he tried
to displace Budzislawski on the basis that he had acted autocratically as editor
of *Die neue Weltbühne*. In doing this Pol had the support of the majority shareholder, Stein, and a number of veteran writers for *Die Weltbühne* and *Die neue
Weltbühne*, among them Ernst Bloch, who had become increasingly discon-
tented with the editor in chief. But Pol did not succeed in his attempt to push
Budzislawski out of the editorship in the same way as the latter had driven out
Schlamm eighteen months earlier.

The incumbent editor in chief initially defended himself by legal means
against the decision of the owner, Stein, to dismiss him. He had no intention
of allowing himself to be deprived of the position he had energetically fought
to obtain ever since the end of 1933 and to sink back into the position of a
common or garden journalist in exile who had to keep his head above water as
best he could by selling articles to a variety of newspapers and magazines.
Uncertainties about his right to remain in Czechoslovakia were an additional
concern. As before, Budzislawski made use of extremely hard-hitting methods
of attack; he saw himself as being "at war." In February 1936 he accused Stein
of using the export earnings of the journal "for his own private purchases" and
"transferring them abroad," and he threatened to report him to the Czech
authorities for currency offenses.[91] But he simultaneously offered to refrain
from doing this if Stein was prepared to sell his shares. Under this pressure,
Stein agreed to Budzislawski's demand. A few weeks later, accompanied by his
wife, he hastily immigrated to the United States.[92] Pol no longer had any backing, and Budzislawski was now able to remove him from the staff of the
journal.[93]

After this, the editor in chief himself acquired a part of Stein's majority
shareholding to a total value of 215,000 crowns, which was then equivalent to
£2,000, selling the remainder to Helene Reichenbach.[94] It was "an exceptional
opportunity," he wrote to her. He financed the acquisition of the rest of the
shares with the help of a credit of 100,000 crowns granted to him by the Swiss
Banking Association on 27 March 1936. Hanna Budzislawski—in person,
apparently—transferred to the bank as security a "pledge in gold" to the value
of $3,000 (present-day value roughly $56,000).[95] The source of this gold is
unclear. Budzislawski wrote vaguely to Helene Reichenbach on 18 March 1936
that he was "now negotiating with people who are supposed to give me gold."[96]
Was he supported by Communist Party members who regarded him as a reliable Popular Front man at the head of *Die neue Weltbühne* and whose presence
would enable them to obtain direct influence over a journal that had previously been independent? This is a tempting but probably a mistaken assumption. It is very likely that the gold that served as security came from Helene

Portrait of Helene "Lo" Reichenbach by the British artist Hubert A. Finney. The picture was painted after the Second World War.

Reichenbach herself, because Budzislawski informed her in October 1936 that there might be tax to pay on foreign gold deposits in Switzerland, referring in this context to her "private situation."[97] But at least the issue of who controlled *Die neue Weltbühne* had been settled, as Budzislawski wrote triumphantly to Alfred Kantorowicz, his former comrade in the Berlin artists' colony: "The attack has been beaten off, and as you know, for the assailants a failed offensive is a severe defeat. Now they are all shitting themselves."[98]

All three of the property changes mentioned above tended in one direction: the previous owners (Nathan, Pol, and Stein) withdrew more or less voluntarily, and Budzislawski, who had already made himself de facto irremovable as editor in chief by virtue of the partnership agreement of July 1935, took over their shares together with Helene Reichenbach, who was advised by him as a trustee. In the summer of 1936, they each owned half the journal.[99] But from the end of February 1936 at the latest Budzislawski was the undisputed head of the enterprise—not just in the editorial office but also as the director of the whole business. In order to refinance the share formerly held by Stein, he now started to write begging letters to exiled friends and acquaintances, among them Ernst Toller, Siegfried Aufhäuser, Emil Ludwig, Alexander Schifrin, and Moritz Loeb, who had fled side by side with Budzislawski to Switzerland in the spring of 1933.[100] He wanted to find new investors so that he could buy Stein out completely, liquidate his Prague debts, and perhaps take over Reichenbach's share, thereby becoming the sole proprietor of the journal. But all his attempts to raise fresh capital in Western Europe and the United States proved unsuccessful. In 1937 Stein was still taking legal action against *Die neue Weltbühne* in order to obtain the final payments due to him, and Helene Reichenbach continued to be a shareholder.[101] The Czechoslovak authorities were also aware of her participation in the business. Thus the Prague police informed the Czechoslovak Ministry of the Interior on 30 November 1937 that *Die neue Weltbühne* was financed both by Budzislawski and by Helene Reichenbach, a woman who came from Berlin but who had in the meantime acquired English citizenship.[102]

In only two years Hermann Budzislawski had succeeded in making himself the editor in chief and publisher of *Die neue Weltbühne*, thanks to his journalistic energy, commercial nous, and lack of moral scruples. Family wealth and the financial support of Helene Reichenbach, as well as the legal and financial know-how he had acquired during his studies and the earlier stages of his career, had given him a decisive competitive advantage in exile power struggles. But all these successes were only worth something as long as *Die neue Weltbühne* could continue to be published, pay its way, and make a political impact. By March 1936, according to Budzislawski, the journal not only was free of debt but also had at its disposal "a considerable amount of working capital."[103] This was remarkable, because the sales figures for the anti-Fascist exile press were in constant decline. All the campaigns the anti-Fascists conducted and all the information leaflets painstakingly smuggled into the country seemed to be ineffective against the regime's propaganda. This not only deprived anti-Fascist journalists of financial support, to the extent that they lived exclusively on the sale of their books, periodicals, and articles, but also increasingly put in question any prospect of successful political engagement.

The left-wing exiles were, however, able to achieve one important symbolic success against Nazi Germany during this period: the award of the Nobel Peace Prize to Carl von Ossietzky, the former editor in chief of *Die Weltbühne*. It was conferred on 23 November 1936 and backdated by one year. The award had been preceded by intensive efforts on the part of a "circle of friends of Carl von Ossietzky" consisting of former colleagues, *Weltbühne* authors, and members of the German League for Human Rights, among them Konrad Reisner, Kurt R. Grossmann, Hilde Walter, Hellmut von Gerlach, and Milly Zirker. The leftist Socialist emigrant and later Federal German chancellor Willy Brandt, who was living in Norway, functioned as contact man.[104] Budzislawski was not a member of this circle of friends in the narrow sense. Nevertheless, as editor in chief and later also publisher of *Die neue Weltbühne*, he reported regularly on the campaign, and indeed he did this even when members of the group emphatically pointed out that his reports would only worsen Ossietzky's situation, imprisoned as he was in the concentration camp of Esterwegen, in the district of Emsland in the north of Germany. International public support was important, but articles in the German-language exile press were counterproductive, they said, especially as there were in fact realistic prospects of achieving his release through the intercession of a sister-in-law of Hermann Göring—presumably, Ilse Göring.[105] The most prominent critic of Budzislawski's approach was Hilde Walter, who had been since 1927 the assistant editor of *Die Weltbühne* and therefore Ossietzky's right-hand woman.[106] In April 1934 she commented angrily that it almost appeared as if Budzislawski was trying "to sabotage the success of our aspirations."[107] A few months later, after all polite attempts to influence the editor in chief had failed, Walter finally wrote a scathing two-page letter that made her position absolutely plain: "There must be no further mention of O[ssietzky] in *Die Weltbühne for a very long time*. In whatever form, and no matter what light he is portrayed in."[108] Budzislawski was not in the least concerned. For him, it was an opportunity to present *Die neue Weltbühne* as supposedly the main publication involved in the Ossietzky campaign.[109]

Budzislawski responded only in exceptional cases to requests for material assistance from the friends of Ossietzky. Only once, on 9 September 1935, did he contribute some money. This was to provide for Maud von Ossietzky and her daughter, who had great difficulty in making ends meet. But the 200 crowns he offered was such a small sum that he received a furious letter from Konrad Reisner accusing Budzislawski of "unreliability" and double standards. "The whole circle of friends, which has devoted itself to this cause for years, [has sacrificed] a considerable amount of time and money," wrote Reisner. He was really shocked by how little *Die neue Weltbühne* was prepared to participate: "After all, we must be clear that even now the paper continues to profit, including in a purely material sense, from the existence of Ossietzky and the special position he enjoys in the world thanks to our work." This was true more for Budzislawski and *Die neue Weltbühne* than for anyone else, Reisner added.[110]

There is no evidence that the editor in chief replied to these comments.[111] In the next few months there was no perceptible change in his attitude, outwardly at least. When at the end of November 1936 Ossietzky was finally awarded the Nobel Prize, Budzislawski celebrated this as the "first clear victory of a just, humane cause." The pacifist Ossietzky had been wrested away from the concentration camps, Budzislawski wrote. With a modesty that was only apparent, the editor in chief wrote in *Die neue Weltbühne*: "Let us admit, not just by us. We were silent for a year, because we feared that if we called for his release, he might have to pay dearly for it in Germany. In April 1934 we realized that it was no use staying silent, and we therefore decided to speak up."[112] That was a double misrepresentation of the course of events. First, as we have seen, Budzislawski did not become editor in chief until the spring of 1934. Hence, he took the first opportunity available to get hold of the Ossietzky case for himself and *Die neue Weltbühne*. Second, he had by no means been the driving force behind the Nobel Prize campaign. That was rather Ossietzky's circle of friends. Budzislawski's only comment on this point was the spiteful assertion that "Ossietzky's previous German friends" had "faded into the background long ago."[113] Budzislawski was less interested in achieving the release of the persecuted former editor in chief than in heightening Ossietzky's symbolic value for present-day politics. Budzislawski therefore interpreted the award of the Nobel Prize as a result of the policy propagated by himself and others of bringing the political Left together. It was not Ossietzky the outstanding individual but the collective group of determined opponents of Hitler, including Budzislawski himself, who could feel they had been honored by the award, he argued: "It is our first great victory, a recompense for the fact that we did not sink into lethargy, that we abandoned no one, that we left no stone unturned. I would not have made this point but for the very understandable presence among us, outside and inside Germany, of the discouraged, the disappointed, the downcast, whose courage can only be restored by a success, a proof of the world's solidarity. Ossietzky's tenacity and the international campaign for the incarcerated German pacifist have proved to these people what can be achieved by tenacious determination."[114]

Budzislawski publicly interpreted the award of the Nobel Prize as a confirmation of the political course he had consistently championed as editor in chief of *Die neue Weltbühne* since 1934, despite all the reverses it had suffered. One example of a political propaganda failure after 1933 was the outcome of a plebiscite over the future of the Saar district, which had been under League of Nations administration since 1919. In January 1935 90.5 percent of the local electorate voted in favor of the Saar's incorporation into the German Reich. Neither the violent suppression by the Nazis of the opposition in Germany nor the intensive propaganda campaign of the Left parties before the vote was able to prevent Hitler from gaining prestige from this success. Nothing more could be expected from the German bourgeoisie in the struggle against National Socialism, Budzislawski wrote disappointedly in the spring of 1935. Rearmament and rampant national chauvinism were simply being accepted, if not openly supported.[115] The Anschluss of Austria in March 1938 and the enthusiasm of broad sections of the local population for the new "Großdeutschland" were also in blatant contradiction to the expectations previously stirred up by *Die neue Weltbühne*. Authors writing in the journal continued to foretell the early collapse of Nazi rule, thereby making themselves almost ridiculous in the eyes of some critical readers.[116] Budzislawski also understood that it was impossible to continue in this way. In view of the sustained foreign policy successes of the National Socialists, he insisted again and again that the German exiles had to develop a positive, future-directed program if they wanted to work politically in Germany during the coming period. His starting point, as outlined on 28 May 1936 in a letter to the Communist writer and *Weltbühne* author Rudolf Leonhard, was the observation that only three years after Hitler's takeover of power the language spoken by political emigrants was already different from that used by the "German people" who remained behind in the Reich:

Expressions such as "honor of Labor" and "national honor" have penetrated into the language use of previously Marxist strata, and when we sneeringly ignore such changes, we cut ourselves off from the German people. These days, many German workers no longer say, "Honor of labor is rubbish, I want higher wages," but ask rather, "How can it be compatible with the honor of labor that wages are being kept so low?" If we want to win influence over the German people, and this is what we do want after all, we must take the given situation into account and learn from the changes that have occurred. . . . The purely negative criticism practiced by the emigration so far is useful but not sufficient. I am looking for colleagues who are able to make positive proposals for propaganda. . . . In order to have an impact and make an impression on the intellectuals, one must appropriate catchphrases from the National Socialists and perhaps say something like this: You also have talents of one kind or another under National Socialism. But with you in Germany they can lead nowhere; there it is always the untalented and the time-servers who push themselves forward. We could develop all the forces lying dormant in the German people if there were to be a new flowering of culture among us. What I mean is this: the German intellectual who has not yet been won over should be able to see a starting point for positive reconstruction in the kind of criticism we make so that together we can think out the shape of the Germany of the future.[117]

Considerations of this nature, which Budzislawski had already put forward in a very similar form in his January 1934 letter to Tucholsky, lay behind the noticeable tendency of *Die neue Weltbühne* to come out explicitly in favor of the Popular Front in the second half of the 1930s. The new slogan meant that disagreements within the Left, which had previously been extremely sharp, must now cease. Only a transnational united front of all anti-Fascists, which should include moderate Social Democrats and dogmatic party-line Communists, could prevent the rise of Fascist movements, thereby also avoiding a new war. The government alliances between Social Democrats, Communists, and trade unions formed in 1936 in France and Spain—the Front Populaire and the Frente Popular, respectively—were seen in the left-wing camp as spearheading a development that could act as a precedent internationally. A central element of the Popular Front ideology was an unconditional rapprochement with the Soviet Union as the protector and the leading force of anti-Fascism in Western and Central Europe. This was something the editor in chief of *Die neue Weltbühne* regarded as inescapable.[118]

At the suggestion of Franz Dahlem and Walter Ulbricht, Budzislawski took part in the first Popular Front Committee, formed in Prague in 1934–35, which also included the writer Oskar Maria Graf, the Communist Anton Ackermann, and the Social Democrats Siegfried Aufhäuser and Max Seydewitz. The last two were leading members of the group known as the Revolutionary Socialists on the extreme left wing of German Social Democracy, who advocated reaching an understanding with Moscow, an idea resisted by the party leadership of the SPD in exile (SoPaDe), which even expelled Aufhäuser from the party in January 1935 for supporting it. The Revolutionary Socialists considered, entirely in line with the Popular Front conception, that only a "united front" of the fighting Left could set out on the "road to a Socialist Germany." Budzislawski was seen as the connecting link between these groups; thus a mediating role between Communists and Social Democrats fell to him in exile in Prague that was similar to the role he had played some years before in Berlin.[119] Budzislawski traveled to the Soviet Union at least twice during 1935. He tells us that during his first stay, in March, he spent hours discussing issues and arguing with Communist authors on the occasion of an evening meal on the premises of the International Union of Revolutionary Writers. He already knew many of these writers, including Ernst Ottwalt, György Lukács, and Andor Gábor, from his time in Berlin. Béla Balázs, Hans Günther, Franz Leschnitzer, Frieda Wolf, and Willi Bredel were also present. A few days after his return, Budzislawski wrote to the American journalist Louis Fischer that he had encouraged the Communists to write more for *Die neue Weltbühne*, although he called on them to preserve some critical distance in their reporting. Most of the submissions from the Soviet Union, he said, were unusable because paeans of praise to the country met with little response in Western Europe. One could still be a friend of the Soviet Union "while acknowledging and investigating the weak points of developments there," Budzislawski argued. Yet he considered it unlikely that he would in fact obtain any balanced articles of this kind in the future from that source, as no one there would dare to approach difficult subjects: "I gained the general impression that the German writers who had not yet spent much time in the Soviet Union felt obliged to provide exaggerated demonstrations of their Soviet loyalty."[120] The Communist writers in Moscow were likewise dissatisfied with *Die neue Weltbühne*, which they found insufficiently committed to the party. When Budzislawski refused to print the contributions they sent in, the authors took this as a personal affront. It also meant they missed the opportunity to be taken seriously as an internationally important voice, which would have demonstrated their political usefulness to the host country.[121]

In October 1935 Budzislawski traveled to the Soviet Union again, this time with Oskar Maria Graf, to take part in a meeting of the exiled KPD in Moscow that was referred to for security reasons as the Brussels Conference. He claims that he took this opportunity to speak directly to the general secretary of the Comintern, Georgi Dimitrov, who gave the keynote address at the conference, titled "The Offensive of Fascism and the Tasks of the Communist International."[122] Following the new guidelines laid down by the Seventh Comintern Congress in the summer of 1935, Dimitrov called for all leftist forces to come together in the spirit of the Popular Front. The "theory of Social Fascism," which had prevented alliances between Social Democrats and Communists in previous years, was from that time onward no longer obligatory. Instead, Communists should in the interests of unity of action overcome or at least shelve their reservations about Social Democracy.[123]

Budzislawski saw this development as a confirmation of the course he had followed and already propagated in *Die neue Weltbühne*. In the next few years, he intensified his attempts to bring together a Left united front of this kind, first while in exile in Prague and later also in Paris. His approach was expressed most clearly in the appeal titled "For the German Popular Front!," which was printed in *Die neue Weltbühne* on 14 January 1937.[124] Budzislawski's repeated use of the pronoun "we" in his articles and letters of the time shows how much he had adopted Communist linguistic mannerisms and the increasing degree to which he had internalized the Communist program. Under Budzislawski's editorship there was no longer a place in *Die neue Weltbühne* for previous authors such as Leon Trotsky; instead, Budzislawski printed the contributions of leading KPD functionaries such as "Walter" (Ulbricht), "Franz" (Dahlem),

and Wilhelm Koenen, who wrote under the pseudonym Heinz Wilhelm.[125]
He also received information on illegal actions against the regime in Germany
through Communist Party channels. The KPD provided material for a series
of articles on the chemical industry in central Germany, which was published
at the end of 1937 in *Die neue Weltbühne*.[126] He had many meetings with
Walter Ulbricht during these years—first in Marienbad (now Mariánské
Lázně), then at the Brussels Conference, and later, repeatedly, at his house in
Prague. But the relationship was and remained a complicated one. According
to information from Budzislawski, Ulbricht had personally agreed that Moscow would in future definitely take five hundred copies of the journal for
distribution in the Soviet Union, which would have signified a "real stabiliza-
tion" from the financial angle. But by September 1937 this had still not happened, despite repeated reminders from Budzislawski.[127] For 1938 Ulbricht
promised that two hundred copies would be taken, but even this number
was reduced in the course of the year to fifty by the Soviet distributors. For
1939 he canceled the arrangement completely.[128] At first Budzislawski was able
to talk to Ulbricht on a level of equality, but the relationship quickly evolved
into one of political and eventually even financial dependency on the part
of *Die neue Weltbühne* editor. Later on, in the GDR, they almost became
enemies.

Despite the way in which his power position had become consolidated, or
perhaps rather because of it, Budzislawski's energetic Popular Front endeavors
after 1935 hardly developed any political impact. He complained in August
1937 that after three and a half years in Prague he had still not succeeded in
"bringing about any friendly cooperation between the different tendencies of
the German opposition as manifested in exile."[129] Something that was easy to
advocate in the pages of *Die neue Weltbühne* could only be achieved with
difficulty in political practice. The Prague police recorded in October 1937
that the Communists' unification attempts had so far been completely "dilettantish" and that they had not been taken seriously by the political intelligentsia in general.[130]

It was not long before Budzislawski's opponents among the exiles became
convinced that the editor in chief who had held the office since 1934 was a
"Communist agent" who had "KPD funds" at his disposal. Only in this way,
wrote Willi Schlamm, could he have been in a position to take control of *Die
neue Weltbühne*.[131] Schlamm had described Budzislawski as a "Stalinist" as
early as January 1934, allegedly on the basis of information from the Socialist
Workers' Party (SAP).[132] The liberal lawyer and journalist Rudolf Olden also
began to suspect, only a few months after Budzislawski had taken over *Die
neue Weltbühne*, that he was attempting to edit the journal "in accordance

with a Comintern resolution." For Olden, the call for the formation of a united front sounded like a Communist Party slogan: "The tone, the style, and certain omissions appear to indicate this. Am I mistaken?"[133] Ten years later, the former Communist Ruth Fischer, who after her break with Stalinism agitated relentlessly during her American exile against actual or presumed Communists, claimed that Budzislawski was not just a Communist but also a top party official. His value to the strategists in Moscow was all the greater, she wrote, precisely because he had never officially belonged to the KPD. Under his editorship, *Die neue Weltbühne* was a disguised Stalinist periodical in which "anti-Stalinists" could not have published even a single line.[134]

In examining such accusations, one must bear in mind that Schlamm and Budzislawski spent much energy in attacking each other with an unflagging hatred, which started in 1934 and continued for the rest of their lives. The intensity of their mutual detestation was equaled only by their shared abhorrence of Hitler and the Nazis.[135] Ruth Fischer's comments also lose some of their significance when seen in the light of her extremely anti-Communist position at that time. Even the US military intelligence service, the Office of Strategic Services (OSS), regarded her accusations as highly exaggerated, and they kept their distance, referring ironically to Budzislawski as "Miss Fischer's contact man."[136] The writer Lion Feuchtwanger was intimately familiar with the rivalries and enmities among left-wing intellectuals at that time. In his novel *Exil*, published in 1940 by the Querido-Verlag in Amsterdam, he wrote that even exiles "who had the same inner destiny and the same goals" were worn down by constant proximity and became disappointed with one another. "There was hatred, sometimes deadly enmity, among the exiles, and each of them, more or less in good faith, suspected the other of negligence or treachery to the common cause."[137]

During Budzislawski's lifetime, none of his opponents was able to produce any proof that he was politically or financially dependent on the Comintern. Statements by those directly affected and in exile in the United States and evaluations given by leading German Communists in connection with Budzislawski's return to Germany are therefore more convincing than imputations motivated by anti-Communism. They make it clear that since the end of the 1920s he had been a Socialist who spoke out strongly in favor of cooperation between the parties and groups to the left of the main body of the SPD but was not prepared to tie himself to a political party. In spite of his closeness to representatives of the KPD in exile, he did not wish to become dependent in a financial sense on a political grouping, and as we have seen, he had no need for this, at least initially. After all, he wrote in August 1941 to Heinrich Mann, alluding to the Hitler-Stalin Pact of the summer of 1939: "Experience has shown that it is pointless to negotiate with a party's middle-level functionaries; indeed, occasionally even those at the top of the party do not entirely keep their word."[138] This statement indicates that Budzislawski had engaged in discussions with leading Communists during his time as editor of *Die neue Weltbühne* and that he had also made agreements with them. But throughout his life he rejected any accusation that he had ever committed himself or *Die neue Weltbühne* to a party-political line.

In relation to his fellow exiles, too, Budzislawski distinguished clearly between those who were dependent on a political party (such as, for example, his old colleague from the artists' colony Alfred Kantorowicz and the Communist journalist Bruno Frei) and "highly regarded personalities who enjoyed full freedom of action," such as the lawyer Kurt Rosenfeld, who had been Prussian minister of justice for a short time during the November Revolution of 1918 and was later an SPD deputy in the Reichstag before he helped set up the SAP in 1931. During the Weimar Republic Rosenfeld had belonged to Carl von Ossietzky's team of lawyers and was thus a member of the wider *Weltbühne* circle. In exile in the United States starting in October 1941, he published a periodical called *The German-American*, together with the exiled Communist Gerhart Eisler, who was the brother of the renowned composer Hanns Eisler.[139] Budzislawski saw himself as belonging to the second group, the independent personalities. If he needed to establish *Die neue Weltbühne* in the United States, he explained in the above-mentioned letter to Heinrich Mann, independence from the Communist Party would be an imperative requirement, especially after the traumatic experience of 1939: "I would not like to serve as the front man or the covering label for a group whose sudden shift of policy I found very painful two years ago, when they abandoned the principles of the Popular Front from one day to the next for reasons I won't now go into." A possible new edition of *Die neue Weltbühne* would therefore have to be "somewhat more broad-minded" than the old one, he added self-critically. He even wanted to offer a forum in the restored journal to representatives of the old majority Social Democracy such as Albert Grzesinski, the former Prussian minister of the interior, and liberals such as Emil Ludwig and the writer Thomas Mann.[140]

The KPD functionary Albert Schreiner, who in his later GDR career saw himself as a historian, insisted in October 1948 that in 1944 and 1945, as a member of the Council for a Democratic Germany, Budzislawski had occasionally voted with a few other independent leftist Socialists against the Communist exiles even though his political stance had been in general "advantageous" to the Communist Party. Budzislawski, continued Schreiner, was a "convinced journalist" whose character was still "strongly individualistic." He was a vain man with a pronounced craving for recognition: "The decades he spent as a lone wolf who did not want to tie himself to a party are a part of the reason for that."[141] Schreiner was well-disposed toward Budzislawski, and he would certainly have picked out membership of the KPD in exile as a positive feature if that had been the case.

It can therefore be maintained that from 1935 at the latest Budzislawski as an exile journalist was a consistent advocate of the Popular Front policy and that he repeatedly took Moscow's side in this context, but that as the publisher and part owner of *Die neue Weltbühne* he wanted to avoid financial or political dependence, partly because he had to consider the attitude of the authorities in the host countries.[142] He knew that this position tended to make the journal's articles less convincing, as can be seen from a letter he sent in 1938: "It is tremendously difficult today to put the paper together as an editor, because it must not be empty of content but it must also avoid being confiscated."[143] To put it in another way, running *Die neue Weltbühne* was a complicated business—figuratively as well as literally. Possible financial difficulties or acts of political imprudence therefore had greater weight for him than compromises over the quality of the journalism. If one leaves aside the personal insults, Kurt Hiller also came to this conclusion after the Second World War, when he called Budzislawski a "writer of leading articles who was versed in economic history, not ignorant of history in general, and completely uneducated in philosophy and literature" and who was "neither a Left Social Democrat nor a free-standing Socialist nor a Leninist nor an ideologist of any kind, hence not a Stalinist either" but a "speculative newspaper entrepreneur who saw things from the viewpoint of his desire for money and recognition, who did not want to get into financial difficulties, and who had placed his bet on Stalin."[144]

For Budzislawski, as for many other opponents of the Nazis, until the summer of 1939 one element of the situation was absolutely unquestionable: the unequivocal hostility of the Soviet leadership to the hated rule of Adolf Hitler. And that was ultimately what mattered.

Parisian Impasse

The End of Die neue Weltbühne, *Internment, and Flight*

H OW LONG WOULD they be able to continue publishing their journal in Prague? Hanna and Hermann Budzislawski discussed this subject intensively both in the editorial office and at the dinner table. Tensions between the German Reich and Czechoslovakia had been increasing continuously since 1937, and this posed a great danger to the German exiles, particularly to those who were Jewish. In March 1938 the National Socialist Press Service described Czechoslovakia as the "European center of world Jewry," and the Reich Security Main Office in Berlin renewed its efforts to seize the editor of *Die neue Weltbühne*.[1] It was allegedly only the intervention of the current Soviet ambassador, Sergei Alexandrovsky, that prevented the government of President Edvard Beneš from giving way to pressure from Berlin as early as December 1937 and prohibiting the journal.[2] Even so, the censor repeatedly stepped in during the next few months. The Czechoslovak authorities confiscated *Die neue Weltbühne* on one occasion in March 1938 and then three more times in May, and in each case they only allowed it to reappear after changes in its contents. Contributions from Berthold Viertel and Lion Feuchtwanger were substantially shortened, and an article by Rudolf Olden was deleted in its entirety. One of the censor's interventions was probably directed against Viertel's angry article "Suicides," which was printed in the journal's final April issue. In this text, Viertel, who was Austrian, commemorated those of his fellow citizens who, having been forcibly included in the German Reich in March 1938, had not been carried away by German nationalist feeling and who had preferred to kill themselves rather than be "forced into line" under the National Socialists. In addition to the well-known suicides, among whom he mentioned Egon Friedell, the Austrian writer and cultural philosopher, there were many nameless victims, "faceless martyrs," who had suffered "the crushing burden of humiliation and rightlessness."[3] Although there is no precise indication of exactly what the censor took exception to, the motives behind his intervention were clear: to make sure that no further provocation of the German Reich would come from sources in Czechoslovakia, especially now that German troops had marched into Austria.[4]

At the turn of 1937 to 1938, the heightened danger led Budzislawski to give increasing thought to the idea of shifting his journal's headquarters to Paris. But he continued to delay the decision, not least on account of the extra expenditure involved in finding fresh editorial offices and the significantly greater printing costs in the French capital. "I will only leave here when I have to," he wrote in January 1938. Eventually, however, the situation became too dangerous. The censor's requirements became increasingly strict, and the news of Austria's Anschluss with Germany made a National Socialist march on Prague more and more likely.[5] Budzislawski's financial difficulties also increased. His own resources were insufficient to cover a move, as the financial reserves held in Switzerland had apparently been exhausted. In the first months of 1938, therefore, he accepted "a kind of loan or a form of participation in *Die Weltbühne*" of an amount that is unknown but that amounted to 50,000 crowns at most from a certain Egon Rudolf Feigl. In return, he later employed Feigl's girlfriend in Paris as a secretary for several months. Budzislawski recalled in 1967 that the involvement of this financier had come about through the agency of Wilhelm Koenen, who had been a leading KPD functionary since 1920 and who was, in Kurt Hiller's colorful description, "the paramount chief of all the German Communist exiles in Central and Western Europe" in the 1930s.[6] In 1968 the Central Committee of the SED discussed whether Feigl should be given compensation for part of the loan he had made thirty years ago, Budzislawski having admitted in 1967 that he had been unable to pay the whole amount back to Feigl owing to the police prohibition of Budzislawski's journal at the outbreak of the Second World War.[7] At the end of the 1960s, therefore, the SED assumed that the move of *Die neue Weltbühne* to Paris was made on party instructions, and it was ready to take financial responsibility for it even after several decades had elapsed. This also means, conversely, that Budzislawski can be proved to have accepted money on this one occasion, a time of extreme emergency, from a person who was very close to the KPD.

After the question of costs had been settled, Budzislawski rapidly pushed forward with the relocation of *Die neue Weltbühne* to Paris, which brought him into what had in the meantime become the most important center for Hitler's German-speaking opponents. In the practical aspects of the move, he had the help of Maximilian Scheer and Milly Zirker, faithful *Neue Weltbühne* colleagues who had long been resident in the French capital. Both of them would also accompany Budzislawski two years later to New York, where they again worked as journalists and where Zirker occasionally made ends meet by working as Budzislawski's "secretary."[8] On 13 May 1938, "after consultation with the Czechoslovak authorities and with their agreement," as he emphasized later in a letter to the Czechoslovak consul general in New York, the editor in chief finally left his previous place of work on the banks of the Vltava.[9] Having been provided with fresh identity papers by the Prague authorities, he flew first to Switzerland under a false name, then traveled from there to France on his genuine passport. His wife, Hanna, and his daughter, Beate, followed shortly afterward, but the details of the route they took are unknown. His father, Isidor Budzislawski, who had traveled to Prague at the end of 1937 to live with his son and his son's family after the death of his wife, Jenny, also made the move to Paris.

Although Budzislawski tells us that he had received backing from Yves Chataigneau, who was secretary general under Prime Minister Édouard Daladier in the early summer of 1938, as well as from other people, *Die neue Weltbühne* was not at first given permission to be published in France.[10] Each issue was therefore put together in a hotel room in Paris, and copies were then run off in Brussels. To change this situation, Budzislawski made a personal appeal on 4 June 1938 to the press chief of the French foreign ministry, Pierre Comert. Budzislawski's efforts were successful in the medium term, despite the diplomatic pressure exerted on France by the Third Reich. Beginning with 10 November 1938, *Die neue Weltbühne* could be printed in a normal manner in Paris.[11] In France, as in Prague, it was urgently necessary for Budzislawski to reach a political understanding with the government of the host country if he wanted to ensure the survival of his paper. Its circulation was falling continuously: by this time it was around nine thousand at most and perhaps considerably less than that.[12]

In the 1930s France was one of the last of Germany's neighbors where foreigners who had fled the Nazi regime could feel comparatively safe. One extra reason for this was the easing of entry requirements for those subject to political persecution that the governments of the Left-inclined Front Populaire had pushed through, particularly in view of the Spanish Civil War. Even in France, though, the situation of political refugees worsened after 1937. For example, the French minister of the interior and former prime minister, Albert-Pierre Sarraut, without mincing words, called for prompt and energetic intervention by the authorities "to cleanse our country from the excessive number of foreign undesirables who are hanging around here, agitating against the laws or taking part in an unacceptable manner in political conflicts" that concerned the French people themselves and no one else.[13] There was also an increase in complaints against foreigners by the locals. At first, political exiles were often greeted with sympathy; later, they were merely tolerated at best.[14]

Budzislawski was now one of these unwanted aliens. He was highly exposed politically, and not just because of his leading articles and his editorship of *Die neue Weltbühne*. He was also the chair of the Action Committee of German Oppositionists, presided over by Heinrich Mann, and the author of a "Memorandum by German Friends of Peace on Hitler's War Policy and the German People's Desire for Peace," written together with Willi Bredel, Anna Seghers, Ernst Toller, and others. Furthermore, Budzislawski acted as the director of a KPD-financed publishing house that went by the name 10 May, an allusion to the date in 1933 when books were burned in Germany.[15] He received 9,000 francs from Moscow on at least one occasion to pay for the distribution of its publications.[16] Budzislawski attempted during this time to gain readers within Germany by producing a disguised special issue of *Die neue Weltbühne* that was printed in an edition of several hundred copies and smuggled into the German Reich in the form of packages supposedly containing samples of Lyons Red Label Tea.[17] The journal was also read in the Nazi Ministry of Propaganda, sometimes even by the minister himself. Goebbels, though, was unimpressed, noting in his diary under the date 24 May 1939: "A typical Jewish émigré sheet. Uninteresting and insipid."[18]

During his two years in Paris, Budzislawski developed a more long-term political perspective than he had shown in Prague. Now he no longer hoped for the rapid overthrow of National Socialist rule by a united working class. He expected instead that the Nazis would be defeated in a military conflict. He was convinced that the aggressive policy of expansion and occupation pursued by the National Socialists in Central Europe since 1938 would soon lead to war. In line with this, he sharply criticized the appeasement policy of the Western European democracies. Hopes for peace, as entertained in Western Europe in the summer of 1938, "lacked any real foundation," he said. The National Socialists regarded diplomatic negotiations merely as providing a "temporary interval of peace," and they sought to use the postponement of hostilities to secure a better starting position for the coming war, which was inevitable.[19] As far as the Soviet Union was concerned, Budzislawski did not permit any debate in *Die neue Weltbühne* over the Moscow trials of alleged "Trotskyists" or over any other aspect of the Stalinist purges. As early as 1936 he took the view that one should hold one's nerve over "unwanted occurrences in the allied camp," and he kept to this approach in the three years that followed.[20] All that counted for him was the struggle against the National Socialists, which could only be won in association with the Soviet Union, owing to the West's hesitancy. The Soviet Union was not in a position to exercise decisive influence on political developments in Central and Western Europe, he conceded at the beginning of November 1938 in *Die neue Weltbühne*, but he went on to say: "This power is nevertheless present, and one must reckon with it if there is a change in the constellation of forces. And one must also be aware that it will be available to us, particularly if it is directly attacked. The National Socialists pretend to the German people that Russia is powerless, but this illusion may be a matter of life and death to them. It would not be a walk in the park to get to Moscow, or even to Kharkov [Kharkiv] or Kiev [Kiiv]. And it is also possible that Western Europe may one day be happy to remember the existence of this power, if it is needed."[21]

As an observer of foreign policy, Budzislawski considered any cooperation between the Soviet Union and Hitler's Germany to be out of the question— until 22 August 1939, that is. On that Tuesday morning, as he recalled some years later when in exile in the United States, he received a telephone call from Georg Bernhard, formerly editor in chief of the *Vossische Zeitung* and Reichstag deputy for the liberal German Democratic Party (DDP), informing him that "he had just heard on the radio that Ribbentrop had flown to Moscow to conclude a treaty with Stalin." Budzislawski was utterly amazed: "I was groggy. This pact was a bombshell that overturned the whole European structure." The anti-Nazi front, which had only been cemented back together with difficulty after the Munich Conference of 1938, was now shattered "into a thousand tiny fragments" by the "shock of the Moscow treaty." The Communists "were no longer allies. But the other groups also wavered or abandoned the cause." The impending war, as Budzislawski noted accurately in his analysis, would no longer be waged by an international anti-Fascist front but by various powers in defense of their national interests. In France "every German . . . was now an enemy, every Popular Front supporter a traitor. . . . It represented the complete collapse of our policies."[22] The memoirs of the later Central Committee member Albert Norden confirm Budzislawski's version from the perspective of the exiled KPD. In 1962 Norden related that he had taken part at that time in a crisis meeting of the Popular Front Committee in the house of "present-day comrade Prof. Dr. Hermann Budzislawski" on the party's instructions. It was also attended by Georg Bernhard and Maximilian Scheer. All those present had demanded of him, Norden, that he "reject the German-Soviet Non-Aggression Pact, concluded on 23 August 1939, in the name of the party and that the KPD give public expression to this rejection." Since he was not ready to do this, even after many hours of argument, the Popular Front Committee disintegrated that very day.[23]

Budzislawski tells us that he spent the next few days sitting in front of the radio in a state of nervous tension. He continued to inspire his family with optimism, but inwardly he no longer hoped for either the success of his political cause or the retention of his personal freedom: "Basically I am completely discouraged, and I am focusing on the prospect of a long period of imprisonment."[24] On 25 August 1939 he again invited the members of the Action Committee of German Oppositionists to attend a meeting at their regular café, Au Vieux Saumur, which was located on the rue de Belleville in the city's twentieth arrondissement.[25] It would be the last meeting of this kind, because only five days later, on 30 August and thus even before the official declaration of war on the German Reich, the French government, under its prime minister, Édouard Daladier, resolved to arrest all men between the ages of seventeen and fifty who had been born in an enemy country if war broke out. This plan was announced on large red posters that appeared everywhere on the walls of the country's cities, and it was put into effect on 1 September.[26] The daily newspaper of the French Communist Party, *L'Humanité*, the evening paper *Le Soir*, edited by Louis Aragon, and *Die neue Weltbühne* had all been prohibited on the previous day and their archives confiscated. On 5 September Budzislawski was instructed to report to the detention camp to which he had been assigned, the Maisons-Laffitte Racecourse, west of Paris, "because I was born in Germany and because Czechoslovakia was regarded at that moment as an integral part of the Great German Reich," as the man who was "stateless" owing to the Nazi occupation of Czechoslovakia later bitterly noted.[27] He was deeply offended that he of all people, a man who had agitated unswervingly against the Nazis, was now counted by the French as part of the Fifth Column.

In the Maisons-Laffitte camp, the detainees had to sleep on the cold flagstones of the stable floors. Twelve of them were crammed together in a single stall.[28] The French Foreign Intelligence Service began its interrogations, and it held out the prospect of immediate "release" to anyone who volunteered for the Foreign Legion. Budzislawski discussed with his fellow prisoners, among them the art historian Willi Wolfradt and the former Communist Reichstag deputy Peter Maslowski, how they should react to this. Most of the detainees were united in refusing to give way to French pressure, especially as the military gave no assurances, nor did it promise possible French citizenship in connection with membership of the Foreign Legion, which would have been an enticing prospect for a stateless Jew like Budzislawski.[29]

The next stage for him and hundreds of others was their transfer in what has been described as cattle wagons to the internment camp of Athis-de-l'Orne in Normandy, which had been set up in an empty factory building.[30] Instead of fighting Hitler with words, large parts of the German opposition were now stranded in French camps. But waves of optimism repeatedly broke through the initial feeling of hopelessness, as reported later by Henry Jacoby, a former internee. He had previously been Budzislawski's school friend, and he too had come to France via Prague and been locked up at the beginning of the war. It was particularly the Jewish internees who had fled from Germany and who could be identified as such through an appropriate endorsement on their documents—*réfugié provenant d'Allemagne*—who entertained the hope of an early release. But Budzislawski was not one of this group. Like other internees, he recorded that the camp commandant was a man of humanity and that the work they had to do was comparatively easy. The internees also organized lectures and concerts, and even members of the local population came into the camp to attend these occasions.[31] One of the star turns of these evenings was the German Jewish pianist Ernst Engel, who in the early 1930s had worked as house pianist at the fashionable Jockey Bar on Wittenbergplatz, playing in front of the cultural celebrities of Berlin and their international guests such as Ernest Hemingway and André Gide.[32] Budzislawski too counted as a famous prisoner. The internees valued his opinion, as Jacoby recalled: "It was the custom of the camp inmates to gather together in the dining hall after the evening meal, and Budzislawski's chair was lifted onto a table. From there he explained the military situation on the basis of the newspapers we were able to obtain from a neighboring village. Although he had nothing to add to what could be read in them, he knew how to make their meager contents appear interesting to his listeners."[33]

But these nighttime sessions of political enlightenment quickly came to an end. Budzislawski informed his audience one evening that Willi Münzenberg, who had also fled to France and had meanwhile been expelled from the KPD, had denounced him as a Communist agent and that the camp commandant had responded by banning his evening lectures. Later, in the summer of 1950, Budzislawski even claimed that Münzenberg had promised through intermediaries that Budzislawski would be freed if he gave a public "declaration against the Soviet Union." But he had refused to do this. The internment camp's interpreter of the war situation therefore fell silent, "procured the necessary tools, started to repair the camp inmates' shoes, and ostentatiously avoided any kind of discussion."[34] Jacoby's memoirs show that Budzislawski enjoyed a good reputation among the political exiles interned in France and was a convincing political commentator. This man who knew all the tricks of the trade as a journalist could also be impressive in direct personal contact with other people.

Later on, in the GDR at the start of the 1950s, Hanna Budzislawski gave a detailed account of Münzenberg's alleged denunciation of Budzislawski and the background to it. She asserted that she had had "extremely serious disagreements" with Münzenberg during her husband's internment.[35] According to her statement, the tensions between them dated back to 1937, when Münzenberg wanted to set up a central publishing house for the German emigration in Paris, which was a direct threat to the business model of *Die neue Weltbühne*, then still located in Prague: "When Walter Ulbricht visited our Prague house, Hermann complained about this plan. . . . Ulbricht said at that time that he was not free to reply to this complaint but that he would prevent Münzenberg's plan from coming into effect, and he assured him that *Die Weltbühne* would not suffer from any action taken by the party." Notwithstanding such conversations with KPD leaders in exile, Hanna insisted that *Die neue Weltbühne* did not receive financial support from the party. This was probably true as regards the regular financing of each issue, but, as we have seen, it was not true for exceptional items of expenditure such as the cost of transferring the journal from Prague to Paris.[36]

A final attempt to resolve the dispute with Münzenberg by a one-to-one discussion in the summer of 1939 ended in failure. At that time, Münzenberg was publishing the weekly periodical *Die Zukunft*, and he had broken with Stalin's policies—not least because of the Moscow trials—without initially making this decision public. According to Hanna Budzislawski's version of the meeting, Münzenberg had telephoned her husband and asked him to meet for a discussion in a Paris café: "Münzenberg attempted to win Hermann over by presenting his differences with the KPD as internal matters that did not need to interest a nonparty journal like *Die Weltbühne*. Hermann replied that he regarded him, Willi, as an agent, and that was the end of the conversation. Directly after this discussion, as we learned later, Münzenberg denounced Hermann to various official French bodies, saying that he was a Communist and an agent of the Comintern." Hanna Budzislawski claimed to be convinced that Münzenberg and his wife, Babette Gross, had been active agents of the Deuxième Bureau, the French foreign intelligence service. She even suspected Münzenberg of having worked for the Gestapo as a double agent. She had, she said, received direct information to that effect at the beginning of 1940 from Henri Guernut, the former general secretary of the French League for the Defense of Human and Citizens' Rights who was also minister of education for a brief period.[37] Similar accusations against Münzenberg and against the journalist Leopold Schwarzschild and other exiles who still remained at large were making the rounds of German exile circles in France at that time, and they were later repeated by high-ranking Communists in the GDR, including, among others, Albert Norden.[38] From a present-day perspective, however, these accusations must be regarded as groundless, as no incriminating material against the alleged informers has ever been found.[39]

Münzenberg himself emphatically protested against "the spreading of such rumors." He conceded to Hanna in a letter of 22 December 1939 that he had

had serious disagreements with Hermann that had escalated in the spring of
1939 when they had a conversation in the Paris apartment of Georg Bernhard:
"During this discussion I vainly attempted to convince Herr Budzislawski that
his political attitude and his vehemence against me could only benefit Communism and Stalinism, consciously or unconsciously, willingly or unwillingly.
I regret that I was unable to convince him with my arguments." Münzenberg
announced at the same time that he would continue the political fight against
the editor in chief of *Die neue Weltbühne*, but "only when the opponent is in
a position to reply," in other words, when he was no longer interned. Münzenberg also asked the Budzislawskis to operate a similar policy of "fair play"
toward him.[40] Ten months later, Münzenberg's body was found near Grenoble
in an extreme state of decay; he had died from being hanged. After the war,
unsurprisingly, Hanna did not associate the Communists with this event: "In
discussions among the exiles in Lisbon, the following theses were put forward as possible explanations: (1) suicide, (2) robbery followed by murder,
(3) removal of a double agent by the French authorities."[41] Anyone thrown out
of the party no longer existed—or if they still existed, it was only as an enemy.
The Budzislawskis subscribed to this logic—at least they did in 1950. Münzenberg could no longer defend himself, and now the Budzislawskis claimed that
he was responsible for all the possible problems of the Popular Front era. By
doing this, they were able to present themselves as good Communists, which
in 1950 meant faithful disciples of Stalin.

Between September 1939 and June 1940, the French authorities interned
thousands of Germans as well as those whom the Nazis had made stateless. This
affected Nazi Party members just as much as it did convinced anti-Fascists who
had fled to France to escape persecution in the German Reich. Although Budzislawski was stateless, he was treated as a German national, despite the intercession of influential representatives of the exiled Czech government. The Berlin
lawyer Rudolf Olden, who had made his name in the Weimar Republic as a
journalist for the *Berliner Tageblatt* specializing in legal affairs, described conditions in France in the second half of 1939 in a letter from London to Prince
Hubertus zu Löwenstein, who had founded the American Guild for German
Cultural Freedom, a kind of German Academy of Arts and Sciences in exile. It
acted as an aid organization for German writers, artists, and scientists subjected
to Nazi persecution in the second half of the 1930s.[42] Olden's survey of the situation was couched in tones of resignation and sarcasm: "From Europe, dear
prince, I only have depressing news to report. Leaving aside all the big worries,
the small ones are bad enough. All our friends, or almost all of them, are stuck
fast in France. One of them, Berthold Jacob, has received the special honor of
solitary confinement, without books, in the prison of La Santé. It has evidently

been discovered that he is a dangerous spy." Jacob, he added bitterly, had been "one of the most faithful supporters of France and of peace in the whole of Germany." He was a man "who had taken the most extreme risks in order to be true to his convictions. I cannot help it, but I don't think the French are acting wisely. My brother [the writer Balder Olden], Leonhard Frank, Leo Lania, and Willy Speyer are sitting in internment. Kurt Kersten is in prison (he, like Jacob, is in La Santé). An internment camp is an excellent place to stay, as long as it is warm and the sun is shining. But yesterday snow fell for the first time in central France. What is to be done? Tell this to the people France has to pay attention to, Dorothy Thompson, Walter Lip[p]mann. You will know whom to approach better than I do."[43]

Arnold Zweig also expressed his regret that the "most resolutely and explicitly anti-Nazi organs" such as *Die neue Weltbühne* were no longer available owing to the decisions of the French government. But he remained optimistic in the medium term, because one result of the war, he hoped, could be the emergence of a genuinely democratic Germany—to the extent, that is, that the country could catch up with the year 1789, when the French Revolution began, and that the hold of the traditional elites, the "Prussian Junkers and the feudal nobility," could be broken.[44]

Budzislawski remained in the internment camp of Athis-de-l'Orne until the end of January 1940, when he was transferred along with the Communists Albert Norden and Alexander Abusch as well as a number of independent right-wing intellectuals such as Karl Otto Paetel to a camp at Damigny near Alençon, also in the department of Orne.[45] Here the treatment of the internees was notably harsher. According to Budzislawski's description, the camp commandant, a certain Major Alliez, was a "Prussian Junker in French uniform." Corruption, mistreatment, eavesdropping on prisoners' conversations, and antisemitic harassment by the camp guards were the order of the day at Damigny.[46] Budzislawski described his experiences in a short vignette dated 10 May 1940, to which he gave the ironic title "A Journey through France": "The Damigni [*sic*] camp combines two different strata. Within the barbed wire there are the prisoners, an ethnically mixed group who dwell in wooden barracks without a solid floor. When it rains, the clay surfaces in the living and sleeping areas become soft, and we wade to our camp with muddy feet. From the outside, the barracks on the other side of the barbed wire look identical to ours. We built them ourselves, and they are made of wooden planks covered with roofing felt. But they are more comfortable inside. They have wooden floors, rooms, and cupboards. That is where the 'guardian nation' lives."[47]

As he himself stated, Budzislawski was one of the "privileged prisoners" who were occasionally allowed to leave the inner section of the camp, which was rigidly fenced in with barbed wire, and to speak to the "guardian nation," in other words, the French camp guards, as well as to smoke with them and make all kinds of bargains. Compared with other French internment camps, not to mention the concentration camps of the Third Reich, conditions at Damigny were at least endurable. Henry Jacoby, who was also interned there, reported that life in that environment was "not a big problem psychologically," at least as long as one did not fall seriously ill: "Certainly, the food often did not taste good, the sleeping arrangements were bad, and the toilets were unhygienic, but nothing was unbearable. It cannot be said that we suffered bad treatment."[48] Another detainee, in contrast, reported that they had to get used to living like animals, "keeping lice and fleas in check and defending food supplies successfully against the mice."[49] Budzislawski later wrote that during his period of imprisonment he had worked first as a woodcutter and a stonebreaker and then as a plasterer until he was finally sent to the camp's mail room.[50] The last-mentioned employment allows us to conclude that after some time the prominent internee was accorded relatively favorable treatment. Moreover, the job of postman provided the journalist Budzislawski with privileged access to information.

A long thank-you letter from Hanna Budzislawski, written on 18 April 1940 to Hubertus, Prince of Löwenstein, provides some information on the situation of the members of Budzislawski's family who had not been interned. Löwenstein's organization had been trying since the autumn of 1939 to secure Hermann's release, and in March 1940 it had temporarily relieved the family's material distress by sending one hundred US dollars to Sèvres, near Paris, where Hanna continued to live with her child and her father-in-law. Hanna's letter also provides a thorough description of the political situation and her own future prospects. There was no mention of an early reappearance of *Die neue Weltbühne*. Instead, she concentrated on settling political accounts and on plans for emigration and possible ways of making a living in a new place of exile: "You know all the finer points of politics, and you know the honorable fight our journal has waged for years. It is certainly not necessary to assure you that you are campaigning for a completely just cause. . . . Our situation is fairly miserable. I have not seen my husband for almost eight months. He is only allowed to write one postcard a week—and he is forced to live alongside his deadly enemies, the Nazis. . . . Money would have been available to cover living costs if my assets had not been sequestered since November. If my husband is not rehabilitated, I shan't receive a single sou. And today I don't yet know what I shall be able to live on next month. I have used the American donation first of all to pay the rent and the deposit for the current quarter."[51]

When Hanna Budzislawski wrote these lines, she had already been forced to move house yet again. After arriving in France, the family's first address had been an imposing villa on a hill in Sèvres. This house, 95, rue de Ville d'Avray, was a splendid property with no fewer than fourteen rooms. It was pithily referred to in emigrant circles as "The Castle." When she was reproached later about this luxurious exile accommodation, Hanna justified herself by pointing to pragmatic considerations: "It was an old mansion in a big park, certainly, but it was much cheaper than the corresponding amount of space in Paris. . . . The editorial office and the publishing house were accommodated in three rooms: we delivered copies to the subscribers ourselves. In addition, there were other exiles who worked in the house from time to time, preparing leaflets for Germany and sending them off."[52] After the prohibition of the journal at the beginning of September 1939, it was no longer possible to pay the rent. The money for "moving house in a proper manner" was admittedly available, but the account had been blocked. Hanna dug out the emergency reserve of 25,000 francs buried in the garden, but this money too was seized by the French police during a house search.[53] The police allegedly carried out further raids on the house and the business premises of the prohibited *Neue Weltbühne* in the next few months; Hanna again ascribed these police actions to a denunciation by Münzenberg.[54] She said that she was forced by lack of money to use a wheelbarrow to move the whole establishment, including thousands of books and business papers, "from one hill in Sèvres to another." This took weeks of effort. Her new accommodation, in 3b, rue du Point de Vue, was an ordinary kind of family home, with four rooms. Measured against the living conditions of many other exiles, however, it was still very comfortable.

The Budzislawskis now no longer believed that their future lay in France: "My husband, who until then has always refused to leave Europe, now asks me in every postcard whether there is a possibility of emigrating. I am helpless here. San Domingo or Shanghai are probably out of the question. All other overseas countries can only be reached by paying a large amount of money. The only hope left is to secure an appointment. On this subject I would be most grateful if you could tell me whether our friends over there could arrange something of this kind. (My husband speaks perfect English; many years ago he edited a journal in the English language.) I would willingly agree to be separated from my husband and hold out here if I knew that he could recover his liberty in this way."[55] The influential politicians, writers, and journalists who according to her would be ready to write a reference for Hermann included Thomas Mann, the holder of the Nobel Prize in Literature; Henry

Wickham Steed, the former editor of *The Times* of London; Richard Freund from the Left-liberal *Manchester Guardian*; François Crucy, former head of the foreign press section at the Quai d'Orsay; the biographer and successful author Emil Ludwig; Émile Kahn, the general secretary of the League for Human Rights; Arne Laurin, the former editor in chief of the *Prager Presse*; and finally Hubert Ripka, the former editor of the Prague *Lidové Noviny*, who had in the meantime become a member of the Czechoslovak National Committee in Paris.[56]

But it was impossible to predict whether Hermann Budzislawski would be released or when this would happen. At the end of April or the beginning of May 1940 he was once again transferred, this time to the internment camp of Bassens, seven and a half miles from Bordeaux, which had been set up for "foreign undesirables." At times, up to eleven hundred internees were locked up in this camp, which was located on the premises of a former gunpowder factory in the Gironde. The vast majority of them were Jewish refugees from the Nazi regime, but there were also roughly 350 captured German military personnel.[57] Jewish exiles and Nazis had to do forced labor together and unwillingly sleep side by side. The inmates of the camp included Georg Bernhard; the renowned lawyer Alfred Apfel; the Social Democratic politician Erich Ollenhauer, who later became chair of the SPD in the Federal Republic; the art critic Carl Einstein; the historian Kurt Kersten; the writer Wolf Franck; and the theater critic Julius Bab, who was almost sixty years old and had earlier been a contributor to *Die Schaubühne*. According to Budzislawski, their main job was to unload frozen meat in the port of Bordeaux, but unlike the regular workers, they had to use their bare hands.[58]

The biggest danger he faced was not conditions in the camp but the evolution of the military situation after the end of the Phoney War on 10 May 1940 and the rapid advance of German troops into French territory that followed during the next few weeks. The Wehrmacht occupied Paris on 14 June and was preparing to bring the rest of the country under its control within a few days. The sound of the Luftwaffe's nightly bombing raids on nearby Bordeaux was part of everyday experience in the camp during the early summer of 1940. This strengthened the imprisoned opponents of the Nazis in their conviction that they must get away from there sooner rather than later. A delegation of "political" internees went to the camp commandant and threatened to rise in revolt if they were not released immediately or brought to a place of safety. German troops were already as close as eighteen miles away: if there were no obstacles, their tanks could reach the camp in no more than two hours.[59] Then Hitler's opponents in Bassens would have been handed to the German occupiers on a plate. Internees such as Budzislawski were faced with the direct prospect of interrogation by the Gestapo, transportation to the Reich, and a long period of incarceration and mistreatment in a German concentration camp. He was sitting in a trap, and he was under a triple threat: first as a well-known anti-Fascist journalist, second as a stateless person, and third as a Jew.

But once again luck was on Budzislawski's side, because he got out of the internment camp just before 22 June 1940, when the Franco-German Armistice was concluded. It is not entirely clear how he managed this. Some sources report that the camp commandant had decided to free his prisoners because he was under no illusion about what the Germans would do with their political enemies. A few days later, under article 19 of the armistice agreement, the Vichy government did in fact undertake to hand over to the Third Reich all opponents of the Nazi regime living on French territory.[60] But according to other sources, the gentleman in question, a certain Capitaine Cardineau, had little or no interest in the fate of the internees and despite the general environment of dissolution surrounding the camp wished to proceed strictly on the basis of the official files in administering the release of the prisoners. It was rather his subordinates who created facts on the ground by spontaneously opening the camp gates, at least for the group of internees who were "in particular danger." That is how Albert Norden, who also made his escape, recalled these events after the war, when he wrote that in the second half of June 1940 the internment camp disintegrated.[61]

According to Budzislawski's own version, the liberation of "political" internees who were in particular danger was called for first by the Mexican consul and then by the US ambassador, William Christian Bullitt Jr. A few days later the camp commandant released a select group of prisoners. Budzislawski was one of the lucky ones who were able to pass through the gate of the camp on the evening of 20 June 1940. They had been furnished with regular release papers dated the previous day and thirty francs.[62] In his own words, though, the end of his period of incarceration sounded more exciting than an orderly release from prison : "We prisoners rose in revolt, demanded our release, were rebuffed, put off with fine words—and finally they let us go. I threw a rucksack over my shoulders—it contained nothing but rags, the remains of clothes I had worn previously—and marched off."[63] In addition to Norden, Budzislawski was joined in his escape by Paetel, Apfel, the liberal democratic journalist Carl Misch, and Alexander Abusch.[64]

Budzislawski's initial objective at that point was to find his family. A few days earlier, on 15 June 1940, a telegram sent by his wife from Paris had reached him in the camp, informing him of her new address: "Domé Dordogne chez Madame Ducroix." To begin with, he took a train from Bordeaux to the town of Montauban, which lay a good 125 miles to the southeast, so as to put some

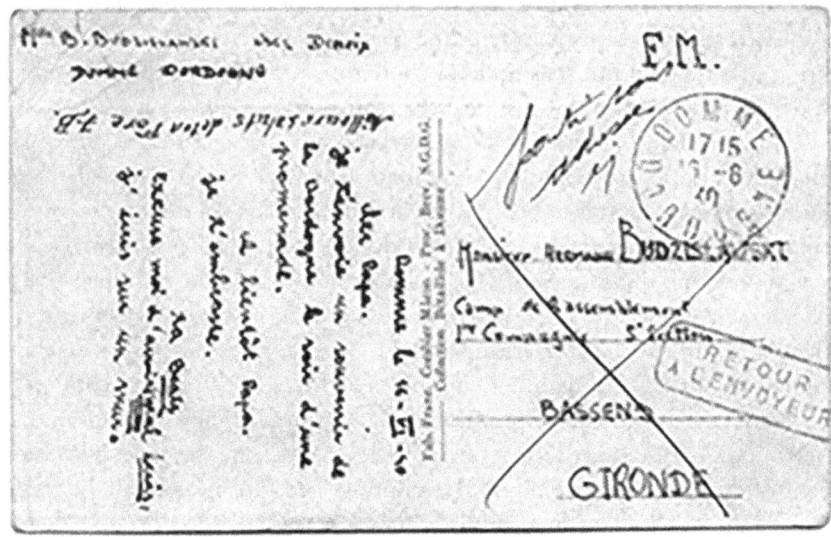

Postcard sent by Budzislawski's ten-year-old daughter that failed to reach him in the Bassens internment camp in June 1940 and was returned to the sender.

distance between himself and the front. From there he went on foot in the direction of the Dordogne, which meant going directly toward the advancing German troops. On the way, he met French soldiers and refugees traveling in motor cars and on motorcycles who repeatedly advised him to turn around. He claims that he was the only person traveling on foot and that he managed up to twenty-five miles a day. At night he found accommodation in farmhouses, where the inhabitants gave him food and wine. It was important later for Budzislawski to make a sharp distinction between the repression carried out by the French state and the eagerness of broad sections of the French population to give assistance to the refugees. Although he looked like a vagrant and could easily be identified as a foreigner from his accent, people had repeatedly spoken to him in the street, invited him into their houses, and given him advice as far as they were able to.[65] He could only identify himself with his release papers from the internment camp as well as with a membership card of the PEN club signed by Jules Romains and Heinrich Mann, which was very helpful on several occasions. As he recalled in 1964, it had been the "best passport" to use in dealings with the authorities, with soldiers at roadblocks, and with the civilian population.[66]

Since no one knew of a place called Domé, Budzislawski struggled through to a village with the similar-sounding name of Domme. He arrived there, he says, around midday on Sunday, 23 June 1940, a day after France and the German Reich had concluded the armistice at Compiègne. At first his search for members of his family was unsuccessful. The small village of Domme, which normally had a population of eight hundred, was now bursting at the seams. Budzislawski estimated that there were several thousand people seeking shelter there. Having sat down on a park bench, exhausted from his vain attempt to find a Madame Ducroix who was possibly living in the village, he suddenly recognized the old man sitting beside him as his seventy-six-year-old father. The Budzislawski family—his father, Isidor, his wife, Hanna, and their daughter, Beate—had in fact found accommodation in Domme with a certain Madame Denoix after they had fled from the German occupiers. The flight from Paris, which they had undertaken in company with the wife and child of Maximilian Scheer, had started on 11 June. It had taken several days under chaotic conditions. If the two women had not succeeded in hiding overnight in a brothel for French colonial troops near Périgueux, eighty miles to the east of Bordeaux, the attempt to flee would have ended quite possibly with their arrest.[67] The armistice a couple of days later was a stroke of luck. "We had lost everything, but we had found each other again": that was how Budzislawski later described the reunification of the family on a park bench in an American newspaper article written in the autumn of 1940.[68] His wife described it as a "cinematic ending no one could have invented."[69]

Immediately after his arrival in Domme, Budzislawski contacted the American Guild in New York as the first step toward the family's immigration to the United States. This is how such efforts were described by the writer Walther Victor, who was in a similar situation at that time: "One hurled appeals for help into the unknown while making one's way through the nerve-wracking chaos" of the French collapse.[70] Communication was difficult and could only be done in a conspiratorial manner if one wanted to avoid being arrested and transported to Germany. Budzislawski therefore instructed the American Guild on no account to mention his and his family's legal name in any correspondence. All letters should be sent instead to a Fräulein Marie Röselova at the address of Madame Denoix. At the beginning of July 1938, the Budzislawskis had invited a twenty-two-year-old woman named Röselova to visit them in Paris. She was probably the family's Czech housemaid, whom they had continued to employ in Paris and who had perhaps gone on ahead to find somewhere for them to stay in southern France. Hanna Budzislawski later stated that they had found accommodation with "Czech comrades."[71] In Domme their quarters were exceedingly spartan: a room with an open fire, which was also used for cooking. In other respects, too, the hygienic arrangements left much to be desired, if we can believe Budzislawski's later account: his daughter suffered from skin rashes, and head lice made the rounds in the family. In order to buy food and to cover other items of expenditure they were forced to sell their last pieces of jewelry—which Hanna had smuggled out of Paris— including rings that had belonged to Budzislawski's late mother.[72]

The situation became still more oppressive when a new ordinance was issued prohibiting all foreigners from leaving their place of residence, thereby making foraging trips into neighboring villages illegal. The family's fear of renewed arrest increased every day. Now they wanted to leave France as quickly as possible. On 6 August 1940 Hermann Budzislawski therefore wrote directly to the State Department in Washington, DC, both in English and in French, asking it to rapidly issue a transit visa for himself and his family, as they were in great danger. However, he did not say whether they would travel on to another country after arrival in the United States.[73] A month later, on 10 September, a telegram actually arrived in Domme for the supposed Marie Rösel-ova. It stated that the visas were ready and could be collected in Marseille. But the telegram could not be delivered, as the Western Union Telegraph Company explained on 17 September to the sender in New York: the addressee had moved away to an unknown location.[74]

The Budzislawskis had in fact already set out southward on 22 August because they were worried that they might fall into German hands if they stayed in Domme. They now aimed to get to their ultimate objective, which was the United States, by leaving France and traveling through Spain. For this, they needed papers. The word had spread quickly among the refugees that such things were available—if at all—in Marseille. In the course of a few weeks, that city had become the goal of mass migration. It had turned into an "anxiety zone" for tens of thousands of Europeans who wanted to reach a place where they would be safe from the approaching army and the German occupation regime and where they could hope for an early opportunity to travel even farther away.[75] The Budzislawskis were able to raise the cost of the journey to Marseille because an American Express carrier had handed them 2,000 francs in Domme on 19 August. They found out later that the money had been sent by the League of American Writers.[76] During a fact-finding tour to Montauban, which briefly became a "gathering point for Central European Socialists," Budzislawski heard a rumor that there was a list of refugees who had to be saved in the American consulate in Marseille and that the names of the most important journalists who had worked for the German-language exile press were on it.[77]

Relief operations in Marseille had been coordinated since the middle of August 1940 by Varian Fry and, on behalf of the exiled KPD, by Lex Ende (real name Adolf Ende), who called himself Philippe Gautier in France. The aim was to bring to safety the most important leaders of the German opposition using unbureaucratically issued emergency visas for the United States.[78] On 23 August, when the Budzislawskis arrived in the port city of Marseille, their visas were already in the American consulate, which immediately handed them out. They were, admittedly, slightly bogus, according to Hanna. Hermann's profession was given as novelist and not, as would have been more appropriate, as political journalist.[79] Supposedly, nonpolitical literati were far more welcome as refugees to the United States than Communists and their sympathizers.

Visas for Spain and Portugal could quickly be obtained on the black market in the Old Port neighborhood. But the Budzislawskis' situation was still not without risk, as Hermann later recalled. When he first arrived at the railway station he had to go through a checkpoint, which he only passed with difficulty. The whole city was swarming with policemen and spies, with the result that many refugees lived holed up in their rooms. Even so, he was able to meet many friends and acquaintances again in Marseille: Emil Julius Gumbel, the well-known mathematician and pacifist, "who thinks that no one can recognize him because he has grown a long beard. Heinrich Mann, about whom the wildest stories are circulating, is also there. Lion Feuchtwanger is in hiding; I cannot get through to see him. But Czechs, Poles, and even an Indian friend whom I last saw in Prague are all popping up. We are exchanging information, trying to gauge the situation, and asking each other questions, such as whether there is a ship about to leave the country or whether the Spaniards will let us through."[80]

Even after the Budzislawskis had acquired the necessary visas, by no means had all their problems been solved, because the family did not have enough money for the expensive transatlantic journey. Here too help was at hand, thanks to the network of former *Weltbühne* authors: the journalist and former *Weltbühne* employee Carl Misch left behind a letter in Marseille in which he advised the Budzislawskis to present themselves to a certain Mr. Bohn from the American Rescue Committee, which was known locally as the Centre Américain de Secours. The contact Misch mentioned was the former American trade unionist and Socialist Frank Bohn, who until Varian Fry arrived had been endeavoring to bring refugees persecuted by the Nazis into the United States on behalf of both the German Labor Delegation and the Jewish Labor Committee in Marseille. At first, the committee did its work in the rooms of the Hôtel Splendide, where its members were staying, since no offices had yet been rented.

Hanna recalled in 1950 that Hermann had met with a friendly reception at the hotel. But she claimed that the Social Democrat Rudolf Breitscheid, who was an active member of the American Rescue Committee, prevented the payment of their travel costs from being authorized because he wanted first and foremost to rescue "top Social Democratic functionaries and their secretaries or mistresses," not Communists or emigrants who sympathized with them.[81] In fact, it was for reasons of US internal policy that Bohn and his colleagues mainly provided trade unionists and moderate Social Democrats with emergency visas; Communists or their sympathizers were often at a disadvantage.[82] Hanna's later spitefulness toward Breitscheid appears out of place, especially as she knew that he had been arrested a few weeks later and handed over to the German authorities; he died on 24 August 1944 in the concentration camp of Buchenwald during an American air attack. Her defamatory remarks show once again the depth of the chasm between the reform-oriented wing of the SPD and the Socialist Left after 1945 at least. In February 1942 Hermann Budzislawski could still denounce the French, in a reader's letter printed in the *New York Times*, for handing over Breitscheid and Rudolf Hilferding to the Third Reich. Eight years later, this solidarity no longer existed.[83]

In the summer of 1940 the Budzislawskis finally succeeded in starting their onward journey using 1,500 French francs donated by the American Rescue Committee. They were probably included among the "small number of important cases" of Jewish refugees whom the committee had decided to help, even when these cases were "definitely political."[84] The Budzislawskis promptly set out for Perpignan, close to the border between France and Spain. In addition to the money from the committee, the cash they were traveling with included some pounds sterling that Hermann had arranged to be paid out of the British editorial account of *Die neue Weltbühne*, which was held in the London Westminster Bank. In previous years the journal had often operated complex billing practices, as its international readership made it necessary to open numerous foreign accounts; this now turned out to be a stroke of luck.[85]

Nevertheless, there was still no possibility of leaving the country legally. The Budzislawskis were, it is true, now permitted to migrate to the United States. But they were not allowed to leave France without the obligatory exit visa. In Perpignan such a document could be obtained after weeks of waiting at best; in addition to that, the Budzislawskis would have had to give up their papers to the authorities, and it was uncertain whether they would get them back. Against this background, the family of four decided to risk the arduous journey across the Pyrenees into Spain on foot.[86] The most dangerous part of the route was the illegal border crossing between Cerbère in France and the Catalan town of Portbou along a mountain track used by smugglers.[87] The family was unable or unwilling to pay the sum of 15,000 francs demanded by the criminals who organized escapes in Perpignan. It was, moreover, extremely doubtful whether the traffickers would hold to their promises. The Budzislawskis therefore decided to climb the mountain on their own, together with a married pair of journalists who had befriended them, Elsbeth and Herbert Weichmann (the husband later became the mayor of Hamburg). They chose to undertake this journey on 8 September 1940, which was a Sunday, hoping that the border guards might be otherwise engaged. The small group was among the first people to choose this way of fleeing from France into Spain, which soon afterward became a popular route.

The refugees left their luggage behind in Cerbère. Only Budzislawski's seventy-six-year-old father, Isidor, refused, it seems, to be separated from the tools of his trade, which absolutely had to be brought along.[88] Even without extra burdens to carry, scrambling over slippery rocks and vegetation was an extremely strenuous activity. Budzislawski wrote later that his father fell down at least thirty times. He tore his trousers, and his hands were severely scratched by thorns; it was a "frightening sight I shall never forget."[89] At the end of September 1940, when he was waiting in Lisbon for the ship to the United States and in good spirits, the memory of those terrible days was still vividly present in his mind: "I literally brought my seventy-six-year-old father 'over the mountain'; to be honest, my wife pulled him up a steep slope when my strength failed me. But my daughter thought it was great fun, and when we were finally on the insecure soil of Spain, she hugged me, saying 'Now they will no longer be able to catch Papa.'"[90]

By the end of September, the news of the Budzislawskis' method of escape had spread among the German refugees, and it had repeatedly shown its effectiveness in the meantime. Who had managed to get out of France, when they had done it, and how were major topics of conversation in those weeks. As Budzislawski reported at the end of the month, "Heinrich Mann also traveled on foot over the mountains, three days after us, together with [Franz] Werfel. But Feuchtwanger is still over there in France. . . . And not just him. Friedrich Wolf, Rudolf Leonhard, and others are stuck in the concentration camp of Le Vernet in the Pyrenees under intense French surveillance. They are at the disposal of the Gestapo, who have already interrogated them four times. Mehring was arrested in Perpignan when he finally decided to make the attempt to walk over the Pyrenees. He was brought to the camp of St. Cyprieux—though I heard yesterday that he has probably escaped again. Every day it becomes harder to get out of France. No one can renew his papers because it is necessary to hide. No one among us has received the French *visa de sortie*. The Spaniards have recently started to refuse transit visas to everyone under the age of forty. . . . And in Marseille people are constantly meeting friends—without money, without papers, and all looking for a way out. We should not have got as far as here without the help of some Americans. They gave us money for the journey to Lisbon and a fair bit of useful advice. Happy as we are to have got this far, it is heartbreaking to know that the others are still in France."[91] One of the victims of the increasing severity of Spain's visa regulations was Walter Benjamin. Owing to his fear of being sent back to France and despite his initial success in crossing the border, he took his own life on 26 September 1940 in the Catalan town of Portbou with a morphine overdose.[92]

The Budzislawski family traveled southwest from the Franco-Spanish border region as quickly as they could, passing through Barcelona and Madrid and finally reaching Lisbon, the "port of last resort." Between forty thousand and one hundred thousand refugees entered Portugal during that year, often with nothing more than the clothes they were wearing. They were obliged to rely on the support of charitable associations, consulates, shipping companies, and, last but not least, the Portuguese state, which issued temporary residence permits with relative generosity in view of the bureaucratic challenges this involved. Not until 1942 did the Portuguese start to intern refugees who were unable or unwilling to leave the country. The following documents were required as a rule for the onward journey: an identity card, an exit visa from France, a transit visa for Spain, and an entry visa for the United States. For many of the refugees from Central Europe, the "hunt for the correct papers," during which there was always the danger of failure at the last moment, induced feelings of extreme dislocation, leading to a crisis of identity.[93] They had arrived at the edge of the European continent after an often hectic and improvised flight. Nothing lay before them except the wide Atlantic Ocean and a future in America that could at best be vaguely imagined, while the whole of their previous life lay behind them. The coordinates of their existence had to be radically recalibrated.

By 1940 the Budzislawskis were already experienced refugees, and they coped better than other people with the atmosphere of uncertainty—not least because of their chutzpah. During the two and a half days' journey through Spain they presented themselves to the local officials as Russian emigrants and "refugees from Bolshevism."[94] No one in Spain seems to have noticed that none of them spoke Russian. The surname Budzislawski, with its Polish origin, was evidently Eastern European enough to sound credible. Their good command of French, traditionally the preferred language of the Russian upper classes, also appeared to fit the picture.

In Lisbon the phony Russians stayed at the Pension Alcobia, 15, Poço do Borratém, in the heart of the city. There they soon met other prominent refu-

In September 1940 the Budzislawskis reached Lisbon, and they started their journey to the United States from there at the beginning of October. This contemporary photograph shows the bustling activity around Rossio Square, which is centrally located in the downtown area.

gees such as Lion Feuchtwanger, Konrad Heiden, and Emil Julius Gumbel; they were also able to arrange excursions to visit Heinrich Mann, Franz Werfel, and the latter's wife, Alma Mahler, who had found accommodation in the fashionable coastal town of Estoril, farther to the west.[95] Budzislawski, who had only just escaped the French "mousetrap" and felt he was now "reasonably safe," wrote a long letter to the prince of Löwenstein on 21 September 1940. It reveals how much the former editor of *Die neue Weltbühne* was worried about the colleagues and friends he had left behind

who are still sitting in concentration camps at the disposal of the Gestapo. . . . The worst fate is suffered by the prisoners in the camp of Le Vernet, in the Pyrenees, where Friedrich Wolf and Rudolf Leonhard have been interrogated four times during one week. Bruno Frei is also there. His wife was killed in the bombardment of Paris, and his children are in an orphanage somewhere. Friedrich Wolf, Rudolf Leonhard, and a few others have visas for Mexico—but this does not help them, as the French are keeping a sharp lookout. Other people who are still at liberty, for example [Siegfried] Kracauer, are unable to summon up the courage to cross the border in secret. There is great material deprivation, and I do not know what will become of the many people who do not have special connections. The German *réfugiés*, who are after all under particular threat, are everywhere at an extreme disadvantage.[96]

Budzislawski's concern for his fellow countrymen was matched by his fury over the favorable treatment given to the Russian émigrés: "The Russians have received the most American visas. They can travel out of France legally; they can receive their *visa de sortie*—and they have been fortunate enough to be able to bring their luggage with them. We, on the other hand, who have sat in internment camps for a long time and no longer possess anything, have crossed the border with nothing. We have no change of shirts, no coats, nothing. And when we arrive in Lisbon, there are fresh difficulties."[97] The Jewish refugees from Russia had their passages paid for immediately, since their names stood on lists that had been deposited at the Lisbon office of the HICEM, an association of three Jewish emigration assistance organizations founded in 1927. Budzislawski's family had also been promised at first that they would be able to cross to the United States in a Greek steamer, the *Nea Hellas*, as third-class passengers. But then a signature was missing somewhere. "We were told in the meantime that this would not work because the American organizations had not given appropriate instructions. The organization mainly responsible is the Emergency Rescue Committee, under Kingston, its president—but unfortunately this office does not reply to cables. So we sit here in a terribly awkward situation. I continue to hope that they will take us after all—but this is extremely doubtful in the absence of instructions from America."[98] At least they were safe for the time being and no longer had to fear imprisonment and deportation to the Third Reich, unlike in France and Spain during the previous weeks and months.[99] Two weeks later, on 4 October 1940, the Budzislawskis were finally able to travel to New York on board the *Nea Hellas*. The journey was not entirely free of danger, however, because it was feared that a ship bearing the Greek flag might be attacked by ships of the German or Italian navy.[100]

The Budzislawskis had not at first known how they could raise the 800 US dollars that, according to the aid organizations, were required to pay for a passage across the Atlantic by a family of four. By the beginning of October the American Guild in New York had only received an anonymous donation of ten dollars for the Budzislawski family. But Budzislawski's sister-in-law, Erna, the former wife of his deceased brother Martin, had started work in the meantime in Hollywood as the secretary of the actor and director William Dieterle, and she brought the case to the attention of the European Film Fund. Although the main aim of this welfare organization, founded in 1938, was to support European actors and directors who were in financial difficulties, Dieterle's wife, Charlotte, and Liesl Frank, the wife of the writer Bruno Frank, made efforts to collect money for the Budzislawskis' journey. Whether substantial amounts of money accrued from this source is not known.[101] We can assume from the papers of the American Guild that the journey of Hermann Budzislawski and his family across the Atlantic was financed at the last minute by the Hebrew Immigrant Aid Society (HIAS), one of three organizations that operated under the HICEM umbrella.[102] According to the family's HIAS "arrival card," issued on their entry into New York, all four of them were supposedly born in the Soviet Union, a statement that was incorrect but that may well have served the purpose of enabling the costs to be authorized more rapidly.[103] As we have seen, Hermann Budzislawski proceeded on the assumption that funds would more easily be forthcoming for a crossing of the Atlantic by Russian refugees; moreover, the family's pretense of a Russian identity had already proved its value in Spain.

The Budzislawskis entered the United States on 13 October 1940 together with many other famous refugees, among them the writers Franz Werfel, Heinrich Mann and his nephew Golo, Alfred Polgar, Friedrich Stampfer, and Lion and Marta Feuchtwanger. These prominent exiles were set down in the port of Hoboken, New Jersey, opposite Manhattan, and they received the full red-carpet treatment: it is said that entrance tickets to the pier were already sold out the previous day.[104] But this enthusiastic reception by no means reflected the mood in the country as a whole. Thus the *Ladies' Home Journal* asked its readers in June 1941: "What are we to do with these intellectual refugees who are flooding into the country and who put on such an intolerable air of superiority?"[105] Hermann Budzislawski at least was so prominent—or his passage cost the HIAS so much—that his arrival was mentioned by name in the bulletin of the Jewish Telegraphic Agency for 14 October.[106] He again compared himself self-mockingly to a great historical figure, not Napoleon, as he had done at the end of 1933, but this time Columbus. It was a well-known fact, he said, that Columbus had discovered America on 12 October 1492 (celebrated as Columbus Day), but he, Budzislawski, had made the discovery a day later.[107] His sister-in-law, Erna, also emphasized the tragicomic aspect of the situation, particularly as regards her Prussian Jewish father-in-law: "Thus the seventy-five-year-old Isidor Budzislawski, who was already unable to bear the Austrians because to him they were foreigners, who hated Prague and ranted about Paris because there too absolutely nothing was happening ('What a village, bad roads, bad lighting, impossible bread! There is only one Berlin!'), will now get to know New York and learn to grumble about it."[108] His son Hermann, on the other hand, did not take long to adapt himself to the new circumstances. By the summer of 1941 he was again a man much in demand.

Protected by the Class Enemy

Exile in the United States

T HE AMERICAN GUILD for German Cultural Freedom, which Prince
Hubertus zu Löwenstein initiated in 1935 and directed, had played a
significant part in rescuing Budzislawski and his family. It had provided them with the necessary visitor visas and with US stateless person's
certificates, arguing to the US authorities that, quite apart from humanitarian
considerations, the continuing publication of *Die neue Weltbühne* would be
important for the success of the struggle against the Nazis.[1] The prince had
already used similar arguments a few months earlier, in January 1940, when he
spoke to the French ambassador in Washington, DC, in support of Budzislawski's release from internment. One might have certain reservations about his
political attitude, said Löwenstein, but he was convinced of the integrity of this
important journalist—not least because he had unequivocally castigated the
Hitler-Stalin Pact in *Die neue Weltbühne*, thereby proving that he belonged to
the democratic camp. The prince also used arguments of realpolitik: he indicated that Budzislawski was a "personal friend" of Edvard Beneš and that Arne
Laurin, who had in the meantime become an official of the Czechoslovak consulate in New York and a member of the European Council, had recommended
him to the guild "most emphatically."[2] At that stage in the war, Löwenstein's
arguments had been ineffective. The French ambassador agreed to examine the
case seriously but refused to make any promises.[3] It was only with the worsening of the situation in the summer of 1940 that attitudes began to change.

Alongside Hermann's political contacts with influential people and organizations, it was the provision of material guarantees that finally tipped the balance in favor of granting the Budzislawskis a permit to enter the United States.
Hanna's uncle Adolf Levy, who lived in New York, vouched for the whole
family, telling the authorities that once they had arrived in the city, he would
accommodate them for an unlimited period and provide them with "pocket

money" so that they would not become a burden on the state's finances.[4] Other German exiles as well as American artists in Hollywood also put in a word for the refugee family. Refugee assistance work on the West Coast of the United States was coordinated by the actor and screenwriter Salka Viertel, the wife of the author Berthold Viertel, who was an acquaintance of the Budzislawskis and would soon become a close friend. The Viertels had already lived in the United States since 1928, and they dedicated themselves throughout the 1930s and 1940s to supporting artists and intellectuals persecuted by the Nazis.[5] It emerges from the papers of the American Guild that the screenwriter George S. Kaufman had also declared his readiness in principle to swear an affidavit for Budzislawski, as long as this did not involve Kaufman in any financial obligation. The German Jewish Social Democrat Siegfried Marck, formerly professor of philosophy at Breslau (now Wrocław) University, had been in the United States since 1939, and he also wanted to help. In spite of *Die neue Weltbühne*'s connections with "Communist circles" in previous years, he regarded Hermann Budzislawski as a comrade in need and a political journalist with "good qualities" who had "proved himself by publishing *Die Weltbühne* in Prague and later in Paris."[6] Another sponsor in Hollywood whose name was not given—Budzislawski surmised at the end of 1940 that this was Berthold Viertel himself—declared his readiness to take financial responsibility for the refugees.[7]

For over a year, owing to his imprisonment, followed by his flight through southern Europe, Budzislawski had been unable to publish anything. But he returned to active journalism immediately after his arrival in New York. On 18 October 1940, only five days after he had disembarked the *Nea Hellas*, a short report on his experiences during his flight from France appeared in the German-language exile newspaper *Der Aufbau*, which was edited by Manfred George. In the article, Budzislawski portrayed his escape from the Bassens internment camp and the subsequent search for his family, which culminated in their happy reunion in the small town of Domme.[8] Within the month that followed his arrival in the United States he had rented a three-room apartment at 181 West 183rd Street, in Hudson Heights, a residential neighborhood in the Washington Heights area of the city that was popular among German exiles, had written a book proposal, and had put himself forward as a conference speaker for numerous German American organizations. Shortly before Christmas Eve 1940, he met with Thomas Mann in Princeton, New Jersey. They went for a walk, had a midday meal together, and discussed their respective plans for the New Year.[9]

Just over two weeks later, on 12 January 1941, it was announced that the "anti-Nazi journalist" Budzislawski would deliver a guest lecture at Harvard

University at which he would describe the flight of his family from France to the United States and take part in a discussion with the literary scholar Francis O. Matthiessen. All proceeds from the event would be turned over to the League of American Writers, the organization that had helped the Budzislawskis out of severe financial difficulties during the previous year, when they were in hiding in Domme.[10] The text of the speech, which, like so much else, Budzislawski preserved and later brought with him into the GDR, indicates that he had made rapid progress with his English and that he could already make jokes in this foreign language. "I hope you will understand this refugee story," he wrote, "even if it is told in bad English and with this German accent that Hitler could not take from me."[11] He also signed himself up with the Emergency Committee in Aid of Displaced Foreign Scholars as a lecturer on Fascism. The person who accepted his application noted his subject areas of expertise, adding her first impressions of the new arrival. Despite mentioning a few communication problems, the verdict was not unfavorable: "poor English, quiet, gentle, very nice smile." It is not clear from the documentation whether she was able to procure any lectures for him in the months that followed. In any case, he did not receive a grant.[12]

In the spring of 1941 Budzislawski also began to contact publishers and literary agents in New York. His aim was to publish an autobiography about his youth and his adventures in exile. He managed to interest the distinguished publishing house Simon & Schuster in this project, which bore the working title "Democracy Underground: The Adventures of an Anti-Nazi Editor." He was sitting at work "with a heavy heart," he wrote to Heinrich Mann, doing something he was forced into by economic necessity rather than inclination. In any case, he did not get any further than sketches and chapter outlines. The same applied to another literary project to which he gave the working title "Twenty Years of Going Crazy—or How Did He Get the Way?" Budzislawski wanted this book to consist of twenty minibiographies. They were intended to provide a mosaic that would help people understand the atmosphere in the Weimar Republic. The overall purpose was to answer the question of how it had been possible for Hitler to rise to power. Budzislawski envisaged biographical sketches of the following people, among others: the *völkisch* feminist and esoteric Mathilde Ludendorff; the clairvoyant Erik Jan Hanussen, who was murdered by the Nazis in 1933; the Communist social revolutionary Max Hölz, who lost his life in Soviet exile the same year; the serial killer Fritz Haarmann; the former corvette captain and radical right-wing terrorist Hermann Ehrhardt; the industrialist Hugo Stinnes; and the fanatical antisemite Julius Streicher. It was an early version of the recent television series *Babylon Berlin*, only in book form, but it remained unwritten.[13]

These activities are a clear indication that Budzislawski was not one of those exiles who aged prematurely in America, as noted by the actor and emigrant Ernst Josef Aufricht in his autobiography. The latter had seen many formerly important people who soon after their arrival were spending their days on the park benches of New York "in search of lost time," as he put it, alluding to the title of Marcel Proust's masterpiece.[14] These people formed a striking contrast to most other New Yorkers in the seven-million-strong metropolis. The tempo and vitality of the city could be infectious, but for a considerable number of political emigrants who were mainly between forty and sixty years old, the new environment induced paralysis. The writer Hans Natonek, who entered New York in the spring of 1941, felt very insecure at first, as if, having been robbed of all his previous moorings, he might fall into the void. He regarded himself as a "damaged European," stumbling and bumping everywhere he went.[15] There is no evidence that Budzislawski suffered from any such insecurity. He used his network from the Weimar Republic and the journalistic fame he had achieved as the editor of *Die neue Weltbühne* to get in touch immediately with the right people in New York. The commodity he had to offer was himself or, more precisely, his previous life, which he enterprisingly presented as a model for his generation.

This approach is formulated most clearly in the third book project, dating from 1941–42, which bore the working title "Adventurers against Will: The History of a European Generation That Lost Its Chance." The ideal type of this generation was no one other than Budzislawski himself. He well understood how to summarize his previous life in such a dramatic way that the reader was forced to regard the German Jewish social climber with his thirst for educational improvement and a doctorate as a revolutionary daredevil:

> The amazing experiences I have to report are characteristic for my generation and for the agitated continent on which I was born in the year 1901 rather than just for myself. . . . That I became involved in revolutions and wandered through Switzerland, Czechoslovakia, France, Spain and Portugal as a refugee, that I often risked my very existence and that it was only by chance that I escaped two attempts on my life—all this is typical for several thousand political people of our epoch, and only throws a stronger light on the fate of millions of refugees who are wandering through the world today. . . . What was extraordinary in my life has become the commonplace of an epoch.[16]

It is noticeable that in his first months in America Budzislawski only came before the public with (auto)biographical texts and lectures but did not publish any political analyses in the style of his previous leading articles in *Die*

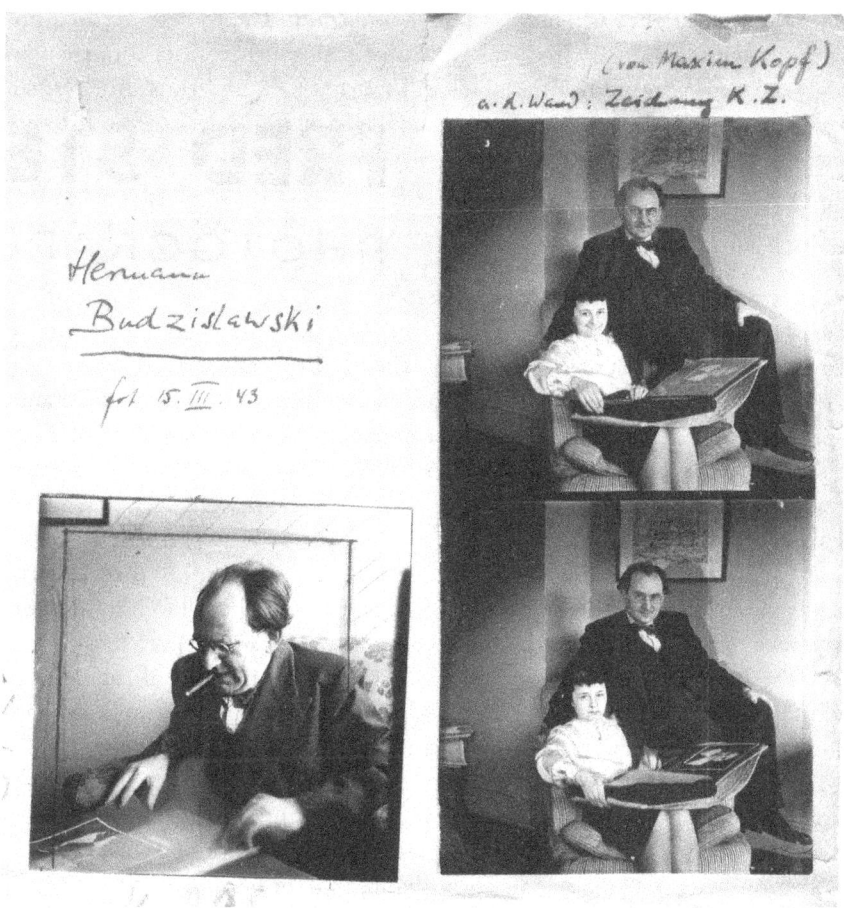

Pictures of Hermann and Hanna Budzislawski taken at a 1943 session with the photographer Fred Stein. Hanging on the wall of their New York apartment is a drawing by Maxim Kopf entitled *Im KZ*.

neue Weltbühne.[17] There was no lack of opportunities, as can be seen from a detailed memorandum by the US Army's Counter Intelligence Corps (CIC) that was drawn up in 1951. According to this memo, the well-established liberal weekly *The Nation* had offered Budzislawski the opportunity to write several articles about Soviet foreign policy at the beginning of 1941, but he had refused.[18] Writing in 1943, he ascribed the widespread tendency of the German exiles in the United States to remain silent about public affairs to their experience in France during the first year of the war: "The whole of the German political emigration has not overcome the shock of those first weeks of the war.

After their experience in France, these men did not dare to take up their political activities again in free America, unless they received encouragement from the American authorities. This did not happen, and thus the German opponents of Hitler here have remained in a state of lethargy until very recently."[19]

A letter sent by Hanna Budzislawski in September 1941 to the writer Balder Olden, who was living in exile in Argentina, provides some additional personal background to Budzislawski's partial silence. Balder was the older brother of Rudolf Olden, who had been drowned during the sinking of the British passenger ship *City of Benares* on 18 September 1940. According to Hanna's letter, the Budzislawskis had "already been denounced by our old enemies" when they arrived in New York in October 1940. "Hermann's hands were therefore tied at first, and he did not yet publish a single line. Old but dubious friends prophesied that he would make a good start if only he wrote an article against the S[oviet]U[nion]. Some of them were very persuasive. This episode now lies behind us. For a whole year, Hermann has kept his political analyses to himself and a handful of friends. (We lived off the Committee)."[20] Hanna's parenthetical remark was a reference to the monthly support payment of $72—this corresponds in current purchasing power to $1,250—that the National Refugee Council provided to the families of refugees. In addition, there were occasional items of extra income, and probably the support promised by American family members was also forthcoming.

The precise identity of the above-mentioned "old enemies" of the Budzislawskis is unclear. Hanna was very probably alluding to German exiles who had previously arrived in the United States and who—like William S. Schlamm—were seeking to pay her husband back for booting them out of *Die neue Weltbühne* or for some other item of unsettled business. Someone did indeed make a threatening telephone call to the private number of Budzislawski's New York apartment one early morning in the summer of 1941. It was taken by Milly Zirker, who was his subtenant at the time. When she asked the caller to identify himself an unknown voice replied in perfect English: "You ought to know, Miss Zirker, who is calling. We will find Mr. Budzislawski wherever he might hide. This is the German Gestapo." The German Jewish exile newspaper *Der Aufbau* received similar threatening calls. Its editor in chief suspected that former terrorists from the Organisation Consul, active in Germany in the 1920s, were behind the threats, which remained unexplained and were not followed by any further action.[21]

It is also possible that the supposed "novelist" Budzislawski stayed silent at first because he did not want his true identity as a political journalist to be exposed and because he feared that any political statement could be seen as breach of the Alien Registration Act, which came into force in the United States in June 1940. It was advisable for a man who only had permission to remain in the country for six months not to expose himself to the public gaze too quickly, and certainly not if he had Socialist convictions. This was also the reason why he could not (yet) take the easy route of joining the American anti-Communist mainstream. Budzislawski was therefore a kind of publicist in waiting during the first half of 1941, cautiously sounding out the terrain but by no means abandoning his ambition to intervene politically as both a journalist and possibly an editor. During this transitional period, however, he had to find another way of earning money. An American aid organization suggested that he take up the practical trade of upholsterer, but it is hard to imagine that he might have been inclined to follow this advice.[22] He worked for a short time as an encyclopedia salesman but failed miserably at the job. As he later put it, jokingly but also somewhat arrogantly, he had simply been unable to explain the practical use of such a reference work to the Americans.[23]

The invasion of the Soviet Union by the German Reich and its allies on 22 June 1941 brought about a decisive change in Budzislawski's attitude. He felt that this attack, which he only half-ironically compared to divine intervention, confirmed his political assessment from the previous years. On 14 August 1941 he wrote enthusiastically and not without a touch of vanity to the man who had helped him flee Europe, his friend Berthold Viertel:

> You see, my analyses and my opinions have essentially been proved correct. Two bitter years have gone by during which I had to exercise considerable self-restraint. The Russia pact was a great mistake on Stalin's part, and it brought Communist politics into an appalling position. How different would the world's readiness to help have been, how much further we should have advanced everywhere, if people's brains had not been clouded by the baloney about the imperialist war and the practical identity between Churchill and Hitler. And as a response to Moscow's mistaken policy the opposite kind of nonsense equating Stalin with Hitler has been circulated. There was only one correct line: a consistent attack, always and under all circumstances, on our main enemy, Hitler. The Russia pact led in France to the onset of the campaign against "L'Allemagne éternelle," aimed at the elimination of everything that was German, the dismemberment of the Reich, the rule of reaction over the European continent— and as a logical consequence the internment of the German opposition in French concentration camps. For Schwarzschild, Schlamm, Konrad Heiden, and others like them this was a triumph.[24]

This comment tells us three things. First, it makes plain that the Hitler-Stalin Pact of August 1939 resulted in the temporary disavowal of the Popular Front policy resolutely promoted by Budzislawski in the previous years. In addition, the existence of the pact exposed him between 1939 and 1941 to the suspicion that his well-known advocacy of the Soviet Union might now be combined with sympathy for its National Socialist alliance partner. Second, Budzislawski left no doubt in the summer of 1941 that he considered the cooperation of the Soviet Union with the National Socialists to have been an unforgiveable error that had inevitably led to political misjudgments in Western Europe and the United States and had reawakened anti-German feelings in France. "Reactionary" France, which craved hegemony over Europe, just as it had in the early nineteenth century, was again endeavoring to "dismember" Germany, and it was persecuting and interning Germans, irrespective of whether they were supporters or enemies of the Nazi regime. Budzislawski thus ascribed a share of the guilt for his period of imprisonment in various French internment camps over almost a year to Soviet policy toward Germany between 1939 and 1941. Third, the memory of the personal injuries he had suffered during his exile continued to resonate, notwithstanding his bird's-eye perspective on world politics, as is clear from his sideswipes at journalists and publicists such as Leopold Schwarzschild, William Schlamm, and Konrad Heiden. Schwarzschild's journal *Das neue Tagebuch* was in direct competition with *Die neue Weltbühne*, and he had branded the defenders of the Moscow trials as "amoral" people; Konrad Heiden, the successful author of a biography of Hitler, had sat with Budzislawski in French camps and escaped in October 1940; while Willi Schlamm, Budzislawski's immediate predecessor as editor in chief of *Die neue Weltbühne*, was in any case certain of occupying the top spot in his personal blacklist. All these men were recognized intellectuals who had never made a secret of their unconditional hostility to the National Socialists. When Budzislawski suggested in his letter that they had openly celebrated his internment, he demonstrated not only his pent-up anger against sections of the German-language exile community but also his recognition of Communists and unreservedly Soviet-friendly Socialists as the German opposition; bourgeois anti-Fascists no longer qualified.[25]

At the same time, however, Budzislawski emphasized when writing to the moderate left-winger Carl Misch that he "had not identified himself with Bolshevism, nor did he want to," and that he had no desire to "establish a regime of a similar type in Europe."[26] He wanted the unconditional maintenance of the territorial integrity of Germany based on the right of national self-determination. This is how he understood the eight points of the Atlantic Charter, issued jointly by the American president Franklin D. Roosevelt and the British prime minister Winston Churchill on 14 August 1941. Budzislawski had heard about the charter on the radio, and he welcomed it:

> This is a war . . . only against Nazi rule and not against the German people. . . . Economically: improvement of living conditions and access to raw materials for all whether victor or vanquished. I know that a declaration does not yet signify a reality and that everything depends on how it is implemented. All in all, however, the war has now taken on the anti-Fascist face it ought to have had from the beginning. I already told some of my friends in 1937, and I repeated this in Paris in 1938, that we may well be locked up at the start of the war and then put into office in its second half. I do not know whether the second part of the prophecy will come true. But in principle we have now reached that point.[27]

Budzislawski did not, it is true, take on any public duties in the years that followed, but he did succeed in using the West's new view of the Soviet Union as the point of departure for a remarkable journalistic career in the United States. Dorothy Thompson, a stellar figure in American journalism, was made aware through the agency of the actor and film director Fritz Kortner of Budzislawski's political analyses, which at that time were circulating on the quiet in New York.[28] Thompson had made her name as an international journalist in the spring of 1932 through an exclusive interview with Adolf Hitler.[29] Her fame increased two years later when she was expelled by the National Socialist authorities during a visit to Germany. In the 1940s she was regarded in the Anglo-American world as the leading expert on Germany, and she had a great influence on public opinion.[30] She telephoned Budzislawski on 22 June 1941, the day of Germany's invasion of the Soviet Union, after she had already made his acquaintance several weeks earlier.[31] Her telephone call was a big opportunity for him. As Hanna recalled, "She twice invited him to visit her, and by the third evening we were already on her magnificent property in Vermont. We have now been living here for almost three months in the midst of German forests tinged by American exoticism, and we are starting to love America (I mean the landscape). Hermann is working with Dorothy, he is having great fun, and he is entirely satisfied with the role of the man acting behind the scenes. In autumn we shall be in New York again."[32]

It is hard to imagine that Budzislawski would have been happy with his new occupation for long. Hanna's view of the situation was rather the result of initial euphoria. As time went by, the former editor in chief and proprietor of *Die neue Weltbühne* began to find it offensive to lead a shadow existence as a journalist and see his analyses of world politics printed under someone else's name. The new arrangement paid very well in material terms, however. He started under Thompson with a fixed salary of $300 a month (just over $5,000 in today's values), which he further improved in the next few years by engaging in "independent literary activity." He also received forty dollars a week for organizing broadcasts by the Columbia Broadcasting System to Germany.[33] Furthermore, he had the very welcome opportunity, through Thompson, of meeting influential individuals and gaining access to important insider information. For example, he claims to have had personal discussions in Vermont with Wendell Lewis Willkie, the 1940 Republican presidential candidate, who was one of Thompson's friends.[34]

Despite these opportunities, Budzislawski felt that he was badly placed as a man in the second rank, especially behind a woman. This is shown by the jokingly spiteful tone of a draft article he wrote in Leipzig at the end of the 1940s. Thompson, he writes, had always been "a kind of actress, who from one day to the next, indeed even from one hour to the next, could slip into a different role, which she would play equally vigorously. Dorothy Thompson only becomes a mysterious personality when she is seen as a personality." If one is to believe Budzislawski, he was only one of several European exiles and journalists she made use of in the course of the 1930s and 1940s. It was indeed true that she had built up a circle of advisors, including the economist Gustav Stolper, who came from Vienna, and the Italian anti-Fascist Max Ascoli of the New York–based New School for Social Research. But it was undoubtedly presumptuous and impertinent of Budzislawski to assert disparagingly that he and his colleagues had only made use of this lady's "collective name" to get printed. He alleged that Thompson had never possessed an independent character as a journalist and that she was at most a good stylist and a skillful arranger of material who was able to manufacture a journalistic end product from the analyses he gave her in writing or in conversation.[35]

It was not until the Second World War had ended that arguments of this kind over questions of literary competence began to surface. The Budzislawskis appeared at first to be entirely happy with the new arrangement, especially as Thompson actively assisted them on more than one occasion. When her new colleague and his family moved into another apartment, at 328 East 50th Street, she lent him numerous items of furniture, and, as he himself stated, she made sure that his daughter, Beate, was accepted by a prestigious private school, the bilingual Lycée Français de New York, founded in 1935.[36] Thompson later wrote: "I accepted the agreeable little man with the grey eyes as what he said he was. Journalists have a strong sense of solidarity, and here was a professional colleague who was in a tight corner. He belonged to a persecuted race, for which all decent human beings had the greatest sympathy. He clearly had a well-trained mind and apart from German he spoke fluent

French and English."[37] Like many Americans, Thompson seems to have assumed that an exile like Budzislawski would quickly and easily become assimilated in the United States.[38] Moreover, it can be deduced from her long-lasting
and generous commitment to her new colleague that he really was useful.
Budzislawski also brought her good fortune in her private affairs. He not only
put her in touch with a capable architect to remodel her Vermont house but
also introduced her to the exiled Czech artist Maxim Kopf, who would become her third husband in the early summer of 1943.[39]

Carl Zuckmayer, who was friends with both of them, remarked in his autobiography on how closely they cooperated together from the summer of 1941
onward. According to him, Thompson first engaged Budzislawski as an "advisory colleague" for her newspaper commentaries, which appeared three times
a week, and he helped her very much "with his accurate knowledge of political
and economic conditions in Europe and his astute analyses of the world situation." She only seemed to notice later that he was a Communist, but in those
days one was in alliance with Soviet Russia and had nothing against "left-
wingers," commented Zuckmayer laconically.[40] Thompson soon found her
new colleague indispensable. Her biographers report, on the basis of interviews with former coworkers, that Budzislawski was the only person who was
allowed to dictate to the secretaries the newspaper columns that appeared in
her name without referring back to her. He not only endured Thompson's
sweeping postprandial political monologues right to the end but also was able
to make newspaper articles out of them, which he presented to his chief the
next morning, already fully typed up.[41]

From 1941 onward, the Budzislawskis, as successors of the Kortners, spent
at least four long summers, sometimes lasting from May to October, at Twin
Farms in Vermont, the summer residence of Thompson and her second husband, the author Sinclair Lewis, although she already lived separately from
him by this time. When they first stayed there, their host announced her
departure in the middle of July with the words: "For this summer, the house
belongs to you." Then life really became very pleasant. In the months that followed, they made extensive use of Thompson's library, which included many
modern novels, as Hanna Budzislawski reported on 10 October 1941, shortly
before their return to New York: "The house here is full of romantic novels,
and one thing I now know is that in the United States you get nowhere and
are seen as a piece of trash if you can't booze. Hermann is already brilliant at
it. He works hard with Dorothy, and he drinks even harder with her."[42] Budzislawski also took the opportunity to invite his friend Berthold Viertel, who
had helped them to flee Europe, to come to Vermont. For the time being, he
said, he would be busy with drafting the "situation analyses" for Dorothy

Hermann Budzislawski (*on the left, partially hidden*) at the wedding of Dorothy Thompson and Maxim Kopf in June 1943, held at Twin Farms, Vermont.

Thompson, but soon, after she would have left, he would describe in detail his "project for a journal" to Viertel—in other words, his plan to continue *Die Weltbühne* in whatever form.[43]

Viertel was unable to come to Vermont that summer, so Hermann explained his plans in a letter. In his opinion, he had two options at the end of September 1941: to merge with or, as the case might be, to enter into another project for an exile journal, or, alternatively, to revive *Die Weltbühne* independently. He reacted dismissively when Viertel asked him whether he might want to cooperate with *The German-American*, the journal planned by Kurt Rosenfeld and Gerhart Eisler. He had heard nothing from either Rosenfeld or Eisler about their plan for a new German-language journal in the United States, he said; he had only heard of it indirectly through Heinrich Mann. A "merger" with *Die Weltbühne* would also be difficult: "I have to know who it is I am supposed to be merging with and whether we have the same opinions about a few things in this world. Finally, I have to know who is providing the money. That would perhaps be a tedious question, if the prospect of receiving instructions together with the money did not stand behind it." Rosenfeld is "good, but as we know he is not wealthy," and the allies who might provide him with money "have not so far distinguished themselves by their tolerance." This was a sideswipe at the party-line Communists and their political requirements. But there were other options, too. Julio Álvarez del Vayo, former foreign minister of the Spanish Republic, had invited Budzislawski to collaborate on the periodical *Free World*, which first came out in October 1941. Although this publication was in the Popular Front tradition of the 1930s, and the editorial board was located in New York, a merger of the German cause with the aspirations of "all the planet's emigrant groups" was out of the question for Budzislawski.[44] In spite of his sympathy for the liberation movements of other nations, he wanted to work first and foremost for and in Germany.

Budzislawski held firmly to his goal, which was to start publishing *Die neue Weltbühne* again soon. He did not want to create a "purely party organ or something similar" because then "everything would be tied up so rigidly that it would be impossible to produce anything of any intellectual value." He asked Viertel rhetorically: "But what do we want a paper for? To negotiate over guidelines? Or to produce something new and come to terms with the world in our own way?" If there was a good chance of success, he would set to work with optimism, but he did not want to produce a new journal at any price.[45] He continued to regard his property rights in *Die neue Weltbühne* as too valuable to share with other people; he did not want to lose absolute control over "his" journal. Under no circumstances would he repeat the hectic search for fresh capital he had often had to make in Prague: "This enforced waiting period is probably the greatest undertaking of my life. I am holding on to an object that will soon be very valuable but into which other people can at present penetrate very easily. It is against my wishes that I am making this speculation: I hate this waiting period, and I would like to be engaged in production."[46]

Nothing came of the plan to revive the journal in the United States. Budzislawski estimated the chance of success for such a project as very slight, and he was not prepared to accept financial support from party-political circles. The shock of the Hitler-Stalin Pact of the summer of 1939 strengthened him in his opinion that entrepreneurial independence was a prerequisite for journalistic integrity. This did not, however, prevent him from taking sides politically. He returned to writing extensive analyses of world politics between the summer of 1941 and the spring of 1945, which often focused, as they had in the 1930s, on the need to combat and overcome National Socialism, but he was no longer writing these on his own account. What he wrote was regarded by his employer and patron Dorothy Thompson as background information for her articles, although, according to his own later version, she only edited what he had written and then published it as her own work. Either way, what they produced together was impressive in extent and scope. Thompson's weekly columns appeared in over a hundred American newspapers. As mentioned earlier, there were also broadcasts on the German-language program of CBS, which Budzislawski provided scripts for between 1942 and 1944.[47] These weekly radio broadcasts on behalf of the Office of War Information (OWI) were part of a policy of psychological warfare intended to weaken the attachment of the Germans to the Nazi regime. They were also collected by Budzislawski and appeared in book form at the end of 1942 under Dorothy Thompson's name. The title was *Listen, Hans*.[48] From 1943 onward, Budzislawski had a column of his own entitled "The Diplomatic Front," written under the pseudonym Donald Bell. It was distributed by the Overseas News Agency (ONA), located in New York.[49] This organization, which also employed Maximilian Scheer and Milly Zirker, among other people, was an offshoot of the Jewish Telegraphic Agency, founded by the Zionist Jacob Landau during the First World War. Since 1940 it had specialized in distributing news about persecuted minorities, and it supplied newspapers that had a total daily circulation of five million copies. Of course, only a part of the ONA's income was derived from the distribution of press articles. It also received support from wealthy benefactors, such as the banker Felix M. Warburg. The ONA had also been subsidized since April 1941 by the British Security Coordination, an umbrella organization that covered all British Secret Intelligence Service activities in the Western world. In return, the ONA tailored its reporting to the requirements of the British and a little later the US Secret Service as well.[50]

For Budzislawski, his new career as Dorothy Thompson's journalist and anonymous coauthor marked the end, both professionally and privately, of his precarious existence as an exile. This allowed him to get over the fact that Ernst Bloch, one of his opponents during the winter of 1935–36 in the fight over the control and the course of *Die neue Weltbühne*, had inveighed against "platitudinous journalism à la Budzislawski."[51] The former editor in chief was accustomed to facing headwinds and jealous outbursts; moreover, he now had much more influential friends, including the investment banker Alexander Sachs, vice-chairman of Lehman Brothers and consultant to the OSS.[52] It was therefore not a catastrophe when Budzislawski's fourth book project during his American exile also came to grief. This book, which he was working on during 1942 and 1943, had been intended for publication by the renowned New York house G. P. Putnam's Sons under the title *The Future of Europe*. But, like its autobiographical predecessors, it was never completed.[53] At the beginning of 1944, Budzislawski finally withdrew from the book contract and returned the advance of $250.[54] Despite his occasionally devious business practices, he maintained a Prussian standard of correctness in financial affairs during his exile in the United States.

The Budzislawskis were by no means the only European exiles in the rural idyll of Vermont. In the early 1940s, during the summer months, the isolated villages and farms in the vicinity of Twin Farms became a miniature Mitteleuropa, or a "Sudeten Vermont," not least thanks to Dorothy Thompson's generous invitations.[55] Thus Backwoods Farm, which was only a few miles away, had been worked since the early summer of 1941 by Carl Zuckmayer, who was also a friend of Thompson and received financial support from her, together with his wife. The Zuckmayers, unlike the city-based Budzislawskis, who only came in the summer, turned into actual farmers. They renovated the old farm and bred goats, pigs, and poultry there. In his memoirs, which were published in 1966 under the title *Als wär's ein Teil von mir* (translated and published in 1970 as *A Part of Myself, Portrait of an Epoch*) and became very successful with the German reading public, Zuckmayer described his life on the farm as a hard but fulfilling experience. While the long winter months had been lonely, the summer evenings, when "prominent people dropped in to see Dorothy Thompson," could be very lively. A visit to Backwoods Farm was a welcome change from hectic city life and pressure for many of her guests, whether they were American celebrities or European exiles. Hermann and Hanna Budzislawski and their daughter, Beate, were frequent visitors. There was much talking, drinking, and laughter. The adults swam in the lake with their children and sat together by the campfire in the evenings. Zuckmayer brought out his guitar, and they sang German and American songs together.[56]

Budzislawski repeatedly invited Berthold Viertel to visit Twin Farms, and in 1942 he was finally able to come. This is what Viertel wrote to his wife, Salka, about the idyllic summer months he spent in Vermont:

> The Budzislawskis enjoy the gayest, pleasantest and most good-natured family life that can be imagined. It is a constant pleasure to be their guest. . . . Hanna, as the hostess a[nd] excellent cook, is a model of cleanliness a[nd] order, without one's ever becoming aware of how she slaves away. Everything is done so effortlessly that it seems like magic. People get up and have breakfast at very different

times, but everything is always there a[nd] then immediately cleared away. She sits here smoking her pipe in the sun like a gypsy mother . . . and is always in the pleasantest of moods. . . . In the evenings I always go with [Hermann] Budz[islawski] to visit Dorothy, or she comes over here, a[nd] the atmosphere of the house has a moderating influence on her irrepressible energy; she works with Budz[islawski] uncomplainingly and smoothly. As you know, evenings with her are long, as she never wants to go to bed. But so far the discussions have not touched off any hidden mines, a[nd] I find she is an outstanding personality in so many respects.[57]

After his return to the "social season" in New York in the autumn of 1942 he gushingly thanked his host: "You have spoiled me for the rest of my life, because the idea of living anywhere else but in Vermont with you now seems completely absurd to me. . . . I was indescribably happy with you from the first moment to the last, and since then I have mourned a vanished paradise."[58] Zuckmayer too recalled after his return to Europe that his family had spent "many warm and friendly evenings" with the Budzislawskis, "even though we did not agree politically."[59]

Zuckmayer's additional phrase about politics owed more to the atmosphere of the Cold War than to contemporary disagreements. Between 1941 and 1945 the Budzislawskis ("the Budz"), the Zuckmayers ("the Zucks"), and Dorothy Thompson were close friends. Months before the next visit to Vermont was due, Hanna and Hermann's daughter, Beate, was already counting off each Sunday. She looked forward to the company of Thompson's son, Michael, and Zuckmayer's daughter, Maria Winnetou, who was only a few years older, and she wrote enthusiastically to Alice Herdan-Zuckmayer, Maria Winnetou's mother, about her tortoises, Cléo and Patra, as well as about a cat she had brought back from Vermont to New York. Alice replied to her equally affectionately. She told Beate about the animals of Backwoods Farm, adding comments more directed toward the adults about the problem of flight from the land in Vermont, which was worsened dramatically by the high wages available in the expanding defense industries during the early 1940s.[60]

The adults were also politically active together. Carl Zuckmayer was on the payroll of the OSS, an organization set up in 1941, and he wrote around 150 dossiers for it about individuals of importance in German cultural life. Other emigrants such as Herbert Marcuse, Otto Kirchheimer, Franz Neumann, and Hajo Holborn also worked for the OSS, and in the early years of the Cold War they continued to exercise a strong influence on American intellectual debates.[61] Budzislawski's way of seeing things and his analyses are likely to have entered into Zuckmayer's portrait of the emigration just as much as

Dorothy Thompson and Hermann Budzislawski
barbecuing together at Twin Farms on 20 June 1942.

they did into the first version of the manifesto he wrote in 1943 for the Council for a Democratic Germany.[62] In view of these close intellectual connections, US Secret Service personnel even referred at the beginning of 1944 to a "Vermont conspiracy," and they suspected that the discussions between Thompson, Zuckmayer, and Budzislawski would pave the way to a new kind of Popular Front, especially as Budzislawski was "slowly recovering from his temporary distaste for the communist party."[63]

The friendly political discussions with Zuckmayer and Thompson were also reflected in Budzislawski's "Manifesto of Liberty," written by him in 1941 or 1942 at Twin Farms. This unpublished document, a strategy paper forty-eight typed pages long, puts forward the idea of a new League of Nations, the

"World League of Nations," which should be joined gradually by all the great powers. Another global war would be permanently prevented and the happiness of the whole of humanity promoted by cooperation between the world's significant forces.[64] Budzislawski had already suggested to his fellow journalist Carl Misch in September 1941 that he had begun to concern himself with future issues on behalf of the American government: "The Americans whose guest I am want to know where all this is going. They consider it necessary to create an effective alternative to Hitler's New Order. And they can already afford themselves the luxury of preparing in passing a program they will one day be able to pull out of their pocket. This is not something happening in isolation. It is closely linked with the war of propaganda and the fight against isolationism, but it offers perspectives for the future that go beyond this."[65] The recipient of Budzislawski's conceptual considerations was very probably the State Department's Advisory Committee on Postwar Foreign Policy, which first met on 12 February 1942 under Roosevelt's authority. One subject of discussion at this meeting was the division of the territory of the German Reich after the military defeat of the National Socialists.[66]

Nothing could have been further from Budzislawski's ideas about the future than a possible dismemberment of his homeland. He aspired to develop a political order that would allow the whole of humanity to fulfill "the great yearning of our time for freedom, equality, justice, for bread and prosperity," and that naturally included the population of Germany. The goal of the National Socialists and their allies was the exact opposite, namely, "the eradication of the achievements of the American War of Independence and the French Revolution and the creation of a world state under German leadership without either liberty or equality." The wide extent of the Nazis' ambitions would require an equally global American reply. A "World League of Nations" would be needed to make safe the "new world of organized liberty." The multiplicity of European nation-states was an anachronism, and it should be overcome by the creation of five European blocs. Each bloc would be formed by joining together a number of culturally, linguistically, and economically similar neighbors. Budzislawski named the fourth of these blocs "Germany." The German Reich would admittedly have to give up its territorial claims in Eastern Europe and the Balkans, but it could include Austria in a new federal structure and eventually one or two other neighboring countries. Today this reads like a vision of a slimmed-down Greater Germany, but in the autumn of 1941, when the Nazi policy of expansion was at its height in Europe, it sounded less extreme—even if Budzislawski's proposal undeniably reflected its author's Prussian origin. It was clear at least to him that the smaller states were not capable of surviving without being attached to one of the five European blocs.

It would also be necessary after the war to integrate the Soviet Union permanently into the new security architecture. This would not constitute a danger for the European democracies, Budzislawski argued. The tremendous extent of the devastation caused by the war in Russia would inevitably lead reconstruction to be prioritized over new armaments projects there. Even a "democratization of the regime" in Moscow was a possibility, he claimed.[67]

The unusually passionate and idealistic style of this document was attuned to the political rhetoric of the "internationalists" in the United States. Budzislawski wanted to use it to secure not only the future of the world but also his own future, because this optimistic and very deep-going paper was a way of recommending himself to the US government as a political advisor during the war years and beyond. Between the summer of 1941 and the beginning of 1945, he had good channels of contact to the White House. Budzislawski claimed later, when in the GDR, that Thompson and her closest colleagues even had a part in writing the speeches Roosevelt delivered as the Democratic candidate in the 1944 election. William S. Schlamm, meanwhile, had been signed on as a ghost writer by the newspaper publisher and editor of *Time Magazine*, Henry Luce, and he wrote speeches for the Republican challenger, Thomas E. Dewey. It had been a "grotesque spectacle," Budzislawski wrote later, that ten years after the "battle" over the editorship of *Die neue Weltbühne* the former "Trotskyist" Schlamm and himself were opposing each other in an American election in this way, conducting a feud between rival worldviews "through the largest possible loudspeakers."[68] The former protagonists of the struggle over *Die neue Weltbühne* were now making use of the genuine *Weltbühne*—the world stage—at least indirectly. Neither before nor afterward had Budzislawski the journalist ever come as close as this to political power—and he did this as a refugee who had only arrived recently in the United States, who continued merely to be tolerated there, and whose name was known by hardly anyone.

On 19 April 1944, in order not to put his new career in danger, Budzislawski directly contacted the newly founded FBI. In this letter he defended himself against the assertion repeated by the two renegades from Communism Ruth Fischer and Adolph Weingarten in their short-lived periodical, *The Network— Information Bulletin about Stalinist Organizations and Organizational Forms*, that he had financed *Die neue Weltbühne* with Soviet money and that he had maintained close ties with Soviet secret services since the late 1920s. Faced with these grave accusations, Budzislawski composed a detailed rebuttal. He proceeded on the assumption that the authorities had already built up a dossier about him, and he now explicitly requested that his view of the matter also be heard. Ruth Fischer should by no means be allowed to determine the picture the American immigration authorities or the US Secret Service had of him, especially as the extension of his leave to remain in the country was directly dependent on this. In this letter Budzislawski claimed that the injections of capital repeatedly required in the mid-1930s for *Die neue Weltbühne* had always been provided by private individuals. He mentioned Stein, Nathan, and Reichenbach by name—but he kept quiet about Feigl, the donor whose help had been secured through the Communist Party at the start of 1938. Nor had the Soviet Union indirectly financed the journal, he added. Roughly fifty copies had been sold every week there, and this was less than in smaller countries such as Belgium and Switzerland. Aufhäuser, Reichenbach, and Arne Laurin of the Czechoslovak consulate in New York could testify to all of this. He himself was prepared to repeat his assertions under oath and in a personal confrontation with his accusers.[69]

This preemptive defense of his own cause was also larded with details about Ruth Fischer's life before 1933 and during her period in exile, which Budzislawski could assume were of value to the US Secret Service. He hoped to be able to destroy her credibility and ward off any damage to himself, and he was evidently successful. The head of the FBI, J. Edgar Hoover, sent him a personal letter of thanks, confirming that his wish had been granted, and his declaration had been added to the FBI's files.[70] This did not, however, save him from being called in for questioning a second time by the OSS, on 13 June 1944. A little later the CIC also showed an interest in him because he was recorded there as a "communist." The letters he sent, as well as those addressed to him, his family, and his acquaintances, were intercepted and analyzed.[71]

Budzislawski had first been thoroughly interrogated on 12 April 1943 by FBI agent Thomas S. McGrath.[72] This interview made Budzislawski so worried that immediately afterward he begged his mentor, Thompson, for her support. Only two days later she wrote to Sylvester Pindyck, the official in charge of questions of immigration and citizenship in the US Department of Justice, emphatically supporting her colleague. There was not the slightest doubt about his loyalty toward the country of which he was a guest, she wrote. According to Thompson, Budzislawski was an "outstandingly intelligent man" of "impeccable personal and intellectual sincerity." He was connected with the OWI through his contributions to the radio programs put out by CBS. He had had lengthy discussions with Ernestine Evans of the Overseas Publications Department of the OWI, which was responsible for these programs. If necessary, Thompson could certainly give further information.[73] Notwithstanding these details, Budzislawski's precise role during these years in the interconnected world of politics, journalism, and the secret services remains nebulous. He was certainly involved through Dorothy Thompson in the work of the

West's secret services, but in addition he may possibly have been one of the Communist (double) agents who supplied Moscow with information about internal details of American politics.[74] But there is no concrete proof of this, notwithstanding the accusations of his opponents.

At the beginning of February 1943, after the German defeat in Stalingrad, it was pretty well certain that the Third Reich would lose the Second World War. Postwar planning immediately took on greater urgency both for the Allies and for the German political exiles. From the autumn of 1943 onward, Budzislawski was involved in preparing and helping to set up the Council for a Democratic Germany.[75] This council was a response to the challenge presented by the establishment in the Soviet Union a few months earlier of the National Committee for a Free Germany, and it was the last concerted attempt of the German opposition in the United States to unite the exiled democratic forces and exert influence on the impending reorganization of Europe in the postwar era.[76] Since the German question was inextricably bound up with the future of Europe, the council considered that the Allies must under no circumstances pursue the "enslavement" of the German people. The members of the council demanded instead the strengthening of democratic forces in Germany so that the Germans could liberate themselves from National Socialism independently, in the light of their own historical experience. The council initially had nothing to say about the crimes against humanity committed during the war.[77]

The council's organizers consciously bore in mind the need to appeal to a broad spectrum of opinion; hence, they included former Center Party members such as Friedrich Baerwald alongside representatives of the SPD and the KPD. The chair was the theologian Paul Tillich, a man who was well known in the United States and enjoyed cross-party respect. The State Department was at first "fairly cool" toward the council, but it quickly became "very friendly," as Bertolt Brecht told Heinrich Mann in March 1944.[78] A month later, Brecht told the Marxist theoretician Karl Korsch that the attitude of the new council could be summed up in this way: "Against an orientation of a democratic Germany toward East or West, against the country's division or deindustrialization, against intervention when Germany eventually frees itself from Hitler and the classes behind him, against Pangermanism. . . . In short, the c[ouncil] is a highly entertaining cross section." Unlike many of his fellow participants, Brecht saw the council's main problem as not just its lack of influence but also a certain degree of alienation from events in Central Europe since the outbreak of war: "It has some connection with developments here, but none with what is happening in Germany."[79]

Budzislawski headed the council's press committee until the beginning of 1945. As in the 1930s, he played an important role in building bridges between the Left Social Democrats and the Communists, though this by no means prevented sharp disagreements from breaking out. His attitude toward the Communists was generally sympathetic or at least "loyal," wrote Albert Schreiner after the war. (Albert Schreiner was one of the three Communist Party members on the council, the others being Albert Norden and the medical doctor Felix Boenheim.)[80] Even so, the former publisher of *Die neue Welt-bühne* occasionally voted along with Social Democrats such as Siegfried Aufhäuser against the Communists. Indeed, according to a March 1944 report by an undercover agent of the OSS, Budzislawski was the only person who had spoken out against the inclusion of Albert Schreiner and Felix Boenheim when the council was first constituted.[81] And in February 1945, according to Schreiner, Budzislawski had threatened to break up the whole group after some of Dorothy Thompson's political articles had been severely criticized by the Communist newspaper *The German-American*. Budzislawski managed to get the council to distance itself from the Communists' criticisms of his employer and sponsor and to declare publicly that "the policy pursued by Dorothy Thompson towards Germany for years in both her speeches and her articles is essentially in line with the principles laid down by the Council in its May 1944 manifesto."[82]

Although Budzislawski had defended his boss Thompson from criticism, Schreiner was certain in retrospect that this disagreement had hastened the breach between the two factions on the council. He was convinced that cross-party action had only been possible because its chair, Tillich, along with other supporters of Roosevelt on the council, had received the explicit permission of the US government to bring the Communists on board as well, because it had become apparent that the Soviet Union would have an important voice in postwar planning for Europe.[83] The German Communist exiles, for their part, were working to strengthen the position of the Soviet Union in the international negotiations that would take place in the not-too-distant future.[84] It was clear to all the participants that the council was a short-term strategic alliance intended not just to help the Allies but also to provide the people concretely involved in it with a springboard from which to launch their postwar careers after the collapse of the Third Reich.

Insurmountable differences between the exiles on the council had already surfaced by the summer of 1945 during the Potsdam Conference, when the Allies set the seal of approval on Poland's physical shift westward and the German territorial losses that this move involved. Paul Tillich regarded the Potsdam decisions as marking the "end of Germany" as a "Reich," or empire, and he argued that the council members should sharply dissociate themselves from them. Failing that, it would be better to dissolve the council entirely merely to maintain self-respect. "The advance of the Slavs to the Oder," he asserted, falling back on a familiar topos of nationalist historiography, "had reversed the thousand-year settlement history of the German Volk." In the West, "Anglo-Saxon world domination" had been established "for a long time to come." In view of the situation in the United States and the Soviet Union, it was now impossible "to speak of an age of new democracy."[85] In contrast to Tillich's views, it was emphasized in a proposed public declaration drawn up by the Left Social Democrat Siegfried Aufhäuser jointly with Budzislawski that "cooperation between the Western powers and the Soviet Union" was "the only guarantee for the rebuilding of Europe and a lasting peace." The threatened formation of rival blocs must be avoided. The German people had to take note of the decisions of the Allies, even if the burdens they had to bear were considerable: "The council notes with concern that more than ten million Germans will have to live in a reduced area and that the German economy will be reduced at the same time. These decisions may endanger the ability of the German people to survive."[86]

An OSS agent who could not be identified by name remarked as early as March 1942 that an unchanging "Prussian militarism" often lay hidden behind economic arguments of this nature, even among those who had been turned into refugees by nationalist forces. The German Liberal and Marxist exiles often had recourse to economic justifications because they could not speak of their nationalism directly.[87] Albert Schreiner's view, finally, was that these were all "revisionist protests." German anti-Fascists would do better to ask themselves self-critically whether they had really done all they could in previous years "to denounce the Nazi desecrators of the German name and actively to combat them." What was important now was to tighten one's belt and to make compensation wherever this was possible: "The evacuation of roughly ten million Germans is tragic for everyone affected. But what does it amount to in comparison with the fate of over twenty million Europeans, children and old people, men and women, annihilated in the Nazi death factories?"[88]

Schreiner was one of the few members of the council who explicitly used the Holocaust and the expulsion, enslavement, and murder of millions of Central and Eastern Europeans as an argument. For Budzislawski at that time, these were still matters of lesser political significance. It was not until long after the war that he mentioned that one of his cousins, twenty-two-year-old Herbert Budzislawski, a member of the Jewish resistance group around Herbert Baum, had been executed at Plötzensee Prison in Berlin on 7 September 1943.[89] Budzislawski did make efforts behind the scenes to provide humanitarian assistance to the persecuted Jews of Europe to the best of his ability, as is shown by a letter he sent on 18 January 1944 to Fritz Kortner. But he did not stand out as being particularly committed. He excused himself by referring to his "sometimes slovenly character," adding that he was also suffering from "overwork." He was by no means uninterested, he wrote, but unfortunately there was very little one could do. In the United States only the Joint Distribution Committee had any lists of the Jews deported to Poland, and these were "very incomplete." Moreover, there was "no government institution in Washington which either knew or attempted to do anything. Even the Red Cross had failed in dealing with this question."[90]

Budzislawski even spoke out on 30 April 1945 against only mentioning "Nazi atrocities" during a discussion in the Council for a Democratic Germany of a declaration he himself had drawn up that the group intended to publish on the day the Third Reich capitulated. "We should restrict ourselves to questions of reconstruction, and make no historical assertions," he argued.[91] When he made this statement, thousands of concentration camp inmates were still staggering through Germany on the so-called death marches, during which they were often murdered by fanatical National Socialists or left to die by the wayside of exhaustion, hypothermia, or disease.[92] Budzislawski nevertheless thought it tactically unwise to draw attention to the crimes of the National Socialists—at least at that precise moment. The anti-Fascist postwar order he aimed at could not be created by public denunciations or appeals to the guilty consciences of Germans. This was an early version of the policy of "drawing a line under the past," this time advocated by the Left, which anticipated how wartime atrocities would be remembered a few years later in the GDR, when persecuted Communists would be privileged over all other groups of victims.[93]

But insurmountable differences of opinion soon arose not just in the council but also between Budzislawski and his sponsor, Dorothy Thompson. It was even better to help to shape the future of Europe than to write about it, and Budzislawski, as a political journalist, had worked toward this for many years. Now, at last, the opportunity had arrived. At the start of 1945 he was revolving the idea of traveling to Europe as a correspondent for the ONA, but he could not put this plan into effect, despite Thompson's personal intercession with Eleanor Roosevelt, because he was not given any papers.[94] By 1943 US government circles had already started considering whether to prohibit the return of German political emigrants to Europe for two years after the end of the war in order to avoid having to compete over the reconstruction of Germany with the German opponents of the Nazis, who might possibly have plans different from those of the Americans.[95] Budzislawski later asserted that the US government had deliberately torpedoed his European travel plans in the spring of 1945 and that instead it "had hired as many reactionary emigrants as it could get."[96] He did not want to take the risk of leaving without papers, because he was uncertain whether he would be readmitted to the United States after the end of his journey. The original justification of persecution would have lapsed owing to the directly impending collapse of National Socialist rule.

The personal break between Budzislawski and Thompson took place only a few weeks after the end of military operations in Europe. They met in Vermont during the summer of 1945, as they had in previous years, and discussed the new international political situation over long whisky-lubricated evenings, also attended by Maximilian Scheer.[97] According to Budzislawski's later version, Thompson had now formed the view, after a three-hour conversation with Churchill at Chequers, the country residence of the British prime minister, that a continuation of the wartime struggle of the Western allies was directly imminent and that this time they would be fighting the Soviet Union.[98] She even placed bets on the prospect. If this war was actually to become a reality, they must of course support the West. She even named a target date for the outbreak of the new war: 15 August 1945. Budzislawski, however, was more than ever convinced after the victory of the Red Army that the Soviet Union was a globally leading force, and he had been warning since 1942 at the latest against any violent confrontation between the capitalist and Communist superpowers. Under these circumstances, he was not prepared to cooperate any longer with the American journalist. He set her an ultimatum: either she returned to her previous pro-Soviet position, or she would have to do without his services from now on. Thompson decided in favor of the latter, not least because she had learned during these months from several female friends in occupied Germany about the numerous rapes committed by Soviet soldiers, and this further reinforced her anti-Soviet stance.[99] A little later, rumors of the quarrel also reached Kurt Hiller in London: "Is it true that the boring intriguer Budzislawski, having first succeeded in forcing himself on the delightful Dorothy Thompson as her secretary, has now been seen through and sent to the devil by her? What will the guy do now?"[100]

The break with Thompson led to the loss of Budzislawski's previous main source of income. In the summer of 1945, therefore, he joined the ONA as a full-time editor, thereby returning in a kind of way to his initial starting point as a journalist in Weimar-era Berlin. After the war, the Communist Albert Schreiner, who had been one of Budzislawski's acquaintances during his US exile, remarked dryly that some of his articles during this period, which appeared under the pseudonym Donald Bell, could easily have come from the pen of "a liberal apologist of American imperialism."[101] Budzislawski preserved newspaper cuttings of his publications in thick folders, which he later took with him to the GDR. According to a conspectus he himself drew up, he

wrote a total of 464 articles for the ONA between 1943 and 1948, a large proportion of them in 1946 and 1948 (123 and 92, respectively).[102] Many of his
texts dealt with questions of world politics, particularly with the tension
between the global requirements of the great powers, on the one hand, and the
liberation movements in Asia, Africa, and the Americas, on the other. He
often reported on the attempts made to regulate the spread of nuclear weapons, but he also discussed problems resulting from restrictions on international travel, which he knew only too well from his own experience.[103] European themes included the shortage of food supplies there, early plans for a
European Union (which he described in 1947 as "a concept which is tempting
in theory, but unrealisable in practice"), and the unwavering support of many
Germans for National Socialism. Young people between the ages of twenty-
five and thirty-five could not forgive Hitler for Germany's military defeat, but
in other respects they had moved away very little from the National Socialist
positions of previous years, he claimed. Fascism had also by no means been
defeated internationally, he argued in the spring of 1946, in view of the success
of the army officer Juan Perón in the Argentinian presidential elections, the
staying power of the Franco dictatorship in Spain, and the absolute majority
achieved by conservative and royalist forces in the Greek parliamentary elections.[104] These were not the words of an "apologist for American imperialism,"
as Schreiner thought, nor were they those of a party-line Communist whose
perception of the world was primarily oriented by a guiding ideology.

Budzislawski was soon complaining of overwork. Quite apart from that, it
was high time, now that the war had ended, for him to revisit his own publishing plans.[105] On the whole, he had enjoyed a very respectable career as a journalist in the United States. Unlike most of the political emigrants, who had to
hold out for years in a state of "linguistic exile" (Fritz Kortner) and could do
little more than keep their heads above water, Budzislawski quickly gained a
firm foothold in the world of the American media.[106] From the summer of
1941 onward, he had been able to obtain an above-average income, which
allowed him and his family to enjoy a comparatively high standard of living in
New York. His daughter Beate's school fees alone amounted to an impressive
$550 over the academic year 1944–45, although this amount was reduced by a
$250 scholarship.[107]

Although the Budzislawskis were able to make ends meet, they found the
country's extreme disparities of wealth highly distasteful. Hermann later gave
many lectures deploring the fact that even universities, railroads, and medical
treatment were privatized in the United States. The state refrained almost
completely from intervening in the life of society; hence, it was only fulfilling
its political tasks inadequately, he argued. This would be one of the reasons

why most Americans did not live in freedom; instead, they were trapped on a treadmill kept in motion by a small number of wealthy capitalists. He illustrated this with the example of his father, Isidor, who died on 10 February 1943, in New York, uprooted and at a great distance from home.[108] Shortly before his death, he became severely ill, but the nearby Bellevue Hospital in Manhattan would not accept him as a patient. Budzislawski had been obliged "to run from one hospital to another over several days," but "they refused to take my father everywhere, because I couldn't produce an advance payment." Isidor finally ended up in Harlem Hospital, which was a "black hospital," and that was where he died. As a hospital it was excellent, his son added, but it is clear from his remarks that he would have preferred to see his father in a hospital for "white" Americans. For Georg Bernhard too, who was the former editor in chief of the *Vossische Zeitung* and who had been Budzislawski's friend in Paris, "no well-equipped hospital could be found, because he died in poverty."[109]

The exiled Budzislawski was an attentive United States watcher, but he always looked at the country through Europe-tinted spectacles. Even so, he was a penetrating observer, and he was able to use his personal experiences as vivid illustrations of the general tendencies of the epoch. While he was living in the United States, he explained European politics and European ways of thinking to his readers and listeners there; from 1948 it would be the other way round. Despite all his successes, he never felt at home in America or even fully accepted there. This was a feeling shared by many German emigrants and occasionally mentioned directly in private correspondence. Herman Reichenbach, the husband of Helene Reichenbach and former part owner of *Die neue Weltbühne*, put it in a nutshell in a letter to his friend the musicologist Eric Werner: "In spite of all the advantages of expulsion from Germany," one "is still not at home" in the United States.[110]

The War After the War

Leaving the United States and Starting Afresh in the GDR

"HURRAH! THE WAR has ended!" Budzislawski's daughter, Beate, now sixteen years old, greeted him with this exclamation on 8 May 1945 as he sat at the coffee table, pensively adding, "And what will you do now?" That is how he remembered the conversation in old age. For both of them, it seemed difficult to imagine a life without the Nazis. "Every conversation in the family or in school about a book's value or a person's character revolved around just one thing: Were they capable of holding their own in the fight against the embodiment of evil?"[1]

In the case of the Budzislawskis this statement was by no means a retrospective distortion of history. For over a decade, they had divided the world into supporters and opponents of the Nazis. The political conflict had overlain all private matters, and often enough it had influenced their lives directly. But this ideological touchstone was now no longer necessary, or at least it quickly lost its significance in public affairs. Until May 1945 Budzislawski had played an important role in the United States as an acknowledged expert on Central Europe, but with the end of the alliance caused by the war, the ideological antagonism between the Allies again came to the surface. He was not prepared to become an anti-Soviet US propagandist under any circumstances. According to Albert Schreiner, who discussed with Budzislawski possible ways of getting back to Germany when they were both in New York, the Second World War had barely finished when he realized that there was no possibility of "writing openly" in the United States—in other words, of expressing his left-wing and pro-Soviet political convictions. He had not wanted to pay "the price of being a hireling," which was to allow the owners of the capitalist press to prescribe the subjects he could cover.[2] What more obvious step could now be taken than to resuscitate *Die Weltbühne*? The former editor had always had this plan at the back of his mind.

But events moved more quickly than he would have liked, and entirely without his involvement. The initiative was taken by a Berlin journalist, Walther Karsch, who had worked as an editor for *Die Weltbühne* between 1930 and 1933.[3] On 3 July 1945 Karsch approached Johannes R. Becher, the newly elected president of the League of Culture in Berlin, suggesting that as a former colleague of Carl von Ossietzky he should be allowed to revive the "old *Weltbühne* in a new form." Karsch was at that time still a member of the KPD, but he failed in his effort to appeal to Becher, the "malevolent party bureaucrat."[4] Karsch left the KPD shortly afterward and became involved in publishing *Der Tagesspiegel*, which started to come out in West Berlin on 27 September 1945.[5] But Ossietzky's widow, Maud, now entered the scene. She had greater staying power than Karsch. She had lived through the Third Reich in great destitution, and according to her own account, she had suffered constant persecution from the Gestapo. Her identity documents had been taken away, and she had not been allowed to look for gainful employment. She had only been able to survive on the income she received from giving foreign language lessons on the quiet—Maud was a native of Britain and had been forced to use her maiden name, Woods, during the war. She was convinced that the Nazis wanted her "to die as a pauper."[6]

Immediately after the end of the Second World War, an ad hoc people's committee was formed in Pankow. It took steps both to restore civilian life in that district of Berlin and to provide maintenance for Maud von Ossietzky. A certain Franz Jack introduced himself to her at the end of May 1945, saying that he was a former fellow prisoner of her late husband; he was also personally acquainted with Budzislawski. "Some rooms in a quiet street in Schönhausen" had been "reserved for her," and the committee intended to name one of the nicest streets in the district after Carl von Ossietzky.[7] Maud again adopted her husband's surname, and the next few months were filled with her efforts to gain a license to publish *Die Weltbühne* again in the British zone of occupation. On 21 November 1945 she finally succeeded, but Budzislawski and Helene Reichenbach, who had received news of the new project, announced from New York that they objected to the British authorities' decision. They were the legitimate owners of *Die Weltbühne*, they said, and they had rights in the name. From today's perspective, their protests were valid, but at that time they were ineffective, one reason being that Maud von Ossietzky was supported by Hans Leonhard (actually Hans Julian Lewysohn), who had previously been her neighbor in Pankow. He had had himself baptized, which enabled him to survive the war as a Berlin warehouse employee, and he soon became the strategic brain behind the journal's revival. He had been familiar with *Die Weltbühne* since the early 1920s, when he had been made an intern thanks to the influence of his father, a conductor and composer who was one of Siegfried Jacobsohn's friends.[8] Leonhard received political and financial backing from the KPD in postwar Berlin, and he continued to negotiate on behalf of Maud von Ossietzky for some time with the British licensing authorities as well as with possible publishers in the western part of the city. They were unable to come to any agreement, however.[9]

It wasn't just Budzislawski's objection that gave the British authorities a jolt. Peter Jacobsohn, who was now thirty years old and had immigrated to the United States, also put forward a claim to the name of the journal founded by his father and copyright in any articles it published. Jacobsohn asserted that the sale of *Die neue Weltbühne* by his mother in 1934 had been invalid. He argued that she had inherited only one-quarter of the journal from his father, while he had inherited three-quarters, as recorded in a certificate of joint inheritance issued in January 1927 by the Berlin-Charlottenburg district court.[10] The fact that the son was now the main beneficiary and not the mother, as Siegfried Jacobsohn had decreed in his handwritten will of 1925, was the result, it seems, of a drafting error; in any case, it did not reflect the testator's wishes. It is, moreover, uncertain whether this really invalidated the sale of the journal in the early summer of 1934. That would only have been the case if Frau Jacobsohn had acted against her son's interests and the new proprietors had not acquired the journal in good faith. In other words, Peter Jacobsohn's legal position was by no means certain in the postwar years, although in his view this applied equally to the opposing party in the dispute. As for Budzislawski, Jacobsohn remarked tersely that the latter might like to present his alleged 1934 contract of sale.[11] Budzislawski could not do this, because the business documents of *Die neue Weltbühne* had been seized by the French police in 1939, and after the war they counted as missing.

Peter Jacobsohn successfully repeated his claims on many occasions in the next few decades. Until the early 1990s, he was regarded in the Federal Republic as the legitimate owner of the name of *Die Weltbühne* and as the copyright holder. It was possible to ignore what had actually happened after 1933 on the grounds that the renowned periodical had been "hijacked" by the Communists. In the western part of Germany, too, the battle lines of the Cold War were ultimately more important than legal details.

In such a confused situation, one thing at least was clear immediately after the end of the war to the British occupation authorities: the question of *Die Weltbühne* was a complex one, and its settlement required more time than Leonhard was either able or willing to afford. While continuing to conduct discussions with the British, he reinforced his contacts with the Soviet sector, where legal problems were not regarded as significant but the publication of a new *Weltbühne* promised to be politically advantageous. In mid-February 1946 the British finally canceled the license they had previously issued to Maud von Ossietzky, yet on 1 June of the same year the Soviet occupiers officially gave their blessing to the reappearance of the journal by issuing license number 371. Ossietzky and Leonhard then decided to set up a public company in which she would own 60 percent of the shares and Leonhard would own 40 percent. The agreement would take effect retroactively from 10 January 1946. This was the firm v. Ossietzky—Verlag Die Weltbühne, which was later renamed Verlag der Weltbühne v. Ossietzky und Co. The sole object of the planned enterprise was to publish, print, and distribute a new *Weltbühne* journal.[12]

The editorial staff of the new periodical moved first into a couple of offices in the building of the *Nacht-Express*, a tabloid newspaper that had appeared since 1945 in the Soviet sector and had its headquarters on Mohrenstraße (soon to be renamed Anton-Wilhelm-Amo-Straße). The first issue, which was wrapped in *Die Weltbühne*'s trademark red jacket and retained the old type-faces and the quarto format, came out as early as 4 June 1946 and must there-fore have been put together and printed even before the license was officially granted. There was no shortage of prospective authors, the two editors asserted when they were interviewed a few weeks later. Among *Die Weltbühne* veterans, Axel Eggebrecht had already agreed to contribute, and negotiations with Erich Kästner and Kurt Hiller were allegedly going well. There were also representa-tives of the new generation in the shape of Wolfgang Harich and the theater critic Friedrich Luft. In terms of party politics, the editors wanted to continue the "politically unattached" course of the Weimar Republic's *Weltbühne* while feeling that they belonged within the spectrum of left-wing democracy—though not, of course, that "lukewarm, toothless democracy" that had "once brought the NSDAP to power through the legal route."[13] But these ambitious goals had soon to be abandoned. In May 1947 Walther Karsch, who had been unsuccessful two years earlier, protested against the way "the Socialist Unity Party is laying claim to Ossietzky's name for itself." Leonhard, Karsch wrote, was an "orthodox Marxist" who would trample all over democracy and the right to form one's opinions freely, which had been fundamental features of the old *Weltbühne*.[14] This argument was again put forward a year later in an anti-Soviet propaganda pamphlet printed in West Berlin under the title *Die wahre Weltbühne*, which resembled the old journal in format and presenta-tion.[15] Some aspects of the criticism were rhetorical exaggerations deriving from the Cold War, but one central accusation stuck fast to the newly initiated *Weltbühne*: it was a periodical of high intellectual caliber, but it was politically loyal to the Socialist Unity Party (SED) and therefore in essence "a permanent

desecration of Carl von Ossietzky's memory," as Kurt Hiller argued with his
customary acerbity.[16] An article glorifying Stalin as the "most universal dia-
lectical thinker of our epoch" appeared in *Die Weltbühne* shortly before
Christmas 1949. One would never have had to read such a phrase under
the previous chief editorship of Ossietzky or Tucholsky—at least one would
hope not.[17]

Now that *Die Weltbühne* had been brought back to life in this way, Maud
was able to recoup her losses. Editorial decisions were taken by Leonhard,
seconded by Erich Weinert and for a while by the young Wolfgang Harich,
one of the rising stars of the postwar Berlin intellectual scene. Indeed, in the
summer of 1946 Harich even tried to replace Leonhard as editor in chief,
accusing him of "miserable dabbling" and "dilettantish tinkering." He wanted
to make the resurrected *Weltbühne*, which was at first a fortnightly and later
became a weekly, into an intellectual forum covering all four occupation zones
and to make an explicit link with the political independence it had displayed
under the Weimar Republic. But despite receiving intermittent support from
the propaganda department of the Soviet Military Administration in Germany (SMAD), he was unable to prevail against Leonhard, who enjoyed very
good connections with leading SED politicians.[18]

Maud von Ossietzky had no central role in these disputes and was at most
marginally involved in the daily work of editing the journal. She spent the
next few years commuting between her homes in Stockholm and Berlin-
Pankow, and she covered her living expenses by making withdrawals from the
journal's operating account. "Do you ever lend a thought to the fact that the
business is working hard to earn this money, and I am as well?" Leonhard
beseechingly implored his pro forma partner when the situation threatened to
get completely out of hand.[19] However, he could not and would not forgo the
use of her good name. The question of legal ownership was still unsettled, and
as a result he could make at most a moral claim to be the journal's publisher,
but this inevitably depended on his continued association with Ossietzky's
widow. Not until 1950, when the journal fell into the red and had to be given
financial support by the SED, did he succeed in persuading his partner to give
up her share in return for an annuity of 1,000 marks.[20] But sole ownership did
not mean editorial independence. In 1952 the SED-owned publishing house
Volk und Welt concluded a trustee agreement with him by which it took over
responsibility for all *Die Weltbühne*'s liabilities. In return, Leonhard had to
obey the party's instructions.[21]

All the participants in these negotiations were aware of how complicated
questions of ownership and copyright were in the postwar era. This was also
confirmed by Ursula Madrasch-Groschopp, who was the editor in chief's

assistant for many years in the GDR. She said that with Soviet permission *Die Weltbühne* was not even listed in the trade register until the death of Hans Leonhard in 1966.[22] An entry referring to *Die Weltbühne* was first made on 31 October 1967, with the additional purpose of documenting the GDR publisher's own claim to the journal in view of the emergence of a possible rival journal in West Germany that was at that time the subject of negotiations between Peter Jacobsohn, Walther Karsch, and others with the Munich publisher Kurt Desch.[23] The new company that emerged in 1967 in the GDR, Verlag der Weltbühne GmbH, had two equal partners: Rudolf Barbarino, formerly assistant general director of publishing in the SED's Central Printing, Purchasing, and Auditing Company (ZENTRAG), who subsequently became acting director of the Berliner Verlag; and Wilhelm Türk, ZENTRAG's legal advisor. *Die Weltbühne* was now also officially owned by the state party.[24]

Readers of the journal knew nothing of these background quarrels. The postwar *Weltbühne* initially sold well in all four zones of occupation, and in the second half of 1946 it made a net profit of 235,000 reichsmarks. At the start, its circulation amounted to a respectable 82,000 copies, and a year later this figure had risen to 170,000. Right at the outset, the journal thereby reached four times as many readers as it had in the 1920s and 1930s. But the circulation figures soon began to decline considerably. That was partly a result of the divergent political development of the western occupation zones and the Soviet occupation zone, but a much greater part in the journal's decline was played by its increasingly one-sided Communist orientation.[25] In the immediate postwar years the new *Weltbühne* was read by many people in the Federal Republic and outside Germany who had anti-Fascist convictions; they often read it for nostalgic reasons as well. Lion Feuchtwanger, who was living in the United States, was given a copy by friends and was very moved by reading it, as he informed the new editors in 1947: "To look at the journal was a heartwarming experience. One can see that the new *Weltbühne* has retained the familiar form and color of the old one, both externally and internally."[26] Thomas Mann too found words of commendation for the new *Weltbühne* in September 1949. He said that he did not always agree with its political direction, but he had come across "more than one word and more than one article" that seemed to him good and important.[27]

Meanwhile in New York, Budzislawski could do no more than observe these developments from a distance. He was powerless, as although he could announce his claim to proprietorship, he was unable either to prove or enforce it.[28] Nevertheless, at the start of 1946 he was still determined to republish what he called his *Blättchen*, or "little paper," as soon as possible on his own account. He even contacted the Czechoslovak consulate in the hope that the good connections he had made in the 1930s might help him to secure political or financial support from Prague.[29] Berthold Viertel noted on 20 March 1946 in a letter to his wife, Salka, that Budzislawski wanted to publish *Die Weltbühne* in the United States as soon as postal communications with Germany were fully restored. This would happen within a few weeks, he claimed. Budzislawski's new *Weltbühne* would be from the start a transatlantic project. "It was intended that people from over there would also write, and a cultural bridge would be built, which at the appropriate moment would become a raft on which they could cross the ocean," wrote Viertel, adding that Budzislawski had him in mind for the post of literary editor. Admittedly, the source of finance for the project was still unclear, as was the potential location of the editorial offices. The prospective editor estimated that at least $6,000 would be needed to guarantee the fortnightly appearance of the journal over the first six months. To rely on the Vermont network "had become impossible owing to the break with Dorothy," and for the time being Budzislawski was still tied to the Greater New York area by his "bread and butter work" at the Overseas News Agency. "I hope it will soon be decided whether the project finds any kind of favorable reception (material backing)."[30] At that time, as indicated above, facts on the ground were being created by people on the other side of the Atlantic.

However, the developments in Berlin and the continuing lack of clarity over how a transatlantic *Weltbühne* could be financed were only two of the problems that stood in the way of Budzislawski's ambitious plans. A third problem was that during the McCarthy era of the late 1940s, members of the Communist Party and their sympathizers had less and less room to maneuver in the United States. The German-speaking left-wing intellectuals and Communists in New York—a group that in addition to people already mentioned included Albert Norden, Stefan Heym, Friedrich Alexan (actually Georg Kupfermann), Ernst Bloch, and Wieland Herzfelde—drew together even more closely than before and began to discuss possible future scenarios in terms of both general politics and their own fate as individuals. This small group of like-minded people adopted the name the Tribune for Free German Literature and Art. Its informal venue was Alexan's New York bookshop at the corner of 42nd Street and Sixth Avenue.[31]

This is how the writer Stefan Heym later described the situation: "In view of the constantly increasing mood of hostility in the country toward everything that can be denounced as 'Red,'" any open statement of political commitment would have amounted to an act of "senseless self-exposure" and journalistic suicide. On the other hand, one wanted to be able to look oneself in the mirror while shaving in the morning.[32] Most of the Left exiles found it difficult to imagine that they could have a long-term future in the United

States. This feeling comes through clearly in a 4 November 1947 letter from Hanna Budzislawski to Berthold Viertel. A few days after Bertolt Brecht's appearance before the House Un-American Activities Committee, which the world-famous playwright had planned and rehearsed like a theatrical performance previously with Hermann Budzislawski, she made this comment: "Let us not deceive ourselves. The wheels are in motion. Fascists learn quickly, and next time they will already be better at it."[33] After the hearing in Washington, DC, Brecht hurried straightaway to New York, where he listened to his "performance" on the radio that evening together with Helene Weigel and Hermann and Hanna at the Budzislawskis' apartment. The next day he was already sitting in a plane bound for Europe, never to return to the United States.[34]

In this climate of fear and intimidation, an increasing number of German-speaking left-wing intellectuals contemplated returning to Europe. "We the abandoned ones are sticking close together," Hanna wrote with confidence. But for how long?[35] In the Budzislawski household, too, preparations for leaving the country were now well advanced. Since 1947 at the latest they had been in touch by letter with the lawyer and Harvard University lecturer Horst W. Baehrensprung, a former Reichsbanner leader who, like Budzislawski, had been a member of the preparatory committee for the Council for a Democratic Germany in 1944. Shortly before the end of the war, Baehrensprung was expelled from the United States. He returned to Germany, where in September 1947 he was appointed chief of police in Brunswick. The Budzislawskis sounded him out as to how he viewed the chances of restarting publication of *Die Weltbühne* under its former publisher and editor in chief. Budzislawski enjoyed "a very good reputation," Baehrensprung wrote back, according to an "important man" whom he did not mention by name, but it had not been possible to prevent the emergence in the meantime of a new *Weltbühne* in East Berlin under Soviet license. His pragmatic suggestion was that Budzislawski should come to Germany first, and then it would be possible to come to an agreement with him.[36]

The choice of an occupation zone and therefore of the political regime under which the Budzislawskis were thinking of living—East or West?—had not yet been decided. The only definite decision they had already made was to leave the United States: "We are feeling very lonely here, and we mourn all our old friends. . . . There is really no one left here with whom one can have a calm and rational discussion."[37] In this situation, the arrival of encouraging signals from the eastern part of Germany was very convenient. The author and KPD official Willi Bredel, who had returned to Germany from his Moscow exile in 1945, wrote to Budzislawski to say that "journalists of your caliber" were urgently needed in the Soviet occupation zone "because our newspapers and journals still look utterly dreary." If it proved impossible to find an appropriate position in journalism, Budzislawski could think about a professorship in Greifswald or Rostock.[38]

The decision to return to Germany was made a few months later. Budzislawski's wife, Hanna, reported in February 1948 that her husband had been offered two professorships: one at Rostock, the other at Leipzig. "And the more deeply he reflected on the idea of a chair in the history of the press and journalism, the more tempting did the assignment appear. We have therefore agreed in principle, though we are unlikely to fall in love with the Saxons and remain stuck in Saxony. But it is very good for a start." The Budzislawskis continued to be a working marital partnership—"we" accepted the call, wrote Hanna. But it would soon turn out that the move not only brought the period of exile to an end but also made it increasingly possible for Hanna to dispense with her role of giving background support to her husband.

The Budzislawskis were now Czechoslovak citizens and therefore "foreigners" in Germany. This meant that they needed entry permits from the Soviet military authorities, who were in no hurry. "Without a visa, we can neither book nor pack. So once again, the watchword is: wait." On the other hand, as Hanna remarked in her letter to Viertel, America was becoming more interesting politically: "The political struggle between what are now three parties is sharpening, and no one is standing on the sidelines." Hermann had been sitting close to the "source of good things" for some time, she added. She was referring to Henry A. Wallace, Roosevelt's former vice president who was now the presidential candidate for the short-lived Progressive Party, which focused on achieving an international rapprochement with the Soviet Union. But even the prospect of "influence, success, and later opportunities" was not enough to deter her husband from striking camp on the East Coast of the United States: "Unwise? Perhaps. But resolute."[39] Four months later, even before the crushing electoral defeat of Wallace's Progressive Party, they were ready to leave: "Our suitcases are packed, we have given up our apartment, and our cabin on the Polish liner *Batory* is paid for. We sail on 14 August for Danzig [today's Polish city of Gdańsk], and from there via Warsaw and Prague to Leipzig. In the meantime, we have lived through a wonderful period."[40]

Budzislawski described the reasons for his decision to leave and, still more importantly, his highly ambivalent feelings during the journey and the first few days he spent in his old-new homeland in one of his best texts, which appeared in October 1948 in *Ost und West*. This was a journal published by Alfred Kantorowicz, his friend and former neighbor in the Berlin artists' colony. It was one of the most important intellectual periodicals published in the

German language during the years immediately after the war.[41] There is little sign of euphoria in Budzislawski's essay. On the contrary: "Incidentally, my return was by no means as voluntary as it might appear. It almost felt like a new emigration from a land of asylum that had now become dangerous."[42] His description of the return journey to Europe is pervaded by a yearning for the homeland, despite his awareness that it had been destroyed irreparably:

> I had a great feeling of excitement when I saw the Land's End lighthouse emerge off the coast of Cornwall after an ocean voyage of eight days. . . . Eight years earlier, when after the fall of France and our flight through Franco's Spain, we were watching the disappearance of the last Portuguese hills from our Greek ship, I warned my daughter: "Have a good look. Who knows whether we shall ever see Europe again." . . . But here we now were, back with Mother Europe. She was impoverished and torn to pieces, churned up by passionate conflicts, and most probably demoralized as well. But we had often thought of her, . . . and we yearned for her climate, the smell of her woods, the taste of her apples. It was a triumph to be allowed to reconnect with our past, to knit back together our broken, interrupted lives, and to grow again into whole human beings. In Copenhagen we were greeted by cheering crowds of a kind we had never seen in America, where people live alongside each other as isolated individuals. But the reception was not for us but for some Danes who were returning to the bosom of their families after a lengthy absence, and we experienced the leaden realization that we had no relatives and hardly any friends who could greet us in the old homeland. We were separated from Germany by fifteen years of murder.[43]

Long before the concept of Auschwitz as the "breach with civilization" was frequently used, Budzislawski made it unmistakably clear that after the crimes committed by the Nazis during their policy of extermination it would be impossible to return to a supposedly harmonious prewar era. In 1945, in the Council for a Democratic Germany, he had recommended a policy of tactical reticence, but he now adopted a more uncompromising position. The new attitude, which was shared at that time by many German Jewish emigrants, was expressed still more sharply by the lawyer Ernst Fraenkel in 1946, when he rejected an invitation from the SPD politician Otto Suhr to return to Berlin on grounds of principle. He had decided, he said, "never to return to Germany. . . . I have a sense of solidarity with Jews—and only with Jews—in their relationship with the Germans, especially after 5,000,000 Jews have been murdered. . . . My feelings about this are very bitter. I do not think that this wound can ever be healed."[44] Budzislawski expressed himself less categorically, but he too insisted that the mass murder of the European Jews as well as the relentless persecution of the political Left since the National Socialists took over the government in 1933 rendered any form of reconciliation impossible, unless it was accompanied by a fundamental transformation, a new beginning of a Socialist kind. The German Jewish writer Joachim Chaim Schwarz, who "returned" to the GDR from Israel in 1950, succinctly formulated a position Budzislawski would also have subscribed to: "I returned home as an anti-Fascist, and this new world only interested me insofar as it was anti-Fascist."[45]

Apart from the great devastation of his birthplace, the city of Berlin, Budzislawski was also confronted on his return by the Nazification of the German language. Like Victor Klemperer, who experienced this development firsthand while living in the Third Reich and who made it the basis of his book *LTI— Lingua Tertii Imperii: Notizbuch eines Philologen*, which appeared in 1947, Budzislawski was both astounded and shocked by the success of the National Socialist language policy of the previous two decades:

> I had thought that I would no longer be able to find my way around the ruins of my proper home. But in the humid hothouse of the New York summers, I had looked forward yearningly to the dry, clear air of Berlin, to the people of the city, the humorous, quick-witted "old Berliners," and to the jokes of the streetcar conductors. Things turned out differently. . . . I had never imagined that an inhabited city could be so deserted in the evening. . . . I did not feel like a foreigner when I looked at the houses and even when I read the newspapers, whose German occasionally shocked me. I had yearned to come back to my mother tongue, because even after years of familiarization it remains difficult and exhausting to comply with the requirement to speak and write in a foreign language. But the language used here has changed in the meantime. It has run wild and is often permeated with Nazi expressions, or, in certain intellectual circles, it sounds artificial. . . . We were often unconsciously tempted to speak English with each other, in self-defense, as it were, against the German that was encroaching upon us from all directions. It would have sounded less alien if it had come with a Berlin accent. The mishmash of German dialects and the peevish way many people here make a life that is already difficult enough even uglier do not make it easier for us to feel like members of the nation to which we have returned.[46]

Budzislawski ended his article by saying that in Leipzig, admittedly, he had met young people who had "radically turned their backs on the past" more than was the case in Berlin and that they were involved in the energetic construction of a Socialist society.[47] In view of the fact that he had only arrived in the city a few days earlier, this optimistic conclusion was more an expression of hope than a description of the present based on his own experience. Even so, it was possible during those years to sense an atmosphere of renewal in Leipzig. This showed itself not just in the exceptionally thorough and rapid clearing of the rubble left behind by the war, for which purpose the council employed no fewer than thirty-eight hundred people, but also in the widespread enthusiasm for the city's ambitious reconstruction plans. These plans envisaged a mixed approach involving the reconstruction of the historic buildings along with new, future-directed initiatives. Even schoolchildren wanted to join in, and many older people also found that the watchword of a Socialist future had some appeal.[48] The German Jewish literary scholar Hans Mayer recalled later that this had been a time of optimism. He too, like Budzislawski, had received an invitation from the University of Leipzig in 1948, and he too had accepted: "Now that the Germans had also undergone a bitter experience— after all, I had seen the ruins, the suffering, the dead bodies, and the prisoners of war—I became confident that people would be able to relate differently to each other."[49]

On 4 October 1948 Hanna Budzislawski wrote a detailed letter to her old friend Berthold Viertel, giving her personal impressions of the first few weeks in Leipzig. The returned exiles had moved into Lenaustraße 3, a villa built in the modernist "New Objectivity" style, which had become fashionable in the 1920s, and that had only been cleared a few weeks earlier and then refurbished for the new residents with the assistance of the university: "Yes, there we were, on the spot, so to speak. We arrived in Leipzig with thirty suitcases and a small amount of hand luggage, safe and sound, and feeling very cheerful. We are living in one of the fine modern houses with between seven and ten rooms (depending on how one counts), with lots of windows and balconies, a roof terrace, and a garden right around it. We are in the middle of greenery. The house has its own story: a rich 'Jew' built it (as we were told), a Nazi stole it, and we still don't feel quite at home in this abundance of space."[50]

We can be more precise than Hanna was about the history of the house in which the Budzislawskis were to live during the next sixteen years. The villa at Lenaustraße 3 had been built in 1927–28 on the instructions of the manufacturer Paul Funke, the owner of Dr. Curt Schäfer Nachf., a Leipzig pharmaceutical enterprise. In 1935 at the latest, Funke let the villa to the industrialist Dr. Fritz Ries, who moved in with his family and from 1938 was registered as the owner of the property. He had been a member of the NSDAP since 1933 and, as the responsible shareholder of the Leipzig rubber factory Flügel & Polter, had built up a business empire through "Aryanizations" and other kinds of takeovers. During the Second World War he had profited very substantially from the exploitation of Jewish and Polish forced laborers working in the

Oberschlesische Gummiwerke, located in Trzebinia, west of Kraków, and in the Aryanized Gummiwerke Wartheland in Łódź (then called Litzmannstadt). Later, in the Federal Republic, Ries obtained a considerable amount of money from the Equalization of Burdens Fund and again became an influential entrepreneur as the majority shareholder and soon afterward the chief executive of the Pegulan-Werke AG. He had excellent contacts with leading conservative politicians such as Franz Josef Strauß, Kurt Biedenkopf (who married Ries's daughter Ingrid in 1979), and Helmut Kohl, who was at that time the minister-president of Rhineland-Palatinate. In 1972 Kohl, the later federal chancellor, awarded Ries the Federal Cross of Merit with Star "in recognition of his entrepreneurial achievements and his commitment to society." Ries did not do so well after the war in Leipzig because he was expropriated in the Soviet occupation zone in 1947–48. The Leipzig rubber factory of Flügel & Polter became the publicly owned Leipziger Gummiwarenfabriken, and the house at Lenaustraße 3 became public property. The Budzislawskis moved in shortly afterward.[51]

The attention of the new tenants was focused on the future rather than the past—which in this case meant refurnishing the house and organizing their daily lives. These tasks lay entirely in the hands of Hanna, who had very definite ideas about the shape of the family's future living arrangements. The above-mentioned letter to Berthold Viertel gives her point of view in detail:

To represent our "status" properly, they wanted to provide me with good bourgeois furniture: a dining room with a buffet and highly polished sideboards, a bedroom with a mirrored wardrobe and a night table, and, if possible, a parlor as well. No one understood my resistance. In the meantime, I have collected a few pieces of furniture: a Biedermeier suite, a rococo sofa, bookshelves, a writing table at which at least three managing directors could sit, couches, and so on, and it already looks the same as it always did when times were very good. The bathroom has hot water, all the walls are freshly painted, the windows have been cleaned, and the parquet floors waxed and polished. The whole thing sounds like a fairy tale, but it is not. It was difficult at first. Initially one is placed in a low food supply category, and I have not yet worked out how one can actually live with so little to eat. On top of this, 'new arrivals' are not well served by the small traders in the neighborhood. It is said that Saxons are deceitful. This may be true. Everything will get better when we receive the privileges enjoyed by only a few. Beate, as a student, and Hermann, as a professor, will receive ration card no. 1, the mysterious special packet will be delivered every month, and as a victim of Fascism I will be able to buy provisions in special shops, and all these things, taken together, will improve our lives considerably. And our garden, in which a new strawberry bed has been laid out, will produce so much next year that it will feed not just ourselves but several other people as well.[52]

As far as the material basis for a bourgeois way of life was concerned, then, the prospects were highly promising. Hanna Budzislawski understood that she and her family were living a privileged life in the Leipzig of the late 1940s. She appeared to care little about the hostility of her neighbors, who probably viewed the new arrivals with a mixture of envy, resentment, and awe. Her language makes it clear that she was keeping her distance from the long-established inhabitants and that her self-esteem was based to a substantial degree on her identification with the new order and the feeling of superiority that was bound up with it. As far as the practicalities were concerned, she went on to say that things were going well in Leipzig, but mental attitudes in the city were only changing slowly: "Artisans do their work admirably, but they fail on the most elementary political matters. The university is in a wretched condition. One could say that the conservative professors, predominantly of the old guard, are proud to have kept to a single line since the age of Wilhelm II. No one makes any secret of his opinions. On the contrary, they rant against all who are new and against all that is new. Sometimes it seems that there is too much freedom and that it would be more appropriate to have less of it."[53]

Hermann Budzislawski also emphasized that "90 percent of the professors" at the university "belonged to the old guard." There weren't many progressive people: "The only form of contact is when we occasionally yell at each other in meetings. The other ten percent are admirable people, in part. Eleven years in concentration camps or being condemned to death makes us with our ten months of internment feel petty and sordid. And everywhere people complain. Even so, one feels immensely safe and protected."[54]

Both of them agreed that they were faced with a tremendous job of reconstruction. Hanna in particular seemed occasionally to have worried about the wide range of her husband's new responsibilities:

What is worst of all is the lack of trained workers in administrative and official positions, beginning with the press and radio, and one would like to lend a hand everywhere and immediately. But how much can one person take on? Hermann will start his lectures in mid-October; he is the director of an institute of news-paper studies that has yet to be set up. From the beginning of November, he will give a talk on the radio regularly, once a week, in other words, and his participation in all the relevant newspapers goes without saying. Besides that there are speeches to functionaries and groups of specialists, which one cannot refuse to make. . . . He traveled to Berlin early this morning to say hello to old friends and make political contacts. If we wanted to, we could in addition get involved in *Die Weltbühne* in one form or another. But that needs careful consideration, and for the moment the little magazine is still on hold. If one bears in mind that we only left New York six weeks ago and landed in Leipzig three weeks ago, we have probably achieved the maximum possible. Of course, we have as yet no insights into the trend of politics. Everyone with whom we come into contact is cordial, supportive, and amazed by us. How can one leave the richest country in the world voluntarily? For the present, we are in uncharted territory. Even the climate is as alien to us as the New York climate used to be. And to top it off, everyone speaks German. How peculiar![55]

In the months before their departure, the Budzislawskis had received detailed advice from Albert Schreiner, and they had prepared themselves as well as they could for their new life. They came with masses of luggage, including many domestic items that were in short supply in Leipzig: a radio, an electric iron and hotplates, a pressure cooker, coffee, bars of soap, laundry soap, rubber heels, nails, and thread for sewing and darning.[56] In addition, before leaving the United States they had stocked up "with a consignment of the best cigarettes" of the Lucky Strike and Camel brands. Some of these they shared generously with their friends; the rest were exchanged on the black market.[57] The returnees could not bring furniture with them, but it wasn't long before they possessed a fine collection, not least because Hanna regularly visited the city's furniture dealers, who sold antique furniture and other valuable items in the cellars and arcades around the Thomaskirche, sometimes at bargain prices. The Budzislawskis had already acquired secondhand furniture in 1926 for their first dwelling as a young couple—"seven Biedermeier chairs at seven marks apiece," as Hermann recalled forty years later in a talk on GDR radio. Shortly after that, he had begun to seek information about old furniture in specialist journals in the Berlin State Library, and over the years he and his wife had become experts in this field.[58] In Leipzig the Budzislawskis had "specialized in the best Biedermeier," reported Wieland Herzfelde, who had also returned from America and taken up residence in Leipzig. For his part, he was particularly proud of the Chinese ornamental lions that appeared to keep watch beside the garden entrance of his new house.[59]

A fair number of valuable home furnishings must also have come into the possession of the Budzislawskis through the clearing out of abandoned or expropriated East German lodges, castles, and mansions, a process Hanna "assisted."[60] Since the couple were recognized "victims of Fascism," they received preferential treatment in the provision of furniture and household effects from the Housing Office of the City of Leipzig. A transfer certificate

Hermann Budzislawski became well known in the early GDR for his radio commentaries broadcast by Mitteldeutscher Rundfunk. This photograph dates from 1949 or 1950.

dated 1 October 1949 makes it clear that many of the items involved had previously been the property of people who either had fled from their houses and flats to the West or had their assets seized on political grounds, for instance, because they were former National Socialists. Thus the Budzislawskis obtained carpets, a twelve-piece dinner service, and curtains from the house at Stephanstraße 18 ("Podlas, present address unknown"); a complete twenty-five-volume edition of the encyclopedia *Meyers Konversations-Lexikon* and garden furniture from Walter Fritsche at Papestraße 12 ("present address unknown"); a chaise longue and a stool from Gustav Köhlmann at Friedensstraße 4; and a kitchen dresser, kitchen table, and numerous other items of furniture from Georg Mumme at Jacobsstraße 25 ("seizure of assets").[61] All these objects were valued by the official executor in the years that followed; after that had been done, the Budzislawskis had to pay to the state the amount they owed.

The new power relations were therefore also accompanied by new property relations. Families like the Budzislawskis, owing to their social position, were given not only superior accommodation but also access to furniture and many other requirements of everyday life. According to their own account, they had been "expropriated" three times in the 1930s and 1940s (in Berlin, Prague, and Paris), and on each occasion they had lost most of their personal possessions.[62] Now they found themselves on the victorious side: the side that determined the distribution of the goods. After fifteen years of involuntary exile, they felt that they were morally in the right, and they wanted to take back the things they had long been deprived of. For the Budzislawskis, this meant, apart from public recognition, the recovery of financial independence and an upper-middle-class lifestyle. They succeeded very quickly in achieving both these aims, as Hanna Budzislawski euphorically informed Horst Baehrensprung at the beginning of the 1950s: "When one looks at the life we lead, leaving aside the struggles and dangers of the outside world, it is the absolutely secure life of the *Bürger* in the positive sense, a person who has no worries, who is in a good situation financially, who can afford everything, who is short of nothing, I really mean nothing (we live better than we did then in a city of ten million, and if you were to see how our library has grown in the meantime, you might well be envious)."[63]

Everything was "in excellent order," Hanna assured another friend, the returnee Friedrich Alexan, adding: "Hermann has his mind free to think about the difficult world situation."[64] As professor of international newspaper studies with a "special salary for repatriates," he earned 1,100 marks a month, and in addition he received 1,200 marks a month as a commentator at Central German Radio as well as other side earnings, for example, from the *Leipziger Volkszeitung*. The cost of living, moreover, was low. The Budzislawskis only had to pay 200 marks a month in rent for the villa, which amounted to less than 10 percent of their regular income.[65] Contemplating careers like Budzislawski's, Alfred Kantorowicz referred in 1949 to the "bribery" of the Left intelligentsia in the Soviet zone, though he meant this in an entirely positive sense: "To their own surprise and great satisfaction the intellectuals found that they occupied a place on the social ladder . . . that until now had been the preserve of industrialists, bank directors, big landowners, and army generals (and still remained so to a certain extent in present-day West Germany). Why should they not accept the bribe? It was perhaps the first time in Germany's miserable history that the attempt had been made to assign to intellectual work its true, fitting place in society; it was a step toward society's humanization."[66] Lou Eisler, the wife of the composer Hanns Eisler, who had also returned from the United States, formulated the same thought in a much more down-to-earth fashion. To entertain scruples about their new position was entirely inappropriate, she said, as they formed part of "the very small group of people in the country with a recognized anti-Fascist past" and therefore belonged to the new intellectual elite, with corresponding rights, a point that people should "be kind enough" to bear in mind.[67]

Over the course of the next three decades, the Budzislawskis acquired numerous items of antique furniture as well as paintings and other works of art, the value of which was estimated at the end of the 1970s at nearly a million marks. The family was able to draw on plentiful financial resources and build up a genuine art collection, particularly after Hermann received a much sought-after individual contract at the University of Leipzig. This contract guaranteed a monthly income of 4,000 marks, which for the GDR was a very large amount.[68] They lived in what was in a sense a self-created museum of an otherwise defunct middle-class culture. This had nothing to do with the pursuit of profit or the collection of furniture as a store of value, Hanna assured Peter Viertel, the son of Salka and Berthold, shortly before her death: "The fact that the value of my furniture, pictures, and small-scale artworks has gone up so much in the meantime can be attributed to the unhealthy character of our times. We never bought a single piece because it was valuable. All the objects lying around here were bought for their usefulness."[69] This special home environment preserved the memory of bygone days, for one thing, but the furniture also demonstrated the higher social status the Budzislawskis had successfully achieved despite all the obstacles of the previous decades. One might call it a form of indirect personal reparation.

However, the way the Budzislawskis' family life was actually organized in the next few years indicates that despite the rapid rise in their well-being their initial experience of alienation continued to have an impact and was perhaps never entirely overcome. Berlin in the 1920s, the cosmopolitan world of Budzislawski's early life as a journalist, had perished irretrievably, and his parents and siblings were all dead. There was no contact at all, it seems, between the Budzislawskis and their relatives in distant lands—an aunt was living in Philadelphia in 1950, and there are supposed to have been cousins in Argentina. These people were all "small traders," and they were "apolitical," wrote Hermann in August 1950 in an answer to an SED questionnaire.[70] As will be explained in detail in the next chapter, he was already under pressure within the party by then; hence, these statements may have been deliberate falsehoods or attempts to cover himself. He didn't even mention Hanna's uncle, Adolf Levy in New York, who had vouched for the refugee family in 1940.

The new world of "actually existing Socialism" seemed strange at first to the returning emigrants. Just as many German ex-soldiers who had returned from the war liked to get together with former comrades to exchange stories about their war experiences, so also the political returnees sat together to talk about their long periods of exile. The Budzislawskis sought out the company of other returned emigrants, particularly in their first few years in Leipzig. Georg Friedrich Alexan and his family were frequent guests. Alexan's daughter, Irene Runge, born in 1942, even lived with the Budzislawskis for some time after her mother, Maria, took her own life in 1951.[71] Irene remembers Hermann

Budzislawski as a "witty and entertaining man."[72] His wife, she told me, had been a pipe and cigar smoker, which was unusual in postwar Germany. She was an excellent cook who was able to prepare exotic dishes and managed to obtain the necessary spices for them. She published some of her recipes under the pseudonym Habu in the monthly periodical *Das Magazin*, edited since 1956 by the journalist Hilde Eisler, the wife of Gerhart Eisler.[73] It seems grotesque that Hanna Budzislawski's only publications under her own name were recipes that included cultural-historical information under the heading "Love, Imagination, and the Art of Cookery," a title she herself invented, and it confirms the continued existence of traditional differences in gender roles in both East and West Germany. Women such as Hilde Eisler, who was for more than two decades the editor in chief of a popular periodical, remained the exception in the GDR.[74]

The circle of friends who had returned from exile also included the economic historian Henryk Grossmann. He too had received an invitation from the University of Leipzig and returned to Germany shortly after the Budzislawskis. He moved into a ground-floor flat in the house next door at Lenaustraße 5.[75] Contacts were closer at the beginning with Karola and Ernst Bloch, Wieland Herzfelde, and the medical doctor Felix Boenheim. Hanna had been actively involved in assisting the return of all of them from the United States.[76] The Budzislawskis no longer lived in an artists' colony as they had around 1930, but this was a colony too, an unofficial colony of returned exiles. Owing to the prominent position they occupied in the city, they and their friends enjoyed physical amenities and political recognition. Of course, this arrangement hardly facilitated their integration into mainstream Leipzig society, which had some new Socialists but consisted for the most part of former National Socialists. There were strong feelings of mutual antagonism between those who had remained in Leipzig and the returned exiles. Mistrust was still widespread, as were antisemitic remarks on the part of non-Jewish Germans.[77]

Nor had the Nazis completely vanished from the everyday scene, as Hanna was careful to note immediately after her return from the United States: "A few worn-out pairs of SS trousers, and the occasional Sturmbannführer's cap arouse a sudden feeling of anxiety, while the many white knee-high socks remind one disagreeably of Henlein and the gentlemen with leather breeches, and the rakish little hats are thoroughly unpleasant." Here she was referring to the former Sudeten German gauleiter Konrad Henlein and to the SA, which was particularly strongly represented in Sudetenland before 1945. The "pronounced stress on peasant clothing" in postwar Leipzig led Hanna to think involuntarily of National Socialist propaganda around autarky, "blood and soil . . . back to the land and similar nonsense." But little was now left of the former so-called master race, she noted with a mixture of satisfaction, scorn, and astonishment: "The people one meets on the street are careworn, haggard, and sometimes malicious. In the streetcars they push and shove, treading on each other's toes, and one can only admire the women conductors, who calmly regulate the troublesome throngs."[78]

Critical observations like this about postwar German society in the early days of the GDR as well as the initial tendency of Jewish returnees to prefer each other's company are indications of a feeling of insecurity among this group. The former emigrants, who were mostly between the ages of forty and sixty, felt they had returned not to an old homeland that was also new but to an environment that was hostile, if not politically, then at least emotionally. For many of them, to live in the occupied Germany of the postwar years was to take on a big psychological burden, as left-wing Jewish intellectuals and Communists had been subject to merciless persecution and murder in the country only a few years earlier. Was their return to the land of the perpetrators not inevitably a betrayal of the many millions who had been unable to escape the National Socialist genocide? Even those who avoided asking themselves such questions and did their best to approach their new lives in a pragmatic fashion were forced to notice that hardly anything was left of the once multifaceted Jewish life of previous decades.[79] At the end of 1946 there were only 250 Jews in Leipzig.[80] Many of them, including the Budzislawskis, took no part in the Jewish community's slow return to life during the postwar years. The writer Carl Zuckmayer, a Gentile who only relocated from the United States in 1957 and deliberately avoided applying to renew his German citizenship, instead moving to Switzerland, described the basic experience of returners such as the Budzislawskis after 1945 in his memoirs: the exile "may return to the people he missed, to places he loved and did not forget, to the region where his own language is spoken. But he never returns home."[81]

The new start in Leipzig meant at the same time the end of old friendships in the United States. The most significant loss for Hermann Budzislawski was the definitive break with his former patron, Dorothy Thompson, not least because it was conducted as a public feud between two journalists. While he was still living in the United States, Budzislawski thought it wise to keep the summer 1945 quarrel with Thompson out of the public eye. Three years later, and only a few weeks after his return to Germany, he abandoned such prudent considerations. He now began to mount sharp attacks on his former patron on the radio and in the press. "I was America's most famous woman" was the title of an article printed in the 24 November 1948 issue of *Neues Deutschland*, East Germany's flagship newspaper, with which Budzislawski demonstrated his political reliability, reminding his readers at the same time that he was a distinguished political journalist. Apart from a few intellectuals, politicians, and emigrants, hardly anyone in Germany would have known his name, because *Die neue Weltbühne* of the years between 1933 and 1939 was prohibited in the Third Reich. It had circulated only in a few copies, smuggled illegally into the country. The opportunity for Budzislawski to make a sensational debut as a postwar German journalist was offered by an article from Dorothy Thompson titled "An meine deutschen Freunde" (To my German friends), which she had been invited to write by the US-American Office of Military Government for Germany (OMGUS). It appeared first in the military government's newspaper, *Die amerikanische Rundschau,* and it was reprinted a few days later, on 19 October 1948, in the Munich *Neue Zeitung,* which was also controlled by the Americans. *Die neue Zeitung,* which was produced on the presses of the former *Völkischer Beobachter* in Schellingstraße, was regarded by critics such as the Communist renegade Wolfgang Leonhardt as a "worthy counterpart to the Soviet *Pravda*" because of the unmistakable complexion of its politics.[82] In language clearly borrowed from the vocabulary of German idealism, Thompson invoked the cultural values supposedly shared by Americans and Europeans alike. An era of "creative and cordial comradeliness" would soon arise from the "need for joint self-defense and self-reflection" because unlike the Soviet Union, the United States had never had the intention of "allowing historic European states to sink into the position of the satellites and colonies of a conqueror" and to set up puppet governments directed by their masters in Moscow. The Marshall Plan offered good conditions for rapid reconstruction and a guarantee that the decisively important part of Germany would be able to hold its ground against the Stalinist Soviet Union. "If I were a German . . . I would rather be a citizen of a rump Germany within a European federation than a unified Germany in the iron grip of the Soviet empire." National unity dictated by the "Russian knout" would never be viable in the long term.[83]

Budzislawski replied that in making these comments Thompson was simply repeating "the old commonplaces of American propaganda," advocating for a permanent division of Germany, veiled in tawdry Western rhetoric. But the slogans uttered by his former boss also presented a personal danger. The Soviet zone of occupation was Budzislawski's new sphere of action, and the last thing he wanted was to be suspected of having been a Western propagandist. Therefore, he now claimed that Thompson, in acting as an instrument of the American occupying power, had returned to the "reactionary tendencies of her youth," which was presumably an allusion to her Christian family background, as her father was a Methodist preacher. "This naturally brought to an end the symbiosis that had joined us for four years in daily collaboration." His polemic against her went beyond purely factual disagreements because he also questioned her integrity as a journalist. She had, he admitted, a "great gift for style," but original "creative thinking" was alien to her. "She is, so to speak, a magnificent actress who plays different roles superbly but cannot write her own plays. She has frequently boasted of being the best in the country at picking brains or stealing ideas. Since she acted as an excellent loudspeaker, progressive circles were happy for many years to make use of this megaphone."[84] Budzislawski's reply to Thompson was nothing less than a calculated, personally wounding, frontal onslaught that was both malicious and brilliant. It was also an indication of how severely he had suffered since the beginning of the 1940s from his loss of visible status in the United States: "A writer does not always have it easy in other countries. He occasionally has to write under assumed names, and that is why I used a female pseudonym for four years. The name under which my newspaper articles, essays in periodicals, lectures, radio talks, and even a book appeared was Dorothy Thompson."[85]

Thompson replied with a long article titled "How I Was Duped by a Communist," published in the New York *Saturday Evening Post* on 16 April 1949. It wasn't just a reply to the attack from her former colleague; she also had to defend herself against all those who accused her and other liberal American journalists of having swallowed the bait offered by Moscow-directed Communists during the war. Thompson depicted her experience with Budzislawski as a paradigm case of Communist tactics that called for greater vigilance in the future. She had at first thought that he had been as disgusted by the Hitler-Stalin Pact as she was, not least because he was Jewish. When he took the view during the Second World War that now was not the moment to attack the supporters of the Soviet Union, which was fighting against Hitler, this did not make her suspicious. From Thompson's point of view, a working relationship had quickly turned into a genuine friendship, until the summer of 1945, at any rate. Since then, she had learned a great deal about the Communists, who were utterly immoral people. "I know that deceiving the bourgeoisie, even their 'best friends,' is practiced as a duty, without the slightest twinges of conscience." Budzislawski was stationed in Leipzig, at "communism's westernmost outpost in Europe." Strategically, commercially, culturally, and politically, the city was the "spearhead of Russia into the heart of Europe"—and her former colleague and friend was one of the people who were expected to lead this onslaught in the interests of the Soviet Union.[86]

Thompson initially intended to respond more cautiously to Budzislawski's attack, as is evident from a confidential exchange of letters with the journalist Ben Hibbs at the beginning of 1949. She had become convinced, she wrote, that the Communists had deliberately "attached" Budzislawski to her so as to bring the American public round to their view of the situation and that they

First page of the 1949 article in the *Saturday Evening Post* in which
Dorothy Thompson defended herself against the accusations of
her former colleague.

also intended to use her to gain access to secret government information. But
she did not want to go public with this, presumably because she had no proof,
among other reasons. It is not entirely clear why she changed her mind soon
afterward.[87] It certainly mattered that Thompson too was under criticism in
the intensifying Cold War atmosphere of the McCarthy era because of what
was alleged to be her excessively pronounced sympathy for Communism at
the beginning of the 1940s. This was one further reason, in addition to a sense
of personal injury, why she felt it necessary to distance herself publicly from
her former colleague after his attack on her. Now she regarded him as one of
those dangerous Communists who had shamelessly exploited her kindheart-

edness. She had been unable to believe that someone could "conceal his feeling and beliefs for years . . . or that there existed otherwise civilized human beings who could simulate the most intimate friendship for persons whom they . . . were making use of for their own purposes."[88] Thompson was hit hard by her former collaborator's attack, which occurred at a highly dangerous time in American domestic politics. She cast aside everything that reminded her even remotely of the hours, often very pleasant ones, that she had spent with the Budzislawskis in Vermont and New York. As a result, her archives contain at most rudimentary traces of this very close working relationship, which had lasted for several years.

The public feud with Thompson helped Budzislawski to present himself in the Soviet occupation zone as a reliable Cold War warrior, despite having returned from Western emigration. However, as regards the hoped-for resuscitation of *Die Weltbühne* under his direction, the first few years were disappointing. Internal SED documents show that Walter Ulbricht, whom he had known for a long time, had already made the personal decision at the end of 1946 that the SED could make use of Budzislawski as a scholar but not as an independent journalist. "Not *Weltbühne*. Better to be utilized in teaching activities" was Ulbricht's handwritten note on a memorandum from Franz Dahlem, from which it also emerges that Albert Schreiner had spoken to Budzislawski in New York about his possible return to Germany and that various alternatives were already being considered at this early date.[89] A month later Jakob Walcher specified in a memorandum on "eventual returners from the United States" that in the case of Budzislawski they were dealing with an unusually talented journalist who had "operated very progressively throughout his emigration, including in America," and who could be extremely useful under present circumstances in the Socialist part of Germany. Even so, Budzislawski was not one of the seventy-five emigrants who returned from the West between 1945 and 1956 to pursue their main profession in the mass media of the Soviet zone (later the GDR).[90] The skeptical Paul Merker, concurring with Ulbricht's suggestion, recommended that the SED use Budzislawski "in teaching activities" if he returned and joined the party, but they should keep him away from *Die Weltbühne*: "He regards *Die Weltbühne* as more or less his own private property, and he would probably make a clear attempt to assert his right of ownership."[91] Merker's view prevailed within the party.

While the reestablished *Weltbühne* under Leonhard prospered in the second half of the 1940s, sometimes reaching a circulation of over one hundred thousand copies, Budzislawski, the supposed legal owner—who obviously also regarded himself as the best possible editor in chief—stood on the sidelines. In confidential discussions with leading comrades, he complained that he was

Poster advertising a meeting organized by the Leipzig SED at which Hermann Budzislawski was the main speaker, 17 September 1959. His hostile attitude toward William S. Schlamm, Budzislawski's predecessor as editor in chief of *Die neue Weltbühne*, promised to bring political dividends during the Cold War.

being ignored in postwar Germany, and he insisted on his right of ownership over the periodical, whose publication had been prohibited at the beginning of September 1939. But he also gave the impression that he was ready to compromise: "After all, I am not a person who makes too many difficulties. On the other hand, I do believe that I deserve some recognition for my long period of work and that I am entitled to receive compensation."[92] The SED leadership did not respond to this indirect offer to negotiate. In the next few years, instead of rising to be one of the most important opinion makers in the GDR, Budzislawski, by the wish of those at the top of the party, became one of the political professors whose job it was to reconstruct the university environment on Socialist lines. Even though the political transformation was not supposed to endanger "standards," the loss of intellectual substance had been considerable, recalled the philosopher Hans-Georg Gadamer, who was the rector of the University of Leipzig from 1946 to 1947. As "citizens who owed allegiance to both the party and the subject," the new professors had to be able to demonstrate, in addition to their academic qualifications, a credible commitment to Socialism and—ideally—to show that they possessed moral integrity.[93] Budzislawski could lay claim to the last-mentioned quality because of his long period of enforced exile. His party assignment for the coming years was to produce ideologically reliable and professionally competent journalists for the good of the cause.

The Invention of Socialist Journalism

Budzislawski as University Professor in Leipzig

I N THE LATE 1940s the University of Leipzig was a place full of contradictions. Apart from the old scholars from the Nazi period who had kept their jobs and who were described as the "bourgeois" in the jargon of the new era, the teaching staff included at least three other groups: the returned emigrants from the West; the returned emigrants from the East; and finally the "internal emigrants," in other words, people who had spent the war years in Germany but had not supported the dictatorship of the National Socialists and who now hoped for better times. Because of the need to find qualified scientists with an emphatically left-wing profile, which would enable the university to drive forward the political transformation that was planned, invitations were liberally issued to politically acceptable individuals even if they were not necessarily academically qualified.[1] In view of the shortage of appropriate candidates, Fritz Behrens, the associate dean of the Faculty of Social Sciences (the Gewifak), which was reestablished in 1947, is alleged to have exclaimed at one committee meeting: "There's only one thing to do. We have to bring in a bunch of Jewish emigrants from America!"[2] And they came: in addition to Budzislawski, the philosopher and veteran *Weltbühne* collaborator Ernst Bloch, the physician Felix Boenheim, the jurist Henryk Grossmann, and the publisher Wieland Herzfelde all obtained teaching positions at the university, and the jurist and literary historian Hans Mayer arrived from Switzerland.

Decades later, the historian Walter Markov still remembered the extraordinary mixture of left-wing intellectuals who taught in Leipzig until the mid-1950s as a result of this appointment policy: "Almost every one of them claimed to be a person of significance and to possess a fully formed worldview." But the making of actual university policy, Markov went on to say, had been handed over to people from the "second team."[3] This would soon prove to have been a mistake, because it was the members of this second group, the careerists with

political party ties, who only a few years later held the real power in the institution and made everyday life intolerable for the intellectual leaders who were
often self-absorbed and not always very pragmatic. This is how Hans Mayer, a
representative of what one might call the "first team," summarized the atmosphere in memoirs he published later in the Federal Republic: "It was a time
when foundations were laid, but there was also a lot of quarrelling, doctrinaire
verbiage, and interventions by know-all Russian ideologists whose views were
usually quickly echoed, only a few days later, by German Communists who
zealously supported the pure doctrine of Marxism-Leninism."[4]

For Budzislawski, the remigrant from the West, the promising fresh start in
Leipzig ran into difficulties during the first year after his return. In the GDR,
too, the repressive course of the Stalin era led to internal reviews and "purges,"
which were coordinated by the newly established Central Party Control Commission, directed by Hermann Matern.[5] Budzislawski was again triply threatened, this time as a remigrant from the West, a former leftist Social Democrat,
and a Jew. The SED had, it is true, officially inscribed on its banners that the
"Jewish question" would be abolished. The party's leading elements were of
the view that there could no longer be any place for antisemitic prejudices in
a genuinely Socialist society. In addition, in the late 1940s the party had campaigned in favor of compensating Jews who had been persecuted under the
Nazi dictatorship both symbolically and materially. Yet the group of potential
beneficiaries was largely restricted to Jewish Communists and Socialists, as the
SED leadership rejected claims for reparation to be provided to all Jews persecuted for "racial" reasons.[6] The party purges in the GDR around 1950 had a
definite antisemitic component, although this was not so pronounced as in
some of the neighboring Socialist countries. People who had returned from
exile in the West were now faced with accusations such as participation in
"Trotskyist" deviations within the party and possible collaboration with the
US Secret Service. Returned exiles who were Jewish could also be charged with
support for Zionism.[7]

Critical questions had already been raised about Budzislawski's political activities in exile even before his return to Germany. Thus Willi Bredel, a returned emigrant from the East, reacted in September 1947 to the ongoing
negotiations between the party and Budzislawski over his return by remarking
sarcastically that he was "now evidently making another attempt to get into
paradise" after his "misstep at the start of the war"—a reference to Budzislawski's criticism of the Hitler-Stalin Pact in 1939. However, bearing in mind
the overall situation, particularly the fact that the universities continued to
be dominated by bourgeois professors, it was not advisable to continue bearing a grudge against him "until the Last Judgement." It would be "ten times

better" to employ Budzislawski than to keep "a university professor who had only recently changed his political colors from German nationalist to SED member."[8]

This pragmatic attitude was initially the majority view at the top of the SED, and it was the reason why Budzislawski had been invited to take up the chair in international press studies. Paul Merker, who had returned to Germany from Mexico, campaigned particularly strongly among the top functionaries of the SED in favor of Budzislawski, whom he had got to know when they were both in exile in France at the end of the 1930s.[9] In the university's Faculty of Social Sciences, they also looked forward impatiently to the arrival of such an experienced journalist. Budzislawski was "more suitable as a professor than anyone else" owing to his "wide-ranging knowledge and experience gathered in most of the countries of Europe and the United States," they claimed.[10] He took up his new appointment in October 1948. A few weeks later, on 23 November, he was admitted to the SED. A year after that, he became a citizen of the GDR.

Budzislawski quickly conformed to the new power relationships. On Stalin's seventieth birthday, 21 December 1949 and thus only a year after Budzislawski's return from America, the former critic joined in with the chorus of the Soviet leader's apologists. In his speech on the theme "Why are we celebrating Stalin?" he also indicated the kind of criticism against which he had to argue publicly at that time. Ultimately, he said, it was only the adoption of a Marxist analysis of the inevitable course of historical development that made it possible for him as a German patriot to present a statesman belonging to one of the victorious powers as a model worthy of admiration and a driving force of history. According to the manuscript for the speech, which was not written out in detail but has come down to us as a series of bullet points, he replied as follows to the rhetorical question as to whether in celebrating Stalin in Germany they were not celebrating a "conqueror":

Did not conquer us, because we are not Fascism. We are not capitalism. We are the people of a new era that is emerging, and Stalin has conquered for us. We have conquered with him, we see in him the man who has prepared the way for us. He embodies the experience we need. . . . When we celebrate Stalin we are not sucking up to the statesman of the occupying power, but: our brain. Our lodestar through a difficult time. Not always understood. Because Stalin was in charge of Soviet domestic policy, and our problems were different for a long time. But today we are catching up. We are learning. . . . Illumination. Stalin is a Russian statesman, of course. He should be celebrated if he was nothing more. . . . But he is more: symbol of world history. Hence also of our own development.[11]

In the early GDR, eulogies of this kind for the Soviet leader were obligatory exercises for SED functionaries and for career-conscious academics, yet many people performed them rather reluctantly. Victor Klemperer, professor of Romance languages, noted in October 1949 in his diary that one could hardly fail to notice that fewer than half of the GDR's inhabitants were "really Russophile and really Communist."[12] His diary entries during that period reveal his deep skepticism and disenchantment in regard to the new start in the Soviet occupation zone, soon to become the GDR. It was clear to him, he wrote, that "the democratic republic has a lie at its heart. . . . I know that things sounded exactly the same, and went the same way, under the Nazis. I know how little it means in reality."[13] There is no record of any similar expressions of doubt by Budzislawski, although this does not necessarily mean that he saw things differently from Klemperer. His eulogy of Stalin, however, went beyond what was strictly required by the party, which suggests that as a German Jewish emigrant returned from the West he felt it was particularly necessary to present himself as a comrade who was true to the party line. As early as the beginning of the 1950s, the Polish poet Czesław Miłosz gave a trenchant description of the inner contradictions Eastern European intellectuals within Stalin's sphere of influence had to cope with. He observed that many of those who would have been entirely in favor of the revolution and the new, supposedly fairer economic system struggled inwardly with the fact that they had to "submit" to a nation that "could not even rule itself and had known neither happiness nor freedom however far one looked into the past." This is how the Eastern European intellectual thinks, he says, "even as he pronounces a speech about the 'supreme honor' of being able to live in the 'great Stalinist epoch.' His function, as he defiantly calls it, is to 'inoculate' others with the 'basic principles of enthusiasm.'"[14]

According to Budzislawski's public statements of the time, West Germany had become an insignificant appendage of Western imperialism after the Second World War, whereas the GDR deserved praise for participating in the "peace front" created by the Soviet Union, a front that would stretch from the Pacific Ocean to the Elbe River and include the anticolonialist freedom fighters of Africa and Asia.[15] As he said in a speech made on 11 March 1949 to representatives of the Leipzig cultural scene, he hoped for a peace treaty that would cover all four occupation zones, because otherwise "at least the western half of our homeland" would sink "to the level of a colony." The imperialists would "prevent West Germany from entering the world market, just as previously India and China had been prevented from developing their industries."[16] To judge by his public interventions, he regarded the rapid and extensive economic integration into the capitalist world economy of the western occupation zones and later the Federal Republic as out of the question or at least extremely unlikely.

Budzislawski's speeches on the radio and at mass demonstrations did not deal exclusively with the Soviet Union and Germany's current political problems. He also discussed prospects for the United States, his former host country. As a veteran New York journalist, he was one of the GDR's best-informed experts on American politics.[17] Many East Germans were very interested in the United States and its people, not least because of the constant increase in American propaganda in the western occupation zones of the country. Budzislawski's "eye-witness reports" on the United States were as knowledgeable as they were one-sided, and they were not free of Eurocentric arrogance. "Excessively harsh, but always interesting" was the verdict of Klemperer, who regularly listened to Budzislawski on the radio.[18] Budzislawski candidly admitted that things had not gone too badly for him in America: "My family had plenty to eat, and we were well clothed. We had decent accommodation. But there was also a lot of luck involved." Outside Manhattan he had seen a great deal of poverty in New York and other big cities: "The houses are low when you enter, the wooden stairs are rotten, and the rooms are overcrowded and bug-ridden. They swarm with all kinds of vermin." The slums of New York, Baltimore, Boston, and Chicago were "indescribable" and worse than anything to be seen in the port districts of Europe.[19] Assessments of this kind recall Budzislawski the Socialist eugenicist of the early 1920s and perhaps also the young eccentric with a doctorate who claimed to have hung around the bars and brothels of St. Pauli in Hamburg for a while in 1923.

In view of the widespread poverty in the United States, it was of course necessary to explain why the organized workers' movement was of such modest dimensions there. In Budzislawski's interpretation, this was above all a result of the American workers' lack of "any deeper insight into the mechanisms of the capitalist economy." In America, Budzislawski said, even the Socialists proceeded on the assumption that all that was needed "in order to guarantee a crisis-free and prosperous economy to the end of time" was the removal of some of the "excesses" of capitalism. In fact, he also included the American Communists in his criticism:

This small party, the whole of whose leadership now stands before a court, on the ridiculous charge of preparing the violent overthrow of the government, was not even capable of sustaining the publication of its weekly periodical, *New*

Masses, and even the *Daily Worker* constantly has to fight with financial difficulties. . . . Only a few years ago, the party underwent a severe and extremely characteristic crisis. Its previous leader, Earl Browder, went so far during the war as to throw the whole of Marxism overboard and to try to conduct a policy of domestic political cooperation with big capital. . . . The objective was not a bad one, but the price he was ready to pay was ridiculously high, namely, complete self-abandonment.[20]

This criticism of an actually existing Communist Party was clearly sharper in tone than the SED wanted to hear. The comments just quoted were struck out of the manuscript of the speech. What Budzislawski evidently could say and was expected to say is written there in his own hand, although it is not clear whether he or someone else was the censor: "The Communists are courageous and will play their part. At present they are repressed—the leaders under arrest, the party half illegal."[21]

Despite these efforts to adjust, it was clear only twelve months after his return from the United States that Budzislawski had overstepped the mark with his self-confident demeanor. Albert Schreiner wrote in November 1949 to the SED Central Committee to say that he had unfortunately been too optimistic when he had evaluated the newcomer positively. Budzislawski had given a negative impression in Leipzig owing to his "political pushiness" and his pronounced "craving for material benefits." He would do better to concentrate on his actual work of university teaching. "His academic title was an advance payment, not a free ticket to an undeserved political career."[22] Unluckily for Budzislawski, he also wrote to the party at the very same time to ask for a motor car because he was currently overloaded with work. If necessary, he was prepared to pay for the vehicle. The pace of life in his new sphere of activity was slow in comparison with the bustling activity of the metropolis of New York, he commented sarcastically: "In Leipzig I use the tram, and I spend my time waiting for it to arrive." Later on, he could at least make use of the motor pool of the *Leipziger Volkszeitung*.[23] It was true that the new university professor was on a tight schedule. He had been appointed director of the Institute of Journalism and Newspaper Studies, set up in 1949, as well as administrator of the university archives, and he immediately made detailed proposals for restructuring his special field, which he wanted to promote from being a marginal area within the Faculty of Social Sciences to an independent study pathway.[24] To achieve this, he wanted the teaching of the foundations of Marxism to be cut back in favor of subjects genuinely related to journalism. Greater attention was to be paid to "problems of contemporary cultural politics," and students should study one or, even better, two foreign languages. This program, which was recognizably based on his own life experience, could be summarized as less of Marx and Lenin and more of Budzislawski. The goal was "the education of better-trained press cadres" whose expertise should not be limited to the capacity to "pick up *Pravda* every day and find out from it how we should do things."[25] This was a clear sideswipe at the glorification of the Soviet Union that was prevalent at the University of Leipzig and particularly at its Gewifak. In addition to his university tasks, Budzislawski was also vice-chairman of the "liberal-Communist" League of Culture in the provisional Volkskammer, the East German parliament, and he remained a regular commentator on Central German Radio.[26] On top of that, there were public lectures and party work for the SED. He claimed in a letter that he spoke over the course of only one week in November 1949 in the following places: at the ball-bearing factory in Böhlitz, at the steelworks in Riesa, in the Hall of Culture in Leipzig "in front of ten thousand people," and in the Leipzig League of Culture, as well as in the Volkskammer and at party conferences in Berlin.[27] And he made an appearance at least once as a master of ceremonies at a festive evening organized by the Probstheida SED on 18 March 1949 under the title "We're Going to America," for which the prominent African American singer, actor, and civil rights campaigner Paul Robeson provided part of the musical accompaniment.[28]

In the summer of 1950 the cadre section of the SED Leipzig District Leadership pronounced a devastating verdict on the party's new entrant from the United States. Budzislawski, they said, was an egoist who in all his proceedings acted according to the motto "How do I get what is due to me as an individual?" Although he was an excellent speaker, he could not be counted a "scientific worker" and would in general be regarded as a "Bussines-Mann [*sic*]." He may have been personally accepted into the party by Otto Grotewohl, the first prime minister of the GDR, and Wilhelm Pieck, its first and only president, but caution had to be exercised in his case because he had chosen to immigrate to the United States.[29] Jealousy toward the "American" who had rapidly achieved prosperity played an important role in this negative "appraisal" at the local level. An additional factor—as a group of student devotees of the party line complained—was that there was still no trace of any Socialist education at the university: "Admittedly, many professors assert that they are Marxists, and themselves believe this to be the case, but there is little evidence of it in their lectures and academic work." Hans Mayer, Ernst Bloch, and Wieland Herzfelde were mentioned by name in this complaint. Herzfelde had eked out his existence in New York for some time as a stamp dealer before he was invited to Leipzig, but now he presented himself as a distinguished professor of literature, although he had not created a strong presence at the university.[30]

There is no doubt that these remarks were also meant to apply to Budzislawski, who was not mentioned explicitly, however.

It was probably no accident that all those mentioned were former Jewish exiles and *Bildungsbürger*, or members of the educated middle class.[31] There is some indication that Budzislawski believed he was under particular observation not only as a returner from the West but also as a Jew. In 1950, in one of the numerous questionnaires and résumés he had to submit to the SED in reply to the accusations mounted against him, he described himself for the first time as being "without religious affiliation," adding after that the words "previously Jewish."[32] This act of dissociation appears to have been a tactical move to minimize his vulnerability to attack by opponents within the party, because in both earlier and later times he always entered the word "Jewish" in this column. An ostensible commitment to the "Jewish nationality" could easily be interpreted and sanctioned by orthodox SED members as showing "a lack of ideological clarity."[33]

In August 1950 the Central Committee of the SED, together with the newly founded Central Party Control Commission, charged eleven high-ranking SED functionaries for collaborating with imperialist (i.e., Western) secret services. Four of the accused were of Jewish origin.[34] A few days later, on 24 August 1950, the SED leadership of the University of Leipzig called on Budzislawski to take a public position on this declaration. Investigations began right across the country, and they all followed a similar pattern. For Budzislawski this meant a hearing in the university and an internal party investigation. He had to engage in public self-criticism, and he did this in front of the SED Operations Group of the Gewifak on 18 October 1950 by making a speech on the "connection of SED functionaries with American agents."[35]

According to records that have been preserved in the Budzislawski papers, he conceded on that day that he had shown "ideological weaknesses," but he emphasized that he had "behaved properly, relatively speaking," in practical life. He had never taken a position against the Soviet Union, except for one "moment of faintheartedness"—an allusion to his criticism of the Hitler-Stalin Pact in the final edition of *Die neue Weltbühne* in August 1939. Germans who immigrated to the Soviet Union, he asserted against his better knowledge, had possessed an "unlimited advantage" over their counterparts in the West because they "were in pure, germ-free air. Even so, they still had crises of purification associated with the cleansing of the CPSU [Communist Party of the Soviet Union]."[36] Thus the thousands of German emigrants executed in the Soviet Union within the framework of the People's Commissariat for Internal Affairs' "German operation" of 1937 and 1938, including the former editor in chief of the main Communist Party newspaper, *Die rote Fahne*, Hans

Neumann, and the lawyer Felix Halle, were described in Budzislawski's self-criticism as bacteria that had allegedly contaminated the pure air of Soviet society.[37] On the other hand, the exiles who had returned from Western Europe and America to Germany had "never been cleansed" and had therefore introduced deposits of "petty-bourgeois slag" into the country. In many cases, they were interested in acquiring material benefits and possessed by "unrestrained ambition"; at best, they were "sentimental Socialists."[38]

Budzislawski also used a medical metaphor when he replied to the rhetorical question of how he and other returned emigrants viewed their former host countries in the West: "Sometimes infection can be deep-rooted. Many people felt fine over there: they found new homes, and they spewed out counterpropaganda. Why? Because they were petty bourgeois who did not look behind the scenes. . . . They did not perceive the essence of imperialism. They did not see what there was behind sham democracy, and they believed in the deceptive rules of the game of pure democracy. Here they miss the stimulants abundantly available over there: a variety of n[ew]sp[apers], appalling films, the scent of a decaying society. We need to argue with them. They are not simply agents but elements of our prol[etarian]-revolut[ionary] party who are, first, vulnerable and, second, questionable."[39] Was that also self-criticism? Budzislawski deliberately left this undecided. A back door was kept open, as usual. His speech was not only a self-criticism in formal terms but also a piece of self-promotion, as he pretended that he had understood the weaknesses of the other Western exiles at an early stage.

The Budzislawski archive contains a written statement, preserved in an incomplete form, that he sent to a party functionary some days after his speech at the University of Leipzig. In this statement he made it clear that although he was ready to perform the public act of repentance required of him by his party, he rejected the points made against him, and above all he disliked the tone of this ritual: "This criticism treats me as a suspicious person or a questionable comrade. It is the kind of criticism that is likely to ruin me personally and materially. For two weeks I have been practically incapable of working, and the burden of these accusations makes me feel unable to appear as a radio commentator, a public speaker, or a university lecturer. Because why should other people listen to a man who consciously or unconsciously defends the worst parasites on the working class?"[40] In view of the situation, the tone of these remarks was very self-confident. He regarded the self-criticism he had to undertake as an imposition resulting from the circumstances of the era and an attack on him as an individual. He was, it is true, under considerable pressure in Leipzig, but he felt somewhat protected because of his political networks in

East Berlin, which in his case reached to the very highest level, including Grotewohl and Pieck.[41]

Budzislawski was nevertheless banned from teaching from November 1950 onward. The marginalization he suffered went beyond the purely professional arena. His wife was excluded from the party's housing group evenings, and shortly afterward she was recruited as an informant by the Ministry of State Security, known as the Stasi, under the cover name Gretl.[42] The isolation of the two returned emigrants, who had only recently come to live in the city, was increased by their social exclusion. The prominent new party member from the United States was severely taken to task by the party leadership of the University of Leipzig SED branch in a meeting chaired by its secretary, Hans-Joachim Böhme. After a "discussion" that took place in January 1951, the party committee put it on record that Budzislawski was deficient in class consciousness. He had displayed an arrogant nature, "although he maintains that he has always been an inhibited person." It could not be said of him that he was attached to the party.[43] Even so, the committee wanted to avoid a wholesale condemnation of this man, who was a particularly talented journalist: "From the moral point of view, we know of nothing detrimental to Com[rade] Budzislawski."[44] The newly appointed professor, who promised to learn Russian and said he was ready to attend the party school, was reinstated as a candidate member of the SED at the end of January 1951.

The Institute of Journalism and Newspaper Studies, the setting up of which had been suggested by Budzislawski, was officially founded on 1 December 1950. A certain Dr. Eduard Schulz was initially appointed to head it.[45] The background to this decision is highly obscure, but it soon turned out, for various reasons, that the SED had made a serious error. Budzislawski himself gave a summary of the story in July 1951: Schulz was "a third-rate journalist without any theoretical training in the art of journalism, and apart from that—I mean this literally—he was a common criminal who was subsequently dismissed without notice from the university for rape, sadistic violence against his housemaid, and complete moral degradation, after which he made his way to West Berlin as a political refugee."[46] In stark contrast to Schulz, the former editor in chief portrayed himself as a competent and "clean" alternative candidate, and he pressed the top people in the party to make a quick change in his status. He sent personal letters appealing to Wilhelm Pieck, to Walter Ulbricht, and to Gerhard Harig, who was the state secretary for university education. Budzislawski reaffirmed his commitment to the party, but he pointed out that it was simply impossible "to achieve anything in the university in a vacuum."[47] At the beginning of July 1951, he was once again investigated by a special commission of the Central Committee. He dutifully put it on record that he had benefited from the party's criticism in the last few months, but this criticism had not always been "of the right kind." One comrade (Häusler) had given him a real dressing down; his criticism had left Budzislawski dumbfounded.[48] Two colleagues who had also returned from emigration—Ernst Bloch and Wieland Herzfelde—put in a word for Budzislawski and his wife behind the scenes in Leipzig, describing them as "upright anti-Fascists" whose reliability had been proven, if one looked at their years of emigration.[49] Herzfelde was to receive no thanks for his intercession, however, as only a few years later Budzislawski helped to roughly push him out of the university because his old companion had failed despite repeated invitations "to participate socially within the context of our faculty." Solidarity between the returned emigrants was at most temporary, even among those who had regarded themselves as having been joined in a community of fate when in exile. In the early GDR, Stalinism finally broke many people's moral backbone; it weighed on that generation like a nightmare from which they were unable to free themselves.[50]

In the summer of 1951 Budzislawski's supplications to the powerful were finally crowned with success. Wilhelm Pieck informed him by letter on 26 July 1951 that a decision had been reached about his future work: "I hope that this will finally resolve to your satisfaction the vexatious situation you have been in until now."[51] Despite this, matters continued to drag on. Budzislawski was soon "deeply depressed" again. Indeed, he even suggested to the SED in October 1951 that he should be removed from the area of journalism and appointed to the Faculty of Modern History. He had discussed this idea earlier with Leo Stern, the German Jewish historian who had returned from Moscow to an appointment at the Martin Luther University in Halle, but to put this idea into effect would also have meant leaving Leipzig.[52] Finally, in November 1951, the state secretary for university and vocational education instructed the University of Leipzig to include Budzislawski in the Institute of Journalism and Newspaper Studies, which was now headed by Wilhelm Eildermann, a dogmatic Communist. The two men were very different in character but united by a heartfelt, though subdued, feeling of mutual antipathy. Things were not made easier by the fact that in 1954 it was Budzislawski and not the previous director, Eildermann, who was entrusted with running the Faculty of Journalism, which had been established at a solemn ceremony on 20 September of that year. Budzislawski's former assistant and successor as dean, Franz Knipping, recalled an incident in 1955 that apart from being a charming anecdote also illustrates the conflict between two cultures in the faculty. When Budzislawski was awarded the Franz Mehring Medal of the Association of Journalists, Eildermann pinned on his Patriotic Order of Merit and congratulated his competitor by saying that his own decoration carried greater weight. Budzis-lawski wittily replied: "The difference is this: you were decorated as a good patriot, and I was decorated as a good journalist."[53]

From the winter semester of 1952–53 onward, Budzislawski was again allowed to give lectures at the University of Leipzig. He started his course with an overview of the history of the press in the Weimar Republic and in "foreign capitalist countries." The year before, the Budzislawski couple had translated *Power without Glory*, a novel by the young Australian writer Frank Hardy, who had taken part in the World Festival of Youth and Students held in Berlin in 1951; Budzislawski eulogized the book as an act of anti-imperialist enlighten-ment in a thank-you letter sent to Wilhelm Pieck: "Using the example of Australia, this novel displays the rottenness of decaying capitalism, the corrup-tion in the Labor Party, and the collaboration between big capitalists, political 'machines,' and criminal gangs. The similarity with American conditions is strikingly evident." The Western emigrant Budzislawski insured himself against attacks by cursing the country in which he had formerly taken refuge and reinterpreting the occupations he had taken up out of necessity during his isolation from politics as an active contribution to the political struggle. He closed his letter to Pieck with "deep admiration and gratitude" as well as "with socialist greetings."[54]

A few weeks later it became evident that there were very good reasons for taking this obsequious stance. The Soviet party leadership began to orches-trate the so-called Doctors' Plot: hundreds of mainly Jewish physicians were arrested and deported to prison camps, and some of them were executed.[55] A circle of alleged antistate conspirators was also unmasked in Prague. The accu-sations in this case centered around the former general secretary of the Com-munist Party of Czechoslovakia, Rudolf Slánský. Eleven of the fourteen accused were condemned to death on 27 November 1952 on a charge of Trotskyist-Zionist conspiracy. They were executed on 3 December. One of the victims was Otto Katz, a Jew and a former Western emigrant whom Budzis-lawski had known when they were together in Prague in the 1930s and whom he had perhaps also met when they were both in exile in New York.[56] Eleven of the fourteen defendants were of Jewish origin. As it had to be expected that similar show trials would also take place in the GDR, alarm bells rang loudly for Budzislawski and all the other Jewish emigrants who had returned from the West. On 20 December the Central Committee of the SED specified "the lessons to be learned from the trial of Slánský and his conspiratorial center." Leading returned Western emigrants associated with Paul Merker, Budzis-lawski's earlier champion, had wanted to act as Slánský's extended arm by mounting a conspiracy against Communism in the GDR, the party now claimed. Moreover, Merker was said to be a "Zionist" who supported Israel and had called for Jews persecuted by the National Socialists to receive reparations.[57] The Leipzig District Leadership of the SED responded to these instructions by resolving on 8 January 1953 that in Leipzig, too, a large number of party members should be investigated for their alleged deviations from the party line during the period of exile.

Budzislawski was one of approximately a hundred Leipzig Jews affected by these measures, but things were prevented from getting any worse by Stalin's death, which occurred a few weeks later on 5 March 1953. Three days before, Hanna Budzislawski had commented in a letter to a friend, the writer and associate of Brecht Elisabeth Hauptmann, that it was at present difficult to write any letters at all: "Some people are finding it hard to maintain their mental balance. It is a depressing and unpleasant time."[58] Alfred Kantorowicz was more explicit in his diary, published in the late 1970s in the Federal Republic. He found the parallel with National Socialism impossible to ignore: "This is the language of Streicher, the mentality of Himmler, and the atmosphere of Gestapo interrogations and proceedings in the People's Court of Justice."[59]

Hermann Budzislawski fell into line with the new requirements. In February 1953 he made a public statement at the university condemning the alleged conspiratorial center around Paul Merker. He now reviled the man who had previously championed him, referring to him as "agent Merker." By calling for reparations to be paid to all persecuted Jews, "including the thieves," Merker had shown a gross disregard for the class aspect, and—consciously or unconsciously—he had played into the hands of the Zionists and the antisemites. Budzislawski, who had been able to get from Lisbon to New York in 1940 with the help of the Jewish aid organization HICEM, now claimed that Jewish organizations active in the GDR and Eastern Europe were gateways for the entry of Western agents and were ultimately acting as the extended arm of American monopoly capitalist interests.[60] In the hope of avoiding the line of fire, therefore, Budzislawski contributed in part to the anti-imperialist and sometimes antisemitic campaign that was raging at that time in the GDR.

The insecurity and anxiety felt by the country's Jews were reflected in the Leipzig Jewish community: it had been 300 strong in 1950, but three years later numbers were down to 173. Dozens of Jews had fled to the West.[61] This was not an option for the Budzislawskis. A letter from Hanna to her friend Horst Baehrensprung from around this time makes it clear that her situation, as well as her husband's, had already improved substantially: "Seen from within, we continue to live very peacefully in our beautiful house, which you are familiar with. The Biedermeier furniture has been replaced by Baroque in the meantime, and the impression aroused by the whole thing is as if piece after piece has been collected through many generations until it has reached its present perfection. This is how we deceive the outside world. . . . Hermann has his old job at the university, and he is 'on air' regularly every Thursday."[62] They were becoming older and calmer, she remarked in the same letter. But she ascribed this contrast not primarily to the insecurity of their earlier years but to a completely different, innocuous reason: "Beate has been happily married for over a year now, and married daughters make parents more mature. One day, probably in the summer of 1950, she suddenly informed us, in an entirely friendly manner, that she had finally become intellectually independent and that it was not acceptable to keep on taking on opinions from one's parents. She moved to Berlin, became a student, and six months later she got married."[63]

The Budzislawskis' son-in-law was Horst Eckert, a "working-class student" of German literature born on 19 June 1925 in Berlin-Charlottenburg. He had completed an apprenticeship in technical drawing, and he had joined the KPD in August 1945 after two years of military service in the Wehrmacht and a short period as a prisoner of war in Britain. His nonbourgeois origin meant that he had good career chances in the GDR. After spending the academic year 1947–48 at an institute for preliminary studies in Berlin, he was admitted to Humboldt University Berlin for the winter semester of 1948–49. It was there that the young couple got to know each other, and after a few months they got married, on 18 November 1950. For Hermann and Hanna this was a surprising but welcome occurrence and a further indication of their successful integration into the GDR. Their son-in-law's fundamental political convictions also fitted in well with those of the family, as Hanna emphasized in the spring of 1952: "There have been many journeys between Berlin and Leipzig in the meantime, and intellectual dependence has been transformed into intellectual agreement. We are very satisfied with both of them, especially as Horst has been accustomed to political matters ever since childhood—you know what monomaniacs we are—and his convictions, based on his knowledge, coincide completely with ours."[64]

In the years that followed, Horst Eckert's professional activities, like his father-in-law's, oscillated between the university, journalism, and the role of a party functionary. His career included spells in the SED Central Committee, in the GDR Writers' Union, at the *Berliner Zeitung*, and, from 1966 onward, in Humboldt University's Aesthetics and Art Studies Department.[65] In the doctoral dissertation he defended in 1962 he analyzed articles by German writers that had appeared in *Die neue Weltbühne* between 1934 and 1939. The dissertation was a family affair, as Horst's father-in-law played an essential role in its construction. He contributed background pieces of information that were known to him alone, and in addition he used his son-in-law's dissertation to present the line he had pursued during the 1930s in *Die neue Weltbühne* as having been in perfect harmony with the policies of the KPD in exile and in this way to recommend himself to the SED Central Committee once more as a reliable Communist. Budzislawski's daughter, Beate Eckert, worked as an editor for GDR television after completing her studies. The Budzislawskis could now be described as a two-generation family of journalists with a strong attachment to the party and excellent personal connections to leading politicians.

After Stalin's death and the end of the paranoid search for deviationists within the Communist Parties of Eastern Europe, Hermann Budzislawski was finally fully rehabilitated in the GDR. In the following years, his career advanced at a rapid pace. In May 1954 he took part as a delegate in the congress of the National Front held in Berlin, and between 1955 and 1958 he was on the presidium of the German Press Association, later called the GDR Association of Journalists. He also chaired the Club of Cultural Workers in Berlin and until 1967 the German-Polish Friendship Society.[66] The opening in the autumn of 1954 of the Faculty of Journalism at the University of Leipzig, which was officially described as Karl Marx University after 5 May 1953, finally paved the way to a career in scholarship and research administration for Budzislawski.[67] As dean of the faculty, who was by virtue of his office also a member of the SED leadership, and as director of the Institute for the History of the Press, Budzislawski was in a key position to promote the training of journalists in the next decade. He now had the power—in coordination with the Agitation and Propaganda Department of the SED Central Committee—to develop and remodel the faculty in line with his own ideas, and he was able to set priorities in terms of both personnel and content.

Much of the teaching at the University of Leipzig was devoted to examining the history of the German and the international press and deriving lessons for the future. The aim was to understand the tactics of the capitalist opponent and to improve the performance of one's own mass media while maintaining strict adherence to the party line. This is how Budzislawski summarized his track record in February 1966, in the best language of a party functionary, on the occasion at which he was awarded an honorary doctorate: "We have a doctrine that permits the deliberate expansion of the role of the press, the radio, the television, and the news agency as instruments of progress, as weapons in the proletarian class struggle. . . . We have brought together the principles of a press of a new type and linked these with the progressive elements of the past, also making systematic improvements to the style using scientific methods."[68]

The new faculty was housed in a complex consisting of three villas covering Tieckstraße 2, 4, and 6, at the edge of the Scheibenholz racecourse, about one mile south of the city center. It soon acquired the nickname "Red monastery" because it was constantly "bathed in Red light" and perhaps because of the red color of the porphyry masonry from Rochlitz that had been used to build the villas. The teaching rooms and the living accommodations were only a stone's throw away from each other. The intention was to produce a new generation of Socialist journalists there using not only lectures and seminars but also convivial gatherings in the living areas as well as walking tours and excursions.[69] The hardliners of the SED strove to "eradicate" from student consciousness "everything that was bourgeois or petty bourgeois."[70] Until the building of the Berlin Wall in 1961, however, this was only partially successful. The party's influence in almost every sphere of life did increase, but it still had to compete with other opinions and attitudes, not least because the border between the two Germanys was not yet hermetically sealed, and it was easy to reach West Berlin from Leipzig on weekends. In the city of Leipzig itself there were still places such as the Kaffee Schmalfuß in Katherinenstraße, where student nonconformists from the Faculty of Journalism came and went and—to use the words of the Stasi—met "homosexuals, ruined characters of all kinds, and numerous individuals who are infected in every respect by Western decadence."[71] Some of the students of journalism at the university even publicly condemned the GDR's official recommendations on how to describe the military suppression of the Hungarian popular uprising of November 1956 as "a whitewash," and they described the speaker from the Free German Youth who followed these recommendations as an "opinion manufacturer."[72]

In the 1950s the GDR's professorial body was by no means united over whether the education of journalists should be primarily determined by the need to influence the masses or by the orthodox teaching of Marxism-Leninism.[73] One of the advocates of a rigid party-directed course was Basil Spiru, who had been summoned to Leipzig in the autumn of 1954 from the Lomonosov University in Moscow. Spiru's original name was Josef Hutschnecker. He was born in 1898 in the town of Luzan (now Luzhany), not far from Czernowitz (now Chernivtsi) in North Bukovina, which belonged to the Habsburg Empire at that time. He took part in the short-lived Hungarian Soviet Republic under Béla Kun in the spring of 1919 and subsequently helped to found the Communist Party of Romania. After studying law in Vienna under Hans Kelsen, he began a doctorate on the theme "Problems of Modern Parliamentarism," which by his own account he was unable to finish because he was suspended from the university and expelled from Austria. He then worked in the Soviet Union for more than two decades.[74] Soon after his arrival

The complex of buildings in the Tieckstraße, Leipzig, housing the Faculty of Journalism, 1954.

in Leipzig, Spiru complained that the course of study there had not produced the aspired-for "educational impact" because the "presentation of Marxism" was being done dogmatically and was insufficiently linked with "party life and party resolutions."[75] The strength of the GDR press, he added, consisted precisely in the fact that "it was always and in all respects subject to the party's direction."[76] The task of "progressive journalism" was not, as it was in the subjectivist, interpretative bourgeois press, to entertain but "to find the truth and make it socially effective."[77]

Spiru's idea of truth was inseparably connected with the Marxist narrative of progress and historical determinism; something could only be true if it conformed with this fundamental assumption. Or, in a reversal of Marx's dictum, consciousness had to determine the being that journalism needed to address. Budzislawski regarded that as nonsense. The citizens of the GDR could not be inspired with enthusiasm for their own cause by a journalism that merely printed proclamations and party resolutions. His advice was: "Think of the readers; they ought to be able to enjoy what they read, even if they might be able to learn something in the process!"[78] He reacted to criticism of his work with acute sensitivity, particularly when it was made by party hacks using doctrinaire arguments. Budzislawski advocated a comparatively liberal course of studies that would leave no doubt about the need to adhere to the party line but would still make the GDR's mass media so interesting that in the ideological competition of the Cold War they might stimulate an enthusiastic response even beyond the country's borders. The main emphasis in training the journalists of Leipzig should therefore be laid on the "acquisition of practical abilities."[79]

Every year a good 350 young men and women entered the course as "direct students," and in addition more than 200 "distance students" received tuition while still being in employment. Even at the start only roughly a third of them had a middle-class parental background; approximately every second student was a member of the SED.[80] The students liked the sophisticated and amusing Budzislawski, even if they noticed that he was not a man given to precise and scientific reasoning. One of his early students, the American Communist Victor Grossman, remembered "Budzi" as a "nervous lecturer" who walked up and down in the lecture theater, often cleared his throat, and constantly removed and replaced his spectacles while he was lecturing. Despite this, he knew how to hold his audience's attention: "I learned a great deal about German history from his lectures on the German press."[81] Ingeborg Schmidt, another former student, said that, unlike other lecturers, Budzislawski was thoroughly respected. Many students knew of him from his radio broadcasts. One of them was Heinz Halbach, who would himself go on to lecture in journalism at Leipzig and who had this to say: "I used to listen to his polished way of speaking. But what impressed me most of all was the quality of his arguments. You could not read anything comparable anywhere else. There was something highly distinctive about his approach. When I heard that he was teaching the journalists, I was pleased to be allowed to study under him."[82] But a former staff member of the Leipzig broadcasting station recalled that Budzislawski's radio commentaries did not always receive favorable letters from members of the public. There was criticism both of the "high intellectual level" required of the listener, which some people evidently could not or would not meet, and the sharpness of his enunciation, which was felt by some people to be "strident."[83] Budzislawski relied confidently on his tremendous store of experience and was therefore able more easily than other colleagues to diverge from the written text and intersperse his lectures with anecdotes. On more than one occasion he would stroll into the lecture hall after a weekend in Berlin, a sitting of the Volkskammer, or a radio broadcast and fulfill his teaching obligations satisfactorily without much preparation.

Despite or perhaps rather precisely because of his eminence and the international reputation he claimed to possess as the director of the institute, Budzislawski generally kept a distance from his younger colleagues in the

Faculty of Journalism. His former assistant Karl-Heinz Röhr recalled that the boss had displayed little interest in the books available in the university library but was instead a keen reader of the *New York Herald Tribune*, *Le Monde*, the *Neue Zürcher Zeitung*, and the West German tabloid *Bild-Zeitung*. These were the Western newspapers the faculty subscribed to. Every day at midday he took them home in two black briefcases to the house in Lenaustraße, where Hanna was waiting with lunch. Afterward they indulged extensively in perusing these Western papers. The next day, Budzislawski would bring the hot commodities back to the faculty in the same conspiratorial fashion and exchange them for the newspapers that had just arrived.[84] It was the assistant lecturers and senior lecturers who bore the main burden of day-to-day work in the faculty. This did not mean that their future professorship was assumed, which would have allowed them to plan their careers in the medium term. According to an internal report, this uncertainty was a source of discouragement to many younger colleagues and led finally to a situation in which a tendency toward "indifference" and "not giving a damn" was evident in the teaching body.[85]

Spiru was one of the sharpest critics of Budzislawski and his relatively liberal mode of running the faculty, and he approached the Ministry of State Security as early as 1955 in an attempt to stir up official hostility toward him. Spiru accused Budzislawski of collaborating with the US State Department during his years in exile and also claimed that he now had "his own agent" in the SED Central Committee, as his son-in-law, Horst Eckert, would ring him after every sitting with a firsthand report.[86] Another charge Spiru made, in a letter sent to the SED Central Committee, was that Budzislawski had created "an atmosphere of benign Christian charity" in the faculty. He had even reacted indulgently to the desertion from the GDR of five graduates of the university. His "insouciance" and "political blindness" were dangerous and hindered the successful performance of the party's tasks, Spiru lamented. "There is absolutely no trace of political or ideological control at the Faculty of Journalism."[87]

In addition to the dispute between the professors over the right way of running the faculty, there was also the difficult relationship they had with the younger generation of scholars. There was a generation gap between the middle-ranking academics, who were young German Socialists with a horizon limited to the GDR, and the professors, who had returned from emigration, had lived on several different continents, and referred to the interwar period as their intellectual point of reference. The two groups had little to say to each other across this gap, a situation that did not change despite the need to cooperate in a confined space. Younger academics concerned themselves with practical questions and believed they were committed to pursuing a common goal, but only in exceptional cases was there any genuine interest in the often complicated and fractured life histories of the professors.[88] The situation was also similar in reverse: there are many manuscripts in Budzislawski's extensive archives of speeches and lectures dating from the Leipzig period, but there are no reflections or notes about his relationship with the students or even indications pointing to a genuine interest in the destiny of these young people, the children of the Second World War. This may of course be because the relevant documents have not survived. Siegfried Schmidt, who was a doctoral candidate in 1963 and later a professor at the University of Leipzig himself, remembered Budzislawski as a "fatherly mentor" to whom Schmidt had many personal reasons to be grateful. When Schmidt's wife died during the birth of their second child and the young scholar struggled hard as a single parent, Budzislawski not only reacted with sympathy and understanding but also used his own connections to enable his protégé to be allotted a new dwelling in the immediate vicinity of the faculty so that he could combine his duties as a parent and a teacher more effectively.[89] Gottfried Braun, another former assistant of Budzislawski, still has the neatly typed text of the speech his former boss delivered at his wedding celebration.

One of the young people who studied under Budzislawski in the early 1960s was Alfred Eichhorn, later to become the last managing editor of GDR radio. After 1990 he worked at Radio Free Berlin and then at Berlin-Brandenburg Radio. He recalls that his parents "were proud that their son had managed to get from a small mining village to the university at Leipzig." Half a century later, one particular remark by his lecturer Budzislawski remains in Eichhorn's memory: "The impact of the *Mona Lisa* is different when it is in the Musée du Louvre from when it is housed by Henry Robinson Luce in the magazines *Time* or *Life*."[90] This statement makes it clear that even in the GDR, Budzislawski's journalistic points of reference were the Western rather than the Socialist press, although he dutifully stressed the lack of authenticity of the popular American illustrated magazines owned by the conservative publisher Henry Luce. Their mass circulation would bring great art to the people with the sole aim of maximizing the publisher's profit, and in any case Luce's magazines were "stuffed full of rubbish." Budzislawski gave the impression of being a superior, sophisticated connoisseur of art who had carefully examined the masterworks of European art and culture on the spot. Museums like the Louvre in Paris were inaccessible to his students and colleagues at that time, particularly in the years immediately after the building of the Berlin Wall.

In view of the difficult situation in the faculty and despite the prominent position he enjoyed in the university, Budzislawski repeatedly tried to return to his previous career as a political journalist. Walter Ulbricht, who in the late

1940s had expressly rejected Budzislawski's return to the post of editor in chief or even as publisher of *Die Weltbühne*, was not to have the last word. In the middle of the 1950s, Budzislawski made a new attempt to obtain a leading position in GDR journalism with the support of Otto Grotewohl, the prime minister, who was well disposed toward him.[91] Budzislawski's goal was to publish a weekly newspaper to be entitled *Die Republik*. This idea had been discussed within the party since the end of 1953 and was reportedly first suggested by Albert Norden, a Communist Party functionary who had also returned from emigration in the West. This former fellow prisoner of Budzislawski had meanwhile risen to the position of director of the Agitation and Propaganda Department, attached to the SED Central Committee.[92] The new paper was to be launched as a direct competitor to the West German *Die Zeit* and, like the latter, was to be modeled on the British paper *The Observer*. They were even prepared to borrow from Goebbels, as the prospective title was deliberately reminiscent of Goebbels's flagship weekly, *Das Reich*—although, of course, the new paper simultaneously distanced itself from it.[93]

Documents from a meeting devoted to this topic in the Agitation and Propaganda Department of the SED Central Committee under the leadership of Horst Sindermann on 21 June 1956 are revealing. Discussion papers presented by Budzislawski and Bertolt Brecht demonstrate the opportunity that the GDR leadership failed to grasp on that occasion. Budzislawski's proposal began by stating that the new periodical should be "an organ of struggle against imperialism," with its "main thrust directed against imperialism in the United States and West Germany." This was little more than the politically necessary act of homage to the hard-liners of the SED. But what he went on to propose might have revolutionized the GDR journalism of the 1950s and had little in common with the triteness of standard propaganda. The new periodical should provide a platform for Socialists from both inside and outside the country, including contributions by well-known journalists from Western countries. Socialists from the GDR would be required to stick strictly to the party line, but "a certain degree of toleration" would have to be exercised toward the contributors from the West. Still more important was the aspiration that the new periodical might provide facts and items of information that "are not mentioned at all in our press or are treated too briefly." The target readership would be educated and middle-class people in general, not just GDR citizens: "In its presentation, the paper must be of such a level that it also attracts interest in West Germany, Switzerland, and Austria."[94] Budzislawski had in mind nothing less than a quantum leap in GDR journalism. Building on his experience as a journalist and as the editor of *Die neue Weltbühne*, his plan was to produce a newspaper that would not only present global developments to its readers from a party perspective but also cover the maximum permissible spectrum of opinion for the GDR: "Genuine questions must receive genuine answers, as in a discussion panel. At the same time, the readers' horizons must be extended. It is necessary to ensure that they are constantly informed about the most important events in the imperialist and neutralist countries, imperceptibly so to speak, without noticing it. . . . The haphazard presentation of information that is unfortunately so characteristic of our press ought not to be tolerated."[95] To put it differently, the GDR press must finally emerge from its self-chosen isolation. Instead of boring the reader with unvaryingly identical announcements of GDR successes, Budzislawski wanted to discuss the country's development in a global context—from a party point of view, but without blinkers.

Whereas Budzislawski submitted highly practical proposals for the creation of this new weekly, even going so far as to include possible column headings, Brecht approached the question from the cultural policy angle, saying that the GDR needed a major weekly that could, "if not be read, at least be quoted in the whole of Germany." A partisan and polemical voice that spreads confidence was needed:

> Our difficulties are in the highest degree honorable, we have taken on a gigantic undertaking, and there is little that can stimulate imagination and sympathy as much as the confident presentation of unsolved problems of all kinds. . . . In almost all questions we must not forget that we have quite a bit of the Western with us, in the GDR, because Socialism is still alien and scary to many intellectuals, most of the petty bourgeoisie, and even sections of the working class and because Western radio broadcasts and the immense number of letters exchanged between relatives play an evil role.[96]

Few people in the GDR of 1956 could afford to express themselves so openly. Brecht was protected from serious attack by his position as a living national monument and an artist of international standing. Budzislawski, too, was not entirely unknown outside the GDR. But in view of his experience during the party purges only a few years earlier, it was a courageous act to put forward a plan of this kind. However, little remained of the ethos of the 1944 Council for a Democratic Germany's postwar planning just a decade later in the GDR. In the "Memorandum on the Press and the Information System in Germany," Budzislawski and his colleagues in the United States had back then demanded that the future German press should "exclusively serve the purpose of giving true information to the public and allowing the free formation of opinion." They accused the National Socialists of subjugating the press and using it as the instrument of their "party dictatorship."[97] Now, in the mid-1950s, a political party—this time the SED—was again determining the content and the form of reporting. For *Die Weltbühne* in 1957, this meant "to struggle against new and old Fascism[,] . . . [t]o take the side of the working class also outside the GDR[,] . . . [t]o neutralize all the treacherous forces and agencies of imperialism and capitalism that are working to split the working class, and to unmask those forces, in which connection *Die Weltbühne* must be particularly careful in its dealings with bourgeois intellectuals."[98] In the light of such requirements, Budzislawski's plan for the new periodical ventured right to the edge of what was permitted under the dictatorship without questioning it in any fundamental way.

In the next few months, events developed in line with his hopes. On 23 October 1956 the Agitation and Propaganda Department of the SED Central Committee, headed by Norden and Sindermann, recommended to the Central Committee that a weekly journal be issued. Two floors of Mauerstraße 85 in Berlin were cleared for the editorial offices of the new journal in a building that was the former headquarters of the Julius Kahlbaum Liqueur Factory and Wine Shop. One of the prospective editors involved at that time recalled that they had already started to buy furniture and typewriters on a large scale: "We were swimming in money, and everything happened as in a fairy tale. The publishing manager, Hermann Leopold, an old warhorse from the Berlin newspaper district, almost tore his hair out over the expenditure."[99] The first issue of the new paper was planned for 1 March 1957. It would comprise sixteen sides in Rhenish format, be printed "on well-glazed paper," and have an initial print run of 120,000 copies. It was intended that Budzislawski would be the editor in chief while at the same time retaining his position as dean at the university—even if he would only be able to continue in this function temporarily at most. Furthermore, it was envisaged that there would be two assistant editors: Bernt von Kügelgen, a graduate of the Central Anti-Fascist School at Krasnogorsk near Moscow, who was then editor in chief of the *Neue Berliner Illustrierte*, and Arno Rehan, who was working in the Committee for German Unity, set up in the GDR in 1954. At fifty pfennigs, the new weekly would have been considerably cheaper to buy than its West German competitor, *Die Zeit*.[100] The Secretariat of the SED Central Committee adopted the proposal, and at a sitting held on 28 November 1956 it asked the Politburo to give its formal approval.[101] Ulbricht, however, opposed the idea for reasons that are still unclear today. Even a decade later, Budzislawski did not want to talk about the failure of his attempt to establish the new periodical and merely replied to a question from a former associate by saying that the project had fallen through "for reasons of a nonjournalistic nature."[102]

To judge by an entry in his cadre file, Budzislawski fell seriously ill in 1958, perhaps as a reaction to the failure of this project, along with the increasing severity of the internal disputes at the Faculty of Journalism.[103] The observations of the writer Joachim Schwarz about the situation in the GDR in the 1950s also applied to Budzislawski. Schwarz noted that it had always been the "best comrades" who "paid for the conflict between discipline and criticism with stomach ulcers, heart attacks, and clinical raving madness, that the open contradictions . . . were nothing compared to the secret ones, by which the best were literally eaten up."[104] While noticeably reducing his involvement in the university, Budzislawski began to take on new tasks in politics and the media. In 1957 he ensured his election to the Executive Council of the World Federation of Scientific Workers. He was also one of the founding members of the International Society for the Study of Mass Media, an affiliate of UNESCO. In 1958 he spent a few months standing in for Eduard von Schnitzler, the director of the television show *Treffpunkt Berlin*, who had fallen ill, and in 1961 he traveled as a member of the GDR delegation to a session of the World Peace Council held in India, where on 27 March 1961, accompanied by his thirty-two-year-old daughter Beate, he was given a personal audience with Prime Minister Jawaharlal Nehru.

Hermann Budzislawski and his daughter, Beate, were received on 27 March 1961 by the prime minister of India, Jawaharlal Nehru (*center*), and they had a private conversation with him at his residence in New Delhi, Teen Murti Bhavan.

Hermann Budzislawski giving a talk to the Indian Council of World Affairs in New Delhi, March 1961.

On this occasion, Budzislawski also addressed the Indian Council of World Affairs, a high-level think tank founded in 1943. The title of his speech was "The Role of the GDR Press in Promoting International Understanding and Cooperation," and he expressed his conviction that in the foreseeable future there would be a "confederation" between the two German states and that Germany would ultimately be reunited. A nation that had achieved unity in the past could not be prevented from regaining it. That was an allusion to the German national movement of the nineteenth century and perhaps also to the division of British India in 1947 into the two successor states of India and Pakistan, which his audience would have been more likely to recall.[105]

The journey to India was a part of the GDR's continuing endeavor to gain international recognition through trade, development assistance, cultural contacts, and, in this case, meetings with top-level Indian politicians. To reach broader strata of the population as well, the Politburo even thought of issuing an illustrated magazine in Hindi, the first issue of which was supposed to appear a few days after Budzislawski's trip.[106] For the latter, the visit to Nehru was akin to the closing of a circle, because, as we saw earlier, he had already worked in the mid-1920s as the editor of the anticolonialist journal *Industrial and Trade Review for India*.[107] A German activist from the transnational anticolonialist network of the interwar years had now arrived at the political center of a rising regional power—on a visit, at least—and was thus at the same time part of the increasingly close cultural exchange between the Socialist states of Eastern Europe and the Global South since the second half of the 1950s.[108]

In comparison with such glamorous appearances, Budzislawski found his everyday activities at the University of Leipzig increasingly irksome. He was not particularly enthusiastic about training young people in the Marxist dialectic and preparing them for a career in the party. When conducting admissions interviews, he even warned highly competitive candidates for a university place against studying journalism at the Red monastery. With results as good as this, he said in an aside, you could just as well study something else![109] Even his acceptance speech when the University of Leipzig awarded him his honorary doctorate in 1966 turned out to be somewhat ambivalent, especially when Budzislawski alluded to the fact that the party had prevented him from continuing his career as editor in chief in the GDR:

> I naturally regret the unwritten articles, the loss, so to speak, of my personality as a journalist, if one may be allowed to say something like this. But I am not angry today. I believe the party was right when it indicated to me the path I have followed since then, though admittedly not in a straight line. There were always byways in our society, and I sometimes wandered along them, an action I would also like to defend. Without being involved in political life, one can be neither an active journalist nor a scientific and theoretical one.[110]

Whenever a call came in from an editor, Budzislawski admitted, he still pricked up his ears "like a cavalry horse that has heard the call of the bugle." He was a journalist in body and soul, he said, who since the late 1940s had devoted his research and teaching not only to fulfilling the party's mandate to educate hundreds of new "Socialist journalists" but also to seeking to understand the precise nature of journalism—or, to put it differently, to establishing a theoretical foundation for his practical activity.[111] On that occasion Budzislawski downplayed his previous disagreements with both the SED leadership and his comrades in the faculty, taking refuge in the customary rhetoric of the party functionary: "If a foundation stone has actually been laid, thanks should go first and foremost to the guiding hand of the party, which always set out what was needed and indicated the direction to be taken by education and research. The party set the goal, our state guaranteed the means, and I and all the rest of us ought to express our gratitude."[112]

Reading between the lines, one can perhaps impute a small subversive potential to this reference to the party will. It is undeniable, however, that

Budzislawski made compromises with the state power in the GDR that more than once amounted to self-denial. The "new Socialist journalist," according to the textbook *Socialist Journalism: A Scientific Introduction*, published in 1966 under Budzislawski's name, is distinguished not by originality but by the ability to recognize, categorize, and express in comprehensible language "what is historically necessary. . . . The character of the Socialist journalist is not that of an isolated individual swimming against the current of world history, the hero of the bourgeois drama . . . but as it were the executor of history and its laws in the most diverse spheres."[113] In other words, the demand was not for courageous idealists and principled lone warriors like Tucholsky and Ossietzky but for cautious skeptics like Brecht and Budzislawski.

Budzislawski's textbook on Socialist journalism was one of the few publications of the Faculty of Journalism to enter the mainstream book trade of the GDR.[114] This tendency to keep things secret may have contributed to the unequivocally political reputation of the Red monastery, but it was also a result of the fact that the production of scholarly texts was very slow to get going. At first there was little to publish that might be of interest to a broader readership.[115] The textbook was based in part on Budzislawski's lecture notes from previous years. Other chapters were written by an authors' collective. Budzislawski noted that he also received "some assistance from colleagues" in preparing the book for publication. This was an elegant way of admitting that younger scholars had to do most of the work for him—a situation that had caused years of tension in the faculty. His assistant Karl-Heinz Röhr, who in later years was himself a professor at the university, still had a very vivid memory in 2015 of the way the book originated: "Little of this was of his own manufacture. We had to do the preliminary work. He then tore everything apart, did some dictation, and wrote a little. At the end there was a Budzislawski. He was able to coin phrases that went beyond officialese."[116]

In its content, the book fell entirely within the framework of what the SED required of its new journalists. As stated in the introduction, it was the task of the Socialist journalist "to be a teacher of the whole nation, an educator of the masses in the spirit of revolution," and to enable the individual "to move away from his individualistic way of viewing life and arrive at a collectivist approach."[117] The book endeavored to present journalism as a scientific subject in its own right that would combine a theoretical basis grounded in Marxism-Leninism, an empirical study of the mass media, an investigation of the impact of journalism, and an examination of the way it was practiced in the GDR. The work was additionally intended as a polemic against Western journalism. One can read in it, for example, that it is impossible to speak of press freedom in the mass media of Western Europe and the United States because of the economic pressures they are subject to. But this argument, which was repeated in many variants and with many examples, was significantly weakened by the fact that Budzislawski demanded undeviating commitment to the party line from GDR journalists. What was most important, he bluntly stated, was that "journalists should be able to understand and defend the policy of the state of workers and peasants and its ruling party in its wider context."[118] Admittedly, this did not in principle rule out the possibility of giving voice to divergent opinions on specific questions. But because loyalty to the regime was always paramount, such criticism could only be relative. As a result, even positively inclined reviewers, like Verena Blaum, an expert on communications who was originally educated in Leipzig and later lived in the Federal Republic, concluded that the book had in general been a disappointment, not least because of its failure to exploit the "flexibility of the Marxist-Leninist system of thought, which was definitely available for use." Strict political requirements had prevented the emergence of genuine controversies within the Socialist camp.[119]

On 7 March 1962, four years before the publication of the book, the SED Central Committee had passed a resolution dismissing Budzislawski from the post of dean of the Faculty of Journalism "on health grounds."[120] An unofficial collaborator (IM) who went by the name "Otto" had already reported to the Stasi that Budzislawski had "in practice ceased to perform his function as director of the institute a long time ago . . . owing to his constant absence from the faculty."[121] To "preserve his rank and title in international appearances," the spy's report continues, a special institute had been set up "for research into cooperation between instruments of mass communication." The institute "is located in Berlin and consists only of Prof. B[udzislawski] and a secretary; hence in practice, it does not exist." If we are to believe this assessment by IM "Otto," in the 1960s Budzislawski was concerned above all with his "academic reputation," while he neglected his everyday work in teaching and research:

This aroused fierce discussion (behind his back) among the members of his institute. Many of them have a low opinion of his abilities and consider that they are being exploited (Assistant Röhr, for example). Prof. B instructs Röhr to produce draft papers, he adds rhetorical expressions to them, and he then issues them as his own work. However, since no one expresses his opinion of Prof. B to his face, an atmosphere of hypocrisy has arisen that, I must say, makes one want to throw up. People bow down before him when he is there (they really do), but in his absence they revile him.[122]

Leaving aside the delightful paradox that a spy is apparently genuinely furious about hypocrisy in everyday university affairs without realizing that he or she has just denounced him- or herself, the report touched on a sensitive point: the observation that Budzislawski was distinguished by a strong "craving for recognition," combined with a pronounced sensitivity to criticism and a generally "petty bourgeois attitude," runs right through the various assessments made not only by the party but also by his journalistic and academic opponents since the 1930s.

After his final defeat by the post-Stalinist hard-liners at the Karl Marx University in the long-standing struggle for power within the Faculty of Journalism, Budzislawski increasingly withdrew along with his wife to his antique-filled house in the Lenaustraße and his weekend cottage in Buckow. A little later, in 1964, he gave up his Leipzig residence and started to live in Berlin again. Plans were being made at this time to launch an "illustrated news magazine" under the title *Profil*, which was intended as a Socialist competitor to the West German magazine *Der Spiegel*, but the project collapsed in 1965 for reasons similar to those that lay behind the failure to publish *Die Republik* a few years before. Budzislawski had not even been invited to take part in this new project. The news of this "treachery" made him foam at the mouth with fury.[123] He also failed to make the grade when other leadership roles were considered. Thus he was one of the candidates to succeed the writer Bodo Uhse as editor in chief of the literary and culture magazine *Sinn und Form*, but the position finally went to the Wilhelm Girnus, who had previously been state secretary for university and vocational education.[124] One does not need much imagination to perceive that for a man of the world with broad cultural and political interests the now hermetically sealed GDR, which did not allow his talents as a journalist to come to their full fruition, must have appeared narrow and stuffy, especially after the Eleventh Plenum of the SED Central Committee in December 1965, which is known as the "Kahlschlag [clearcutting] Plenum." Budzislawski again found himself in a kind of emigration, only this time it was in his own country and was enforced by the daily dichotomy between the publicly utterable and the privately thinkable. Was not his villa, decked out with oil paintings and costly antiques, an ostentatious, "bourgeois" counterproject to Socialist modernity? And was not Helene Weigel's living room in Buckow, where the Budzislawskis had been regular guests since the 1950s, one of the last refuges in the GDR for the former political and cultural avant-garde of the interwar period?[125]

At the start of his seventh decade, Budzislawski was weary and irritable. He also had to battle again and again with lengthy periods of illness, which sometimes put him out of action for weeks on end. We do not know what he was thinking while his chauffeur was driving him backward and forward between Leipzig, Berlin, and Buckow, but despite enjoying many privileges he will surely have thought occasionally that one cannot live a good life in the midst of falsehood. He was living in a golden cage. Had he really made it in the GDR? Or had the GDR done him in?

Belated Satisfaction

Back in Charge of *Die Weltbühne*

SOME WEEKS AFTER his compulsory retirement, which finally came into effect on 1 January 1967, Hermann Budzislawski took over the position of editor in chief of *Die Weltbühne* again and retained this position for the next four and a half years.[1] He was "very happy" to do this, as the longtime assistant editor Ursula Madrasch-Groschopp recalled, although she added that he was not really interested in any of the financial and organizational details relating to the journal. The "father of the young generation of journalists" in the GDR arrived "with two people from the Agitation Department," but he had been "incorrectly informed about the functioning of our editorial board." Budzislawski himself wrote on 17 January 1967, hence only a few days after he had taken over the position of editor in chief, that he had been very surprised to be offered the job after the death of Hans Leonhard, especially as, for health reasons, he was no longer able to work to his full capacity.[2] But in view of the way his career as a journalist had previously been obstructed in the GDR, he was unable to resist the offer. The paper had been his "training ground," and it was "like a home" to him, he wrote in his first lead article for two decades. What was needed now was to get on with current tasks, to work for peace, to confront the neo-Nazis in West Germany, and to support the "policies of the German Democratic Republic and its leading party."[3] There had long ceased to be any political objection on the part of the SED Central Committee to the return of the former Western emigrant to the position of editor in chief of *Die Weltbühne*. With the building of the Berlin Wall, the rule of the SED had been secured for the foreseeable future, and since it owned the journal, it was clear who would hold the upper hand in case any conflicts arose.

At his own request, Budzislawski was officially identified in the journal's imprint as "Chief Editor, Publishing Director, and Licensee." It was not by chance that he looked back in this way to his role in the 1930s as editor in chief and proprietor of *Die neue Weltbühne*. Moreover, he attached greater value to his academic titles than he had ever done before. After receiving his honorary degree, he was now officially "Herr Prof. Dr. Dr. Hermann Budzislawski," a title his editorial colleagues caricatured behind his back, distorting it into "Professor Dr. Hermann Hermann Budzislawski." Right from the beginning, he intended once again to take the reins of "his" journal firmly into both hands. This is, for example, shown by a disagreement with the poet and travel writer Hugo Huppert, who lived in Austria, which blew up in the first few weeks of Budzislawski's time as editor. Huppert, a Communist, had published regularly in *Die Weltbühne* in previous years, but he had always reacted very angrily to editorial alterations in the texts he sent in. He now attempted to make use of the change in editors in chief to obtain a guarantee that his texts would never be altered, and he also longed a well-funded permanent contract.[4] Nothing came of this, however. Budzislawski sent a sharp answer, pointing out that editorial revisions to Huppert's texts were sometimes unavoidable, especially as the reading public in the GDR differed from that in West Germany or Austria. He also could not produce *Die Weltbühne* in the same way as he had in the 1930s, he added. Nor did he want to. Previously, the language of *Die Weltbühne* had defined the category it belonged to and the class it appealed to, but now the journal was no longer exclusively read by the Left bourgeois intelligentsia. It was also read by "educated workers," and it was necessary to take account of this fact.

Budzislawski insisted on having the last word in all editorial matters, just as he had done thirty years earlier.[5] The tone of the letters the two men exchanged escalated rapidly. Huppert was particularly worked up over the accusation that sitting as he did in Austria he would not be able to judge what was important or interesting for GDR readers. He knew the GDR "better than some of the people who live there," he insisted, and he loved it as a "spiritual fatherland" that was his "adopted country politically." He was not prepared to tolerate the polemical tone of Budzislawski's letters and the accusations in them.[6] It was apparently only thanks to the assistant editor in chief, Madrasch-Groschopp, who intervened to smooth things over, that the two old men were able some weeks later to have a personal discussion in Berlin, at which they again thrashed out the issues that divided them. The minutes of this meeting leave no doubt as to who won the power struggle: Budzislawski had his way on all the points in dispute, not least because Huppert, who had also fallen out of favor with the Austrian Communist Party, could not really afford to give up the fees he regularly received from East Berlin.[7]

During the next four years, anyone who wrote for *Die Weltbühne* and lived in Berlin had to personally submit their articles to Budzislawski. He then examined the text, in most cases straight away and in the presence of the author sitting opposite, who was often nervous, and quickly and unmistakably gave his verdict. Many articles went back to be revised, but if the writer was lucky, Budzislawski said, "I will print this—not under its present title, of course!" The formulation of titles and headlines was one of Budzislawski's strengths as a journalist, and it was a task he undertook without being asked. He almost always remained polite in his interaction with other people, but at the same time he placed a high value on keeping his distance and maintaining hierarchical relationships. In the editorial office, which comprised only four permanently employed journalists and a few freelancers, the new editor in chief's word was law, and there was no point in contradicting him. Just as during his time at the University of Leipzig, he had no confidential dealings with anyone, not even with long-standing colleagues. There were no invitations to visit the apartment in Treptow or the weekend cottage in Buckow, and if his *Weltbühne* colleagues ever proposed anything of this kind, he appeared to be utterly terrified.[8]

Budzislawski's behavior in his office was characterized by extreme restlessness. He could only sit still occasionally, and he often did not know what to do with his hands. Involuntary hand movements seem to have been practically a characteristic feature of this generation of SED cadres, in stark contrast to their generally immobile facial expressions.[9] They had fallen victim to an inner tension, an "enslavement through consciousness," which was expressed physically, in Budzislawski's case too, by the movement of their hands.[10] He preferred to think while in motion, and when he was speaking to someone he paced the floor of his office. He spoke so softly that his interlocutor was well advised to move around as well. You had to stay physically close to the boss so as not to miss a single word. Personal closeness, though, was hardly possible, recalled Richard Christ, a journalist whose career began at *Die Weltbühne* in 1970. He admired Budzislawski as the "most independent, fearless journalist" Christ had got to know "in a period of rigid censorship," but he had never come into close contact with him privately. The rather odd appearance of the small man in the old-fashioned suit with the obligatory bow tie had at first sight inspired confidence, Christ remembered, but "hard eyes" lay behind the thick, horn-rimmed glasses.[11] Ursula Madrasch-Groschopp also regarded Budzislawski as a person to be respected, but she evidently had had a more cordial and trusting relationship with his predecessor Leonhard and with Albert Norden from the Agitation and Propaganda Department of the Central Committee. She called Budzislawski an "impersonal individual" whom it was difficult to warm to. "But you could clown around with him or tell jokes. He was a very polite man but very distant. Always impersonal."[12]

As editor in chief, Budzislawski was able to take the liberty of avoiding the press briefings of the Agitation and Propaganda Department of the SED Central Committee, which were held every Thursday and were actually obligatory. He regarded these events as "a national misfortune." Their official purpose was to provide "guidance for state Socialist argumentation," an expression that was shortened by the journalists to "Argu." Budzislawski also skipped the annual meetings of all the GDR's editor in chiefs, held in the Haus am Werderschen Markt in Berlin, which had been the headquarters of the SED Central Committee since 1959. According to Madrasch-Groschopp, he told the editorial staff that such meetings made him so upset that "he would have had a heart attack" if he had gone. But at the same time he was reputedly proud to know that the whole of the Politburo read his journal. He discussed important questions directly with individual members of the Central Committee apparatus instead of collecting obligatory instructions from official channels every week on the language to be used, like the other leading editors of the GDR's mass media.[13]

Thus, although *Die Weltbühne* under Budzislawski always followed the party line, it was still worth reading, not least because the standing and reputation of its editor allowed a freedom of maneuver that would disappear under his considerably younger and less distinguished successor, Peter Theek. In the 1970s approximately 30,000 copies of each issue were printed, although the editorial staff estimated—very optimistically—that the number of actual readers of *Die Weltbühne* amounted to between 300,000 and 450,000.[14] Scoffers in the Federal Republic maintained that the sole purpose of the East Berlin *Weltbühne* was to prevent the establishment in the West of an independent rival publication that would genuinely be a continuation of the Weimar *Weltbühne*. But this is a far too superficial judgment.[15] Even if the GDR *Weltbühne* was always obliged to follow the course set by the SED when any doubt arose, it still contained relevant material, especially if one could read between the lines, an ability that most of its readers in the GDR possessed. At the same time, this version of the periodical no longer had much of a connection with the uncompromising desire for truth, courage, and readiness to engage in confrontation that had distinguished the Weimar journal of the same name. The vice president of the Central Administration for People's Education, the writer and poet Erich Weinert, put it in a nutshell in 1952 in a letter to the then editor in chief, Hans Leonhard. Weinert wrote that the reestablished *Weltbühne* was a journal that through its "special way of dealing with problems and its cultivated mode of expression acts on certain strata of the intelligentsia who are difficult to reach with other forms of propaganda."[16] Before 1989 there was no fundamental change in this approach.

After a short settling-in period, Budzislawski set about the task of developing new perspectives for his new but also old journal. Yet his attempts to influence the Central Committee's Agitation and Propaganda Department came to nothing. In September 1968 he lamented to Albert Norden that many of his ideas, which in part continued the design recommendations he had made for *Die Republik*, were now being used in a new periodical, the weekly journal *Horizont*, which, like *Die Weltbühne*, reported mainly from abroad. Budzislawski complained that the editorial board of *Horizont* under its editor in chief, Ernst-Otto Schwabe, a man barely forty years old who had previously been director of the press department at the Ministry of Foreign Affairs for several years, could draw on a plentiful supply of personnel, whereas *Die Weltbühne*, which could not, took a long time to be printed and distributed. When it appeared every Tuesday, all the contributions in it were always at least a week old, and they were therefore never fully topical. But the biggest problem was the lack of qualified staff, because in the GDR "there are too few genuinely literate and knowledgeable people who can also find time to write."[17] Budzislawski evidently felt that even the next generation of journalists, educated under his leadership in Leipzig (by 1968 over a thousand journalists had already graduated from the "Red monastery"), were not suited to join the editorial staff of "his" journal. This evaluation of people he himself had educated and decisively influenced makes it clear that he had little use for journalistic artisans who were working according to party instructions. His ideal was and remained the writer-journalist of a Left bourgeois orientation.

Foreign policy was very definitely the main focus of *Die Weltbühne* under Budzislawski. Anyone in the GDR who wanted to read well-informed reports on Western Europe, the United States, and what were then known as the developing countries (i.e., the Global South) could find what they were looking for there. In the first few months of serving as editor in chief, Budzislawski produced nuanced obituaries of Henry Morgenthau Jr. and J. Robert Oppenheimer.[18] He analyzed the strategic reorientation of the West German company Fried. Krupp AG in the light of the structural changes that were beginning to transform the Ruhr, and he examined the volatile political situation in France.[19] The financial expert Dr. Heiner Winkler wrote on the "dark sides of the Japanese economic miracle," Ulrich Makosch reported from Cambodia about the next moves to be expected from the United States in the region, the British journalist Gordon Schaffer offered insights into the "English newspaper world," and from Montevideo Pedro Fuentes denounced the destruction of the Amazon rain forest and the displacement of the indigenous population.[20] By contrast, developments with the GDR's eastern neighbors were a taboo subject. *Die Weltbühne* did not report at all about the reform discussions within the Socialist camp. As far as it was concerned, the Prague Spring, the attempt to create a "Socialism with a human face," simply did not happen.

Even so, it was impossible to avoid mentioning the invasion of the ČSSR (Czechoslovak Socialist Republic) by Warsaw Pact troops on 21 August 1968, in which the GDR leadership would have liked to participate, and the forcible overthrow of the Czech reform Communists under General Secretary Alexander Dubček in the months that followed. On 27 August, under the headline "What Happened in the ČSSR?," which appeared to promise some enlightenment on the subject, *Die Weltbühne* simply printed an extract from a report by the official Soviet news agency, TASS, without giving any further explanation. According to the TASS report, Czechoslovaks in positions of authority had appealed to the Soviet Union and its alliance partners, begging them to give "urgent assistance," including "the help of their armed forces."[21] In this case, the absence of any commentary from *Die Weltbühne* was a commentary in itself. Moscow's official statement was also printed in the GDR's daily newspapers. It was apparent in this case that the editorial board of *Die Weltbühne* had done only the minimum of what was expected of it by the SED Central Committee. This remains true even if we consider the fact that *Die Weltbühne* opened its next issue with an article in which it condemned the propaganda of the Western powers in Central Europe and justified the military intervention into Czechoslovakia as an act of self-defense against the counterrevolution, in line with the official version.[22]

A letter of 25 September 1968 from Budzislawski to Hugo Huppert indicates that the editor in chief was in something of a dilemma at this time. He had spent the previous weeks in hospital and had therefore not been present at the editorial board, perhaps not entirely by coincidence. On the one hand, he now wrote, *Die Weltbühne* unquestionably had to support the line taken by the GDR government, and it would be impossible now to print articles by long-established authors such as Bruno Frei, who had publicly criticized the invasion. On the other hand, he had known Frei for a long time, and he "had often later corrected mistaken views he had previously disseminated." Budzislawski would therefore make efforts to restore Frei to the group of authors at a future date.[23] On this issue, Huppert was plainly closer to the party line. He sarcastically and indignantly recorded what he thought of the editor in chief's conciliatory attitude: "He would like to 'make efforts' on behalf of this highly regarded scoundrel!!" Frei's return to *Die Weltbühne* would be "eerie and bizarre. . . . Someone who holds out their hand to the devil" (in other words, makes common cause with the West) can never come back.[24]

As was to be expected, coverage of events in Germany itself differed significantly, depending on whether they took place in the West or the East of

the country. Under Budzislawski, every issue of *Die Weltbühne* attacked the
allegedly imperialist Federal Republic, concentrating in particular on its "militarism," the continued influence of the old elites, and the alleged "brutaliza-
tion" of society by filth and trash.[25] Concerns about morality dating from the
1920s continued to plague a man who had by now reached the sixty-sixth year
of his life. In an article published in 1967 on present-day youth, Budzislawski
claimed that "since 1950 the Federal Republic has been deluged with around
three billion magazines containing the worst kind of trash, and extremely
bloodthirsty so-called adventure novels and detective stories." More than two-
thirds of the films shown in the Federal Republic's cinemas in 1965 and 1966
revolved around "gangsterism, sex, and military adventures." The rise in the
number of "teenage hooligans" and other young people with criminal tendencies was the logical consequence of this "poisonous deluge" produced by the
mass media. Budzislawski's views were thus located in the early twentieth-
century tradition of cultural criticism, which was also fashionable in the Federal Republic in the 1950s. He interpreted these aspects of the modern industry of mass culture as "products of the decay of bourgeois society." They were,
in his final analysis, signs of the collapse of democracy in the Federal Republic
and its western neighbors.[26] Whether younger readers of the late 1960s in
particular had a taste for cultural criticism of such an old-fashioned and condescending character is more than doubtful, to put it mildly. On this subject,
the views of the old Socialist Budzislawski were more in line with West Berlin's
Bild-Zeitung, of which he was a regular reader.

Die Weltbühne did, it is true, display a greater understanding of the situation of young people in the Federal Republic in the following months, for
instance, in a two-part article series on the "student revolt," although there the
predominant perspective was that of an imagined anthropology that emphasized the author's remoteness from the young rebels and failed to display any
empathy with them—not least because the article denied that the students
had any power to influence events.[27] The East Berlin *Weltbühne* was in a certain sense a journal of the past, despite all its analyses of the present, because
it always viewed current developments in the capitalist countries against the
background of the political and ideological conflicts of the interwar period.
There was little readiness to reflect in an unbiased way on the social liberaliza-
tion of the 1960s in West and East or at least to regard the process as an open-
ended one. Errors of fact were compounded by a tone that implied the possession of superior knowledge.

As far as the GDR was concerned, critical discussion was almost completely
absent from *Die Weltbühne* between 1967 and 1971—leaving aside theater criticism, where it was indeed possible to allude indirectly to the domestic situa-

tion.[28] One of the rare exceptions was an article on the rehabilitation of youthful delinquents penned by the writer and journalist Elfriede Brüning. She praised the successes of the new state in this area, but she also addressed the problems that still existed.[29] In the main, however, the journal was dominated by supposedly nonpolitical material, preferably treated in the satirical manner favored by the East Berlin magazine *Eulenspiegel*. This allowed shortcomings in GDR society to become a subject of discussion, at least to a degree, but only at the price of trivializing topics once raised more bluntly by critical journalists of the Tucholsky and Ossietzky type and leaving many areas blank.[30] Under the SED's dictatorship this "flight into the humoresque" (Renate Holland-Moritz) was ultimately necessary if one wanted to guarantee the continuing publication of *Die Weltbühne*, and therefore there was actually no alternative, unless one considered the illegal distribution of samizdat literature produced without official permission as a realistic possibility.[31]

The political harmlessness of *Die Weltbühne*'s humor took much of the sting out of its biting and often disproportionately exaggerated criticism of the Federal Republic because it was clear that double standards were operating here. Another reason why this reliance on humor was ineffective in the long run was that many readers already took a very critical attitude toward the reports produced by the GDR mass media on internal politics. Readers were aware of the problematic relationship between censorship and self-censorship, and they were watchful and selective about what they accepted as true. The articles in Budzislawski's *Weltbühne* show what could be written in the GDR of the late 1960s—and what could not. The journal therefore definitely served as a yardstick for the relation between intellectuals and political power under actually existing Socialism, although not at all in the same way as its renowned predecessor had under the Weimar Republic.

During Budzislawski's time in charge, *Die Weltbühne* remained the journal preferred by the members of the intelligentsia who were loyal to the state. As in the 1920s, the readers were sometimes also authors, and the authors were regular readers. Alongside the small number of permanent editors, many professors and specialists of other kinds worked for the paper on a freelance basis. The list included the lawyers Friedrich Karl Kaul and Hans Nathan, the latter being one of the people who financed Budzislawski's 1934 takeover of *Die neue Weltbühne*; the architect and town planner Hermann Henselmann, who as chief architect of the municipal administration of East Berlin decisively influenced modernist urban development in the GDR; and the historians Fritz Klein and Walter Markov. They were not dependent on the fees paid by the journal, but over the years they became known throughout the GDR through their work in *Die Weltbühne*, at least among people who mattered. To see one's name in print in *Die Weltbühne* and to bask in the glamour of its reputation were attractive prospects promising added distinction, even for established specialists, especially if they wanted to present themselves to the wider reading public as intelligent people with cultural interests devoted to the Socialist cause. But many of these authors were of Budzislawski's age or thereabouts. One could hardly expect protest or resistance from this generation. That was one reason why the Agitation and Propaganda Department of the SED was able to loosen the reins a little in the case of *Die Weltbühne*, especially as it could count on the editors' fundamental "solidarity with the state and its system." *Die Weltbühne* was not a "dissident journal," opined one of its longstanding contributors, the historian Fritz Klein, but a weekly that, despite occasionally printing critical articles, submitted to the ruling party's discipline. Indeed, it sometimes obeyed the party's injunctions even before they were issued.[32] In addition to professors and notabilities, many of Budzislawski's long-standing friends and traveling companions from the days of emigration wrote in the journal while he was editor, including the Serbian Jewish writer Theodor Balk, who lived in Prague and had already published in *Die neue Weltbühne* in the 1930s; Elfriede Brüning and Bruno Frei, whom we have already mentioned; and the former prime minister of Saxony, Max Seydewitz.[33] Then there was Greta Kuckhoff, who published important contributions on the history of the resistance group the Red Orchestra, of which she had been a member. She also penned an eye-witness report on the anti-Jewish pogroms of November 1938.[34] *Die Weltbühne* printed an extract from Simon Wiesenthal's book *The Murderers among Us* in advance of its publication.[35] In addition, Budzislawski asked the Russian writer and university teacher Alexander Dymschitz for a contribution. Dymschitz had been a leading cultural official in the Soviet Military Administration in Germany (SMAD) from 1945 until his recall in 1949, and he had made a considerable contribution to the restoration of Berlin's artistic and cultural life in that capacity until, like Budzislawski, he was attacked from the orthodox Communist side and forced to return to the field of scholarship and literary activity.[36] The editor in chief now wanted Dymschitz to write an extensive article to celebrate the sixty-fifth birthday of the author Günther Weisenborn, who, like Kuckhoff, had been actively involved in the Red Orchestra at the beginning of the 1940s. Weisenborn was a pacifist, and after the war he became known in both German states as a theater director and scriptwriter. His work had also been printed by Budzislawski.[37] Right from the beginning, one of Budzislawski's aims had been to commemorate the international Left's resistance to National Socialism in *Die Weltbühne*, and he had in the meantime begun to care increasingly about the need to commemorate the Holocaust for both biographical and cultural reasons. He probably also sensed that he would not be able to set his own priorities for much longer.

Budzislawski finally resigned as editor in chief of *Die Weltbühne* on 28 September 1971, having by then reached the age of seventy. His replacement was Peter Theek, a journalist and author of children's books who was twenty-three years his junior. This was more than a change from one generation to the next. Theek had spent several years in the Hitler Youth before he was obliged to join the Reich Labour Service. He became a party candidate for the NSDAP in late 1942. After the war and a brief period as a prisoner of war, he joined the KPD/SED in 1946 and declared that he would "engage in anti-Fascist activities" to prove that he had "nothing to do with Nazi ideas."[38] Theek owed his second chance at a career to the GDR and was already for this personal reason unconditionally loyal to the ruling party. He had acquired his first experience as a journalist by working for *Junges Leben*, an anti-Fascist youth magazine in the French sector of Berlin, and later as a local editor for the Soviet army's newspaper, *Tägliche Rundschau*, which had ceased publication in 1955. He then moved to *BZ am Abend*, where he rose to the level of assistant editor in chief. From 1959 to 1971 he held the office of editor in chief of the SED-financed daily *Die Wahrheit*, which was the mouthpiece of the Socialist Unity Party of West Berlin (SEW). He therefore had the necessary international experience, and he had also proved himself by working in what the party regarded as "enemy territory."[39] Budzislawski, his granddaughter claims, was not pleased that a former member of the Hitler Youth and candidate of the NSDAP had taken over the running of Budzislawski's "little magazine," even if he might have conceded that Theek's membership in the Hitler Youth had been a youthful sin that could be forgiven. Even though their relationship was not free of tension at first, things seemed to improve quickly between the two men. In a personal congratulatory note on Theek's fiftieth birthday three years later, Budzislawski thanked him "from the bottom of my heart" for remaining true to the *Weltbühne* traditions "in such a likeable way."[40] In 1971, however, Budzislawski refrained from saying a personal farewell in the pages of *Die Weltbühne*, and he did not take the opportunity of introducing his successor to the readers of the journal with a few kind words. Once again, as in March 1934, readers could only speculate about what had actually happened behind the scenes. Budzislawski's name remained on the masthead as publishing director and licensee in the coming years, and he continued to contribute articles on current political issues.

Even though Budzislawski had regained his visibility as a journalist, he was acknowledged and marginalized at the same time in the official GDR history of *Die Weltbühne* produced in the 1970s and 1980s. In 1986, when a special edition was brought out to celebrate the journal's fortieth anniversary in the Soviet occupation zone and then the GDR, Maud von Ossietzky and Hans Leonhard were verbosely commemorated, but there was no mention at all of Budzislawski's important role in exile or his later time as editor in chief in the GDR.[41] In the final years of his life, Budzislawski himself went along with this official reading of history. At the memorial service for Maud von Ossietzky held on 16 May 1974, he was allowed to mention his achievements as editor of *Die neue Weltbühne* in the 1930s, but his back-door expropriation or, to put it another way, the SED's decision to ignore his claims to the editorship after 1945 remained a taboo subject. Meticulously adapting his words to the official narrative, Budzislawski instead praised the alleged savior of the journal, Maud von Ossietzky. She had felt "an inner obligation" to continue *Die Weltbühne*, he said, and she had given Hans Leonhard the job of "carrying out this political task." In this way, she had prevented the journal from falling into "unauthorized hands" through a possible revival in West Berlin or the Federal Republic, for instance.[42] The praise of those who had bypassed him after the war will not have passed easily through the lips of the former owner, who had been booted out and only very late reinstated as editor in chief. Budzislawski had finally lost his fight for control over the narrative of the revival of *Die Weltbühne* after the Second World War.

Former colleagues and younger members of the family remember the old Budzislawski as a likeable but embittered old man who had reconciled himself to his situation on a personal basis but had little to say of what was really on his mind. This character trait had always turned out to be wise politically, and it seems that Budzislawski scarcely ever acted against it, even in the most intimate family circles. He had been utterly depressed, it is said, after the suppression of the Prague Spring in 1968, but he had not wanted to have anything to do with the idea of leaving the GDR: "I cannot live out of a suitcase again. I am now too old for that." Two decades earlier, the Czechoslovak politician and former emigrant Jan Masaryk had given a similar but more dramatic reply to the question of whether he wanted to leave Communist Czechoslovakia, in whose government he was foreign minister, especially as there were some people there who wanted to kill him. His succinct response was: "Better dead than réfugié again."[43]

In the Ambience of Power

The Final Years

THE BUDZISLAWSKIS LIKED to spend their weekends at Buckow, in the Märkische Schweiz, an hour east of Berlin by car. They had regularly visited the resort as guests of Bertolt Brecht and Helene Weigel since the 1950s. Their friend, the theater director Hans Bunge, had started to live next door along with his family in the house where Brecht formerly did his writing after the latter's death in 1956. Some years later, Helene Weigel quarreled with Bunge over the correct way of dealing with Brecht's archive, finally ordering him and his family to leave. She welcomed Hermann and Hanna Budzislawski as new tenants and neighbors in 1961.[1] In view of the Budzislawskis' advanced age, Weigel offered self-mockingly to compete with her long-standing acquaintances "in gradually increasing foolishness." At the same time, she took care of the practical problems in her usual energetic manner: "As far as I know, the roof has been freshly tarred. The central heating is in order, but the house is fairly large, and I fear that things will not work out unless you receive assistance. It is hard to get help during the summer, but you could perhaps bring your Leipzig maid with you."[2]

The Budzislawskis had given the interior of the house a thorough examination in January 1961, and because "our worry that we would have to invest too much" in its upkeep had immediately disappeared as a result, they were very happy to accept Weigel's offer. Hermann showed on this occasion that he was also capable of making flippant remarks: "Once again: expressions of gratitude, shaking of hands, and other marks of genuine enthusiasm."[3] Now, just as in Vermont at the beginning of the 1940s, the Budzislawskis had a summer retreat in a privileged location. They also had neighbors in the shape of their friends the Brecht family, who were equally interested in cultural and political matters and who in addition took care of the house. Years later, when Weigel's

Hermann and Hanna Budzislawski (*on the sofa at the left*) in Helene Weigel's living room in Buckow (*she is at the right*), 1968.

daughter, Barbara Brecht, laid claim to the property, the Budzislawskis bought and moved into the adjoining "tower villa" at Clara-Zetkin-Straße 42.[4]

Buckow was to be Hermann Budzislawski's ideal place of refuge. At the beginning of August 1961, a few months after he had acquired his new week-end residence, the political leadership in Moscow decided to erect the Berlin Wall. The barrier works began on 13 August; the government of the GDR thereby deprived its population of the last remaining trace of freedom to travel to the West. The hard-liners in the SED had finally prevailed. This also applied to the University of Leipzig Faculty of Journalism. The affair of the Council of the Scoffers, a Leipzig student cabaret that included several students from the Faculty of Journalism, tipped the balance in the internal power struggle during the autumn of 1961.[5] A new program by the Scoffers that should have had its premiere a few weeks later was now prohibited and labeled as being counterrevolutionary. No one had objected to it before the building of the wall. Now the SED leadership at the university even went so far as to make the absurd accusation that the students had conducted "organized enemy activity." The main performers of the cabaret, including its leader, Peter Sodann, who later became the director of the Halle State Theater, were taken into custody and given prison sentences in the summer of 1962. The whole affair, the SED leadership at the university concluded, had revealed "serious weaknesses in educational work."[6] Budzislawski was also taken to task by the university's disciplinary committee. It was clear, it stated, that he "no longer possessed the energy required" to lead the faculty.[7]

Budzislawski only defended himself half-heartedly.[8] Franz Knipping, his longtime assistant who succeeded him as dean, wrote later that Budzislawski "had been contemplating the idea of a permanent move to Berlin" for a long time, not least, he claimed, because the "air in Leipzig" did not suit him.[9] This comment should be understood politically rather than literally. After the building of the wall, Budzislawski suffered more than ever from the atmosphere at Karl Marx University, which was now dominated by doctrinaire party members and led both the literary scholar Hans Mayer and his fellow returned emigrant Ernst Bloch to leave the city and the GDR at the beginning of the 1960s.

From 1964 onward the Budzislawskis lived once again in Berlin, the city where they were both born. They exchanged the house in Lenaustraße, Leipzig, for a spacious old apartment at Am Treptower Park 21. Their initial euphoria of the late 1940s had long since evaporated. The attacks from within the party on emigrants from the West, which began almost immediately after the family's return from New York, were not the only reason for this change of mood. Hermann was also afflicted by the country's intellectual narrowness. The writer Edith Anderson compared the political atmosphere that prevailed in the GDR in the 1950s to a refrigerator that urgently needed to be cleaned out. A distinctive odor had developed there: it was "unmistakably cold and rancid." Irene Runge, the child of returned emigrants and part-time guest at the home of the Budzislawskis, recalled that she had experienced the early GDR as an "alien" country, "cold and gray." Even more explicit comments were made by Budzislawski's old friend Alfred Kantorowicz, who had worked for some years as professor of literary history at Humboldt University after his journal *Ost und West* ceased publication. Immediately after he moved to the Federal Republic, in August 1957, he complained in a broadcast transmitted by the radio station Freies Berlin about the "lack of legal rights, the exploitation of the workers, and the intellectual enslavement of the intelligentsia" in the GDR, and he spoke, in reference to the SED, of the "arbitrary rule of a clique of unworthy people who defile the quintessence of Socialism."[10]

The Budzislawskis often argued within their immediate family circle over whether it had been the right decision to leave the United States and move back to Germany. There were also tensions between different family generations that found expression in letters, such as the one sent by Hermann Budzislawski to his daughter, Beate, on 3 July 1953 while he was on holiday in Ahrenshoop on the Baltic Sea. Two weeks earlier, on 17 June 1953, there had been protests by workers over the whole of the GDR that had been violently suppressed by the regime with the aid of Soviet tanks. In official party circles they spoke of "counterrevolution." Twenty-four-year-old Beate, who as a young mother had a child to take care of and in addition was suffering from examination stress at the university, had evidently argued with her parents about political developments, and she had also complained about the shortage of goods in the country.

Although this was not his normal way of dealing with things, Budzislawski decided to use his letter to Beate to deliver a "lengthy lecture about morality." He severely rebuked his daughter, who in his view was materially spoiled and politically unreliable:

> I am not at all satisfied with you. I understand your anger over all the difficulties that have suddenly piled up. No help with the housework, no refrigerator, the wrong milk, and examinations . . . and on top of that the political situation. One can respond to that with depression, with hysteria or panic, or with courage. For a good comrade there is only courage. When have we ever let ourselves be overwhelmed by difficulties? . . . Out of a million infants, only a few dozen are able to get hold of Humana or Babysan. We would like to obtain more. But, devil take it, other mothers also bring up their children. . . . The 17th of June was certainly a horrible business. Even far from the firing line it gave us a powerful shock. But where are you, you fighters? The party has gone through more crises than this one, even if you have not yet experienced any of them personally. Now we shall see who possesses strength of character.[11]

It was unfair of Budzislawski to lecture his daughter in this way not only because he was claiming a political steadfastness he himself had often enough failed to display but also because the young woman could hardly reply to the charge that she had insufficient experience of life. He appears to have noticed this point, because at the end of the letter he apologized, saying that he was "also a bit ashamed" that he had allowed himself to be tempted into delivering such a harangue.[12]

This letter provides evidence that at least in 1953 Budzislawski was defending the official party line not just in public statements but also in writing to the closest members of his family. Even so, this explanation still does not tell us anything about why he wrote this letter. Perhaps he was genuinely anxious about the possibility of an attempted "Fascist" coup in the same way as Victor Klemperer, who recorded in his diary that for him in 1953 the Soviet tanks had seemed like "doves of peace," adding: "I shall feel safe in my skin and position for just as long as Soviet dominion lasts here."[13] But perhaps Budzislawski also assumed that he was under surveillance and therefore deliberately emphasized his loyalty to the party line for the benefit of potential secret readers of his correspondence. In any case, he wanted to warn his daughter against criticizing conditions in the GDR too openly. At the beginning of July 1953 no one could foresee what might be the result of statements like Beate's if they came to the attention of the wrong people.

Budzislawski continued to maintain a loyal attitude toward the GDR over the next two decades. He possessed the elephant's hide so indispensable to a life under Socialism.[14] After what he had experienced during his first few years in the GDR, he was scrupulously careful to avoid exposing himself to further public attack. Within the party he was loyal to the party line, but in the manner of a man of the moderate Left who, despite the firmness of his own judgment, was aware of the fragility of human beings and the precariousness of their social position. The Hitler-Stalin Pact of 1939 had taught him that even a well-informed and astute tactician can make a faulty evaluation. Even when one was fully committed to Socialism, one had to leave a back door open. After the failure of the *Republik* publishing project in 1956, Budzislawski did not venture to introduce any further ambitious initiatives in the field of journalism until 1967, largely devoting himself instead to his official duties. In 1957 he proposed the transfer of the University of Leipzig Faculty of Journalism to Berlin, allegedly to give it a more intensively practical orientation but perhaps also to escape the pressure coming from his opponents at Karl Marx University.[15] By 1961, with the building of the Berlin Wall, it was clear to him that the further development of the GDR would proceed within narrower horizons than he had initially hoped.[16]

Despite all his disappointments, Budzislawski settled into the country as well as he possibly could, especially bearing in mind his advanced age and the lack of any genuine alternative.[17] The party rewarded him financially: it generously permitted him to make trips abroad, and it appointed him to a series of prestigious official positions. In view of the multiplicity of tasks Budzislawski took on after the failure of *Die Republik* and his difficulties at the faculty, it is safe to assume that minor ways of escaping from the routine of his professional life were very welcome to him. In 1958, when the third legislative period began, he returned to the Volkskammer of the GDR as a representative of the Free German Trade Union Federation (FDGB). For the next two decades, until his death in 1978, he was uninterruptedly a member of that assembly, which only met a few times each year. From 1958 until 1966 he was also vice-chair of the Volkskammer Committee on Culture, after which he moved to the Volkskammer Committee on Foreign Affairs. He had occupied a place on the presidium of the GDR Commission for UNESCO since 1963, he was a member of the

German Peace Council and the World Peace Council, and after 1965 he was vice president of the World Federation of Scientific Workers, of which he had been a founder-member ten years earlier. This organization, which was financed with Soviet money but had its headquarters in Great Britain, had an early commitment to disarmament and the protection of the environment. Its official publication, *Scientific World*, appeared in five languages, which illustrates its claim to exert influence in both East and West. According to its statutes, its main task was "to develop a feeling of political responsibility for science, to study the political conditions that are required for genuine and democratic scientific and technological research, and in addition to investigate the political consequences of scientific and technological progress."[18] In 1976 Budzislawski was again elected to the Volkskammer Committee on Culture as a representative of the FDGB. He also remained until his death the chairperson of the interparliamentary friendship group between the GDR and Great Britain.[19] He was flattered by the deference and the many honors given to him as the doyen of GDR journalism, in spite of all the compromises associated with such accolades. It was ultimately too important for him to promote the legacy of *Die Weltbühne* and his own image to endanger them by taking any ill-considered steps.

But there were one or two extra reasons why Budzislawski was committed to the GDR. One was the value he set on culture in the broadest sense, which was indirectly related to his family background, his schooldays, and his student years. Higher education and the development of aesthetic standards, as well as the ability to enjoy things of beauty in general and art in particular, were not inborn in the son of a master butcher. He had had to acquire these qualities through hard work, and for a long time he struggled to secure intellectual recognition, even though he was, for obvious reasons, unwilling to let this struggle become apparent. The work he put in to acquire the habitus of a middle-class intellectual is perhaps demonstrated most impressively by the fact that as a young man he had studied books about antique furniture in the reading room of the Berlin State Library. Journalistic opponents, such as the manufacturer's son Kurt Hiller, instinctively sensed where Budzislawski the social climber was most vulnerable when they vilified him as an intellectual upstart, as a "nobody who has barely emerged from nothingness."[20]

Budzislawski's experiences as a child and a young man were part of the reason why he put so much effort into supporting the endeavors of the GDR to become a "cultivated nation." In the 1960s, as vice-chair of the Volkskammer Committee on Culture, he repeatedly undertook so-called tours of inspection through the residential areas of Magdeburg, Dessau, and Görlitz. The Bitterfeld Path slogan, he declared in 1964 on GDR radio, was backed by an "immense popular movement."[21] This was a huge exaggeration, and it reveals the social distance between Budzislawski as the representative of the GDR elite and the rest of the population, especially as he failed to mention the repressive aspect of the party's initiative: the pressure that was exerted on established writers and intellectuals by requiring them to be close to the workers.[22] But what is decisive here was the justification Budzislawski used in order to give public legitimacy to the SED's efforts in the cultural sphere. His justification should not be dismissed as pure propaganda. He started off by asking rhetorically whether and how far workers had been able to concentrate on "general aesthetic matters" in earlier times. They had received very little encouragement to do so, he went on. Now, in the GDR, things were completely different: "Today, there are lectures on paintings everywhere in our museums. . . . Art is brought nearer, and an understanding of art is promoted, so that it can be absorbed and comprehended. The advantage of the previously privileged classes is removed not through taking something away from them but by giving the whole of the people a share in their cultural assets." What was formerly a privilege has now become everyone's right. People educated in this way can enjoy life more than they did before: "After all, they are not just working animals but human beings who absorb life with all their senses. And we are making sure that they can. We do not use compulsion, but who needs to be forced to eat well?"[23]

Budzislawski's undiminishing loyalty to the GDR was also a reaction to the personal continuity between National Socialism and the Federal Republic displayed by Germany's political and economic elites, as well as the temporary strengthening of right-wing radicalism there. Between 1966 and 1968 the right-wing extremist National Democratic Party of Germany (NPD) was directly represented in seven state parliaments, with a total of sixty-one deputies.[24] According to Budzislawski, this development showed that West Germany was undergoing an "immense process of contamination."[25] His warnings should also be seen in the context of the Brown Book campaigns of the 1960s, through which the SED aimed to reveal the identities of former National Socialists in the Federal Republic and thereby demonstrate the historical continuity linking the West German state to the Third Reich.[26] These campaigns were directed by the returned Jewish exile Albert Norden, who had been Budzislawski's fellow internee in France. In common with many other Socialists of their generation, the historical events up to 1945 remained for these two men the background of experience against which they assessed German-German developments during the Cold War. For Budzislawski, the rule of the SED was the necessary continuation of the political struggle for a democratic, more socially just Germany that had been proceeding since the late nineteenth century, not only in the narrow Communist sense but also as inheriting the Left liberal bourgeois tradition. Like Arnold Zweig, Budzislawski bore witness to this alleged necessity through his life's work as an anti-Fascist and, in his case, involvement in *Die Weltbühne*.[27] After he had been replaced in the autumn of 1961 as dean of the Faculty of Journalism, this was his most important role in the GDR, and he played it with bravura as long as he had sufficient energy to do so.

Two examples will serve to illustrate this. A week after the extreme right-wing NPD had obtained 9.8 percent of the votes cast in the Baden-Württemberg elections of 28 April 1968 and had entered the legislative assembly with twelve seats, enough to form a parliamentary group, Budzislawski as a member of the GDR Peace Council delivered a speech to accompany the laying of a wreath beside Ossietzky's grave in Berlin-Niederschönhausen. Having posed the rhetorical question "What does Ossietzky mean to us today?" he replied as follows: "In constantly varying ways, and precisely now with the elections in Baden-Württemberg, we are made aware that the enemies of Ossietzky, the enemies of the German people, the nationalists who are lusting after revenge, in short, the neo-Nazis, are again closing ranks and that what Ossietzky wrote about their fathers at the beginning of the 1930s applies again. . . . As the attempted assassinations and murders in West Germany demonstrate, Ossietzky's sufferings are not simply history."[28] The shooting by a policeman of the student Benno Ohnesorg almost a year earlier, on 2 June 1967, at a demonstration in West Berlin against the state visit of the shah of Iran to the Federal Republic was also grist to his mill.[29] Not until 2009 did it transpire that the shooter from the ranks of the West Berlin police force was also working for the Stasi. Budzislawski had a one-sided perspective on right-wing extremism in the Federal Republic because he always looked for historical continuities first and foremost but at the same time attached little importance to tracing out divergent developments. Moreover, he avoided mentioning the actually existing right-wing extremism in the GDR altogether.

Budzislawski reimagined not only Carl von Ossietzky but also Kurt Tucholsky as precursors of the GDR. It was impossible to do this without misrepresenting history. For example, he argued in a talk transmitted by the Berliner Rundfunk to commemorate the eightieth anniversary of Tucholsky's birth that only the heavily Communist-dominated Popular Front movement of the 1930s had brought humanity closer to the "positive goal" that Tucholsky had "aimed at for the whole of his life." The Popular Front had been a "remedy against despair and decadence." This was easy to say politically but dishonest. Budzislawski knew all too well from the letters Tucholsky had sent to him and

other people from his Scandinavian exile in the early 1930s that he had mocked
and ridiculed political maneuvers of this kind. Tucholsky, like most Berlin
Weltbühne authors, expected little and in any case nothing good from a KPD
that had been devoted to Stalin since the late 1920s.

Budzislawski even went a step further, asserting that a basis for the "cultural
accomplishments" and the "humanity" Tucholsky had vainly attempted to promote in the Germany of the Weimar Republic had now been laid in the "Socialist society" that was "under construction" in the GDR.[30] Such an act of political
appropriation was in the highest degree problematic in view of the SED's
repression and persecution of artists and intellectuals who, like Ossietzky and
Tucholsky during the Weimar Republic, had pointed to problems in the state
and society of the GDR that either really existed or were subjectively perceived
by them to exist.[31] Yet the claim was not as crude as it appeared at first sight,
because Budzislawski did not regard the development he had outlined as having reached its conclusion. Instead, he saw it as a current commitment, as the
values of "honesty" and "humanity" called for by Ossietzky were goals that had
yet to be achieved. Even the GDR was not without its shortcomings.[32]

But in the SED-controlled mass media it was only rarely possible to report
on one's own mistakes.[33] It was much less risky to discuss events that had happened a long way away. The party used political rallies to emphasize its international solidarity with the world's oppressed people and at the same time to
denounce the "imperialism" of the capitalist West.[34] As an expert on foreign
affairs, Budzislawski was repeatedly called upon to speak at meetings of this
kind—for example, against the American war in Vietnam or the murder of
Patrice Lumumba, leader of the Congolese independence movement and later
the first prime minister of the Democratic Republic of the Congo.

Budzislawski was still able to offer his listeners an enthralling presentation
of the world political situation, just as he had done in the French internment
camps at the end of the 1930s.[35] For this reason, he was a sought-after expert
on GDR radio and television up to the end of the 1960s. It was above all
through his regular appearances on the *Sunday Discussion* program transmitted by Radio Germany that he was a household name to the politically interested public in East Germany.

The urbane and sophisticated Budzislawski continued up to a ripe old age
to be useful to the GDR in the areas of cultural and foreign relations. Thus in
November 1969 he headed a five-strong delegation of Volkskammer deputies
who spent a week in the United Kingdom at the invitation of the Great
Britain–GDR parliamentary group chaired by the MP Renée Short, a member of the ruling Labour Party, with the aim of developing friendly relations

Hermann Budzislawski speaking in the Congress Hall in Leipzig on 16 February 1961 at a "rally in honor of murdered Congolese freedom fighters," including Patrice Lumumba. The slogan on the wall reads "Down with the Imperialist Murderers of Lumumba and His Fellow Fighters—Africa for the Africans."

between the two countries. The group had existed since 1965, and it initially comprised twenty-three MPs who all belonged to the "forces of the left in the Labour parliamentary party."[36] Great Britain was of particular interest to the GDR because it had not yet joined the European Economic Community (EEC), and there was therefore a chance that the GDR could obtain recognition in London without the need for a simultaneous change of course in Brussels. In the spring of 1969 it became more urgent for the GDR to achieve this because the new Social Democratic–Liberal coalition government in Bonn and the Labour government under Harold Wilson in London were thinking of strengthening their mutual relations. It was therefore necessary to conduct counterpropaganda, or in the language of the SED: "The discriminatory measures of ruling British and West German circles against the GDR must be made ineffective through a heightened offensive by all institutions directed towards Great Britain."[37]

There were, however, no official state relations between the GDR and the United Kingdom. In order to avoid annoying the Federal Republic, the British Foreign Office therefore classified the visit of the GDR delegation at the end of 1969 as "unofficial." It was clear, nevertheless, as Budzislawski argued in his report on the trip, which was also published in *Die Weltbühne* on 16 December 1969, that both sides had an interest in closer cooperation, particularly in the policy areas of trade, education, and training. The GDR delegation had a packed program that included both appointments at Westminster and discussions with representatives of British consumer cooperatives and trade unions. There were also visits to the grave of Karl Marx at Highgate Cemetery in North London and the cathedral of the industrial city of Coventry, which had been heavily bombed by the German Luftwaffe in the Second World War. The press photographs that have come down to us leave no doubt that Budzislawski cut a good figure during the trip; this was a man who spoke excellent English and was still extremely well informed about both events in Britain and world affairs.

In spite of the friendly atmosphere created by their hosts, the visit was, as Budzislawski explained, a mission of some delicacy. This applied particularly to a prospective interview with the BBC news program *24 Hours* and an apparently large number of interview requests from the international press. The journalists "did not want so much to explore the essence and character of our republic as to construct an antagonism between private and official opinions, and in their attempts to trip us up they rivaled the tactics of the roughest players on the football field." He did not reveal what had actually been discussed in the semiprivate sessions, but he claimed on behalf of both his companions and himself that they had carried out the party's assignment to pave the way to a normalization of relations with Great Britain. He shrewdly left it to the SED leadership to make a political assessment of the visit: "How should we describe this episode as a whole? Some English newspapers have chosen to entitle it 'a breakthrough.' They have taken note of the existence of the GDR and its Volkskammer. Many people, perhaps a hundred thousand or even millions, have understood that it is no longer possible to prevent a flourishing state with a Socialist social order from growing stronger."[38] The British newspapers were much more cautious, emphasizing the economic aspect of the

A GDR delegation led by Hermann Budzislawski visits the grave of Karl Marx at
Highgate Cemetery in London, 1969.

discussions above all. There was no mention of a possible recognition of the
GDR as an independent state.[39]

It was on such occasions that Budzislawski appeared at the top of his form.
When he was in contact with international scholars, politicians, and experts,
he sometimes diverged from the SED's official party line. For example, he gave
the last big speech of his career at the ABC Weapons Conference of 1971 in
East Berlin, organized by the World Federation of Scientific Workers, in which
he participated as the chair of the GDR delegation, who were the hosts of the
conference, and as the spokesperson of the federation's disarmament committee. In his closing address he appealed to the attending scientists to display a
sense of social responsibility, and he called on them to advocate peace through
disarmament rather than a "balance of terror." The conference had shown, he
said, that it was possible to find a "common language" between East and West,
"the language of a genuine search for real ways of removing a terrible threat."
Collective security could no longer be achieved in the twentieth century
through individual treaties between states—the same thought had characterized Budzislawski's conception of a global postwar order in the 1940s—but

instead required overarching regulations that should be agreed upon in a "world disarmament conference."[40]

The Central Committee of the SED regarded balancing language like this as dangerous, especially at a time when West Germany, under Willy Brandt, was pursuing a policy of détente that was also popular in the GDR. The Politburo was put on the spot, and it had to take a position, especially as the Social Democratic–Liberal government of the Federal Republic had already concluded treaties with the USSR and Poland in the previous year. A memorandum from the SED's Department for University and Technical College Affairs on the ABC Weapons Conference records that certain "differences of opinion" had come to the surface because comrade Budzislawski "wanted to fit in better with the Western members of the W[orld Federation] of S[cientific Workers] in his tone and use of language," whereas the party representatives wanted "above all else" to make a clear statement of the "Socialist class standpoint."[41]

The West naturally remained an important reference point for Budzislawski's thought and professional activity right to the end of his life. He repeatedly traveled to Geneva, The Hague, and Vienna during the 1960s as a Volkskammer deputy and a delegation leader. At the beginning of the 1970s he visited Paris, using that opportunity to have a final look at the family's former house in Sèvres.[42] He very rarely missed Werner Höfer's program *Der Internationale Frühschoppen* (International pre-lunch drinks), which was transmitted every Sunday on the Federal Republic's television station ARD, the joint organization of West Germany's regional public-service broadcasters.[43]

Since the mid-1950s, honors had been accumulating for Budzislawski the anti-Fascist journalist. His life and work, as the embodiment of historical veracity, were regarded as legitimizing the rule of the SED. Soon after his return from the United States he had been accepted again into the East German PEN Club (known officially as the PEN Center East and West).[44] He was in addition the recipient of many medals: the Fritz Heckert Medal of the FDGB (1955); the Franz Mehring Badge of Honor of the German Press Association (1956); the National Order of Merit in silver (1957); the Medal for Fighters against Fascism (1958); the Banner of Labor Order (1959); the Carl von Ossietzky Medal, awarded by the Peace Council of the GDR (1963); and the Johannes R. Becher Medal in gold, endowed by the League of Culture (1966). After the anguish and humiliations of his first few years in the GDR, these decorations were more than symbolic compensations. Every honor he received from the state was a fresh guarantee that the degradation of the early 1950s would not be repeated. After 1965 he also received an "honorary pension" to add to his "higher additional old-age pension." In 1970 he was honored with the National Order of Merit in gold, and finally in 1976, shortly

Hermann Budzislawski's seventy-fifth birthday is celebrated in the editorial office of
Die Weltbühne, 1976. Those seated at the table are, in a clockwise direction, Hanna
Budzislawski (*at the back, on the left, partly obscured*); a certain N.N.; Ursula
Madrasch-Groschopp (*under the portrait of Carl von Ossietzky*); Hermann
Budzislawski; his successor as editor in chief, Peter Theek; and Werner Lamberz,
head of the Agitation and Propaganda Department in the SED Central Committee
(*viewed from the back*). Thomas Eckert, the grandson of Hanna and Hermann
Budzislawski, is standing at the right-hand edge of the picture.

before his death, he received the Gold Star for International Friendship. He
was only denied the much sought-after Order of Karl Marx, the order that
carried the greatest prestige in the GDR. As the "Nestor of GDR journalism,"
Budzislawski enjoyed a high reputation and great public esteem, particularly
after his departure from the University of Leipzig. He showed that he appreciated his numerous decorations: on official occasions he was happy to wear the
various medals on his coat lapels. Dripping with tinsel like a long-serving
general, the little man with the bow tie and the emphatically nonmilitary
appearance was of course a slightly ridiculous figure.[45]

In view of the many honors he received and the material prosperity he was
guaranteed by the SED, Budzislawski too can be described in his later years as
a "highly cultivated cynic" and a member of the "red aristocracy of the
GDR"—expressions used in 2008 by the journalist Christoph Dieckmann to
describe the former GDR minister of culture Klaus Gysi. Like Budzislawski,
Gysi came from a Jewish family, had risked his life by committing himself to

oppose the National Socialists, had been interned in 1939 and 1940 in France, and had achieved office and influence after the Second World War in the GDR.[46] This generation of German Jewish intellectuals, who grew up as members of the bourgeoisie, were deeply marked by the antisemitic persecution of the National Socialists and their subsequent exile. After the end of the Second World War, they spent the evening of their lives in the GDR and were involved in a fundamental contradiction, as the author Barbara Honigmann has pointed out in recent years. For her father, Georg Honigmann, a journalist who later ran the cabaret Die Distel in Berlin, the situation was the same as it was for Budzislawski. They lived "a classically bourgeois life" in their prewar villas and their prestigious old apartments. At least, this is how it was "seen from the outside, except that in addition they preached the virtues of a Socialist society of which they could only have had vague notions."[47] The Socialism they lived was a Socialism with maidservants.

Ever since the 1950s, public perceptions of Budzislawski have been neatly divided along Cold War lines. In West Germany he was regarded as one of the many Communist cadres for whom the enjoyment of material and symbolic benefits provided a degree of solace for the ambivalence and sometimes the misery of their political existence. This point of view was initially very much influenced by two former *Weltbühne* editors who were also Budzislawski's personal enemies, William Schlamm and Kurt Hiller, and later reinforced by Brigitte Klump's autobiographical account of the "Red monastery," which was first published in Hamburg in 1978.[48] The SED elite, on the other hand, saw him as a deserving veteran fighter for Socialism whom they were happy to utilize as a source of political legitimacy. To penetrate behind Budzislawski's public facade is close to impossible. In the last two decades of his life, he only occasionally received private letters from people who remembered what he had achieved as the editor in chief of *Die Weltbühne* or introduced themselves as its readers.[49] The former Leipzig colleague Franz Knipping reported in 2001 that Budzislawski's secret wish had been to represent the GDR as its ambassador in the United States once he had come to the end of his active university career.[50] This declaration can be read in two ways: it implied either a sense of responsibility toward the state, which was Knipping's interpretation, or a desire to live in the West again without having to cut his connection with the GDR. How Budzislawski himself saw the situation is something we shall never be able to know. For the whole of his life, he reacted to questions like this "by smiling and shrugging his shoulders"; the answers he took with him to the grave.[51]

Budzislawski's social and political influence in the GDR had never been particularly powerful, and despite his many official functions it was further reduced after the late 1960s, partly but not exclusively because of problems with his health. As chair of the Club of Cultural Workers he avoided taking any kind of public stance, for example, when in 1965 Robert Havemann, the professor of chemistry who had been expelled from the SED, applied to him for admission to the club or when a year later the author Stefan Heym asked to be allowed to give a talk there. Behind the scenes, he worked assiduously to make sure that the appropriate procedures were brought to the attention of the SED's Central Committee.[52] He was now an aging intellectual involved in cultural politics, and he did not take part—at least, not publicly—in the debate about "Socialism with a human face," which, originating in Czechoslovakia, aroused the hopes of many people in the second half of the 1960s, including in the GDR. Perhaps this was out of conviction or fear and perhaps simply because he was exhausted.

According to a 1971 memorandum preserved in the documents of the SED's Department for University and Technical College Affairs, Budzislawski was now suffering from "serious problems of concentration," and he was "only capable of doing a limited amount of work." The party therefore decided to give him an associate in the person of Karl-Heinz Wirzberger, at that time the rector of Humboldt University in Berlin. The party also determined that Wirzberger would replace him in the presidium of the World Federation of Scientific Workers at the next opportunity.[53] In 1974, according to a statement by his youngest granddaughter, Budzislawski was committed to the Bernburg psychiatric clinic. After he was discharged from there, he was no longer the same person, she recalled.[54] It was said that the aged Budzislawski suffered under the harsh regime of his wife, who ordered him about and even mistreated him physically. But Hanna Budzislawski wrote shortly before her death in a private letter that she "had lived and worked with her husband for fifty years in a very happy marriage."[55] Hermann himself also declared publicly that if he had his life to live over, he would again marry the same woman.[56] It is impossible to deduce from such statements how things really were in their marriage. The Budzislawskis lived a very secluded life in their old age and were visibly lonely. Hanna suffered from age-related depression. In the late 1960s she became dependent on painkillers and narcotics. These were officially prescribed to her for intestinal problems, and she obtained the required opium solution from the government hospital in East Berlin.[57] The few old friends who were still around, including Jacob Walcher and his wife, Hertha, Helene Weigel, Lilly Becher, the second wife of Johannes R. Becher, Greta Kuckhoff, and Anna Seghers, seldom came to visit them. Contact had been entirely broken off with many other long-standing comrades in arms, such as Maximilian Scheer. When in November 1976 the SED deprived the songwriter Wolf Biermann of his citizenship, Hermann Budzislawski, who was already severely afflicted by illness, had no public comment to make.

Something that did start to be of great interest to him in his final years was his Jewish origin. He corresponded intimately with the Marxist economist Jürgen Kuczynski, who wrote regularly for *Die Weltbühne* in the 1960s and 1970s, and they both described themselves semiderisively as "two old Jews." The partially ironic tone of these letters was only apparently a way of distancing themselves from Judaism; in reality, it was a form of self-protection. It made it possible for them to use external events to exchange comments on their experiences and lives as Jews in the GDR.[58] Jewishness was a conscious element of Budzislawski's identity throughout his life. In this he differed, for example, from the German Jewish returned emigrant and journalist Georg Honigmann, who described his Jewish origin as a "miserable inheritance" and only began very late in life to resign himself to accepting that his apparently inescapable position of "sitting between two stools" had been forced upon him by destiny.[59]

Budzislawski's approach was not always easy to take politically. "No Jew is free as long as not all Jews are free," as Hannah Arendt had recognized in 1943 when she was analyzing the situation of Jewish refugees in the United States. An "individual exit from Jewishness" did not exist.[60] Budzislawski knew that. But like many other Jews who were politically on the Far Left, he regarded the Zionist national solution as the wrong path to take. In line with this, he had argued in 1939 in *Die neue Weltbühne* that the emigration of the European Jews could at most be the solution for a minority, particularly for the younger Jews, who were capable of being assimilated. In the medium term, a return to their "old homeland" in Europe was the only alternative for the most persecuted Jews, and this would become possible more quickly if the persecuted Jews and their organizations were to join the "anti-Fascist movement" and thus contribute actively to Hitler's overthrow.[61] Budzislawski conceived his Jewishness in a cultural rather than a religious sense. He did not belong to a Jewish community in the GDR, and he did not go to a synagogue, although he respected the Jewish holidays. His ideal was a fraternal world society to which Jews would naturally belong, whatever country they lived in. He thought that the best, perhaps indeed the only way to this goal was Socialism. It was on the basis of such youth movement convictions that he repeatedly criticized Zionism and the policies of Israel when writing in the GDR in the 1950s and 1960s, continuing a stance he had taken in his *Neue Weltbühne* articles of the 1930s, although he only very rarely revealed that he himself was Jewish.[62]

Budzislawski gave the clearest statement of his position in 1967 in a letter to the British Labour MP Renée Short, the very politician who would welcome him to Great Britain in person two years later. Short had complained that the GDR mass media reported very one-sidedly on the Six-Day War between Israel and its Arab neighbors.[63] Budzislawski replied on 13 July 1967 in an unusually personal letter:

> I am one of the journalists of the GDR warned by you to remember the persecu-tion of the Jews under the Nazis before condemning Israeli aggression. Please believe me that I will never forget this persecution. I am myself of Jewish origin. The whole of my family was killed, one of my cousins [Herbert Budzislawski] was guillotined. But I do not regard what happened to my family as a justification to break the law in my dealings with my fellow human beings. And thus I believe that international law also exists for Israel, although it has often been perse-cuted. . . . It is not easy for a person of Jewish origin to turn against a state in which there are many Jewish refugees. I have never accepted the saying "My country, right or wrong!"[64]

Budzislawski and Short had fundamentally different conceptions of what political lessons should be drawn from the mass murder of the European Jews. While Short, whose mother was Jewish, called on European Jews to practice solidarity with Israel, this is exactly what Budzislawski rejected. In line with the official foreign policy of the GDR, he regarded Israel as an aggressive nation-state that had formed a close alliance with the United States and the Federal Republic and therefore could only expect a very limited amount of political support from him. He did not, however, sign the "Declaration by Jewish Citizens of the GDR," printed in *Neues Deutschland* on 9 June 1967, in which the alleged "aggression" of "Israel's ruling circles" against its Arab neigh-bors was denounced.[65] And he repeatedly impressed upon his grandchildren that one "should know where one came from," or, to put it differently, that they were a German Jewish family and this was an important aspect of their own identity.

This identity included a continuing awareness, even after 1948, that they never completely belonged, despite every attempt to adapt and to conform. It is true that open antisemitism was no longer tolerated in the GDR after the end of Stalinism, but antisemitic prejudices from the Nazi era continued to exist in everyday life in many cases. The East hardly differed from the West in that respect. As late as 1986, Budzislawski's grandson, Thomas Eckert, who was by then living in West Berlin, complained to his Stasi case officer, to whom Eckert reported as an unofficial collaborator named "Martin Kunze" on political, cultural, and scientific developments in West Berlin as well as on the Jewish community there, that his girlfriend and later second wife, who lived in Buckow, had repeatedly been abused as a "Jewish whore" who would "have her arse ripped open." After that they would deal with him, the "Jewish sow." In at least one case, his girlfriend had been threatened with a knife by extreme rightist youths. Now she was scared even to leave the house after dark.[66] The GDR security services had known since at least 1982 that there was a problem with extreme right-wing youths in Buckow. One group of young people, according to an internal report, were in the habit of giving the Hitler salute when they entered two of the local pubs and were in possession of Fascist propaganda material. "Furthermore, it is known that these youths molest citizens of Jewish origin." Everyone in Buckow was aware of their behavior.[67]

The trauma of antisemitic persecution was deeply ingrained in Hermann and Hanna Budzislawski, and it preoccupied them literally until their last breath, although reality and delusion became increasingly intertwined. For example, when Hanna was an old woman, she asserted that the Nazis had "murdered" her disabled brother, Fritz, in 1935.[68] And when Hermann telephoned his daughter from the hospital in East Berlin a few days before his death it was evident from what he said that he was convinced the Fascists would now come and deport him. The Budzislawskis were not the only people to suffer from this kind of trauma. In his autobiography, written during the 1980s, the returned Jewish exile Stefan Heym aptly remarked that "human anxieties" were implanted in "layers of consciousness" he found impossible to control: "One may attempt to forget or repress them; but they always re-emerge, often in the most curious form."[69] It is impossible to understand the political life of Hermann Budzislawski and his wife, Hanna, after 1945 without acknowledging this deeply rooted fear of incarceration, deportation, homelessness, and death, which could not be completely controlled and which continued to exist like a cancerous growth in the Jewish former exiles, irrespective of the level of actual security they enjoyed in the GDR.

If we leave aside his attempts to tell his story in the early 1940s, attempts that owed their existence more to material circumstances than to a personal desire to communicate, Budzislawski did not leave behind autobiographical fragments, let alone a complete manuscript that might have given a more precise picture of his views. His was not an isolated case. He was part of a hidden generation that had been taught by life that the security provided by trusting in other people and human closeness might at any time turn out to be deceptive. Georg Honigmann, who was two years younger than Budzislawski, had a similar attitude. His daughter wrote that her father never made an effort to write down his memories or to pull together the many fractures in his life into a biographical whole by means of a coherent life plan. It was as if he "did not trust the written word, or no longer trusted it. There was only oral

transmission, the stories he told during our walks or during car journeys. . . .
Travel, and the movement it involved, appears to have given him a sense of
security and provided an incentive, because such conversations seldom took
place when we sat at a table, face to face, so to speak."[70] Honigmann, who was
an enthusiastic motorist, thereby created a free zone in the interstices of existence, a protected area in which he and his daughter could fleetingly exchange
views on the questions that really moved him. In contrast to this, Budzislawski, who was driven back and forth between Leipzig, Berlin, and Buckow
by a chauffeur, remained silent about the earlier stages of his life.

From his point of view, this reticence was a political strategy that had demonstrated its value. Budzislawski the Socialist had already had the pertinent
experience of secret police surveillance when in exile, and he himself had fed
these bodies with allegations against other people. By the early 1950s at least,
he knew that as a member of the SED in the GDR he was under observation.
He wanted to be perceived as a public intellectual, and he was eager to add his
own name to the list of renowned *Weltbühne* editors alongside Jacobsohn,
Tucholsky, and Ossietzky while at the same time disavowing his immediate
predecessor, the "Communist basher" Schlamm. Budzislawski's prestige in the
intellectual field was important to him, yet the life of the German Jew Hermann Budzislawski was of no public significance and of no concern to anyone. He had written these words in 1949 about Stalin: "His life story is not the
person he married or the food he likes to eat or the films he likes to watch. His
life story is world history."[71] Budzislawski saw his own life story in similar
terms, but obviously on a far smaller scale. He ultimately subordinated almost
everything else to the effort to secure his place in the history of German politics and journalism. Only in this way can we comprehend his conformity to
the party line of the SED and the fact that he did not hesitate to make public
attacks on close companions such as Dorothy Thompson if doing so served to
advance him professionally or politically.

We do not know what was discussed in the 1960s and early 1970s in Helene
Weigel's sitting room and in the Budzislawskis' summerhouse next door. In his
speech of congratulations made on 12 May 1970, which was "Heli's" seventieth
birthday, Hermann made a few vague references to their past: "At weekends
we were neighbors, and we talked of many things: Picasso and mushrooms,
music and fashion, cooking and art, and naturally politics as well. And as so
often, these discussions stimulated Weigel's zeal, combativeness, and sense of
civic obligation."[72] The meager amount of surviving correspondence between
the two shows that they occasionally intervened behind the scenes in favor of
former prisoners of war or students who had been punished in order to make
their lives easier in the GDR.[73] But they were unable to achieve any structural

changes. We can assume that Budzislawski saw his current way of life as a form of internal emigration, only partly chosen of his own free will. "You live everywhere as an *enemy alien*, always in exile," wrote Honigmann in one of his letters.[74] Budzislawski's silence about his life history was a result of this fundamental experience. His political and personal freedom of action was naturally restricted in the GDR, but that was not the only reason. First and foremost, perhaps, he was the prisoner of his own craving for recognition.

Budzislawski died early in the morning of 28 April 1976 in Berlin, the city where he was born. Erich Honecker, the general secretary of the SED, and Willi Stoph, the chair of the Council of Ministers, sent official letters of condolence to his widow.[75] *Die Weltbühne* took its leave of an "honored teacher, friend, and comrade," emphasizing that, right up to his final hour, he had devoted his life "to social progress and the struggle for peace."[76] The obsequies were conducted to the accompaniment of the second movement of Beethoven's Third Symphony, the "Eroica," and "The Internationale." In conclusion, workers' songs and battle hymns rang out on the organ.[77] The SED Central Committee proclaimed that the deceased had served "the development of our state in an outstanding manner." The statement recalled the decisive stages in Budzislawski's life, and in this case not just as a matter of form; he had been "a consistent anti-Fascist" and had "earned special recognition for his work in training the GDR's young journalists." In his later years he had returned to editing *Die Weltbühne*, which he had done in a praiseworthy fashion, fulfilling Ossietzky's legacy.[78] He would certainly have been very happy to read this last comment in particular. Although the SED had hindered his career as a journalist after 1945, he did at least succeed in securing recognition in the GDR as the savior of *Die Weltbühne* between 1934 and 1939.[79] He was not to know that, like the East German state, this reputation would have ceased to exist within a few years.

The death of her husband worsened Hanna's feelings of depression, for which she had been receiving medical treatment since 1965.[80] Now seventy-seven years old, she sent a get-well letter from the government hospital in East Berlin to her son-in-law, Horst Eckert, who was also undergoing treatment at the hospital, on 13 November 1978. She herself, she said, "could be helped by no one, because I shall never get over the loss of Hermann." At the same time, she insisted on her independence: "I determine everything that concerns my life, and I would not like anyone to interfere in this. I do not wish it, I cannot allow it, and I do not have to."[81] Comrade Johanna Budzislawski, holder of the Fighter against Fascism medal, the golden badge of honor, and the Distinguished Service Medal of the GDR, died a few months later, on 30 March 1979.[82] The exact cause of her death is unclear. The State Security Service announced on 4 April that according to a statement by the chief physician of the government hospital she had been admitted to the intensive care department early on the afternoon of 30 March after her grandson, Thomas Eckert, had called for a doctor to visit the house. "In the course of the next few hours, the patient gradually lost consciousness and then went into a coma. Death occurred at 20:15." Her death was a surprise, insofar as she was constantly under treatment for her dependency on narcotics and only a week earlier had attended as an outpatient for a medical examination, at which no abnormalities had been detected. The doctors initially assumed that the cause of death was the "rupture of an aneurism of the abdominal aorta." But an autopsy carried out on 3 April by the Institute of Pathology at the Hospital of the People's Police "was unable to clarify the cause of death." The doctors felt that a rupture of the aorta was now unlikely to have been the cause of death, while the chief physician at the Institute of Pathology explicitly refused to rule out poisoning. The internationally famous forensic pathologist Otto Prokop found in addition that there were signs of considerable physical violence: "Spots and signs of bleeding were found, particularly in the area of the head, which must lead to the conclusion, in the framework of a differential diagnosis, that there has been a forcible compression of the neck—in the sense of a means of strangulation—with acute congestion of the blood above the site of compression." Rumors of an unnatural cause of death soon spread as far as Leipzig.[83]

Immediately after the autopsy on 5 April 1979, Hanna Budzislawski's body was cremated. The interment took place on 26 April.[84] The couple's grave is located at the Socialist Memorial Site in the Central Cemetery Berlin-Friedrichsfelde. Hanna only acquired a place there after her daughter intervened with the Politburo, finally getting her way by referring to the explicit wishes of both her parents.[85] The area around the Pergolenweg, or Pergola path, in the cemetery also contains, in addition to the Budzislawskis' graves, the remains of the following people: the former KPD dissidents Herta and Jacob Walcher; the miner Adolf Hennecke, who was well known in the GDR because of the "activist movement" named after him; the second wife and the sons of Karl Liebknecht, murdered in 1919; and Greta and Adam Kuckhoff from the resistance group the Red Orchestra. This area was planned and used for decades as a kind of pantheon of German Socialism, and until the beginning of the 2000s tens of thousands of people, in some years even hundreds of thousands, made a pilgrimage to the site on the anniversary of the murder of Rosa Luxemburg and Karl Liebknecht. Nowadays the atmosphere there is calmer. Like few other places in Germany, the cemetery represents the ambivalent inheritance of Socialism as one of the formative ideologies of the twentieth century.

What Remains?

A Twentieth-Century German Life

H ERMANN BUDZISLAWSKI WAS a German Jew who had belonged to the Socialist movement since the days of his youth. He shared its aspirations and its expectations, but he also experienced its defeats. He used others, and he was used by them; he was interned, and he was liberated; he was persecuted, and he was courted by the powerful. From time to time, he too had influence, but even then he knew that he could never place his trust in power. He was a left-wing intellectual and at the same time a bourgeois, a calmly reflective businessman who was also a master tactician. He had devoted himself to the struggle against Fascism and National Socialism since the early 1930s. This struggle gave meaning to his life, and it continued to do so long after the Third Reich had ceased to exist in 1945. Even so, he well understood that many of the networks he joined as a political emigrant were precarious alliances with a limited half-life. Throughout the course of his life, he displayed little loyalty even to his closest associates when the direction of the wind appeared to be changing. That is how he was able to keep his head above water in different political systems. He was always oriented toward what was feasible because he did not want to wait for "original truth" to appear, as he put it in 1934. In his view, any vision of society had to be based on an "undogmatic" analysis of reality. Being committed to this credo, he left behind an extensive journalistic oeuvre but no lasting mark.

Budzislawski was a journalist with burning ambitions for whom politics was first and foremost and sometimes also ultimately a means to an end. Like many members of his generation, he was marked by the "lessons of cool conduct" taught by the First World War.[1] Hopes, enthusiasms, and a dedication to higher aims are found—if at all—in Budzislawski the high school graduate. The ideals of his youth fell into the background as soon as he had completed his doctorate and was faced with the problem of establishing himself as a journalist in Berlin. Budzislawski's idealism, which may well not have been very strongly developed anyway, suffered considerably from the explosive events of the critical year of 1923, which was marked by hyperinflation, the occupation of the Ruhr, and the Hitler putsch. On a closer look, there is not such a great difference as one might first assume between his coolly argued, eugenicist doctoral dissertation and his economic thought of subsequent decades, characterized as it was by realpolitik and occasionally astute predictions of the future course of events. One constant element since the mid-1920s, when he worked for a year for the anticolonial journal of the Indian exile nationalists, was a pronounced interest in the Global South to which he later reverted when he lived in the GDR. This enabled him to make a small contribution to "Eastern Europe's global vision of a socialist civilisation" after the Second World War.[2]

Notwithstanding all his tactical flexibility, Budzislawski remained surprisingly consistent in his political realism. One unchanging aspect of his way of thinking was a form of Prussian patriotism that was further accentuated by his experience as an exile.[3] The feeling of tenderness for his own country, "above and beyond all politics," which Kurt Tucholsky had invoked at the end of his angry and bitter book, *Deutschland, Deutschland über alles*, written in 1929, remained one of the impulses behind Budzislawski's political engagement throughout his life as a German and as a Jew: "Of course, in order to be able to place any of one's hopes on Germany, one has to believe that barbarism is a transient phenomenon that one day will again give way to humanism." That is how he formulated his position on the eve of the Second World War. Even the murder of six million European Jews was unable to deal a lasting blow to this hope.[4]

Budzislawski pursued his political and professional goals resolutely, perhaps in part because he never forgot the smell of his father's butcher's shop. It was a reminder of the milieu he came from and to which he never wanted to return. He was completely unwavering in his rejection of National Socialism. He was always a Socialist, but what did that mean to him personally? He only spoke or wrote about this belief in exceptional cases. From the perspective of a later generation of historians, Budzislawski left behind both too much and too little: too much, if we look at his extensive archive and his impressive journalism, which ranged over five decades of German and international history, and too little where the feelings, hopes, and disappointments of Budzislawski the man are involved. It almost seems as if, by choosing which documents to preserve, he had wanted to determine which parts of his life would be visible to future generations and which would not. He preserved everything that demonstrated his importance as a public figure or the political compromises he had to make. But the nature of his private life in the context of his immediate family is very difficult to grasp. Even for the 1920s, his surviving personal correspondence offers extremely meager pickings. There are no love letters to his wife in the publicly accessible archive. He did not write any diaries. The early death of both his brothers, the loss of his beloved mother (whose grave he was only able to visit for the first time in 1948, eleven years after her death), and even the birth of his only child in 1929 receive at most a simple mention in the written testimonies we have. In 1940, as an emigrant, he undertook an arduous flight along with his aged father through half of Europe and then to the United States, but there does not seem to have been any close emotional bond between them even in the harsh circumstances of refugee life. It was difficult for Budzislawski to show his feelings, and he rarely wrote of them. Did he want to avoid confronting his own mirror image, his desires and anxieties? Was he in love with himself—or did he only want to make something of himself? Such questions mark the limit for a historian who can and must make use of fictional, aestheticizing means but at the same time must bear in mind the veto right of the sources.[5]

Budzislawski's course of action in 1933 and 1934 after becoming the editor in chief of *Die neue Weltbühne* was determined not only by a strong desire to become a powerful journalist but also by the need to secure a regular income in exile for himself and his family. After the failure of his earlier attempts to achieve fame as a writer and a political commentator, he seized the unique opportunity he had created for himself. Until the prohibition of the journal by the French authorities at the beginning of the Second World War, Budzislawski did everything he could to keep *Die neue Weltbühne* in existence and to strengthen his own position in the arena of the German-language exile press. The reputation he achieved thereby as an influential, experienced, and comparatively independent journalist opened several doors to him from the autumn of 1940, when he came to live in exile in the United States.

After the Second World War, however, the same reputation became a burden, too. For two decades, the fact that he had previously insisted on remaining independent prevented his return to becoming the editor in chief of *Die Weltbühne* when it was reestablished in East Berlin in 1946. The SED leadership under Ulbricht made a political decision to pass over Budzislawski's morally and legally justified claims, and the disappointed editor in chief accepted Ulbricht's fiat, not least because there was no other alternative. He was made a professor at the University of Leipzig instead and, after the end of the Stalin era, rose to become the dominant figure in its Faculty of Journalism, founded in 1954. Even so, he did not abandon his ambition to regain a top position in journalism. When he returned to *Die Weltbühne* in 1967 for a final four-year stint, this marked the culmination of a remarkable career, although it hardly

fulfilled the former editor in chief's dreams, because it took place under different circumstances from those he had envisaged. It was certainly a worthy position, but the sphere of activity was very limited. Budzislawski's professional
skill and the credibility of his anti-Fascist record did allow his journal to operate with a degree of flexibility that was somewhat greater than that enjoyed by
many other GDR newspapers and periodicals, particularly in foreign affairs
reporting. But neither *Die Weltbühne* nor its editor were able to exert any
noticeable influence on the country's political and social development.

Some questions about Budzislawski's life have been left undecided in this
book, and this cannot be otherwise. As Ernst Toller wrote in his autobiography, *Eine Jugend in Deutschland*, which appeared in 1933, biographies that
portray "people in public life" are only rarely able to depict "the complexity of
an individual's existence." Many contours of the "complete human being"
inevitably remain unilluminated.[6] That would not have worried Hermann
Budzislawski, who was a smooth operator and a survival artist. Indeed, he
would probably have preferred to see fewer contours than have been exposed
in this book. He did not want to show his hand, not to anyone, and not at any
time. He expressed this attitude most clearly in a triumphant letter sent in
March 1936 to Heinz Pol, his defeated rival for the position of editor in chief
of *Die neue Weltbühne*: "People can say about me, if they want, that I have
made this or that mistake. Nothing more. It has been their bad luck that I
have always known a great deal about all the people involved, while about me
they have known nothing."[7]

When he was an old man, the editors of the GDR illustrated magazine *Für
Dich* (For you) asked him to give a personal answer to the hypothetical question "If I were to start my life again . . . ," and he agreed to do this. There is no
question that calls for more self-criticism than this one, he stated by way of
introduction, but the words that followed were marked by a complete absence
of that quality. Instead, writing with wit and self-confidence, he linked his
biographical data to generalities, and he avoided replying to any personal
questions, referring instead to the laws that allegedly determine life in society:
"As with so many people, my life was an inevitable, law-governed reaction to
the circumstances of the time. If repeated under the same conditions, the same
results would occur. With my present experience I could easily have embel-
lished these results to some extent. But I would have had the same profession
of an active journalist, including the move to the university, which enabled me
to digest the profession theoretically and make it easier for the next generation. I would have had the same political attitude, and with more experience
I would have supported Socialism more effectively and more powerfully. . . .
My back would perhaps have been less bent because I would have done more

sports, and in general I would not have left out so many of the fine things of life. Like so many people, therefore, with more experience I would have lived a better variant of my present life."[8] Should one believe this? Did he believe it himself?

When he was looking back on his past three decades earlier, he had been still more circumspect. "Subjectively, everything is true," he wrote in one of his attempted autobiographies of the 1940s, "but motives change in the memory. Sometimes, what was a pure accident acquires meaning after time. Moreover, an apparent political connection may also be a matter of interpretation. It must be enough to report with honesty. Pure truth does not exist on this planet."[9] When he had grown old, Budzislawski was no longer able, for reasons of both health and politics, to write an honest autobiography of this kind. Like many people who postponed writing the story of their life until they grew old, he lacked the strength to undertake the task when any further delay was impossible. Much therefore remained unspoken. Even so, Budzislawski, the "careerist" who crossed so many boundaries, retained a few bedrock character traits; the course of his professional life bears witness to this. Since taking over *Die neue Weltbühne* in 1934 he had worked indefatigably to secure his place in the history of political journalism, and for him private affairs were largely a means to an end. He himself was aware of this, as we can see from what he wrote at the beginning of the 1940s in retrospective contemplation of the months immediately after the Hitler-Stalin Pact, those months that saw "the collapse of my existence": "My personal collapse was a punishment for attempting to live on too large a scale. I had sacrificed my private life to create space for the big things. My plans for the world hardened me against the concerns of my own family, the burden of the political struggle caused me to forget about art and beauty. Inner impoverishment was the price to be paid for involvement in the great game. And the game ended in defeat."[10]

These are impressive words. He is severe on himself, he is cool, he is objective, yet he adopts a literary style appropriate to the genre of autobiography. Moreover, the words are perhaps not as seriously meant as first appears if one looks at his life in the United States and later in the GDR, in exile from exile, as it were. Had he succeeded, as he wrote in 1948, in his attempt "to restore the connection with our past, to knit our broken, interrupted lives together, so that we can develop once again into whole human beings?" Could this be done? Could it be done in Germany, and if it could not, was there any other country where he and his family could have begun their lives again? The journalist Hilde Walter, who like the Budzislawskis was living in New York in 1941, wrote to a woman friend that as an exile from any country, one brought to the new land "the concerns of those who had remained behind," and therefore one remained "doubly alien."[11] If that is correct, then Hermann Budzislawski was a quadruple alien when he returned to Germany, or at least a man repeatedly uprooted. Was there still a homeland for this Prussian Jew, this journalist who sympathized with anticolonialism, despised Hitler, despised Stalin, praised Stalin, wrote in English, thought internationally, and lived a very bourgeois existence in the GDR in a villa stuffed with antiques?

And do members of a later generation, living comfortably in a peaceful situation, have the right to judge the attempts of such a man to lead his life? There is no doubt that Budzislawski was a man of ruthless decisions. He was a businessman who operated with all the tricks in the book and an unreliable friend. But he lived at a time when harshness toward both oneself and others appeared advisable if one did not want to go down in defeat. This applied to an even greater extent if, like him, one was a man of politics who wanted to remain consistent and for that very reason had to act with flexibility. But it has to be asked whether his own ideal goals of human coexistence and the building of a better society could be achieved by these methods and whether Budzislawski thought they had been realized at least in part in the GDR. He knew the answer that was publicly required from 1949 onward, but he kept his private opinion to himself.

With all these contradictions, Hermann Budzislawski, the "impersonal personality," was perhaps a more typical Socialist than many others whose names are better known today. His story demonstrates that there is not much to be gained by making cut-and-dried verdicts and hastily imposing political labels when the objective is not only to do justice to someone's lifetime achievement but also to understand the opportunities, constraints, and frustrations of the twentieth century. His was a life of a century, lived and not lived, at the same time individual and universal.

Epilogue

"Operation Legacy"

WHEN HERMANN BUDZISLAWSKI died, a will signed by the couple in 1969 came into force. It provided that each partner would inherit from the other. The will also stated that when the surviving partner also died, the couple's only child, their daughter Beate Eckert, who was born in 1929, would be their sole heir.[1] But this was not what happened. The Budzislawskis' grandson, Thomas Amos Eckert, born on 12 April 1953, had known at least since the death of his grandfather that a codicil had been added to the will, as he frankly explained to his Ministry of State Security handler on 12 May 1978. The latter made a note of the conversation, which read: "Hermann Budzislawski's wife had the right to change the will according to her wishes. Frau Eckert's son, Thomas Eckert, is at present endeavoring to make use of the last-mentioned possibility, that is, to obtain an alteration of the will in his favor through the agency of Frau Budzislawski." As the family's lawyer did not want to undertake such a change, Thomas Eckert was now in the process of "winning over another lawyer to support his objective."[2]

By the time Hanna Budzislawski died, less than a year after the death of her husband, the will they had originally drawn up together had been altered. The name of Thomas, who had been Hanna's favorite grandchild for many years, was inserted into the new version, dated 16 November 1978, as the sole heir. And in this case sole heir really meant sole heir, because, according to the Civil Code of the GDR, which had just come into force in 1976, the mandatory portion of the inheritance reserved for close family members in the German Civil Code was only to be given to them if their interests needed to be protected, if, for example, they were not yet adults. Hence Beate Eckert, the Budzislawskis' only daughter, went away empty-handed, as did her own two daughters, Thomas's sisters. Two months before her death, Hanna Budzislawski, who was now in a weak physical state, wrote as follows in a private letter: "The only person who stands by me is Thomas, the oldest grandchild, who works at the GDR radio station." It also appears from her letters that her grandson was just then furnishing a new place to live, which she felt would "cost a small fortune." Even so, she was evidently prepared to pay for the renovation and even give up some of her valuable furniture, because "if someone barely earns 600 marks, as he does, and an ordinary set of shelves costs 1,300 marks, even with the best will in the world he won't be able to afford it."[3]

Hanna Budzislawski's youngest granddaughter visited her occasionally, but she was, Hanna wrote, "just as incited . . . as the others."[4] Whether that was a reference to political differences between the generations is unclear. In any case, even before the inheritance dispute blew up, there was a complete absence of harmony between members of the Budzislawski-Eckert family. The relationship between Beate Eckert and her son had broken down after his parents had thrown him out of the house they shared when he was still a student.[5] Shortly before her death, Hanna wrote with bitterness that her daughter and the grandchildren were all "after the inheritance," even though they had already been provided with antique furniture and similar objects of value during her lifetime. She was clearly aware that her power of disposition was the last trump card she could play in the family game: "According to the will, I am the sole heir, and I can make any disposition I regard as right and proper."[6]

The inheritance was both materially and culturally substantial, and Hanna Budzislawski's death was followed by an acrimonious feud over its true destination. Over the next thirty years, not only the family but also German courts, publishing houses, top SED functionaries, and the Stasi were all kept busy by the case. Material interests, the wish to safeguard the cultural legacy of *Die Weltbühne*, and the need to ensure that Hermann Budzislawski was properly appreciated as an important political intellectual were all inextricably intertwined in this dispute. Thomas Eckert, the grandson who had been made sole heir by his grandmother, occupied the central position in these disagreements. His is a story of isolation and decline that is intimately linked with both the quarrel over the inheritance and the specific configuration of relations between the two Germanys in the second half of the twentieth century. To understand why the story of Hermann Budzislawski and *Die Weltbühne* again aroused a considerable amount of public interest after the fall of the Berlin Wall, one needs to know about a series of events and quarrels that stretch back as far as 1979 but that were scarcely known to the public. They were described for the first time in detail by the journalist Andreas Juhnke in 1990.[7]

At first, it looked as if Thomas Eckert had gained the most from the latest developments. He was a young man who was well connected in cultural circles and who spent his time within the ambience of the playwright Heiner Müller, for example. He was twenty-five years old when his grandfather died, well educated and charming.[8] After gaining his Abitur and doing his military service in the National People's Army, he had studied philosophy at Humboldt University between 1973 and 1979, completing his degree by writing a thesis entitled "Problems of the Strategy and Tactics of the KPD during the 1930s."[9] He was the third generation of his family to work on the subject: his grandfather had been actively involved in these historical events, and his father, Horst, had gained his doctorate by analyzing a very similar topic in the early 1960s. After his studies, Thomas Eckert received a job in the GDR's broadcasting service, perhaps through the influence of his mother, who was also employed there, but he did not have a good career. It was only the inheritance he received from his grandparents that enabled him to indulge permanently in a casual lifestyle. He enjoyed status symbols such as his grandparents' Volvo and the inherited tower villa in the idyllic town of Buckow, and he regularly received rent from the twenty-five tenants who lived in an apartment building at Kaiserin-Augusta-Allee 87 in Berlin-Charlottenburg, which his grandmother Hanna Budzislawski had inherited in January 1969 from her mother.[10] The rental income from the house in West Berlin amounted to approximately 5,000 deutsche marks a month at the beginning of the 1980s.

This wealth not only made it easy for Thomas to give assistance to needy friends and acquaintances and thereby secure the goodwill, affection, and regard of those around him but also allowed the descendant of a prominent grandfather to approach the SED leadership and the Ministry of State Security with confidence. Thomas had been recruited by the Stasi as an informal collaborator (IM) in 1973 at the age of twenty. He was of interest to that organization because of his membership in the October Club, a state-promoted political folk music group. The connection between Eckert and the Stasi continued to exist in varying forms until the end of the GDR in 1990.[11] The Stasi made use of Eckert in the 1970s "to provide information about and to safeguard cultural-political events and intellectual circles of political interest." According to his Stasi handler, Eckert was an "intelligent, critical, and to some extent politically loyal individual . . . who was always well informed in all political, social, and cultural spheres [and] had always been confronted with the whole range of Western literature through his grandparents."[12] Even so, his spying activities had not produced any outstanding results, the Stasi concluded.[13]

The dispute over the family inheritance broke out immediately after the last will of Hanna Budzislawski had been revealed. Thomas Eckert initially suggested that his mother and his two sisters be allowed to have a share in the inheritance in order to keep peace within the family. But Beate Eckert did not wish to accept any "handouts"; she wanted sole power of disposition.[14] She contested the will with the assistance of a well-known medical expert on the grounds that her mother had supposedly been of unsound mind when she altered the provisions. Thomas Eckert suspected that leading figures in the SED Central Committee had helped her to do this. What had "originally been a family dispute about an inheritance" had thereby taken on a political significance, and according to a 1987 report by the Stasi, it had permanently alienated Thomas Eckert from the GDR.[15]

After the medical expert's report on Hanna's testamentary incapacity had been submitted, the State Notary's Office decided to reinstate the 1969 will. Beate Eckert again became the heir, as her parents had jointly provided, but that was not the end of the story. Thomas Eckert complained bitterly to his Stasi handler; he went in person to a member of the Politburo, Kurt Hager; and he now made use of the courts himself. The Stasi documents covering "Operation Inheritance" for the months that followed are missing. According to the journalist Andreas Juhnke, this was probably because the matter was dealt with at the highest levels of the Office of Reconnaissance. The organization was able to destroy a lot of highly sensitive documents before the Stasi archives were seized in January 1990 by Citizens' Committees, which made sure no further destruction of the files could occur.[16]

The archives do at least record the result of "Operation Inheritance." On 10 March 1980 the Treptow District Court found in favor of Thomas Eckert. Four days later, Hanna's final will, which made him the sole heir, was entered into the records of the State Notary's Office in Berlin-Treptow as a valid document.[17] Only a few weeks later, however, Thomas had to sell a large part of the moveable estate to the GDR export company Kunst und Antiquitäten GmbH to raise the money to pay an inheritance tax assessment of 832,056 marks issued by the responsible tax authorities.[18] This company, founded in 1973, was part of the Commercial Coordination Sector (KoKo), managed by Alexander Schalck-Golodkowski. One of its tasks was to obtain currency for the financially embarrassed GDR by selling antiques, works of art, and other commodities to the West. The GDR was, in a sense, selling part of its family silver in order to satisfy the rising expectations of the country's consumers.

But this family silver did not just come from the public coffers; it was often taken from private possessions, which in the GDR were only very inadequately protected from the grasp of the state. In practice, the SED regime's self-imposed obligation "to prevent the creation of accumulations of wealth that are detrimental to the people" allowed it a fairly wide margin of discretion and a great deal of room for maneuver.[19] Kunst und Antiquitäten GmbH, in collaboration with the Ministry of State Security, made thorough use of this provision, as was reported after reunification by the lawyer and politician Gregor Gysi, who had great insight into the way the business was conducted, not least because he had acted as attorney for the state-run art trade in the GDR. Since the end of the 1970s, tax demands had repeatedly been used in the GDR as a means of pressuring reluctant sellers: "The principle was always the same, as far as I could observe. . . . One never had the impression that genuine tax liabilities were involved. The aim was rather to gain possession of these objects so as to be able to sell them to the West in return for foreign currency."[20]

It quickly became clear to Thomas Eckert that he had been deliberately deprived of his wealth by the GDR authorities in the spring of 1980. These proceedings were conducted according to a system, he said, and he could, if necessary, have divulged information about this to interested parties in the Federal Republic, which would inevitably have inflicted reputational damage on the GDR. This is how we should understand the cautious formulation he used in a letter sent in 1983 to the GDR minister of culture: "This GmbH has a clear-cut financial remit. This is still true even today."[21] The Stasi had recorded a few years earlier that it was necessary to be self-critical and to admit that Thomas Eckert "has meanwhile come into possession of documents on the matter of the inheritance and its transfer that demonstrate in black and white that there have been breaches of the law that could actually lead a citizen like him to despair. It should also be pointed out in this connection that the documents in question could represent a political weapon against our judicial organs or be used against us if they were made available to the class enemy."[22] And on 10 April 1980, after a conversation with Eckert, the Stasi representative made the following note: "He holds the view that after his victory in the proceedings over the inheritance the sole aim of the relevant state agencies is now to suck his blood by imposing inheritance and property taxes."[23]

The sum of money demanded by the authorities consisted of an annual property tax on the house in Buckow, the Volvo inherited from his grandparents, and the as yet unsold antiques. The money had to be paid immediately. In addition, property taxes for 1978 and 1979 were retroactively imposed on the bank deposits of his deceased grandparents.[24] Eckert regarded these demands as exorbitant, and he also complained bitterly that the payment deadlines he had been given were very tight. He had had only eight days since the house had been allocated to him in which to deliver the antiques and historic art treasures he had inherited to the Mühlenbeck purchasing office, to those neighbors and acquaintances who were interested in purchasing them, and, as the Stasi put it, to "well-connected profiteers from the underworld of the antiques trade" so that he would be able to pay his inheritance taxes by the due date and thereby avoid incurring interest on arrears of payment. The Stasi report goes on to say that Eckert did not understand why the state agencies of the GDR "were unable to reach an agreement with him calmly and over a period of time" on handing over named works of art and antiques to GDR museums. He had repeatedly approached the Ministry of Culture and other party institutions with requests for a postponement. But because since 1976 the Kunst und Antiquitäten GmbH had enjoyed an unlimited right of pre-emption, he had met with a categorical refusal everywhere. After all the taxes had been paid, he was left with no more than approximately 60,000 marks, reduced still further by the cost of court proceedings and lawyers' fees.[25] A grandfather's services in the fight against Fascism did not prevent the state from plundering the possessions of this German Jewish family.[26]

Budzislawski's grandson, who had until then lived well and happily in the GDR, felt that this was more than he could bear. In 1982 he put in an application "on personal and political grounds" to be allowed to renounce GDR citizenship and move to West Berlin. The response of the authorities was to deprive him of his membership in the SED and his job at the GDR radio station. Over the next few months he took a number of odd jobs, working at the Jewish cemetery in Berlin–Prenzlauer Berg and as a butcher in the kosher butcher's shop of the East Berlin Jewish community.[27] Finally, in June 1983 he was able to move to the western half of the city "with the agreement of the organs of the GDR."[28] He transferred the tower villa in Buckow to his wife as part of ongoing divorce proceedings. When she in turn wanted to leave the GDR at the beginning of 1984, she did not have to search very long for a buyer for the tower villa, as Gregor Gysi, the Eckerts' lawyer who had acted first for Thomas's mother and then for Thomas himself, was interested in it. According to Gysi's version of the story, he heard of the favorable opportunity by accident. Eckert's former wife had telephoned the actress Barbara Brecht-Schall, a daughter of Bertolt Brecht, "while I happened to be there and asked whether she was still interested in the property. She said no and asked me if I was interested in buying a house. As I did not have one, I nodded. In this way I got to know the divorced wife of Budzislawski's grandson, and I then concluded a contract of sale with her so that I became the owner."[29] According to the information given by Gysi, the purchase price was approximately 60,000 GDR marks.[30]

The Ministry of State Security was very well informed about all these trans-actions. There is an entry for 31 January 1984 in the handwritten service diary of Günther Lohr, the assistant director of Main Department XX, Division 9 of the Ministry of State Security, that records the minutes of an internal meet-ing. According to this document, "IM Notar" was instructed to give a report on Thomas Eckert. It also states that "if the house has already been sold to

'Notar,' then the contents of the four cabinets (cultural assets of the GDR) must be reported to the authorities."[31] In 1995 the news magazine *Der Spiegel* claimed that "IM Notar" was Gregor Gysi, basing this assertion mainly on the above document.[32] Three years later, the Immunity Committee of the Thirteenth German Bundestag came to the same conclusion: "Officers Lohr and Reuter of the Ministry of State Security were solely responsible for Dr. Gysi during the period of his unofficial collaboration between 1978 and 1989 using the cover names 'Gregor' and 'Notar' for him, as well as the IM categories GMS [societal collaborator for security], IMV [IM pre-run], IMS [unofficial collaborator for security], and IM side by side and in various combinations. The committee has no knowledge or any reliable indication that these cover names were applied to any other person than Dr. Gysi."[33] In recent years, the courts have seen this differently: they have stated on several occasions that it is not absolutely certain that Gregor Gysi was "IM Notar." In March 2010 the Hanseatic Higher Regional Court Hamburg concluded that by making a critical report to that effect in 2008, the TV program *Heute-Journal*, broadcast by ZDF, the German public-service television broadcaster, was "spreading suspicion without permission." It would not be a proven fact that Gysi had engaged in IM activities, the court ruled. It was especially necessary "to avoid making a prejudicial report that would give rise to the impression that the person in question had already been found guilty."[34]

Thomas Eckert's departure from the GDR was preceded by a continuous series of attempts on the part of the SED and the Ministry of State Security to keep this grandson of a prominent former emigrant and party cadre within the territory of the GDR. However, despite the imposition on him of "long-term political and ideological pressure," it proved impossible to prevent his "relocation," as the Stasi noted. In any case, his departure brought a little more money into the coffers of the bankrupt state, although not as much as had been hoped. Eckert was permitted to leave "with a generous allowance of household goods" after he had agreed to provide the GDR with a total of 125,000 marks. He made a partial payment of 35,000 marks, and he promised to settle the rest of the account after his relocation had taken place. However, there were no further payments by Eckert from West Berlin in the years that followed.[35]

This process did not, however, end the connection between Thomas Eckert and the Stasi, because in the next few years he remained in close contact with the organization, despite the fact that he now lived in West Berlin. According to his Stasi handler, Eckert regarded these contacts as "an opportunity to retain a connection with the GDR and a way of justifying in his own mind what he himself described as an act of political treason toward his country."[36] For "security reasons," the Ministry of State Security did not give him any more targeted assignments, but he remained useful for the Stasi, since he had evidently established contact very quickly with politicians from the SPD and the Greens, and he also reported on the Jewish community in West Berlin. He claims to have worked for some time in the Journalism Department of the Free University of Berlin and for Radio Free Berlin. Conversely, he attempted to make use of the Stasi for his own purposes, apparently threatening repeatedly to publish incriminating material he had found in his grandfather's archives about top GDR officials of the 1950s and 1960s. This tactic was at first successful. After he immigrated to the West, Eckert was allowed to travel back into the GDR with no apparent restriction. There he continued friendships and engaged in love affairs, and these had consequences, as the Stasi reported: he got married for the second time to "a woman ten years younger than him . . . whom he helped to move to West Berlin beforehand by exerting massive pressure on the state organs of the GDR." His divorced first wife had already left the country in 1985.[37]

In 1987 this remarkable cooperation between Budzislawski's defecting grandson and the Stasi came under threat for the first time, probably because Thomas started to make a serious effort to settle in his favor the disputed question of who held the copyright to *Die Weltbühne*. He informed universities and state archives in both West and East that he intended to do research into the history of *Die Weltbühne* and his grandfather's life. He hoped to find in the journal's former editorial archive the contract with which he could prove that his grandfather had bought *Die neue Weltbühne* in the 1930s—in other words, to do what the latter had not managed to achieve immediately after the Second World War. The editorial archive of *Die Weltbühne* had been confiscated by the French police in the autumn of 1939, it had come into the hands of the Gestapo the year after that, and it had then passed through Poland to Moscow and been placed in the Special Archive there. Finally, in 1967 it had been transferred from Moscow into the archives of the East Berlin Institute for Marxism-Leninism.[38]

Thomas Eckert must have known about this before 1989.[39] He told the Ministry of State Security in 1984 that he hoped to be able to acquire not less than half a million marks by suing the Athenäum Verlag, a West German publishing house with headquarters in Königstein near Frankfurt that had reprinted the Weimar *Weltbühne* some years earlier and had made an agreement with Siegfried Jacobsohn's heirs, who presented themselves in the Federal Republic as the owners of the rights to *Die Weltbühne*.[40] At that time, Siegfried's son Peter Jacobsohn had received from the Athenäum Verlag the fabulous sum of 225,000 marks in return for permission to reprint the journal.[41] By 1987 at the latest, the Stasi was of the opinion that in the case of their long-standing IM "Martin Kunze," alias Thomas Eckert, political questions (and perhaps the interests of historical scholarship) played "a subordinate role to the achievement of his own personal goals."[42] As former close friends recall, Eckert was by then no longer capable of doing concentrated work on his eminent grandfather's archive, not least because he suffered from progressively worsening alcoholism.[43]

In September 1986 the Stasi cut off contact with Eckert for at least two years, and it banned him from reentering the GDR, although this decision was reversed soon afterward.[44] This prohibition came at the most inconvenient time possible because it prevented him at first from gaining access to the former archive of *Die neue Weltbühne*, although preparations for his admission had already been made. At the end of 1986 the SED leadership and Eckert agreed on a deal that both sides thought would be to their advantage. Eckert was assured that on 27 January 1987 he would receive copies of his grandparents' correspondence from the period of immigration to Prague and Paris, as well as "a selection of bank documents" relating to the former *Neue Weltbühne* that were housed in the Central Party Archive of the SED, free of charge, after he had signed a declaration. The SED planned to hand over 361 photocopied pages, only a fraction of what was actually available.[45] In return, Thomas agreed that Rolf Harder, the party secretary in the East Berlin Academy of Arts, could visit him in his West Berlin apartment and examine Budzislawski's manuscript archive stored there "in order to complete" the Heinrich Mann Archive of the GDR Academy of Arts. This would be a way of correcting an omission made in 1979. After Hanna Budzislawski's death, the former director of the Staatsbibliothek Unter den Linden in Berlin had "taken over" valuable books from the Budzislawskis' former house, but no one had paid any attention to the manuscript archive, which contained "some documents of value." As a result, Thomas Eckert had been able to take these documents with him to the West when he left the GDR in 1983.[46] Harder's proposed visit to Thomas Eckert in the Kaiserin-Augusta-Allee did take place on 12 February 1987, but Budzislawski's grandson refused to allow Harder to examine the documents he wanted to look at. Thomas also failed to sign the declaration he was expected to make that he would use the archive material he received exclusively for his projected dissertation.

During these months Thomas Eckert's second marriage also broke up. Moreover, he only maintained contact sporadically with his mother and his two sisters; their relationship had suffered irreparable damage. The memory of injuries he had suffered in his childhood and youth also played its part in the quarrel. He told close friends that his mother had regularly locked him in the cellar and that his grandfather had delivered him more than once from his plight. Eckert's friends, however, soon noticed that "not everything Thomas Eckert said . . . was necessarily true."[47] In any case, by the end of the 1980s he was an increasingly isolated and desperate man whose outbreaks of alcoholism were increasing in frequency and severity. He had quarreled with his mother and his sisters, his two marriages had collapsed, and he was never able to get out from under the long shadow of his grandfather, to whom he wanted to erect a memorial. When the Berlin Wall came down, he also had to count on being "exposed" as a long-standing unofficial collaborator with the Stasi.

Thomas Eckert fled from the GDR, but he was unable to get away from himself. During the Wende period of 1989–90, when the borders between the two German states were opened, he sold the large apartment building in Berlin-Charlottenburg and withdrew to Fréland in the Kaysersberg valley near Strasbourg in France, where he acquired a large, isolated house named Ferme Cou Cou. There he deposited the twenty-eight file folders containing the archive of *Die neue Weltbühne*. These files had been handed over to him on 13 October 1990 by the former party archive of the SED, with the personal authorization of Gregor Gysi. His former lawyer, who as we have seen had bought the tower villa in Buckow a few years earlier, had in the meantime become chair of the former SED, which was renamed the Party of Democratic Socialism in December 1989. In other instances, too, Gysi dealt quickly and unbureaucratically with the task of handing over SED documents to journalists and private individuals at the time.[48]

Eckert now made another serious attempt to promote his grandfather's journalistic legacy.[49] The Berlin journalist and author Barbara Felsmann visited him in France in the summer of 1990 in order to help him with his dissertation and to prepare a complete reprint of *Die neue Weltbühne*. She was supposed to organize his grandfather's archive and compile a register of all the documents.[50] But on the day she arrived Eckert got so drunk that he had to be taken to the hospital. In the years that followed, phases of productive work alternated with lengthy intervals of sickness.[51] His mother, Beate, and her two daughters dashed madly from Berlin to France several times in the early 1990s, partly because they felt a personal duty of care but also because they were terrified that Thomas might sell or destroy the valuable archive. On 19 July 1991, during one of these visits, when Thomas lay once again in a hospital bed, either the mother or the sisters are alleged to have taken possession of the files. But Beate Eckert rejected this accusation as far as she personally was concerned in a rebuttal printed in the *FAZ Magazin*.[52]

Here is how Thomas Eckert described his situation in a letter sent in March 1993 to a former lover:

> As you know, two years ago, while I was working in the literature archives in Marbach, my "mother" broke into my house and stole absolutely all the archives

Beate Eckert in her Berlin apartment around 1992.

and papers. Three lawyers from Paris and Berlin are endeavoring to secure their return. They are paid a lot of money. The "other side" are continuing to hurl around indescribable filth in the manner of the article in *TransAtlantik*, and they are threatening to appeal to a higher court if the lawsuit has a positive outcome for me. . . . I am rather tired of the whole business with the Ju[h]nkes, the judges, and the lawyers. I have no idea how I managed to stop drinking in those circumstances. Perhaps out of the subconscious awareness that to continue drinking would only provoke the worst case of all.[53]

Seriously ill, Eckert was able to win his lawsuit in 1993 and compel the family to return the former editorial archive of *Die neue Weltbühne*.[54] But he himself stated that by then he was already "at rock bottom financially." He was now living in a flat in Strasbourg and being cared for by the welfare service of the local Jewish community. His friend the writer Barbara Honigmann, who occasionally visited him, recalls that his conversation was limited to "his grandfather and the *Weltbühne* archive," subjects that were interesting at first but that became tedious the third time around. "His sisters had warned me by telephone against anything their brother might say, which I found very peculiar." According to Honigmann, Budzislawski's grandson often walked through the city wearing a conspicuous sky-blue kippah, and sometimes he even showed off a sort of concentration camp number, which she assumes he must have drawn on his upper arm with ink. It is also possible that the number depicted the date of his grandfather's birthday or death, she suggested.[55] Thomas Eckert died a broken and lonely man on 5 December 1994 at the age of only forty-one. He was laid to rest at the Jewish cemetery of Cronenbourg in Strasbourg.[56] Apart from Honigmann, the only people who came to the funeral were his second wife and a few friends. Eckert had made his only child, a son from his second marriage, his sole heir, imposing the condition that he could not inherit until December 2011, when he would have reached the age of twenty-five.[57]

By this time, *Die Weltbühne* was already history. It ceased publication after the 6 July 1993 issue came out because Peter Jacobsohn, who had meanwhile turned seventy-six, had written from the United States, once again claiming copyright in the title. Thomas Eckert was already either too ill or too exhausted by the continuing conflict with his family to make any objection, and in any case he no longer had the money to pay a lawyer. Bernd F. Lunkewitz, the new owner of Aufbau-Verlag since the autumn of 1991 and from the spring of 1992 also the (supposed) owner of the publisher Weltbühne GmbH, did not want to engage in a dispute with Peter Jacobsohn because he was an exile who had been persecuted on racial grounds in 1930s Germany, he said.[58] Even so, the end of the journal came as a surprise, because Lunkewitz had at first planned to make a fresh start with a new editor in chief and an advisory board of celebrities, "well-known personalities" who he thought would include the writers Christa Wolf, Günter Grass, Christoph Hein, Jurek Becker, and Stefan Heym. He was quoted to that effect in March 1992 in the Berlin *Tagesspiegel*. It was time, he had said then, to link up with the glittering days of the "most wonderful and most intellectual journal" of the Weimar Republic and to "become daring again."[59]

In reality, what characterized *Die Weltbühne* of the early 1990s more than anything else was disillusionment. At the beginning of January 1990 its supporters had hoped that, despite all of problems in the GDR, Socialism "in the sense of its ideals and with many practical achievements as well" had put down roots in German society. The commitment of the former bloc parties to Socialism, it was claimed, was also "vigorous and promising."[60] Ten weeks later, on 18 March 1990, the conservative Alliance for Germany, which was supported from the West by the ruling parties in the Federal Republic, the Christian Democratic Union of Germany and the Christian Social Union in Bavaria, won the first free elections for the Volkskammer with the slogan "Socialism Never Again!" The *Weltbühne* authors drew a bitter conclusion. Even before the results of the elections had become known, they considered that the "dictatorship of the Politburo" had been replaced by the "dictatorship of money." The "consumer-oriented growth society" of capitalism had proved its superiority. For that reason, it was more important than ever to challenge the new conditions, to act from below as a "left-wing thorn" in the side of the new regime, because "the Left will not be able to provide lasting proof of its need to exist" if it remains merely "the best defender of the German dacha."[61]

After German unity was formally accomplished on 3 October 1990, thereby largely determining the lines of future political development, *Die Weltbühne* became a backwater. Many of its independent contributors migrated to wealthier newspapers or higher-circulation periodicals or withdrew from journalism altogether. Those who remained were visibly still attached to the GDR, a state that had now been liquidated, and they wrote with an underlying bitterness about the new social reality, which from *Die Weltbühne*'s point of view was the equivalent of a "total sell-out—politically, economically, and culturally."[62] The journal wanted to offer an alternative to the new situation and insisted that the "German democratic potential" had not yet been completely exhausted. This was a recognizable reference to a GDR that no longer existed. The approach was consistent, but it did not constitute the forward-looking breakthrough that might perhaps have made *Die Weltbühne* an important organ of opinion in the years immediately after unification.[63] The emphatic appeals it printed, for example, from the pen of the German-Spanish writer Heleno Saña, went largely unheard. The German intellectuals, he wrote in an article published in September 1992, must finally reflect on their responsibility and return to the "field of battle they have abandoned." They should not be ashamed "to have big ideals and be naive enough to believe in them. . . . We must again seize hold of the concept of enlightenment, discredited by postmodernism, and offer people meaningful and viable alternatives and countermodels to the current situation of reification and alienation."[64]

But most people did not want to take up any of the new alternatives volubly being extolled by intellectuals, especially when those alternatives looked suspiciously similar to well-known old slogans. In the so-called new federal states, many citizens had enough to do to cope pragmatically with the transformation

in their lives in the here and now. The West Germans felt that they were history's victors: criticism of the West German model was seen as unseemly—
especially if it came from the East. Hence *Die Weltbühne* and its authors com-
municated nearly exclusively with each other in the early 1990s, and their
words found little resonance in the country at large. Members of the editorial
staff suggested making moderate changes while maintaining the journal's traditions, but they were ignored by the man who was editor in chief then,
Helmut Reinhardt.[65] Nothing is more fascinating about *Die Weltbühne* than
its illustrious name, wrote the journalist Jan Ross in 1993 in the *FAZ* with
subtle irony. Many of the journal's authors had found it difficult to come to
terms with the political changes of the post-Wende years; what they were
engaged in, he said, was a kind of "historical group therapy."[66]

The alleged copyright holder, Peter Jacobsohn, had no interest either in
continuing to publish *Die Weltbühne* in its current form or in remodeling the
legendary journal for a reunited Germany. Another reason was perhaps that he
blamed the early death of his mother on the disputes of the 1930s. From his
point of view, he had been deprived of his inheritance first by the National
Socialists and then by the Budzislawskis. The behavior of the latter had been
hurtful not only financially but also in interpersonal terms, because both the
Jacobsohns—the mother and her son, who was then a teenager—had regarded
Hanna and Hermann Budzislawski as close friends and allies until at least the
second half of 1934. They had lived with them in Switzerland as direct neighbors and had thus shared the worries of exile at close quarters.[67] When Edith
Jacobsohn died of a heart attack in London on the last day of 1935 at the age
of only forty-four, nothing more was left of the upper-middle-class world in
which Peter Jacobsohn had grown up and to which he felt he belonged. The
seventeen-year-old orphan inherited only twelve pounds sterling from his
mother. Instead of starting his university studies and then taking over a famous
publishing house, he had to struggle through life in Great Britain as a badly
paid apprentice doing odd jobs. He spent part of the Second World War in
internment, being deported as far away as Australia. Until 1947 he often had
to rely on support payments from Jewish charities.[68]

There is little point in speculating on whether Jacobsohn, who now lived
near Boston, Massachusetts, was making a last serious attempt at an advanced
age to become the editor of *Die Weltbühne* when he insisted on his right to the
journal's name. It had by then a print run of fifteen thousand copies. Perhaps
he was mainly concerned to make money for the last time from his paternal
inheritance, something he had succeeded in doing at the end of the 1970s with
the reprint of the Weimar *Weltbühne*. In the spring of 1993, in any case, he
could have obtained the company that published *Die Weltbühne* for the sym-

bolic price of 1 mark, together with a loan of 350,000 marks from the previous owner, Lunkewitz, to ensure the journal would come out over the first few months, as Jacobsohn lacked the financial means to keep the loss-making paper going for very long.[69] Yet a compromise arrangement proposed by Lunkewitz also fell through at the last moment. At a conciliation hearing held on 18 June 1993 before the Higher Regional Court in Frankfurt am Main, Jacobsohn initially accepted Lunkewitz's proposal, which would have saved *Die Weltbühne* (provisionally) and made him the lifetime chair of the board of management. Ten days later, however, he revoked his agreement, perhaps because under the proposed arrangement Lunkewitz would have remained the owner of *Die Weltbühne* publishing house, but also perhaps because he had never regarded the East Berlin *Weltbühne*, which had been appearing for four decades, as a legitimate continuation of the Weimar journal founded by his father.[70]

Lunkewitz now liquidated both the journal and the publishing house, which "like so much in this country could definitely have continued in existence," as he wrote in the last issue. Some doubt had been cast a few weeks earlier on whether he was in fact the legitimate owner of *Die Weltbühne*. On 24 May 1993 the Independent Commission for Investigating the Property of the Parties and Mass Organizations of the GDR determined that the Trust Agency had not been entitled to sell the Verlag Weltbühne GmbH to Lunkewitz the year before. On the qualifying date of 7 October 1989 it had formed part of the property of the SED and was therefore subject to administration by the agency; the sale was therefore null and void.[71] When asked today, Lunkewitz says that his decision to cease publishing the journal was also connected with his disappointment over the behavior of Helmut Reinhardt, the man who was managing the publishing house at that time, because he had at first concealed the dispute with Jacobsohn and then later, when the conciliation hearing was due, he preferred to go on holiday. Lunkewitz had finally decided according to his "sense of what was right," and for him that meant leaving the last word to Peter Jacobsohn. *Die Weltbühne*, he had already declared in the spring of 1993, "fights for justice, even if it has to perish as a result." The journal's editorial board saw things differently; it felt betrayed by "Halunkewitz" (Lunkewitz the rogue), and it printed an angry farewell to its readers: "We have nothing more to say about this wicked game!"[72] The repeated changes in ownership between 1934 and 1936 were only a marginal consideration in this final dispute. It would have been possible to reconstruct what happened from the business records of *Die neue Weltbühne* stored in Thomas Eckert's house. But the conflicts of the past, which took place when the anti-Fascists were in exile and later in the GDR, were entirely irrelevant to the proceedings in the Frankfurt court. They were a contaminated legacy, and in 1993 it was seen as best to not even mention them. Thus, the story of *Die Weltbühne* ended—not untypically for the journal—in a dispute marked by a renewed confrontation between the claims of the law, morality, politics, and journalism.[73] It is understandable that for Lunkewitz the moral capital of the western emigrant Jacobsohn weighed more strongly in the balance than the possibly well-founded legal rights of the exposed Stasi spy Eckert. But his decision had grave consequences. What neither the National Socialists nor the SED had been able to accomplish came to pass in reunited Germany: *Die Weltbühne*, Budzislawski's lifelong project, finally reached the end of the line.

Notes

Prologue

1. On the style of *Die Schaubühne/Weltbühne* as a product of the tempo of life in Berlin, see Ruth Greuner, "Über Jacobsohns Schaubühne," *Die Weltbühne*, 21 March 1967, 373–78. All translations are mine unless otherwise noted.

2. István Deák, *Weimar Germany's Left-Wing Intellectuals: A Political History of the Weltbühne and Its Circle* (Berkeley, CA, 1968), vii.

3. Ralf Dahrendorf, *Versuchungen der Unfreiheit: Die Intellektuellen in Zeiten der Prüfung* (Munich, 2006), 21–22.

4. Martin Sabrow, "Memoiren der Macht: Gedachte Geschichte der Autobiographik kommunistischer Parteifunktionäre," in *Geschichte denken: Perspektiven auf die Geschichtsschreibung heute*, ed. Michael Wildt (Göttingen, 2014), 195; Catherine Epstein, "The Production of 'Official Memory' in East Germany: Old Communists and the Dilemmas of Memoir-Writing," *Central European History* 32, no. 2 (1999): 181–201.

5. On the concept of "narrative identity," see Rolf Haubl, "Autobiographisches Erzählen: Sprechen und Schreiben," in *Das eigene Leben als ästhetische Fiktion: Autobiographie und Professionsgeschichte*, ed. Dietrich Erben and Tobias Zervosen (Bielefeld, 2018), 334.

6. Written record of a discussion between Simone Barck and Ursula Madrasch-Groschopp on 21 June 1999 at the Leibniz Centre for Contemporary History, Potsdam, in Bibliotop der Universität Leipzig (Bibliotop), Ehemaliges Redaktionsarchiv der *Weltbühne* der DDR (yellow file "Die Weltbühne," no call number).

7. Levke Harders, "Migration und Biographie: Mobile Leben beschreiben," *Österreichische Zeitschrift für Geschichtswissenschaften* 29, no. 3 (2018): 20; Claudia Ulbrich, Hans Medick, and Angelika Schaser, "Selbstzeugnis und Person: Transkulturelle Perspektiven," in *Selbstzeugnis und Person: Transkulturelle Perspektiven*, ed. Claudia Ulbrich, Hans Medick, and Angelika Schaser (Cologne, 2012), 1–19.

8. One of the exceptions is the excellent study by Axel Fair-Schulz, *Loyal Subversion: East Germany and Its Bildungsbürgerlich Marxist Intellectuals* (Berlin, 2009). See also Daniel Siemens, "Elusive Security in the GDR: Remigrants from the West at the Faculty of Journalism in Leipzig, 1945–1961," *Central Europe* 11, no. 1 (2013): 24–45; Toralf

Teuber, *Ein Stratege im Exil: Hermann Budzislawski und die "Neue Weltbühne"* (Frankfurt am Main, 2004); Marita Krauss, "Hans Habe, Ernst Friedländer, Hermann Budzislawski—drei Schicksale," in *Zwischen den Stühlen? Remigranten und Remigration in der deutschen Mediaöffentlichkeit der Nachkriegszeit,* ed. Claus-Dieter Krohn and Axel Schildt (Hamburg, 2012), 245–66.

9. Kurt Hiller, "Aufstieg, Glanz und Verfall der Weltbühne," vol. 4, *konkret,* June 1962, in Landesarchiv Berlin (LAB), E Rep. 200-63, no. 23d.

10. Erich Mühsam "Gruß," *Die Weltbühne,* 9 September 1930, 400. On post-1945 nostalgia for *Die Weltbühne,* see Alexander Gallus, *Heimat "Weltbühne": Eine Intellektuellengeschichte im 20. Jahrhundert* (Göttingen, 2012), 62–79. By contrast, the Catholic philosopher Josef Pieper offers a sharply negative view in *Noch wusste es niemand: Autobiographische Aufzeichnungen 1904–1945* (Munich, 1976), 106–7.

11. Klaus Behling, *Spur der Scheine: Wie das Vermögen der SED verschwand* (Berlin, 2019), 117.

12. For a seminal study of transnational historical interdependence, see Michael Werner and Bénédicte Zimmermann, "Vergleich, Transfer, Verflechtung: Der Ansatz der Histoire croisée und die Herausforderung des Transnationalen," *Geschichte und Gesellschaft* 28 (2002): 607–36; on the analysis of historical networks, particularly in relation to biographical studies, see the contributions in *Handbuch Historische Netzwerkforschung: Grundlagen und Anwendungen,* ed. Marten Düring et al. (Münster, 2016); and Friedrich Lenger, "Netzwerkanalyse und Biographieforschung—einige Überlegungen," *Bios* 18 (2005): 180–85.

13. On the situation of the bourgeoisie in the GDR, see Thomas Großbölting, *SED-Diktatur und Gesellschaft: Bürgertum, Bürgerlichkeit und Entbürgerlichung in Magdeburg und Halle* (Halle an der Saale, 2001); and Ralph Jessen, "'Bildungsbürger,' 'Experten,' 'Intelligenz': Kontinuität und Wandel der ostdeutschen Bildungsgeschichten in der Ulbricht-Ära," in *Weimarer Klassik in der Ära Ulbricht,* ed. Lothar Ehrlich and Günther Mai (Cologne, 2000), 113–34.

14. See Jürgen Dinkel, "Erben und Vererben in der Moderne: Erkundungen eines Forschungsfelds," *Archiv für Sozialgeschichte* 56 (2016): 81–108; Stefan Willer, "Kulturelles Erbe: Tradieren und Konservieren in der Moderne," in *Erbe: Übertragungskonzepte zwischen Natur und Kultur,* ed. Stefan Willer, Sigrid Weigel, and Bernhard Jussen (Berlin, 2013), 160–201; and Jens Gieseke, "Soziale Ungleichheit im Staatssozialismus: Eine Skizze," *Zeithistorische Forschungen / Studies in Contemporary History* 10, no. 2 (2013): 171–98.

15. Frank Wolff, "Die unsichtbare Ruine des Kalten Kriegs: Die 'Mauer in den Köpfen' 30 Jahre nach dem Mauerfall," *Geschichte der Gegenwart,* 15 September 2019, https://geschichtedergegenwart.ch/die-unsichtbare-ruine-des-kalten-kriegs-die -mauer-in-den-koepfen-30-jahre-nach-dem-mauerfall/; and, with a specific concentration on the history of the GDR's mass media, Christoph Classen, "DDR-Medien im Spannungsfeld von Gesellschaft und Politik," in *Wie im Westen, nur anders: Medien in der DDR,* ed. Stefan Zahlmann (Berlin, 2010), 386.

16. See most recently Axel Schildt, *Medien-Intellektuelle in der Bundesrepublik,* ed. Gabriele Kandzora and Detlef Siegfried (Göttingen, 2020), 224–40; for a contrary view, see György Konrád and Ivan Szelényi, *Die Intelligenz auf dem Weg zur Klassenmacht* (Frankfurt am Main, 1978) (English translation: György Konrád and Ivan Szelé-

nyi, *The Intellectuals on the Road to Class Power*, trans. Andrew Arato and Richard E. Allen [New York, 1979]); Werner Mittenzwei, *Die Intellektuellen: Literatur und Politik in Ostdeutschland von 1945–2000* (Leipzig, 2001); and Czesław Miłosz, *Verführtes Denken* (Cologne, 1955) (English translation: Czesław Miłosz, *The Captive Mind*, trans. Jane Zielonko [London, 1985]).

17. Kurt Tucholsky to Arnold Zweig, 15 December 1935, in *Kurt Tucholsky: Ausgewählte Briefe 1913–1935*, ed. Mary Gerold-Tucholsky and Fritz J. Raddatz (Reinbek bei Hamburg, 1962), 333–39, here 336–37.

18. Hermann Budzislawski to Edith Jacobsohn, 14 January 1934, in Archiv der Akademie der Künste—Literaturarchiv, Berlin (AdK), Die neue Weltbühne, box 1, preliminary signature 1, 70–72.

Chapter 1. Jew, Socialist, Eugenicist

1. As reported in the *Vossische Zeitung*, Berlin, 11 February 1901, 1–2.

2. The family moved shortly afterward from Gerichtsstraße into Angermünder Straße and then a little later into Rochstraße 17. When Budzislawski was twelve years old, he lived with his family in yet another place, this time in the second rear courtyard of Kochstraße 17, just a stone's throw away from what would later be called Checkpoint Charlie. Hermann Budzislawski, questionnaire for Socialist Unity Party members, 29 September 1970, in Bundesarchiv Berlin (BArch Berlin), SAPMO, DY 30/90300, 44; *Adressbuch für Berlin und seine Vororte*, 1901 and 1913 editions, https://digital.zlb.de/viewer/image/34115316_1901/; https://digital.zlb.de/viewer/image/34115495_1913/.

3. Hermann Budzislawski's grandfather had worked as an upholsterer in what was then the Prussian town of Bromberg (now Bydgoszcz). See Hermann Budzislawski's autobiographical record, 14 January 1951, in BArch Berlin, SAPMO, DY 30/90300, 170–73.

4. Isidor Budzislawski's brother Adolf, father of Herbert Budzislawski, was executed in 1943 by the National Socialists on account of his membership in the Communist resistance group around Herbert Baum, who was also a master butcher in Berlin. Hermann Budzislawski to Ramer Peglow, 21 May 1970, in Bibliotop, Ehemaliges Redaktionsarchiv der *Weltbühne* der DDR, Budzislawski 1, ZZF I.1.448.

5. Hermann Budzislawski, "Meine Meinung: Stunden zum Totschlagen?," typescript in AdK, Hermann-Budzislawski-Archiv, no. 414.

6. Henry Jacoby, *Von des Kaisers Schule zu Hitlers Zuchthaus: Erlebnisse und Begegnungen. Geschichte einer Jugend links-außen in der Weimarer Republik* (Frankfurt am Main, 1980), 15.

7. Hermann Budzislawski, "Scheidung ohne Schuld," *Das Magazin* 13, no. 3 (March 1966): 53; Hermann Budzislawski to Greta Kuckhoff, 25 February 1966, in AdK, Hermann-Budzislawski-Archiv, no. 414. For biographical data on his mother, see https://www.myheritage.com/names/jenny_lewin.

8. Budzislawski, "Meine Meinung."

9. These data are derived from Budzislawski's temporary passport issued on 31 October 1969, in AdK, Hermann-Budzislawski-Archiv, no. 413.

10. Regina Scheer, "Ein Klassentreffen," *Die Weltbühne*, 20 November 1990, 1535–37.

11. Hermann Budzislawski's *Abitur* certificate, 13 September 1919, in LAB, A Rep. 020-20, no. 61, 161; for his *Abitur* assignments, see A Rep. 020-20, no. 110.

12. See the collection of *Abitur* and emergency *Abitur* certificates from 1911 to 1919 in LAB, A Rep. 020-20, no. 61, 161. An impressive group photograph of a class of students in the neighboring *Gymnasium* some years earlier is to be found in Momme Brodersen, *Klassenbild mit Walter Benjamin: Eine Spurensuche* (Munich, 2012).

13. Budzislawski, questionnaire for Socialist Unity Party members, 29 September 1970, 44. Other Jewish families also lived in Sybelstraße 5. At least eleven occupants of the house were deported in 1942–43 and murdered either in Auschwitz or near Riga and Minsk; see https://www.berlin.de/ba-charlottenburg-wilmersdorf/ueber-den-bezirk /geschichte/stolpersteine/artikel.179530.php.

14. Budzislawski's autobiographical record, 14 January 1951, 170–73.

15. Hans Sahl, *Memoiren eines Moralisten—das Exil im Exil* (Munich, 2008), 26–27.

16. Information given by Jay Geller to the author by email on 21 June 2019.

17. Minutes of the General Conference of the Leibniz-Oberrealschule on 19 January 1917, in LAB, A Rep. 020-20, no. 38.

18. Memoirs of Jacob W. Ewer, in Leo Baeck Institute, Center for Jewish History, New York (LBI), Ruth Barash Collection, AR 11754, 7.

19. The Budzislawski quotations are taken from Hermann Budzislawski, "Adventurers against Will: The History of a European Generation That Lost Its Chance," 2, in the author's private archive. In addition, see Teuber, *Ein Stratege*, 194, with further references; and Gert Billing, "Gespräch mit Prof. Dr. Hermann Budzislawski," *Die Weltbühne*, 9 February 1966, 176–80, here 176. The concept of an *Erfahrungseinbruch* (rupture of experience) is borrowed from Reinhart Koselleck, "Erinnerungsschleusen und Erfahrungsschichten: Der Einfluß der beiden Weltkriege auf das soziale Bewußtsein," in *Zeitschichten: Studien zur Historik* (Frankfurt am Main, 2003), 265 (English translation: Reinhart Koselleck, "Sluices of Memory and Sediments of Experience: The Influence of the Two World Wars on Social Consciousness," in *Sediments of Time: On Possible Histories* [Stanford, CA, 2018], 207).

20. Budzislawski's autobiographical record, 30 August 1950, 164.

21. Jacoby, *Von des Kaisers Schule*, 22–24. On opinions prevailing at the time among final year classes outside Berlin as well, see Pieper, *Noch wusste es niemand*, 37–46.

22. Helmuth Kiesel, "Die literarische Verarbeitung der Novemberrevolution in der Weimarer Republik," in *Zusammenbruch, Aufbruch, Abbruch? Die Novemberrevolution als Ereignis und Erinnerungsort*, ed. Andreas Braune and Michael Dreyer (Stuttgart, 2018), 252–53.

23. Sahl, *Memoiren eines Moralisten*, 38.

24. Siegfried Schmidt, "Hermann Budzislawski und die Leipziger Journalistik," in *Biografisches Lexikon der Kommunikationswissenschaft*, ed. Michael Meyen and Thomas Wiedemann (Cologne, 2017), http://blexkom.halemverlag.de/schmidt-budzislawski/. See also Willy Walther, "Hermann Budzislawski," in *Namhafte Hochschullehrer der Karl-Marx-Universität Leipzig* (Leipzig, 1982), 1:62–71.

25. Schmidt, "Hermann Budzislawski." Schmidt calls the journal in question *Der Anfang*, but this journal was only published in 1913–14 under the editorship of Georges Barbizon (Georg Gretor) and Siegfried Bernfeld. Schmidt must therefore have meant

its short-lived successor, *Der neue Anfang*, which came out a total of five times during the spring of 1919.

26. O.H., "Die grüne Fahne," *Der neue Anfang*, 1 January 1919, 1–2.

27. H.B., "Die neue Schulverfassung," *Der neue Anfang*, 1 January 1919, 8–11.

28. See in particular in this context the "Program of the Free School Students of Berlin," *Der neue Anfang*, 15 February 1919, 63–64. Budzislawski still recalled the names of Siegfried Kawerau and Heinrich Deuters as reform-oriented teachers and educational reformers of the time (Hermann Budzislawski to Fritz Klein, 1 March 1966, in AdK, Hermann-Budzislawski-Archiv, no. 441).

29. Essential here is Ulrich Linse, *Die entschiedene Jugend 1919–1921: Deutschlands erste revolutionäre Schüler- und Studentenbewegung* (Frankfurt am Main, 1981). See also Lutz Sauerteig, "Von Hodann zu Amendt: Vorstellungen von sexueller 'Liberalisierung,' kindlicher Sexualität und Geschlechterverhältnissen in der Sexualerziehung um 1900 und um 1968," in *Lebensreform um 1900 und Alternativmilieu um 1980: Kontinuitäten und Brüche im Milieu der gesellschaftlichen Selbstreflexion im frühen und späten 20. Jahrhundert*, ed. Detlef Siegfried and David Templin (Göttingen, 2019), 227–28.

30. H.K., "Revolutionspredigt," *Der neue Anfang*, 1 January 1919, 3–6; "Erziehung der bürgerlichen Jugend zum Sozialismus," *Der neue Anfang*, 15 February 1919, 55–58.

31. "Erziehung der bürgerlichen Jugend zum Sozialismus," *Der neue Anfang*, 15 February 1919, 55–58. Whether this movement would have had a greater political impact if there had been closer contact with revolutionary working-class youth organizations and parties to the left of the MSPD, as Ulrich Linse argues, is questionable in view of political developments during 1919. Linse, *Die entschiedene Jugend*, 40–41.

32. National Archives and Records Administration, College Park, MD (NARA), RG 319 (U.S. Army, Military Agency Records, Counter Intelligence Corps [CIC] Investigative Records Repository), File 302122 (Report on Budzislawski, 1951); Budzislawski's autobiographical record, 30 August 1950, 164.

33. "Bisherige Entwicklung des Schülers nebst Gutachten über seine Reife," report on Hermann Budzislawski, spring 1919, in LAB, A Rep. 020-110.

34. Sebastian Haffner, *Geschichte eines Deutschen: Die Erinnerungen 1914–1933* (Stuttgart, 2000) (English translation: *Defying Hitler: A Memoir* [London, 2002]); Manfred Gailus and Daniel Siemens, eds., *"Hass und Begeisterung bilden Spalier": Horst Wessels politische Autobiografie* (Berlin, 2011).

35. Otto Flake, *Das Ende der Revolution* (Berlin, 1920), 35. On the self-perception of the wartime youth generation, see also Daniel Siemens, "Kühle Romantiker: Zum Geschichtsverständnis der 'jungen Generation' in der Weimarer Republik," in *Die Kunst der Geschichte: Historiographie, Ästhetik, Erzählung*, ed. Martin Baumeister, Moritz Föllmer, and Philipp Müller (Göttingen, 2009), 189–214.

36. Budzislawski, "Adventurers against Will," 2. Christian Meyer provides a similar interpretation in *Die dunkle Seite der Jugendbewegung: Vom Wandervogel zur Hitlerjugend* (Tübingen, 2013).

37. Immo Eberl and Helmut Marcon, *150 Jahre Promotion an der Wirtschaftswissenschaftlichen Fakultät der Universität Tübingen: Biographien d. Doktoren u. Ehrendoktoren 1830–1980*, im Auftrag der Wirtschaftswissenschaftlichen Fakultät der Universität Tübingen (Stuttgart, 1984), 269.

38. Budzislawski, "Adventurers against Will," 3.

39. Ibid.

40. See the corresponding entries in Budzislawski's student file in Universitätsarchiv der Eberhard Karls Universität Tübingen (UAT), 258/2360; and Martin Otto, "Carl Sartorius," in *Neue Deutsche Biographie* (Berlin, 2005), 22:440–41; Helmut Walter, "Beckerath. Herbert von," in *Biographisches Handbuch der deutschsprachigen wirtschafts-wissenschaftlichen Emigration nach 1933*, vol. 1, *Adler–Lehmann*, ed. Harald Hagemann and Claus-Dieter Krohn (Munich, 1999), 34–36; *International Biographical Dictionary of Central European Emigrés 1933–1945*, ed. Werner Röder and Herbert A. Strauss (Munich, 1983), 2/1:67.

41. Robert Wilbrandt, *Karl Marx: Versuch einer Einführung* (Leipzig, 1918); Wilbrandt, *Sozialismus* (Jena, 1919); Wilbrandt, *Sind die Sozialisten sozialistisch genug?* (Berlin, 1919).

42. Wilbrandt, *Sind die Sozialisten?*, 13.

43. Eberl and Macron, *150 Jahre Promotion*, 269; Hermann Budzislawski, "Eugenik: Ein Beitrag zur Ökonomie der menschlichen Erbanlagen" (PhD diss., University of Tübingen, 1923).

44. For the general context, see above all the pioneering study by Michael Schwartz, *Sozialistische Eugenik: Eugenische Sozialtechnologien in Diskurs und Politik der deutschen Sozialdemokratie 1890–1933* (Münster, 1992); and Birgit Lulay, *Eugenik und Sozialismus: Biowissenschaftliche Diskurse in der sozialistischen Bewegungen Deutschlands und Groß-britanniens um 1900* (Stuttgart, 2021).

45. Budzislawski, "Eugenik," 175, 180.

46. On this point, see Veronika Lipphardt, *Biologie der Juden: Jüdische Wissen-schaftler über "Rasse" und Vererbung 1900–1935* (Göttingen, 2008); Michael Brenner and Gideon Renveni, eds., *Emanzipation durch Muskelkraft: Juden und Sport in Europa* (Göttingen, 2006); Daniel Siemens, "Konzepte des nationaljüdischen Körpers in der frühen Weimarer Republik," *Zeitschrift für Geschichtswissenschaft* 56 (2008): 30–54.

47. Budzislawski, "Eugenik," 173.

48. Karl Binding and Alfred Hoche, *Die Freigabe der Vernichtung lebensunwerten Lebens: Ihr Maß und ihre Form* (Leipzig, 1920).

49. Budzislawski, "Eugenik," 180–81.

50. Ibid., 188, 194.

51. Ibid., 195–96. On the significance of "human economics" for ideas of racial hygiene on the political Left, see Reinhard Mocek, *Biologie und soziale Befreiung: Zur Geschichte des Biologismus und der Rassenhygiene in der Arbeiterbewegung* (Frankfurt am Main, 2002), 310–17.

52. On the US case, see Diane B. Paul, *The Politics of Heredity: Essays on Eugenics, Biomedicine, and the Nature-Nurture Debate* (Albany, NY, 1998). There is an interna-tional overview in Veronique Mottier, "Eugenics and the State: Policy-Making in Comparative Perspective," in *The Oxford Handbook of the History of Eugenics*, ed. Ali-son Bashford and Philippa Levine (Oxford, 2010), 134–53.

53. Budzislawski, "Eugenik," 199.

54. Ibid., 200.

55. Ibid., 210, 229–30.

56. Ibid., 214, 228.

57. Ibid., 237, 243.

58. Ibid., 230.

59. Robert Gaupp to Robert Wilbrandt, 24 February 1923, in UAT, 117/228-1.

60. Robert Eugen Gaupp, *Unfruchtbarmachung geistig und sittlich Kranker und Minderwertiger: Erweitertes Referat, erstattet auf der Jahresversammlung des Deutschen Vereins für Psychiatrie am 2. September 1925 in Kassel* (Berlin, 1925), 21.

61. Gaupp remained professor of psychiatry and neurology at the University of Tübingen until his retirement in 1936. He was an enthusiastic supporter of eugenics, and he endorsed the Law for the Prevention of Offspring with Hereditary Diseases, passed on 14 July 1933 by the National Socialists. After the Second World War he acted as the Stuttgart Municipal Council's expert advisor on matters of health and welfare until 1948. See Claudia Leins, "Robert Eugen Gaupp: Leben und Werk" (PhD diss., University of Tübingen, 1991).

62. On the social position of students in the Weimar Republic and their rapidly worsening job prospects, see Michael H. Kater, *Studentenschaft und Rechtsradikalismus in Deutschland 1918–1933: Eine sozialgeschichtliche Studie zur Bildungskrise in der Weimarer Republik* (Hamburg, 1975); for a summary, see Michael Grüttner, *Studenten im Dritten Reich* (Paderborn, 1995), 23–24.

63. Budzislawski, "Adventurers against Will," 3.

64. Budzislawski's autobiographical record, 30 August 1950, 164.

65. In 1951 Budzislawski asserted that Wilbrandt had offered him a position as his assistant as a route toward his *Habilitation*. He rejected the offer because he "was opposed to bourgeois universities" (Budzislawski's autobiographical record, 14 January 1951, 170–73).

66. Billing, "Gespräch," 176.

67. Communication from the rector of the University of Tübingen to the dean of the Faculty of Law and Economic Sciences, 29 September 1938, in UAT, 117/228-1.

68. Memorandum from Wilhelm Merk to the dean of the Faculty of Law and Economic Sciences, 23 September 1947, in UAT, 117/228-1.

69. Hermann Budzislawski to the rector of the University of Tübingen, 7 July 1947, in UAT, 117/228-1.

70. Minutes of the session of the Lesser Senate of the University of Tübingen, 14 October 1947, in UAT, 47a/3, 47.

71. Theodor Steinbuchel to Hermann Budzislawski, 14 October 1947, in UAT, 117/228-1.

Chapter 2. First Steps as a Journalist

1. Sebastian Haffner, *Defying Hitler: A Memoir*, trans. Oliver Pretzel (London, 2003), 52 (German translation: *Geschichte eines Deutschen: Die Erinnerungen 1914–1933* [Stuttgart, 2000]).

2. See on this firm Marc Zierlewagen's article "Sondheimer, Albert," in *Frankfurter Personenlexikon*, https://frankfurter-personenlexikon.de/node/3822.

3. Budzislawski, "Adventurers against Will," 3–4.

4. Ibid.

5. Letter of recommendation and certificate of employment for Budzislawski, 30 August 1923, in AdK, Hermann-Budzislawski-Archiv, no. 217.

6. Budzislawski's autobiographical record, 10 March 1949, 188.

7. Hermann to Hanna Budzislawski, in AdK, Die neue Weltbühne, box 1, preliminary signature 2, 42–43.

8. Budzislawski, "Adventurers against Will," 4. Hirsch immigrated to the United States in 1941. After that, he worked for the New School for Social Research. It is not known whether he met his former protégé when the latter was in the United States.

9. See Hermann Budzislawski, "'Rasse und Geist' (Buchrezension zu Robert Müller, *Rassen, Städte, Physiognomen*, Berlin: Erich Reiss Verlag)," *Berliner Tageblatt*, 7 September 1924, 17–18; Budzislawski, "Sind Darwins Theorien überholt?," *Berliner Börsenzeitung*, 21 August 1926, 9; Budzislawski, "Staatshilfe für die Schiffahrt?," *Magazin der Wirtschaft*, 26 March 1925, 248–51. When in exile some years later, Schwarzschild would be in direct competition with Budzislawski and *Die neue Weltbühne* as the publisher of the periodical *Das neue Tagebuch*.

10. See, for example, the article "The Awakening of Asia—a Socialist View," *Industrial and Trade Review for Asia*, 16 October 1925 (newspaper cutting in National Archives of India, Home Department, Political Branch, 1926, call number F-125-Ii, 7).

11. Kasper Braskén, "'Whether Black or White—United in the Fight!': Connecting the Resistance against Colonialism, Racism and Fascism in the European Metropoles, 1926–1936," *Twentieth Century Communism: A Journal of International History* 18, no. 18 (2020): 126–49; Nathanael Kuck, "Anti-colonialism in a Post-imperial Environment: The Case of Berlin, 1914–1933," *Journal of Contemporary History* 49, no. 1 (2014): 134–59; Fredrik Petersson, "Imperialism and the Communist International," *Journal of Labor and Society* 20, no. 1 (2017): 23–42.

12. For biographical information on Chattopadhyaya, see Jürgen Dinkel, "'Mecca of Oriental Patriots': Antikolonialismus in Deutschland 1900–1960," in *Weimar und die Welt: Globale Verflechtungen der ersten deutschen Republik*, ed. Christoph Cornelißen and Dirk van Laak (Göttingen, 2020), 53–88, esp. 56–59, 69–75; and Brigitte Studer, *Reisende der Weltrevolution: Eine Globalgeschichte der Kommunistischen Internationale* (Berlin, 2020), 282–83.

13. English translation of a letter (presumably in German in the original) from the *Industrial and Trade Review* to the British Foreign Office (Department for East Asia), 23 July 1926, in National Archives of India, Home Department, Political Branch, 1926, call number F-135-Ii, 28–31.

14. Vappala Balachandran, *A Life in Shadow: The Secret Story of ACN Nambiar, a Forgotten Anti-colonial Warrior* (New Delhi, 2016), 33; Ruth Price, *The Lives of Agnes Smedley* (Oxford, 2005), 124; Kris Manjapra, *The Age of Entanglement: German and Indian Intellectuals across Empire* (Cambridge, MA, 2016), 93–96; Daniel Brückenhaus, *Policing Transnational Protest: Liberal Imperialism and the Surveillance of Anticolonialism in Europe, 1905–1945* (Oxford, 2017), 139–40; and Horst Krüger, "Berlin als Treffpunkt von Antikolonialisten und Antiimperialisten in der Zeit der Weimarer Republik," *Bulletin des Arbeitskreises "Zweiter Weltkrieg"* 3–4 (1987): 95.

15. Brückenhaus, *Policing Transnational Protest*, 140.

16. Budzislawski's autobiographical record, 30 August 1950, 164.

17. On Smedley, see Price, *Lives*; Janice R. MacKinnon and Stephen R. MacKinnon, *Agnes Smedley: The Life and Times of an American Radical* (Berkeley, CA, 1988). Smedley also wrote occasional articles for *Die Weltbühne*, for example, "Verachte das Geld und fürchte nicht den Tod," *Die Weltbühne*, 7 March 1933, 362–66.

18. Billing, "Gespräch," 177.

19. Ibid.; Budzislawski, "Adventurers against Will," 4.

20. Alfred Kurella, who became acquainted with Budzislawski in Berlin during the time of the November Revolution in 1918 and who also worked for a short time as a home tutor, claimed that he used this job as a cover for his political activities. But there is no evidence at all that Budzislawski did the same. See Martin Schaad, *Die fabelhaften Bekenntnisse des Genossen Alfred Kurella* (Hamburg, 2014), 104–5.

21. Heiratsurkunde des Standesamts Tiergarten, no. 1293/1926, in AdK, Hermann-Budzislawski-Archiv, no. 414; and in LAB, P Rep. 812, no. 540.

22. Lotte Pick to Thomas A. Eckert, 11 December 1985, in AdK, Hermann-Budzislawski-Archiv, no. 415; obituary for Fritz Levy (extract from a circular letter by the group, July–August 1935), in AdK, Hermann-Budzislawski-Archiv, no. 415; Fritz Levy to Hanna Budzislawski, 12 January 1934, in AdK, Die neue Weltbühne, box 1, preliminary signature 3, 100–101.

23. Heiratsurkunde des Standesamts Tiergarten, no. 1293/1926.

24. Hanna Budzislawski to a certain Hede, 31 January 1968, in AdK, Hermann-Budzislawski-Archiv, no. 414.

25. Manuscript autobiography of Hanna Budzislawski (probably from 1950), in BArch Berlin, SAPMO, DY 30/90301; Linse, *Die entschiedene Jugend*, 25; Ulrich Linse, *Die Kommune der deutschen Jugendbewegung: Ein Versuch zur Überwindung des Klassenkampfes aus dem Geiste der bürgerlichen Utopie. Die kommunistische Siedlung Blankenburg bei Donauwörth 1919/20* (Munich, 1973), 38–50, 56–68, 78–91, 137–38; Schaad, *Die fabelhaften Bekenntnisse*, 130.

26. Hilde Rohlén-Wohlgemuth, "Die Familie Alexander Levy in Eschwege," *Eschweger Geschichtsblätter* 5 (1994): 51–54.

27. Manuscript autobiography of Hanna Budzislawski.

28. Siegfried Kracauer, *Die Angestellten: Aus dem neuesten Deutschland* (Frankfurt am Main, 1930); but the life story of the eponymous heroine in Irmgard Keun's surprise literary success *Gilgi, eine von uns* (Berlin, 1931) gives a distinctly more emancipated impression.

29. Johanna Budzislawski's SED questionnaire, 14 April 1950, in BArch Berlin, SAPMO, DY 30/90301.

30. Robert Gruenwald to Olga Katunal, 27 September 1928, in Deutsche Nationalbibliothek, Frankfurt am Main (DNB), NL 296–Olga Katunal, EB 2014/091 B.01.0014; Henning Ritter, "Von Berlin-Lichterfelde nach New York," *Frankfurter Allgemeine Zeitung*, 12 December 2007. There are further details in Manfred Voigts, *Oskar Goldberg: Der mythische Experimentalwissenschaftler—ein verdrängtes Kapitel jüdischer Geschichte* (Berlin, 1992), 153–62. On Katunal's life story, see Judith Friedlander, *Vilna on the Seine: Jewish Intellectuals in France since 1968* (New Haven, CT, 1990), 162–83; on the friendship between Budzislawski and Benjamin, see Hermann Budzislawski, "Seven Years of Flight: The Adventures of an Anti-Nazi Editor," 23, in the author's private archive.

31. Fritz Levy to Hanna and Hermann Budzislawski, 15 October 1933, in AdK, Hermann-Budzislawski-Archiv, no. 383.

32. Linse, *Die entschiedene Jugend*, 40, 252–56.

33. Helene's father was called Henry Chai, her mother Margarete Anna Chai, born Bercy. The family lived at that time at 98 Wellmeadow Road in the London district of

Hither Green. It was not possible to establish why Helene Chai went to school in Berlin some years later. These details are taken from an extract from Helene Chai's birth certificate, Lewisham, 23 January 1903.

34. The Reichenbachs too experienced long years of exile after the National Socialists took power. Herman Reichenbach went first to Switzerland, then in 1934 to Moscow, where he taught at the conservatory, going on later to become its director. His wife and their daughter, Susanna Joy, born in Berlin in 1930, remained initially in Berlin so as to be able to transfer the family's property out of the country, occasionally in "adventurous ways." After that they lived for some years in the country where Helene Reichenbach was born, Great Britain. At the turn of 1937 and 1938 Herman Reichenbach emigrated from the Soviet Union to the United States. In 1949 the Reichenbachs divorced. See Linse, *Die entschiedene Jugend*, 45–46; Horst Weber and Stefan Drees, *Quellen zur Geschichte emigrierter Musiker 1933–1950 / Sources Relating to the History of Émigré Musicians 1933–1950* (New York, 2005), 2:98–99; "Reichenbach, Bernhard," in *Biographisches Handbuch der deutschsprachigen Emigration nach 1933–1945*, vol. 1, *Politik, Wirtschaft, Öffentliches Leben*, ed. Werner Röder and Herbert A. Strauss (Munich 1999), 591; "Reichenbach, Hermann," in *International Biographical Dictionary of Central European Émigrés 1933–1945*, vol. 2.2, ed. Werner Röder and Herbert A. Strauss (Munich, 1983), 951; Georg Günther and Reiner Nägele, eds., *Musik in Baden-Württemberg: Jahrbuch 1995*, (Stuttgart, 1998), 5:81; Herman Reichenbach to Eric Werner, n.d. (between 1944 and 1948), in LBI, Eric Werner Collection, AR 2179, box 1, folder 10, 655–56.

35. Hermann to Hanna Budzislawski, 20 December 1933, in AdK, Hermann-Budzislawski-Archiv, no. 383.

36. Teuber, *Ein Stratege*, 194. Martin Budzislawski had been involved in commercial activities in Berlin in the 1920s. He was a member of the directorate of the Industrie-, Vertriebs-, und Aktiengesellschaft "Iwag," which was founded in the summer of 1923. The company specialized in the manufacture, distribution, and export of children's toys. See "Bekanntmachungen," *Berliner Börsenzeitung*, 21 August 1923, 4.

37. DNB, NL Zadek Konvolut B.T. EB 87/089; Linse, *Die entschiedene Jugend*, 24–25.

38. Dorothea Hartz, "Der 'Triumph der Faust' schien damals undenkbar," *taz*, 15 June 1988, http://www.taz.de/!1847177/.

39. Robbie Aitken, "From Cameroon to Germany and Back via Moscow and Paris: The Political Career of Joseph Bilé (1892–1959), Performer, 'Negerarbeiter' and Comintern Activist," *Journal of Contemporary History* 43, no. 4 (2008): 597–616; Studer, *Reisende der Weltrevolution*, 292–94.

40. Aitken, "From Cameroon to Germany," 609. Chattopadhyaya was shot in Moscow in 1937 during Stalin's purges.

41. On Gábor's years in Berlin, see John Neubauer and Borbála Zsuzsanna Török, eds., *The Exile and Return of Writers from East-Central Europe: A Compendium* (New York, 2009), 57.

42. Manuscript autobiography of Hanna Budzislawski; NARA, RG 319 (U.S. Army, Military Agency Records, Counter Intelligence Corps [CIC] Investigative Records Repository), File 302122 (Report on Budzislawski, 1951); Bernd-Rainer Barth, "Budzislawski, Hermann," in *Wer war wer in der DDR?*, https://www.bundesstiftung-aufar

beitung.de/de/recherche/kataloge-datenbanken/biographische-datenbanken/hermann
-budzislawski.

43. "Vernehmungsprotokoll der Züricher Kriminalpolizei vom 19. Mai 1933," in Schweizerisches Bundesarchiv, Bern (SBB), E4320B#1980/77#1398.

44. Budzislawski's autobiographical record, August 30, 1950, 163; Hermann Budzislawski, "Arnold Zweig," *Die Weltbühne*, 3 December 1968, 1537–38.

45. Antje Kuchenbecker, *Zionismus ohne Zion: Birobidžan. Idee und Geschichte eines jüdischen Staates in Sowjet-Fernost* (Berlin, 2000), 113–25; Robert Weinberg, *Stalin's Forgotten Zion: Birobidzhan and the Making of a Soviet Jewish Homeland; An Illustrated History, 1928–1996* (Berkeley, CA, 1998).

46. Heinrich Bruhn, "Hermann Budzislawski: Zu seinem sechzigsten Geburtstag," *Zeitschrift für Journalistik* 2, no. 1 (1961): 2; character analysis of Hermann Budzislawski, March 1948, in BArch Berlin, SAPMO, DY 30/90300, 206; radio broadcast entitled "Orient in Europa," *Vorwärts*, 5 November 1930, 4; radio broadcast entitled "Die Speisekarte Europas," *Vorwärts*, 16 June 1932, 6; radio broadcast entitled "Funkwinkel," *Vorwärts*, 1 March 1931, 18.

47. Billing, "Gespräch," 177; Ohio State University—University Libraries, Rare Books and Manuscripts Library (OSU), Alexander Stephan Collection of FBI Files on German Intellectuals in US Exile, 1933–2003, SPEC.RARE.CMS.0307, box 35, folder 5, 14–15.

48. Kurt Tucholsky, "Was haben wir—?," *Die Weltbühne* 22, no. 1 (5 January 1926), 524–26, here 524.

49. On *Die Weltbühne* before 1933, see István Deák, *Weimar Germany's Left-Wing Intellectuals: A Political History of the Weltbühne and Its Circle* (Berkeley, CA, 1968); Gallus, *Heimat "Weltbühne"*; Anna Antonello, *"Die Weltbühne" als Bühne der Welt: Politik und Literatur im Spiegel einer deutschen Zeitschrift (1918–1933)* (Berlin, 2017); Stefanie Oswalt, *Siegfried Jacobsohn: Ein Leben für die Weltbühne. Eine Berliner Biographie*, 2nd ed. (Gerlingen, 2002); Alfons Enseling, *Die Weltbühne: Organ der intellektuellen Linken* (Münster, 1962); Dieter Tiemann, "Kurt Tucholsky und *Die Weltbühne*," in *Le milieu intellectual de gauche en Allemagne, sa presse et ses réseaux (1890–1960) / Das linke Intellektuellenmilieu in Deutschland, seine Presse und seine Netzwerke (1890–1960)*, ed. Manfred Grunewald (Bern, 2002), 269–85; Joachim Radkau, "Die Weltbühne als falscher Prophet? Prognostische Versuche gegenüber dem Nationalsozialismus," in *Weimars Ende*, ed. Thomas Koebner (Frankfurt am Main, 1982), 57–79; and Axel Eggebrecht and Dietrich Pinkerneil, *Das Drama der Republik: Zum Neudruck der Weltbühne* (Frankfurt am Main, 1979).

50. Hermann Budzislawski, "Professoren in der Politik," *Die Weltbühne*, 6 December 1932, 840–41; Budzislawski, "Devisenschieber," *Die Weltbühne*, 24 January 1933, 141–43; Budzislawski, "Der soziale Syrup," *Die Weltbühne*, 27 December 1932, 949–52. Syrup was later state secretary at the Ministry of Labor from 1 January 1939 onward, and in this capacity he was involved in the exploitation of Jewish and Polish slave laborers. He died on 31 August 1945 in Soviet Special Camp No. 7, Sachsenhausen. See Henry Marx, "Arbeitsverwaltung und Organisation der Kriegswirtschaft," in *Das Reichsarbeitsministerium im Nationalsozialismus: Verwaltung—Politik—Verbrechen*, ed. Alexander Nützennadel (Göttingen, 2017), 282–312.

51. Carl von Ossietzky to Hermann Budzislawski, 14 February 1933, in AdK, Die neue Weltbühne, no. 1, p. 1.

52. Ulrich Schweitzer (Hermann Budzislawski), "Patrizier in Wolle," *Die Weltbühne*, 7 March 1933, 366–69. Budzislawski's other pseudonyms were Herman Eschwege, Herbert Ruland, Georg Haefner, Fred C. Villinger, and, later in the United States, Donald Bell.

53. Teuber, *Ein Stratege im Exil*, 18–19.

54. Ibid., 17. Siegfried Jacobsohn, who died on 3 December 1926, had made a will on 22 May 1925, naming his wife as his sole heir. For a copy of this will, see Privatarchiv Bernd F. Lunkewitz, Frankfurt am Main, annex BK-12.

55. Gustav Regler, *Das Ohr des Malchus: Eine Lebensgeschichte* (Frankfurt am Main, 1975), 178 (English translation: *The Owl of Minerva: The Autobiography of Gustav Regler*, trans. Norman Denny [London, 1959], 143).

56. This is how Budzislawski put it retrospectively in a lecture to mark the eightieth anniversary of Tucholsky's birth broadcast by the Berliner Rundfunk on 9 January 1970. See Deutsches Rundfunkarchiv, Standort Potsdam-Babelsberg (DRA), DZ095 346.

57. The information in this paragraph is taken from Alfred Kantorowicz, *Nachtbücher: Aufzeichnungen im französischen Exil 1935 bis 1939*, ed. Ursula Büttner and Angelika Voß (Hamburg, 1995), 26–27; Karola Bloch, *Aus meinem Leben* (Pfullingen, 1981), 68–71; Stefan Berkholz, "Die Hungerburg," *Die Zeit*, 25 October 1991, https://www.zeit.de/1991/44/die-hungerburg/komplettansichts; Billing, "Gespräch," 177; and Alfred Schumann to Hermann Budzislawski, 2 November 1940, in AdK, Hermann-Budzislawski-Archiv, no. 394. On Kantorowicz's Berlin years, see Mario Keßler, *Westemigranten: Deutsche Kommunisten zwischen USA-Exil und DDR* (Cologne, 2018), 65.

58. Hermann Budzislawski, "Democracy Underground: The Adventures of an Anti-Nazi-Editor," undated typescript, in AdK, Hermann-Budzislawski-Archiv, nos. 306 and 390.

59. Maud von Ossietszky, undated memorandum on Kurt von Ossietzky, in Leibniz-Zentrum für Zeithistorische Forschung, Potsdam (ZZF), NL Simone Barck no. 3/5 (original in AdK, 78/6).

60. All the information in this paragraph is taken from Berkholz, "Die Hungerburg."

61. Budzislawski, "Adventurers against Will," 6.

62. Ibid. The special correspondent of the *Manchester Guardian* in Berlin was Otto Wolff, a Swiss citizen.

63. Manuscript autobiography of Hanna Budzislawski. On *The Brown Book*, see Anson Rabinbach, "Staging Antifascism: *The Brown Book of the Reichstag Fire and Hitler Terror*," *New German Critique* 35, no. 1 (2008): 97–126.

64. Hermann Budzislawski to Hellmut von Gerlach, 14 June 1933, in AdK, Die neue Weltbühne, box 1, preliminary signature 1, 28.

65. "Vernehmungsprotokoll der Züricher Kriminalpolizei."

Chapter 3. Writing Against Hitler

1. Doris Danzer, *Zwischen Vertrauen und Verrat: Deutschsprachige kommunistische Intellektuelle und ihre sozialen Beziehungen (1918–1960)* (Göttingen, 2012), 214.

2. Gerd-Rainer Horn, *European Socialists Respond to Fascism: Ideology, Activism and Contingency in the 1930s* (New York, 1996).

3. The "Großstadtdokumente" offer an ethnographic and sometimes sensationalist view of life in the big cities at the turn of the century. They concentrate particularly on the living conditions of marginal social groups. Loeb also composed a polemic about the future of the Jewish community of Berlin that was published in 1930. See Peter Fritzsche, "Vagabond in the Fugitive City: Hans Ostwald, Imperial Berlin and the Grossstadt-Dokumente," *Journal of Contemporary History* 29, no. 3 (1994): 385–402; Moritz A. Loeb, *Berliner Konfektion* (Berlin, 1904); and Loeb, *Um die Zukunft der Berliner Jüdischen Gemeinde* (Berlin, 1930).

4. Zürich CID Interrogation Record, 19 May 1933, and Swiss Federal Prosecutor's Office to Federal Councillor H. Häberlin, 24 June 1933, both in SBB, E4320B#1980/77#1398.

5. Police Headquarters of the Canton of Zürich to the Swiss Federal Prosecutor's Office, 23 May 1933, in SBB, E4320B#1980/77#1398.

6. Swiss Federal Prosecutor's Office to the Police Headquarters of the Canton of Zürich, 2 June 1933, in SBB, E4320B#1980/77#1398.

7. Swiss Federal Prosecutor's Office to Häberlin, 24 June 1933.

8. "On the Refusal to Recognise Dr. Hermann Budzislawski as a Political Refugee," typescript composed by himself, 10 May 1933, in SBB, E4320B#1980/77#1398.

9. Order by the Swiss Federal Prosecutor's Office, 29 June 1933, in SBB, E4320B#1980/77#1398. Four years later the editor of the NPK was a Dr. Emil Walter (presumably Dr. Emil J. Walter, then a Social Democratic Zürich city councilor); it has not been possible to obtain any further information about the NPK. See SBB, E4320B#C.19.7.

10. Hermann Lewin to Hermann and Hanna Budzislawski, 23 June 1933, in AdK, Hermann-Budzislawski-Archiv, no. 383.

11. Police Headquarters of the Canton of Zürich to the Swiss Federal Prosecutor's Office, 23 May 1933; Emanuel La Roche, *Im Dorf vor der Stadt: Die Baugenossenschaft Neubühl, 1929–2000* (Zürich, 2019), 85–87, 129–130.

12. Budzislawski, "Seven Years of Flight," 4.

13. See the exchange of letters on the subject between Hermann Budzislawski (writing under the name Nepomuk Frisch) and Willi Schlamm in the autumn of 1933, in AdK, Hermann-Budzislawski-Archiv, no. 383. Budzislawski's letter of 23 October 1933 to William Schlamm, in AdK, Die neue Weltbühne, box 1, preliminary signature 1, 33, contains a variety of proposed topics.

14. La Roche, *Im Dorf*, 139–42. Other left-wing emigrants in the Werkbund settlement included the proletarian poet Hans Marchwitza, who was expelled from Switzerland at the end of 1934; the later Bavarian prime minister Wilhelm Hoegner and his family; the SAP politician and fighter for women's rights Anna Siemsen; and the writer Arthur Koestler.

15. Stefan Heym, *Nachruf* (Munich, 2018), 94.

16. Peter Becher, "Exil und Exil-Literatur in der Tschechoslowakei," in *Handbuch der deutschen Literatur Prags und der Böhmischen Länder*, ed. Peter Becher (Stuttgart, 2017), 235–41; Kateřina Čapková, "Zuflucht für Prominente: Die Tschechoslowakei und ihre Flüchtlinge aus NS-Deutschland und Österreich," *Stifter Jahrbuch*, n.s., 29 (2015): 151; Danzer, *Zwischen Vertrauen und Verrat*, 215.

17. Karl O. Paetel, "Eine Grenze. Eine Grenze?," in *Verbannung: Aufzeichnungen deutscher Schriftsteller im Exil*, ed. Egon Schwarz and Matthias Wegner (Hamburg, 1964), 109.

18. Heym, *Nachruf*, 101, 104; Lisa Fittko, *Solidarität unerwünscht: Meine Flucht durch Europa. Erinnerungen 1933–1940* (Munich, 1992), 104–5; Paetel, "Eine Grenze," 108–11. For a contemporary depiction of this milieu and its venues, see Fritz Erpenbeck, *Emigranten* (Berlin, 1954), esp. 67–78.

19. Susanne Peters, *William S. Schlamm: Ideologischer Grenzgänger im 20. Jahrhundert* (Berlin, 2013), 33, 77–114; Rolf Hosfeld, *Tucholsky: Ein deutsches Leben* (Munich, 2012), 311–12; Liselotte Maas, *Handbuch der deutschen Exilpresse 1933–1945*, vol. 4, *Die Zeitungen des deutschen Exils in Europa von 1933 bis 1939 in Einzeldarstellungen* (Munich, 1990), 107–12.

20. William S. Schlamm to Georg Heintz, 1 September 1966, in Institut für Zeitgeschichte, Munich (IfZ), Archiv, ZS-2171-1.

21. Fair-Schulz, *Loyal Subversion*, 297. After April 1935 the editorial office was again relocated to new business premises in the Prague district of Dejvice, to the north of the castle.

22. Horst Eckert, "Die Beiträge der deutschen emigrierten Schriftsteller in der 'Neuen Weltbühne' von 1934–1939: Ein Beitrag zur Untersuchung der Beziehungen zwischen Volksfrontpolitik und Literatur" (PhD diss., Humboldt University, Berlin, 1962), 9.

23. Communication from the lawyer Egon Schwelb (representing Hans Heller) to Jacobsohn's lawyer Wladimir Rosenbaum, 31 December 1933, in AdK, Die neue Weltbühne, box 1, preliminary signature 1, 47–49.

24. According to Budzislawski, Edith Jacobsohn, from her Grunewald villa, had already offered him the editorship of *Die neue Weltbühne* in the summer of 1932, when Ossietzky was in prison. But this is unlikely. Only journalists with greater experience and a higher profile would have come into consideration for the top job. There is no record of Budzislawski's having had close relations with *Die Weltbühne* and its owners before 1933. But the National Socialist takeover created a completely new situation. See Billing, "Gespräch," 177–78.

25. According to the information in Thomas A. Eckert, "Wie Weiter," draft paper, in AdK, Hermann-Budzislawski-Archiv, no. 428. But Schlamm did write to Budzislawski on 16 October to say that he was "definitely interested" in securing his collaboration (in AdK, Hermann-Budzislawski-Archiv, no. 383).

26. If the editorial office were transferred to Geneva, the intention would have been to locate it in the suburb of "Amasse" (presumably this meant Annemasse), which was over the border in France, so as not to have to comply with the requirements of the Swiss immigration police (Edith Jacobsohn to Hellmut von Gerlach, 19 March 1934, in AdK, Die neue Weltbühne, box 7, preliminary signature 30, 60).

27. I am very grateful to Emanuel La Roche for providing additional information about Rosenbaum, Oprecht, Jacobsohn, and Budzislawski from the archives of the Werkbund settlement Neubühl.

28. These transactions are covered in detail in Teuber, *Ein Stratege*, 41–52; see also the letters between Hermann and Hanna in AdK, Hermann-Budzislawski-Archiv, no. 384; as well as the business correspondence in AdK, Die neue Weltbühne, box 1, preliminary signature 1.

29. Edith Jacobsohn to Hermann Budzislawski, 21 December 1933, in AdK, Die neue Weltbühne, box 1, preliminary signature 1, 45; Hermann to Hanna Budzislawski, 21 December 1933, in AdK, Hermann-Budzislawski-Archiv, no. 383.

30. Hermann to Hanna Budzislawski, 20 December 1933, in AdK, Hermann-Budzislawski-Archiv, no. 383.

31. Nepomuk Frisch (Hermann Budzislawski) to Willi Schlamm, 23 October 1933, in AdK, Hermann-Budzislawski-Archiv, no. 383.

32. Hermann to Hanna Budzislawski, 6 January 1934, in AdK, Hermann-Budzislawski-Archiv, no. 384.

33. Hermann to Hanna Budzislawski, 10 January 1934, in AdK, Die neue Weltbühne, box 1, preliminary signature 2, 36.

34. Minutes of the meeting on 8 January 1934, drawn up by Hermann Budzislawski and his lawyer Ernst Gütig, in AdK, Hermann-Budzislawski-Archiv, no. 383, and in AdK, Die neue Weltbühne, box 1, preliminary signature 1, 58–60. This archive also contains a copy of the statement of authorization, but there is no signature, and the lower part of the document has been torn off. We cannot therefore rule out the possibility that Budzislawski compiled this document but that it was never signed by Edith Jacobsohn (AdK, Die neue Weltbühne, box 1, preliminary signature 1, 66).

35. Hermann Budzislawski to Hans Heller, 23 February 1934, in AdK, Die neue Weltbühne, box 1, preliminary signature 1, 78.

36. There are two copies of the arbitration agreement in AdK, Die neue Weltbühne, box 1, preliminary signature 1, 79–88.

37. The account given in this paragraph is based on the information given in Schlamm's letter of 1 September 1966 to Heintz; Peters, *William S. Schlamm*, 106–11; and Teuber, *Ein Stratege*, 41–52, with further references.

38. Hermann Budzislawski to Edith Jacobsohn, 14 January 1934, in AdK, Hermann-Budzislawski-Archiv, no. 384.

39. Ibid., emphasis in the original.

40. Hermann Budzislawski to Kurt Tucholsky, 14 January 1934, in AdK, Hermann-Budzislawski-Archiv, no. 343.

41. Hermann Budzislawski to Hanna Budzislawski, 7 March 1934, in AdK, Die neue Weltbühne, box 1, preliminary signature 2, 51.

42. Later on, in the GDR of the 1960s, he claimed that this was a tactically necessary piece of dissimulation. See Eckert, *Die Beiträge*, 30.

43. Hermann Budzislawski, "Ein Jahr Emigration," *Die neue Weltbühne*, 15 March 1934, 317–21.

44. Hermann to Hanna Budzislawski, 23 April 1934, in AdK, Die neue Weltbühne, box 1, preliminary signature 2, 86–87.

45. La Roche, *Im Dorf,* 130; Hermann to Hanna Budzislawski, 16 March 1934, in AdK, Hermann-Budzislawski-Archiv, no. 384.

46. Document of transfer between Edith Jacobsohn and Frau Marianne Nathan-Ludwig and Herr Dr. Hans Nathan-Ludwig, 23 March 1934, in AdK, Hermann-Budzislawski-Archiv, no. 383.

47. Hans Nathan, "Der Simpl in der Emigration," *Die Weltbühne*, 1 August 1967, 979–84; Hermann Budzislawski, "Hans Nathan," *Die Weltbühne*, 28 September 1971, 1224–25.

48. Hermann Budzislawski's authentication proposals, 16 April 1935, in AdK, Hermann-Budzislawski-Archiv, no. 384; note by Peter Teek on a communication from Johanna Budzislawski, 19 April 1978, in Bibliotop, Ehemaliges Redaktionsarchiv der *Weltbühne* der DDR (yellow file "Die Weltbühne," no call number). See also Edith Jacobsohn's letters of 20 June and 24 June 1934 to Hermann Budzislawski, in AdK, Hermann-Budzislawski-Archiv, no. 384; Hermann to Erna Budzislawski, 2 May 1935, in AdK, Die neue Weltbühne, box 1, preliminary signature 3, 121; and Budzislawski, "Seven Years of Flight," 7.

49. Edith Jacobsohn to Hermann Budzislawski, 6 May 1934, in AdK, Die neue Weltbühne, box 1, preliminary signature 1, 104.

50. As quoted in Thomas A. Eckert, "Die Neue Weltbühne unter der Leitung von Hermann Budzislawski—im Fahrwasser der KPD?," typescript, in AdK, Hermann-Budzislawski-Archiv, no. 382.

51. Teuber, *Ein Stratege*, 179–80. The assertion that occasionally surfaces in the literature that Stein was a physicist is incorrect. It is presumably based on an incorrect translation of the English word "physician."

52. Numerous items of information on the family history of the Steins since the nineteenth century and their post-1945 restitution affairs are to be found in documents in the Ludwig Philipp Cohn Estate Collection, AR 25597, box 1, folder 17, and the Regina Stein Collection, AR 25157, both in the Center for Jewish History, New York.

53. Heinz Pol, "Goebbels als Dichter," *Die Weltbühne*, 6 January 1933, 129–33.

54. See Deák, *Weimar Germany's Left-Wing Intellectuals*, 13–29.

55. Kurt Hiller, "Aufstieg, Glanz und Verfall der Weltbühne," vol. 4, *konkret*, June 1962, in LAB, E Rep. 200-73, no. 23d. On the difficult relationship between Budzislawski and Hiller between 1934 and 1937, see Daniel Münzner, *Kurt Hiller: Der Intellektuelle als Außenseiter* (Göttingen, 2015), 189–94; on Hiller's break with Budzislawski around the turn of the year 1936–37, see the circular he sent to sixty-one *Weltbühne* authors and other interested people, printed in Teuben, *Ein Stratege*, xxvii–xxxii.

56. Publisher of "Die neue Weltbühne" to Hermann Budzislawski, 1 July 1934, in AdK, Hermann-Budzislawski-Archiv, no. 384. See also Sylke Kirschrück, "Republikanismus aus Alternativlosigkeit: Zum Demokratiedenken Gabriele Tergits," in *Vernunftrepublikanismus in der Weimarer Republik: Politik, Literatur, Wissenschaft*, ed. Matthias Weipert and Andreas Wirsching (Stuttgart, 2008), 311–21.

57. On Tergit's court reports, see Daniel Siemens, *Metropole und Verbrechen: Die Gerichtsreportage in Berlin, Paris und Chicago, 1919–1933* (Stuttgart, 2007), 46–49, 74–76, 82, 128, 210.

58. Hermann Budzislawski to Gabriele Tergit, 25 May 1934, in DNB, Deutsches Exilarchiv 1933–1945, EB 93/178.

59. See the exchange of letters between Elisabeth Kadar and Hermann Budzislawski in the spring of 1934, in BArch Berlin, R 8091, no. 1, 5–6.

60. Quoted in Gerhard Zwerenz, *Kurt Tucholsky: Biographie eines guten Deutschen* (Gütersloh, 1979), 226.

61. Hermann Budzislawski to Siegfried Kracauer, 14 May 1934, in Deutsches Literaturarchiv, Marbach (DLA), Handschriftenabteilung, MPF A: Kracauer.

62. Siegfried Kracauer to Hermann Budzislawski, 21 March 1934, 5 July 1934, and 28 April 1935, in DLA, Handschriftenabteilung, MPF A: Kracauer.

63. Quoted in Jörg Später, *Siegfried Kracauer: Eine Biographie* (Frankfurt am Main, 2016), 365.

64. Hermann to Hanna Budzislawski, 30 March 1934, in AdK, Hermann-Budzislawski-Archiv, no. 384.

65. Markus Wegewitz, "Kultivierter Antifaschismus: Nicolaas Rost und der lange Kampf gegen den Nationalsozialismus, 1919–1967" (PhD diss., Friedrich Schiller University, Jena, 2021), 104–5. Anne Friedrichs also calls for greater attention to be paid to "variable levels of discrimination and privilege affecting migratory women and men" in her article "Placing Migration in Perspective: Neue Wege einer relationalen Geschichtsschreibung," *Geschichte und Gesellschaft* 44, no. 2 (2018): 179.

66. See the extensive correspondence between Hermann Budzislawski and Maximilian Scheer from 1934 to 1938, in AdK, Maximilian-Scheer-Archiv, no. 503.

67. Hermann Budzislawski to Maximilian Scheer, 6 April 1935, in AdK, Maximilian-Scheer-Archiv, no. 503; Hermann Budzislawski's authentication proposals, 16 April 1935, in AdK, Hermann-Budzislawski-Archiv, no. 384.

68. Soon after the end of the war, the main perpetrator was revealed to have been Alfred Naujocks, who also took part in the pretended attack on the Gleiwitz (Gliwice) radio tower in 1939. At the end of the 1950s, the Ludwigsburg Central Office started investigations into this and other crimes, the results of which were handed over in April 1960 to the State Prosecutor's Office in Munich ("Schreiben der Zentralen Stelle Ludwigsburg an den Generalstaatsanwalt beim Oberlandesgericht München vom 20. April 1960," in Bayerisches Hauptstaatsarchiv [BayHStA], M JU 11/951). Naujocks was never convicted in Germany. See in detail Florian Altenhöner, *Der Mann der den zweiten Weltkrieg begann: Alfred Naujocks, Fälscher, Mörder, Terrorist* (Münster, 2010).

69. See Andreas Morgenstern, "Hier ruft die Schwarze Front! Der Weg des Rundfunkpioniers Rudolf Formis," *Rundfunk und Geschichte* 42, no. 3–4 (2016): 15–23; Hans Sarkowicz, "Das Radio als Waffe im Kampf gegen Hitler!," *FAZ Magazin*, 22 February 1991, 48–54.

70. Written declaration by Hermann Budzislawski to the Prague Police Headquarters, 25 January 1935, in LAB, E Rep. 200-63-52.

71. His wife did not hand over this pistol to the French police until 5 September 1939, the date of Budzislawski's detention. See the delivery receipt issued by the Sèvres police to Johanna Budzislawski on 5 September 1939, in AdK, Hermann-Budzislawski-Archiv, no. 262.

72. Citizenship deprivation list, 4; decree issued on 11 February 1938 by the Reich and Prussian minister of science, training, and public education concerning the removal of the title "doctor" from persons deprived of German citizenship (UAT, 177/288-1); memorandum of 8 March 1935 from the Prussian Gestapo to the Reich and Prussian minister of the interior, in Politisches Archiv des Auswärtigen Amtes (Sig. 83-7626/3), quoted in Thomas A. Eckert, "Entwurf einer Dissertation o. T." (1994), in AdK, Hermann-Budzislawski-Archiv, no. 382.

73. Gabriela Veselá-Ducháčková, "Hermann Budzislawski," in *Exil und Asyl: Antifaschistische deutsche Literatur in der Tschechoslowakei 1933–1938*, ed. Autorenkollektiv unter Leitung von Miroslav Beck und Jiři Veselý (Berlin, 1981), 159. Budzislawski's first Czech passport bore the date of issue of 25 March 1941.

74. Peters, *William S. Schlamm*, III. There are similar but less enthusiastic comments in Maas, *Handbuch*, 4:106–7.

75. Data from Georg Heintz, *Deutsches Exil 1933–1945*, vol. 1, *Index der "Neuen Weltbühne" von 1933–1939* (Wiesbaden, 1972), 9–14, 41–42.

76. Address by Hermann Budzislawski on Heinrich Mann delivered in the early 1970s, in Bibliotop, Ehemaliges Redaktionsarchiv der *Weltbühne* der DDR, Budzislawski 4, ZZF I.1.770.

77. Hermann Budzislawski to Kurt Rosenfeld, 5 August 1936, in AdK, Die neue Weltbühne, box 9, preliminary signature 40, 141.

78. Statement by Robert M. W. Kempner to the FBI, quoted in a memorandum of 13 February 1947 about Budzislawski from D. M. Ladd, in OSU, SPEC.RARE. CMS.0307, box 35, folder 5.

79. Ivan Pfaff, "Deutsches Exil in der Tschechoslowakei—eine Kulturbrücke," *Frankfurter Allgemeine Zeitung*, 24 February 1983, 11.

80. According to Arne Laurin's 1943 remarks, in OSU, Office of Strategic Services, 1941–45, SPEC.RARE.CMS.0307, box 35, folder 5, 20.

81. According to Budzislawski, "Seven Years of Flight," 4.

82. Hermann Budzislawski to Gabriela Ducháčková, 2 November 1972, in Bibliotop, Ehemaliges Redaktionsarchiv der *Weltbühne* der DDR, Budzislawski 4, ZZF I.1.777.

83. See Hermann Budzislawski's memorandum of 6 February 1936, in AdK, Die neue Weltbühne, box 1, preliminary signature 1, 152.

84. These bonds were issued by Japan to refinance its expenditure on the Russo-Japanese War of 1904–5. On 18 September 1934 the Budzislawskis had Japanese government bonds on deposit in the Swiss Volksbank to the value of 1,400 pounds sterling (this corresponds to a purchasing power of roughly £100,000 at 2022 values). It is not known when the pair came into possession of these bonds (Schweizer Volksbank to Hermann Budzislawski, 18 September 1934, in AdK, Hermann-Budzislawski-Archiv, no. 385.

85. Hanna Budzislawski to the Schweizer Volksbank, 1 July 1935 in AdK, Hermann-Budzislawski-Archiv, no. 385.

86. Herbert Bobreker was born in Berlin on 26 July 1888. His wife was Maria Bobreker, maiden name Bauer, two years younger than him, who was also born in Berlin. It was not possible to obtain any more information.

87. Schweizer Volksbank to Hermann Budzislawski, 17 July 1935, in AdK, Hermann-Budzislawski-Archiv, no. 385.

88. Herman Reichenbach to Hermann Budzislawski, undated, in AdK, Hermann-Budzislawski-Archiv, no. 386.

89. Hermann Budzislawski to Heinz Pol, 30 November 1935, in AdK, Die neue Weltbühne, box 1, preliminary signature 1, 147.

90. Heinz Pol to Hermann Budzislawski, 5 October 1936, in AdK, Die neue Weltbühne, box 9, preliminary signature 38, 131.

91. Memorandum from Hermann Budzislawski, 6 February 1936, in AdK, Die neue Weltbühne, box 1, preliminary signature 1, 152.

92. Stein's father-in-law, Ludwig Philipp Cohn, whose firm was "Aryanized" after 1933, died on 11 July 1938 in Buchenwald concentration camp.

93. See Hermann Budzislawski to Heinz Pol, 6 March, 16 March, 4 April, and 11 July 1936, in AdK, Die neue Weltbühne, box 9, preliminary signature 38, 145, 147, 174, and box 1, preliminary signature 1, 179.

94. Ernst Toller to Hermann Budzislawski, 19 March 1936, in *Ernst Toller: Briefe 1915–1939*, ed. Stefan Neuhaus et al. (Göttingen, 2018), 2:1306–7; Hermann Budzislawski to Václav Bouček, 8 March 1936, in AdK, Die neue Weltbühne, box 1, preliminary signature 1, 160.

95. Schweizer Bankenverein to Hermann Budzislawski, 27 March 1936, in AdK, Hermann-Budzislawski-Archiv, no. 386.

96. Hermann Budzislawski to Helene Reichenbach, 18 March 1936, in AdK, Hermann-Budzislawski-Archiv, no. 386, 171.

97. Hermann Budzislawski to Helene Reichenbach, 1 October 1936, in AdK, Hermann-Budzislawski-Archiv, no. 386, 182.

98. Hermann Budzislawski to Alfred Kantorowicz, 7 March 1936, in BArch Berlin, R 8059, no. 1, 58.

99. Draft contract, 3 August 1936, in AdK, Die neue Weltbühne, box 1, preliminary signature 4, 176.

100. Ernst Toller to Hermann Budzislawski, 19 March 1936, in Neuhaus et al., *Ernst Toller*, 2:1306–7.

101. Helene Reichenbach to Hermann Budzislawski, 20 September 1937, in AdK, Hermann-Budzislawski-Archiv, no. 387, 7. The Budzislawskis and the Reichenbachs were in personal contact at least until the summer of 1941, and they also visited each other in New York. See Carl Misch to Hermann Budzislawski, 21 September 1941, in AdK, Hermann-Budzislawski-Archiv, no. 66.

102. Quoted in Forschungsgruppe Deutsche Exil-Literatur in der ČSR, "Zur Frage der deutschen antifaschistischen Emigration in der ČSR 1933–1939," *Philologica Pragensia* 18, no. 1 (1975): 23; report from the Prague police to the Czech Ministry of the Interior, 30 November 1937, in Tschechisches Nationalarchiv Prag (TNP), no. 225-1116-1, 55–57.

103. Hermann Budzislawski to Alexander Schifrin, 12 March 1936, in AdK, Die neue Weltbühne, box 1, preliminary signature 1, 162.

104. For further details, see Frithjof Trapp, "Konfliktlinien im linksintellektuellen Milieu: Die Ossietzky-Kampagne des frühen Vorkriegsexils," in Grunewald, *Le milieu intellectual*, 479–98.

105. Hellmut von Gerlach to Hermann Budzislawski, 8 May 1934, in AdK, Die neue Weltbühne, box 7, preliminary signature 30, 68.

106. Trapp, "Konfliktlinien," 484.

107. Hilde Walter to Paul Olberg, 27 April 1934, in International Institute of Social History, Amsterdam (IISH), Collection Freundeskreis Carl von Ossietzky, Inv.-No. folder 6 (ARCH 01 448).

108. Hilde Walter to Hermann Budzislawski, 19 October 1934, in IISH, Collection Freundeskreis Carl von Ossietzky, Inv.-No. folder 6 (ARCH 01 448), emphasis in the original.

109. A point also made by Teuber, *Ein Stratege*, 131–66.

110. Excerpts from Konrad Reisner to Hermann Budzislawski, 30 October 1935, in Walter A. Berendsohn Forschungsstelle für deutsche Exilliteratur, Hamburg, P. Walter Jacob Archiv, Signatur: KR/8, 1.

111. For Budzislawski's position, see Hermann Budzislawski to Hellmut von Gerlach, 3 October 1934, in AdK, Die neue Weltbühne, box 7, preliminary signature 30, 80–82.

112. Hermann Budzislawski, "Carl von Ossietzky," *Die neue Weltbühne*, 26 November 1936, 1497–98.

113. Ibid.

114. Hermann Budzislawski, "Der Nobelpreis," *Die neue Weltbühne*, 3 December 1936, 1529–33, here 1532–33.

115. Hermann Budzislawski, "Die Kriegsopposition," *Die neue Weltbühne*, 28 March 1935, 381–84, here 382.

116. For a sharp criticism by one reader, see the Austrian Elias Adolf Palme to the editorial board of *Die neue Weltbühne*, 17 January 1935, in AdK, Die neue Weltbühne, box 9, preliminary signature 37, 48–50.

117. Hermann Budzislawski to Rudolf Leonhard, 28 May 1936, in DNB, EB autograph 631.

118. This is stated explicitly by Budzislawski in a letter of 2 February 1935 to Erich Wollenberg, quoted in Dieter Schiller, "Die 'Weltbühne' im Prager Exil," in *Der Traum von Hitlers Sturz: Studien zur deutschen Exilliteratur 1933–1945*, by Dieter Schiller (Frankfurt am Main, 2010), 274.

119. On the Revolutionary Socialists, see Jutta von Freyberg, *Sozialdemokraten und Kommunisten: Die Revolutionären Sozialisten Deutschlands vor dem Problem der Aktionseinheit 1934–1937* (Cologne, 1973), 51–55, 79–124; on Budzislawski's role, see the Gestapo report of 8 April 1935, in AdK, Hermann-Budzislawski-Archiv, no. 385.

120. Hermann Budzislawski to Louis Fischer, 19 April and 2 May 1935, in AdK, Die neue Weltbühne, box 7, preliminary signature 29, 22, 26–27.

121. Willi Bredel to Wieland Herzfelde, 29 March 1935, in *Prag-Moskau: Briefe von und an Wieland Herzfelde 1933–1938*, ed. Giuseppe de Siati and Thies Ziemke (Kiel, 1991), 27–29.

122. Hermann Budzislawski's SED questionnaire, 30 August 1950, in BArch Berlin, SAPMO, DY 30/90300, 174–75; "Wir stellen vor: Professor Dr. Hermann Budzislawski," in AdK, Hermann-Budzislawski-Archiv, no. 414; Gestapo report of 8 April 1935, in AdK, Hermann-Budzislawski-Archiv, no. 385; David Pike, *German Writers in Soviet Exile, 1933–1945* (Chapel Hill, NC, 1982), 60; Simone Barck, "Internationale Vereinigung Revolutionärer Schriftsteller," in *Lexikon sozialistischer Literatur: Ihre Geschichte in Deutschland bis 1945*, ed. Simone Barck et al. (Stuttgart, 1994), 223–26; Klaus Jarmatz, Simone Barck, and Peter Diezel, *Exil in der UdSSR* (Leipzig, 1979), 70.

123. Freyberg, *Sozialdemokraten*, 134–39. For the background to the difficult relationship between "literati" and Communists, see Simone Barck, "Zur Spezifik des deutschen literarischen Exils in der Sowjetunion unter kommunikationsgeschichtlichen Aspekt," in *Kommunisten verfolgen Kommunisten: Stalinistischer Terror und "Säuberungen" in den kommunistischen Parteien Europas seit den dreißiger Jahren*, ed. Hermann Weber and Dietrich Staritz (Berlin, 1993), 318–26.

124. Angela Huß-Michel, *Literarische und politische Zeitschriften des Exils 1933–1945* (Stuttgart, 1987), 24.

125. On Koenen's articles in *Die neue Weltbühne*, see BArch Berlin, SAPMO, NY 4074/40, 115–17.

126. These appeared in issues 46 through 52 (11 November 1937–23 December 1937) of *Die neue Weltbühne* for 1937. For the background, see Eckert, *Die Beiträge*, 52–53.

127. Schiller, "Die 'Weltbühne' im Prager Exil," 279–80.

128. Hermann Budzislawski to Walter Ulbricht, 31 October 1938, in BArch Berlin, SAPMO, RY 1/607, 183. I am grateful to Ilko-Sascha Kowalczuk, Berlin, for this reference.

129. Hermann Budzislawski to Paul Hertz, 23 August 1937, in IISH, Paul Hertz Papers, Inv.-No. 17-2-5 (ARCH 00 563).

130. Report from the Prague police to the Czech Ministry of the Interior, 27 October 1937, in TNP, no. 207-813-10, 48–50.

131. Schlamm to Heintz, 1 September 1966. In 1939 the Gestapo also regarded editor and publisher Budzislawski as a "KPD functionary." See Chef des Reichssicherheitshauptamtes (Heydrich), "Erfassung führender Männer der Systemzeit, Juni 1939," in BArch Berlin, R 58/3566a, 65.

132. Hermann Budzislawski to Hanna Budzislawski, 19 January 1934, in AdK, Hermann-Budzislawski-Archiv, no. 384.

133. Rudolf Olden to Hermann Budzislawski, 13 July 1934, in IISH, Collection Freundeskreis Carl von Ossietzky, Inv.-No. Mappe 5 (ARCH 01 448).

134. See Ruth Fischer's undated reply to the 23 March 1944 "Memorandum against Ruth Fischer" in OSU, Office of Strategic Services, 1941–45, SPEC.RARE.CMS.0307, box 60, folder 2, 174–79, here 177. Fischer's changing political positions are treated comprehensively in Mario Keßler, *Ruth Fischer: Ein Leben mit und gegen Kommunisten (1895–1961)* (Cologne, 2013).

135. See in particular in this context the pamphlet *Die Grenzen des Wahnsinns: Vorträge zum Buch des William S. Schlamm von Professor Dr. H. Budzislawski und Karl-Eduard von Schnitzler*, Sonderheft des Deutschlandsenders, Berlin 1959–60, in DRA, Pressearchiv Personalia, vol. Budi–Bülz.

136. Charles B. Friediger, "Prince Loewenstein on the ONE Germany, a Riotous Meeting," OSS memo, 5 April 1944, in OSU, Office of Strategic Services, 1941–45, SPEC.RARE.CMS0307, box 60, folder 2, 180–84, here 182.

137. Lion Feuchtwanger, *Exil* (Frankfurt am Main, 1981), 123, as quoted in Danzer, *Zwischen Vertrauen und Verrat*, 222.

138. Hermann Budzislawski to Heinrich Mann, 16 August 1941, in AdK, Hermann-Budzislawski-Archiv, no. 391.

139. These details about Rosenfeld's activities are taken from Hermann Weber, "Rosenfeld, Kurt," in *Neue Deutsche Biographie* (Berlin, 2005), 22:66–67.

140. Hermann Budzislawski to Heinrich Mann, 16 August 1941, in AdK, Hermann-Budzislawski-Archiv, no. 391.

141. Albert Schreiner to Franz Dahlem, 18 October 1948, in BArch Berlin, SAPMO, DY 30/90300, 193–94.

142. As pointed out in Jörg J. Bachmann, *Zwischen Paris und Moskau: Deutsche bürgerliche Linksintellektuelle und die stalinistische Sowjetunion 1933–1939* (Mannheim, 1995), 35–36; and Maas, *Handbuch*, 4:114–15.

143. Hermann Budzislawski to Maximilian Scheer, 2 April 1938, in AdK, Maximilian-Scheer-Archiv, no. 503.

144. Kurt Hiller, *Rote Ritter: Erlebnisse mit deutschen Kommunisten*, afterword by Eugen M. Brehm (Berlin, 1980), 76–77.

Chapter 4. Parisian Impasse

1. Extract from the Nationalsozialistische Parteikorrespondenz, 3 March 1938, in BArch Berlin, SAPMO, NY 4074/88, 158; Gestapo Office, Berlin, to all Gestapo branches, 5 March 1938, in BArch Berlin, R 58/3732, 61–74, here 63.

2. Budzislawski's autobiographical record, 30 August 1950, 165–66.

3. Berthold Viertel, "Selbstmörder," *Die neue Weltbühne*, 28 April 1938, 525–30. The other articles the censor took exception to were probably two contributions in the 12 May issue, both of them obituaries for Carl von Ossietzky, who had died on 4 May 1938. One was Lion Feuchtwanger, "Der Realist," and the other was Berthold Viertel, "Nachruf," both in *Die neue Weltbühne*, 12 May 1938, 577–79.

4. Hermann Budzislawski to Lion Feuchtwanger, 21 May 1938, in AdK, Die neue Weltbühne, box 7, preliminary signature 28, 52; Hans-Albert Walter, *Deutsche Exilliteratur 1933–1950*, vol. 4, *Exilpresse* (Stuttgart, 1978), 28–29.

5. Hermann Budzislawski to Maximilian Scheer, 14 January 1938, in AdK, Maximilian-Scheer-Archiv, no. 503.

6. Hermann Budzislawski to the Central Committee of the SED, Department for International Relations, 22 March 1967, in Bibliotop, Ehemaliges Redaktionsarchiv der *Weltbühne* der DDR, Budzislawski 1, ZZF I.1.90; Hiller, *Rote Ritter*, 91.

7. Central Committee of the SED, Minutes of the Sitting of 10 January 1968, in BArch Berlin, DY 30/J IV 2/3/1363.

8. Report from Hans Schlegel and Manfred George, passed on by Bruce F. Levitch to the US Department of Justice on 19 December 1941, in OSU, Office of Strategic Services, 1941–45, SPEC. RARE.CMS.0307, box 60, folder 1; for the life of Milly Zirker, see Michael Quetting, *Journalistin und Organisatorin, Friedensktivistin und Nazigegnerin, die Nobelpreismacherin Milly Zirker 1888–1971* (Sankt Ingbert, 2007).

9. Hermann Budzislawski to the Czechoslovak consul general in New York, 21 January 1941, in AdK, Hermann-Budzislawski-Archiv, no. 113.

10. Budzislawski, "Seven Years of Flight," 4–5.

11. Budzislawski, "Democracy Underground."

12. Eckert, *Die Beiträge*, 55; Jens Wehner, *Kulturpolitik und Volksfront: Ein Beitrag zur Geschichte der Sowjetischen Besatzungszone Deutschlands 1945–1949* (Frankfurt am Main, 1991), 1:379–80.

13. As quoted in Olivier Clochard, Yvan Gastaut, and Ralph Schor, "Les camps d'étrangers depuis 1938: Continuité et adaptations. Du 'modèle' français à la construction de l'espace Schengen," *Revue Européenne des Migrations Internationales* 20 (2004): 2, http://remi.revues.org/968.

14. See the convincing account in Fittko, *Solidarität unerwünscht*, 161–215; as well as Julia Franke, "De véritables 'boches': Französische und emigrierte deutsche Juden im Paris der dreißiger Jahre," in *Jüdische Emigration zwischen Assimilation und Verfolgung: Akkulturation und jüdischer Identität*, ed. Claus-Dieter Krohn et al. (Munich, 2001), 93–94. According to a contemporary source, the situation of the German and German Jewish refugees had worsened dramatically since the end of 1934: see "German Exiles in France: Lack of Sympathy," *Manchester Guardian*, 8 April 1936, 9.

15. Action Committee of German Oppositionists to Manfred George, Hollywood, 26 July 1939, in DLA, Handschriftenabteilung, no. 75.2320; "Denkschrift deutscher Friedensfreunde über Hitlers Kriegspolitik und den Friedenswillen des Deutschen Volkes," in BArch Berlin, NY 4198, no. 23, 141–64; Hermann Budzislawski to Georg Bernhard, 26 and 29 April 1939, in BArch Berlin, N 2020, no. 35, 67, 73; Budzislawski's autobiographical record, 30 August 1950, 166; Jean-Michel Palmier, *Weimar in Exile: The Antifascist Emigration in Europe and America* (New York, 2017), 363–64; Wieland Herzfelde to Carola and Ernst Bloch, 26 December 1938, in *Ernst Bloch / Wieland Herzfelde, "Wir haben das Leben wieder vor uns": Briefwechsel 1938–1949*, ed. Jürgen Jahn (Frankfurt am Main, 2001), 32.

16. Dieter Schiller, "'Wir konnten nicht mit dem K-Unglück rechnen . . .': Der Verlag 10. Mai in Paris 1938/39," in Schiller, *Der Traum von Hitlers Sturz*, 187n26.

17. Wehner, *Kulturpolitik und Volksfront*, 1:380.

18. Joseph Goebbels, *Die Tagebücher von Joseph Goebbels*, issued under the authority of the Institut für Zeitgeschichte and with the assistance of the Russian State Archive Service, ed. Elke Fröhlich, pt. 1, *Aufzeichnungen 1923–1941*, vol. 6, *August 1938 to June 1939* (Munich, 1998), 357–58.

19. Hermann Budzislawski, "Die Friedensfrist," *Die neue Weltbühne*, 7 July 1938, 829–33.

20. Bachmann, *Zwischen Paris und Moskau*, 345–47, 356, 402–10; Münzner, *Kurt Hiller*, 190–92.

21. Hermann Budzislawski, "Die Russen," *Die neue Weltbühne*, 10 November 1938, 1401–7, here 1406–7.

22. Hermann Budzislawski, "Zweiter Weltkrieg: Im Konzentrationslager," typescript, part of a planned autobiography, composed between 1941 and 1943, in AdK, Hermann-Budzislawski-Archiv, no. 390. On very similar lines, see Heym, *Nachruf*, 198–202.

23. "Einige Erinnerungen des Genossen Albert Norden," 1962, in BArch Berlin, SAPMO, NY 4217/54, 13–14. Norden's information is consistent with the notes made by Wilhelm Pieck at the beginning of September 1939 in Moscow, extracts of which are quoted in Bernhard H. Bayerlein, *"Der Verräter, Stalin, bist Du!": Vom Ende der linken Solidarität. Komintern und kommunistische Parteien im Zweiten Weltkrieg 1939–1941* (Berlin, 2008), 141–42. See also Walter F. Peterson, *The Berlin Liberal Press in Exile: A History of the Pariser Tageblatt—Pariser Tageszeitung 1933–1940* (Tübingen, 1987), 221. On the tensions that had already developed in the Popular Front Committee in previous years, see in addition Ernst Stock and Karl Walcher, *Jacob Walcher (1887–1970): Gewerkschafter und Revolutionär zwischen Berlin, Paris und New York* (Berlin, 1998), 126–33.

24. Budzislawski, "Zweiter Weltkrieg." On the despair felt by the political exiles in Paris during this time, see Kantorowicz, *Nachtbücher*, 305–6.

25. Hermann Budzislawski to Georg Bernhard, 24 August 1939, in BArch Berlin, N 2020, no. 35, 127.

26. Clémence Nannini, "L'internement des indésirables pendant la seconde guerre mondiale: Aspects du phénomène dans les Basses-Alpes. Mémoire de 4ème année," Université de Lyon–Université Lumière Lyon 2. Lyons 2017; Fittko, *Solidarität unerwünscht*, 189.

27. Quoted in Ursula Madrasch-Groschopp, *Die Weltbühne: Porträt einer Zeitschrift* (Augsburg, 1999), 380.

28. Hermann Budzislawski, manuscript for a speech, January 1941, in AdK, Hermann-Budzislawski-Archiv, no. 390.

29. Budzislawski, "Seven Years of Flight," 6.

30. See on this camp Thierry Marchand and Gérard Boudin, *Exils normands: Les "ressortissants ennemis" internés dans les centres de rassemblement des étrangers de Normandie (1939–1940)* (Lisieux, 2014).

31. Budzislawski, "Seven Years of Flight," 7.

32. Matthias Pasdzierny, "Ernst Engel," in *Lexikon verfolgter Musiker und Musikerinnen der NS-Zeit*, ed. Claudia Maurer Zenck and Peter Petersen (Hamburg, 2010), https://www.lexm.uni-hamburg.de/object/lexm_lexmperson_00001808.

33. Henry Jacoby, *Davongekommen: 10 Jahre Exil 1936–1946. Prag, Paris, Montauban, New York, Washington. Erlebnisse und Begegnungen* (Frankfurt am Main, 1982), 77–78.

34. Budzislawski's autobiographical record, 30 August 1950, 166; Jacoby, *Davongekommen*, 78. Jacoby, who worked for the United Nations after the Second World War, was in no doubt, when he looked back, that Budzislawski had been "a Moscow agent" at the time. Indeed, in another passage of his memoirs in which he examines the way *Die neue Weltbühne* reported the Moscow show trials of August 1936, he describes Budzislawski as a "Stalinist agent" and a "skillful journalist who knew how to pass himself off as an honest, democratic fellow, unconnected to any party" (23). Whether he was already of this opinion in 1940 cannot be retrospectively verified. It is likely that the political disappointments suffered by the Left Socialist Jacoby in the 1930s and early 1940s were inextricably linked with the side he took later during the Cold War.

35. Manuscript autobiography of Hanna Budzislawski.

36. Hanna Budzislawski, undated report on Willi Münzenberg, in BArch Berlin, SAPMO, DY 30/90301.

37. Ibid. Guernut died in 1943, and any contradiction from his side was therefore out of the question. Hanna was not the only person who made accusations against Münzenberg. The writer F. C. Weiskopf asserted that Münzenberg and Leopold Schwarzschild were members of a French committee "whose advice was sought on all questions relating to release from the internment camps" ("Material aus einem Brief von F. C. Weiskopf über die Haltung deutscher und einiger anderer Schriftsteller nach Kriegsausbruch," in BArch Berlin, RY 5/553, 65).

38. "Einige Erinnerungen," 14; "Autobiographical Statement by Albert Norden, 27 February 1951," in BArch Berlin, SAPMO, DY 30/IV2/11/v., 5427:162; Peterson, *The Berlin Liberal Press*, 242.

39. On the final years of Münzenberg's life in France, see most recently Bernhard H. Bayerlein, "Kein Antifaschismus ohne Antistalinismus: Willi Münzenberg, 'Die Zukunft' und die antistalinistische Wende in der deutschsprachigen Emigration 1933–1940," in *Global Spaces for Radical Transnational Solidarity: Beiträge zum Ersten Internationalen Willi-Münzenberg-Kongress 2015 in Berlin*, ed. Kasper Braskén and Uwe Sonnenberg (Berlin, 2018), 218–70; and Bayerlein, "Willi Münzenberg's 'Last Empire': Die Zukunft and the 'Franco-German Union,' Paris, 1938–1940; New Visions of Anti-

Fascism and the Transnational Networks of the Anti-Hitler Resistance," *Moving the Social* 58 (2017): 51–80.

40. Willi Münzenberg to Johanna Budzislawski, 22 December 1939, in AdK, Hermann-Budzislawski-Archiv, no. 119.

41. Hanna Budzislawski, undated report on Willi Münzenberg. See also the instructive article by Gerhard Paul, "Der verratene Sozialist: Wie schwer sich ein Kommunist von seiner Partei trennt," *Die Zeit,* 29 June 1990.

42. See Hermann Ehmer, "Löwenstein, Hubertus," in *Neue Deutsche Biographie* (Berlin, 1987), 15:100–101.

43. Rudolf Olden to Hubertus, Prince of Löwenstein, 28 October 1939, in DNB, Deutsches Exilarchiv 1933–1945, EB 86/2 I.A.63.

44. Arnold Zweig to Jürgen Kuczinski, 20 December 1939, in Zentral- und Landesbibliothek Berlin (ZLB), Kuc 8-2-Z52.

45. Hans-Albert Walter, *Deutsche Exilliteratur 1933–1950*, vol. 3, *Internierung, Flucht und Lebensbedingungen im Zweiten Weltkrieg* (Stuttgart, 1988), 77.

46. Budzislawski, "Seven Years of Flight," 9–10.

47. Hermann Budzislawski, "Reise durch Frankreich," in AdK, Hermann-Budzislawski-Archiv, no. 304.

48. Walter, *Internierung, Flucht und Lebensbedingungen*, 77.

49. Copy of a letter from an unknown Communist to Georgi Dimitrov, 14 November 1939, in BArch Berlin, RY5/553, 21.

50. Hermann Budzislawski to Hubertus, Prince of Löwenstein, 18 April 1940, in DNB, Deutsches Exilarchiv 1933–1945, EB 70/117; Hermann Budzislawski's SED questionnaire, 5 September 1953, in Der Bundesbeauftragte für die Unterlagen des Staatssicherheitsdienstes der ehemaligen Deutschen Demokratischen Republik (BStU), MfS, BV Leipzig, AIM 761/65, 32–35, here 33.

51. Hanna Budzislawski to Hubertus, Prince of Löwenstein, 18 April 1940, in DNB, Deutsches Exilarchiv 1933–1945, EB 70/117.

52. As quoted in Madrasch-Groschopp, *Die Weltbühne*, 366.

53. Budzislawski, "Seven Years of Flight," 8.

54. Hanna Budzislawski, undated report on Willi Münzenberg.

55. Hanna Budzislawski to Hubertus, Prince of Löwenstein, 18 April 1940.

56. Questionnaire on Hermann Budzislawski filled out by his wife, Hanna, 18 April 1940, in DNB, Deutsches Exilarchiv 1933–1945, EB 70/117.

57. Data taken from "Camp de Bassens (Gironde)," http:///www.apra.asso.fr /Camps/Fr/Camp-Bassens.html.

58. Budzislawski, "Zweiter Weltkrieg"; Budzislawski, "Seven Years of Flight," 11.

59. Budzislawski, "Seven Years of Flight," 12.

60. Karina von Tippelskirch, *Dorothy Thompson and German Writers in Defense of Democracy* (New York, 2018), 245; Anne Klein, *Flüchtlingspolitik und Flüchtlingshilfe 1940–1942: Varian Fry und die Komitees zur Rettung politisch Verfolgter in New York und Marseille* (Berlin, 2007), 90–92.

61. "Autobiographical Statement by Albert Norden, 27 February 1951," 162.

62. Budzislawski's certificate of release from the Bassens camp, 20 June 1940, in AdK, Hermann-Budzislawski-Archiv, no. 237; Budzislawski, "Seven Years of Flight," 16–17. The date of release given there, 21 June 1940, is presumably incorrect.

63. Hermann Budzislawski, "Europa entronnen: Eine Adresse gesucht," *Der Aufbau*, 18 October 1940, 4, https://archive.org/details/aufbau5619391940germ/page/n406/mode/1up?view=theater.

64. Walter, *Internierung, Flucht und Lebensbedingungen*, 169; Alexander Abusch, "Durch die Partei, getreu der Partei: Albert Norden zum 70. Geburtstag," typescript, in Bibliotop, Ehemaliges Redaktionsarchiv der *Weltbühne* der DDR (blue file).

65. Budzislawski, "Seven Years of Flight," 17–18.

66. As stated by Budzislawski at a meeting organized by PEN on 29 September 1964 at the castle of Cecilienhof in Potsdam with the title "Two World Wars and German Literature," in DRA, no. 2 032 678 (0:30–1:40 mins.).

67. According to Budzislawski, "Seven Years of Flight," 16.

68. Hermann Budzislawski, "Europa entronnen: Eine Adresse gesucht," *Der Aufbau*, 18 October 1940, 4. https://archive.org/details/aufbau5619391940germ/page/n406/mode/1up?view=theater.

69. Hanna Budzislawski to Balder Olden, 19 September 1941, in DNB, Teilnachlass 196 (Balder Olden), EB 2004/043 B.010 002.

70. Walther Victor, *Kehre über die Berge: Eine Autobiographie* (Berlin, 1982), 322.

71. Hermann Budzislawski (Paris) to Rudolf Leonhard, 3 July 1938, in DNB, EB autograph 631, 35; manuscript autobiography of Hanna Budzislawski.

72. Budzislawski, "Seven Years of Flight," 19–20.

73. Hermann Budzislawski to the US Department of State, 6 August 1940, in DNB, Deutsches Exilarchiv 1933–1945, EB 70/117.

74. Telegram from the American Guild to Marie Röselova, 10 September 1940, in DNB, Deutsches Exilarchiv 1933–1945, EB 70/117; telegram from the Western Union Telegraph Company to the American Guild, 17 September 1940, in DNB, Deutsches Exilarchiv 1933–1945, EB 70/117 (literally, "addressee left and present address unknown").

75. Später, *Siegfried Kracauer*, 399–404.

76. Budzislawski, "Seven Years of Flight," 20.

77. Ibid., 19; Victor, *Kehre über die Berge*, 323.

78. On Fry's activities, see Klein, *Flüchtlingspolitik und Flüchtlingshilfe*; on Ende's role, see Edith Anderson, *Liebe im Exil: Erinnerungen einer amerikanischen Schriftstellerin an das Berlin der Nachkriegszeit* (Berlin, 2007), 511.

79. Manuscript autobiography of Hanna Budzislawski.

80. Budzislawski, "Seven Years of Flight," 21.

81. Hanna Budzislawski, report on Rudolf Breitscheid, 1950, in BArch Berlin, SAPMO, DY 30/90 301.

82. Klein, *Flüchtlingspolitik und Flüchtlingshilfe*, 111, 176–77, 185–86.

83. Hermann Budzislawski, "France's Action Condemned," *New York Times*, 18 February 1942, 22.

84. Klein, *Flüchtlingspolitik und Flüchtlingshilfe*, 180; Albrecht Ragg, "The German Socialist Emigration in the United States, 1933 to 1945" (PhD diss., Loyola University, Chicago, 1973), 173.

85. Manuscript autobiography of Hanna Budzislawski.

86. Robin Ostow, "Being Jewish in the Other Germany: An Interview with Thomas Eckert," *New German Critique* 38 (1986): 73.

87. See also Jochen Reinert, "Flucht-Passagen über die Pyrenäen," *Neues Deutschland*, 19 October 2002, https://www.neues-deutschland.de/artikel/25188.flucht-passagen-ueber-die-pyrenaeen.html.

88. Hermann Budzislawski, "Stunden zum Totschlagen?," *Das Magazin* 13, no. 4 (April 1966): 37.

89. Hermann Budzislawski, "How Do We Get Out?," undated typescript, in AdK, Hermann-Budzislawski-Archiv, no. 299.

90. Hermann Budzislawski to Berthold Viertel, 22 September 1940, in DLA, Handschriftenabteilung, no. 1980.1.613/1.

91. Budzislawski to Viertel, 22 September 1940.

92. Später, *Siegfried Kracauer*, 405–6.

93. Marian Kaplan, "Festrede," in *50 Jahre—50 Quellen: Festschrift zum Jubiläum des Instituts für die Geschichte der deutschen Juden*, ed. Institut für die Geschichte der deutschen Juden (Hamburg, 2016), 22–23; Theo Pischke, "Furchtbares Wort Heimat," *taz* (Berlin), 26 May 1994, 12.

94. Manuscript autobiography of Hanna Budzislawski.

95. Budzislawski, "Seven Years of Flight," 24.

96. Hermann Budzislawski to Hubertus, Prince of Löwenstein, 21 September 1940, in DNB, Deutsches Exilarchiv 1933–1945, American Guild EB 70/117.

97. Ibid.

98. Ibid.

99. Budzislawski to Viertel, 22 September 1940.

100. Budzislawski, "Seven Years of Flight," 25.

101. Charlotte Dieterle to W. Sauerländer of the American Guild, 27 September 1940, in DNB, Deutsches Exilarchiv 1933–1945, American Guild EB 70/117. For a comprehensive account of the European Film Fund and the significance of the great efforts made for persecuted artists by the female exiles who were actively involved in it, see Martin Saurer, "Liesl Frank, Charlotte Dieterle and the European Film Fund" (PhD diss., University of Warwick, 2010).

102. The American Guild and the Emergency Rescue Committee began to negotiate over who should pay for the journey while the Budzislawski family were still at sea, although as far as we know they did not reach an agreement, so HICEM or HIAS presumably remained entirely responsible for the costs. See Emergency Rescue Committee to the American Guild, 17 December 1940, in DNB, Deutsches Exilarchiv 1933–1945, EB 70/117. The HIAS also financed the journey to the United States of Budzislawski's journalist friend Carl Misch and his wife in September 1940. It subsequently endeavored to recover the money from the Emergency Rescue Committee. See on this in particular Carl Misch to the Emergency Rescue Committee, 22 December 1940, in DNB, Deutsches Exilarchiv 1933–1945, EB 73/21 (Carl E. Misch), 9; manuscript autobiography of Hanna Budzislawski.

103. Yivo Archives, New York, HIAS Arrivals, microfilm Mkm 27.57.

104. Marje Schuetze-Coburn, "Feuchtwanger's Relocation to Southern California: Frustration & Successes," in *Refuge and Reality: Feuchtwanger and the European Émigrés in California*, ed. Pól Ó Dochartaigh and Alexander Stephan (New York, 2005), 101; Berthold Viertel to Salka Viertel, 12 October 1940, in DLA, Handschriftenabteilung, no. 78 872/12.

105. "Eleanor Roosevelt verteidigt die Refugees," *Der Aufbau*, 30 May 1941, quoted in AdK, Hermann-Scheer-Archiv, no. 1204.

106. "Franz Werfel, Heinrich Mann Arrive on Greek Ships," *News from All over the World by the Jewish Telegraphic Agency*, 14 October 1940, http://pdfs.jta.org/1940/1940 -10-14_157.pdf.

107. Billing, "Gespräch," 179.

108. Erna Budzislawski to Berthold Viertel, 4 October 1940, in DLA, Handschrift- enabteilung, no. 69 2229/3.

Chapter 5. Protected by the Class Enemy

1. Comment by Hubertus, Prince of Löwenstein, undated, in DNB, Deutsches Exilarchiv 1933–1945, EB 70/117.

2. Quoted in Walter, *Internierung, Flucht und Lebensbedingungen*, 99; and in a letter sent on 9 June 1940 to Magda von Gronefeld, in DNB, Deutsches Exilarchiv 1933– 1945, EB 70/117.

3. American Guild to Hanna Budzislawski, 27 May 1940, in DNB, Deutsches Exilarchiv 1933–1945, EB 70/117.

4. Declaration of Guarantee made on 13 August 1940 to the American Guild for German Cultural Freedom, in DNB, Deutsches Exilarchiv 1933–1945, EB 70/117.

5. Louise Mally, League of American Writers, to the American Guild, 15 August 1940, in DNB, Deutsches Exilarchiv 1933–1945, EB 70/117. See also Salka Viertel's autobi- ography, *Das unbelehrbare Herz* (Hamburg, 1970); as well as Katharina Prager, "Amerika ist trotz allem großartig—die transkulturellen Leben und autobiographischen Praktiken der Familie Viertel," *Österreichische Zeitschrift für Geschichtswissenschaften* 29, no. 3 (2018): 37–57. On Berthold Viertel's activities as an American radio propagandist from the beginning of 1942, see Florian Traussnig, *Geistiger Widerstand von außen: Österreicher in US-Propagandainstitutionen im Zweiten Weltkrieg* (Vienna, 2017), 39–43.

6. Siegfried Marck to the American Guild, 26 August 1940, DNB, Deutsches Exilarchiv 1933–1945, EB 70/117.

7. American Guild to George S. Kaufman, 15 August 1940, in DNB, Deutsches Exilarchiv 1933–1945, EB 70/117; Hermann Budzislawski to Berthold Viertel, 22 Sep- tember 1940, in DLA, Handschriftenabteilung, no. 1980.1.613/1.

8. Hermann Budzislawski, "Europa entronnen: Eine Adresse gesucht," *Der Aufbau*, 18 October 1940, 4, https://portal.dnb.de/bookviewer/view/1026559758#page/4 /mode/1up.

9. Entry in Thomas Mann's diary for 20 December 1940, in Thomas Mann, *Tage- bücher 1940–1943*, ed. Peter de Mendelssohn (Frankfurt am Main, 1982), 149.

10. "Anti-Nazi Journalist Will Relate War Experiences," *Harvard Crimson*, 10 Janu- ary 1941, https:///www.thecrimson.com/article/1941/1/10/anti-nazi-journalist-will-relate -war-experiences/.

11. Hermann Budzislawski, manuscript of a speech, January 1941, in AdK, Hermann- Budzislawski-Archiv, no. 390. Feuchtwanger made the same joke (see Keßler, *Westemi- granten*, 80).

12. Filing card for Hermann Budzislawski, deposited on 3 February 1941, in New York Public Library (NYPL), Archives, Emergency Committee in Aid of Displaced

Foreign Scholars, MssCol 922, Bulk 1933–45, series 1, grant files 1927–49, I.B. Non Grantees, b.48f.4: Budzislawski, Hermann 1941.

13. See on this his correspondence with the publisher Houghton Mifflin, in AdK, Hermann-Budzislawski-Archiv, no. 127; and Hermann Budzislawski to Heinrich Mann, 15 May 1941, in AdK, Hermann-Budzislawski-Archiv, no. 391. The typescript "Democracy Underground: The Adventures of an Anti-Nazi Editor" is in AdK, Hermann-Budzislawski-Archiv, nos. 306 and 390; on the tendency of the exiles to write autobiographies, see Joachim Radkau, *Die deutsche Emigration in den USA: Ihr Einfluß auf die amerikanische Europapolitik 1933–1945* (Gütersloh, 1971), 16–17.

14. Ernst Josef Aufricht, *Erzähle, damit Du Dein Recht erweist* (Munich, 1969), quoted in Hans-Albrecht Walter, *Gib dem Herrn die Hand, er ist ein Flüchtling* (Düsseldorf, 2016), 37.

15. Hans Natonek, *In Search of Myself* (New York, 1943), 6, 10; Michael Groth, "Wir unterschätzten Hitler: Journalisten in der Emigration," *FAZ Magazin*, 18 April 1986, 42–45.

16. Budzislawski, "Adventurers against Will."

17. According to his wife, Budzislawski was determined in the autumn of 1941 to write a book that "would be fun to write and apparently fun for the publisher as well." But he was unable to publish a single book under his name throughout the period of exile. See Hanna Budzislawski to the Scheer couple, 10 October 1941, in AdK, Hermann-Scheer-Archiv, no. 42.

18. NARA, RG 319 (U.S. Army, Military Agency Records, Counter Intelligence Corps [CIC] Investigative Records Repository), File 302122 (Report on Budzislawski, 1951); Budzislawski's autobiographical record, 30 August 1950, 167.

19. Donald Bell (Hermann Budzislawski), "Memorandum on the German National Committee in Moscow," 1943, in AdK, Hermann-Scheer-Archiv, no. 1204.

20. Hanna Budzislawski to Balder Olden, 13 September 1941, in DNB, Teilnachlass 196 (Balder Olden), EB 2004/043 B.010 002; manuscript autobiography of Hanna Budzislawski.

21. Report from Hans Schlegel and Manfred George, forwarded by Bruce F. Levitch to the US Department of Justice on 19 December 1941, in OSU, Office of Strategic Services, 1941–45, SPEC.RARE.CMS.0307, box 60, folder 1.

22. According to a letter of 1 February 1949 from Dorothy Thompson to *Die neue Zeitung*, Berlin, in Syracuse University Libraries, Special Collections, Research Center (SCRC), Dorothy Thompson Papers, box 102.

23. Document in DRA, Pressearchiv Personalia, vol. Budi–Bülz.

24. Hermann Budzislawski to Berthold Viertel, 14 August 1941, in DLA, Handschriftenabteilung, no. 69.2231.

25. For criticism of Konrad Heiden's journalism by *Die neue Weltbühne*, see Otto Friedlaender, "Konrad Heiden," *Die neue Weltbühne*, 31 March 1938, 402–5; on the controversy between Schwarzschild and Budzislawski, see Bachmann, *Zwischen Paris und Moskau*, 427–31; and Budzislawski's exchange of letters with Lion Feuchtwanger in 1938, in AdK, Die neue Weltbühne, box 7, preliminary signature 28, 44–46.

26. Hermann Budzislawski to Carl Misch, 18 August 1941, in AdK, Hermann-Budzislawski-Archiv, no. 66.

27. Hermann Budzislawski to Berthold Viertel, 14 August 1941, in DLA, Handschriftenabteilung, no. 69.2231.

28. Billing, "Gespräch," 179.

29. Dorothy Thompson, "I Saw Hitler!" (New York, 1932).

30. Dorothy Thompson was sometimes mentioned in the same breath as the president's wife, Eleanor Roosevelt, in the American media at that time. The literary scholar Karina von Tippelskirch comments critically that this assertion, often quoted in the literature on Thompson, is a forward projection of the gender hierarchy of the 1930s: Thompson's prominence needed to be made clear by reference to the wife of the president, whereas a journalist like Walter Lippmann could simply be counted as "the most influential American journalist of the 20th century" (Tippelskirch, Dorothy Thompson, 20). See also Fritz Kortner, Aller Tage Abend (Munich, 1976), 316–19; on Thompson's particular significance as the "political and intellectual intersection point" for the Germanophone exile community, see Radkau, Die deutsche Emigration, 69–73.

31. Minutes of Budzislawski's examination on 12 April 1943, in Ohio State University—University Libraries, Rare Books and Manuscripts Library (OSU), SPEC. RARE.CMS.0307: Office of Strategic Services, 1941–45, box 35, folder 5, 18.

32. Hanna Budzislawski to Balder Olden, 13 September 1941.

33. Hermann Budzislawski's SED questionnaire, 30 August 1950, in BArch Berlin, SAPMO, DY 30/90300, 174–75; minutes of Budzislawski's examination, 12 April 1943.

34. Hermann Budzislawski to Johanna Kortner, 6 April 1973, in Bibliotop, Ehemaliges Radaktionsarchiv der Weltbühne der DDR, Budzislawski 3, ZZF I.620.

35. Hermann Budzislawski, "Antwort an mein Pseudonym," in AdK, Hermann-Budzislawski-Archiv, no. 287.

36. Thompson asserted in 1948 that she had never received the furniture back. Budzislawski, on the other hand, claimed that at the end of 1947 Thompson had organized the removal of the items she wanted from the family's New York apartment. On Beate's school attendance, see AdK, Hermann-Budzislawski-Archiv, no. 249.

37. Dorothy Thompson, "Wie ich von einem Kommunisten getäuscht wurde," typescript, published on 29 May 1949 in Die neue Zeitung, in AdK, Hermann-Budzislawski-Archiv, no. 287.

38. For a similar view, see Manfred Durzak, "Die Exilsituation in den USA," in Die deutsche Exilliteratur 1933–1945, ed. Manfred Durzak (Stuttgart, 1973), 145–58, here 148–49.

39. Marion K. Sanders, Dorothy Thompson: A Legend in Her Time (Boston, 1973), 298–307.

40. Carl Zuckmayer, Als wär's ein Stück von mir: Horen der Freundschaft (Frankfurt am Main, 1967), 529.

41. Peter Kurth, American Cassandra: The Life of Dorothy Thompson (Boston, 1990), 349; Tippelskirch, Dorothy Thompson, 248; Sanders, Dorothy Thompson, 286–87.

42. Hanna Budzislawski to the Scheer couple, 10 October 1941, in AdK, Hermann-Scheer-Archiv, no. 42.

43. Hermann Budzislawski to Berthold Viertel, undated (beginning of July 1941), in DLA, Handschriftenabteilung, no. 78.892/13.

44. Hermann Budzislawski to Berthold Viertel, 22 September 1941, in DLA, Handschriftenabteilung, no. 1980.1.613/1.

45. Hermann Budzislawski to Berthold Viertel, 24 September 1941, in DLA, Handschriftenabteilung, no. 69.2232/3.

46. Budzislawski to Viertel, 22 September 1941.

47. Minutes of Budzislawski's examination, 12 April 1943, 9.

48. Dorothy Thompson, *Listen, Hans* (Boston, 1942); Petra Liebner, *Paul Tillich und der Council for a Democratic Germany, 1933–1945* (Frankfurt am Main, 2001), 116–18. A German translation of the introduction to Thompson's book was printed in October 1946 in the periodical *Sie*; it therefore continued to have an impact beyond 1945: "Der deutsche Geist: Schöpfer und Vernichter. Eine Untersuchung von Dorothy Thompson," *Sie: Berliner Illustrierte Zeitschrift*, 27 October 1946, 2.

49. The column was finally discontinued by the ONA in March 1948, after five years, as part of a series of economy measures. See a letter sent on 15 March 1948 to Budzislawski by H. R. Wishengrad, the editor of the ONA, in AdK, Hermann-Budzislawski-Archiv, no. 99. The pseudonym "Bell" was probably an allusion to the Bell Syndicate of New York, which distributed Dorothy Thompson's articles.

50. Franz Knipping, "Der Mann, der Amerikas berühmteste Frau war: Erinnerung an den Publizisten und Politiker Hermann Budzislawski zum 100. Geburtstag am 11 Februar," *Neues Deutschland*, 10–11 February 2001, 20; Albert Schreiner, "Betr. Prof. Hermann Budzislawski," Leipzig, 22 February 1950, in BArch Berlin, SAPMO, NY 4198, no. 83, 99. On Landau's life, see the obituary issued by the Jewish Telegraphic Agency, *Daily News Bulletin*, 1 February 1952, 1–2, https://www.jta.org/archive/jacob -landau-founder-of-jewish-telegraphic-agency-dies-in-n-y; on the ONA and the role of the secret services, see Thomas E. Mahl, *Desperate Deception: British Covert Operations in the United States 1939–44* (Washington, DC, 1998), 48–51, 198.

51. See Bloch to Wieland Herzfelde, sent on 2 July 1943, in Jahn, *Ernst Bloch / Wieland Herzfelde*, 89. In a later letter to Herzfelde, Bloch wrote disparagingly: "Someone who is unwilling to make an effort will always prefer to read Budzislawski" (10 June 1945, in ibid., 134).

52. Minutes of Budzislawski's examination on 12 April 1943, 12.

53. "Neue Werke, neue Rollen," *Die Zeitung*, no. 324, 21 May 1943, 7, https://portal .dnb.de/bookviewer/view/1026594170#page/6/mode/2up.

54. Earl H. Balch to Hermann Budzislawski, 24 February 1944, in AdK, Hermann-Budzislawski-Archiv, no. 394.

55. Tippelskirch, *Dorothy Thompson*, 242; Sanders, *Dorothy Thompson*, 294–97.

56. Zuckmayer, *Als wär's ein Stück von mir*, 527; Sanders, *Dorothy Thompson*, 295.

57. Berthold Viertel to Salka Viertel, 1 July 1942, in DLA, Handschriftenabteilung, no. 78.874/9.

58. Berthold Viertel to Hermann Budzislawski, 7 September 1942, in DLA, Handschriftenabteilung, no. 69.2034.

59. Zuckmayer, *Als wär's ein Stück von mir*, 529; Henry Glade, "Carl Zuckmayer," in *Deutschsprachige Exilliteratur seit 1933*, ed. John M. Spalek and Joseph Strelka (Bern, 1989), 2:1043–56, here 1044.

60. See the correspondence on the subject in DLA, Handschriftenabteilung, no. 96.6.654 and 95.1.

61. Tim B. Müller, *Krieger und Gelehrte: Herbert Marcuse und die Denksysteme im Kalten Krieg* (Hamburg, 2010); Raffaele Laudani, ed., *Im Kampf gegen Nazideutschland:*

Die Berichte der Frankfurter Schule für den amerikanischen Geheimdienst 1943–1949 (Frankfurt am Main, 2016).

62. "Memorandum on the Observations of Ruth Fischer," undated, in OSU, SPEC. RARE.CMS.0307: Office of Strategic Services, 1941–45, box 60, folder 2, 169.

63. Interoffice memo by C. B. Friediger, January 1944, in OSU, SPEC.RARE. CMS.0307: Office of Strategic Services, 1941–45, box 60, folder 3.

64. Hermann Budzislawski, "Outlines zu einem Manifest der Freiheit," in AdK, Hermann-Budzislawski-Archiv, no. 394. I am currently preparing an article that will provide a comprehensive assessment of this important document.

65. Hermann Budzislawski to Carl Misch, in LBI, Carl Misch Collection, Personal and Professional Correspondence 1941–66, AR 7214.

66. Diane Clemens, *From Isolationism to Internationalism: The Case Study of American Occupation Planning for Post-war Germany, 1945–1946* (Berkeley, CA, 1993), 1–2.

67. These quotations are all taken from Budzislawski, "Outlines zu einem Manifest der Freiheit."

68. Extract from the manuscript of a speech by Hermann Budzislawski covering his time in New York without a title or a date, in AdK, Hermann-Budzislawski-Archiv, no. 390.

69. Carbon copy of a letter from Budzislawski to the FBI, 19 April 1944, in AdK, Hermann-Budzislawski-Archiv, no. 122. See also D. M. Ladd's memorandum of 13 February 1947 on Budzislawski, in OSU, SPEC.RARE.CMS.0307: Office of Strategic Services, 1941–45, box 35, folder 5.

70. Edgar Hoover to Hermann Budzislawski, 23 May 1944, in AdK, Hermann-Budzislawski-Archiv, no. 394.

71. NARA, RG 319 (U.S. Army, Military Agency Records, Counter Intelligence Corps [CIC] Investigative Records Repository), File 302122 (Report on Budzislawski, 1951).

72. Henry C. Fleisher of the OSS to Budzislawski, 13 June 1944, in AdK, Hermann-Budzislawski-Archiv, no. 150; minutes of Budzislawski's examination, 12 April 1943. Such interrogations, for which the Secret Service agents usually seemed extremely well prepared, could be conducted very politely. For more information, see Alexander Böker, diary, 2 February 1943, in IfZ, Archiv, ED 448/56.

73. Dorothy Thompson to Sylvester Pindyck, US Department of Justice, 14 April 1943, in SCRC, Dorothy Thompson Papers, box 36. On Pindyck, who was involved among other things with the investigations into the National Socialist organization called the German American Bund, see "Sylvester Pindyck, 64, Is Dead; US Immigration Investigator," *New York Times*, 5 November 1968, 47.

74. Mahl, *Desperate Deception*, 54.

75. For details, see Ursula Langkau-Alex and Thomas M. Ruprecht, eds., *Was Soll aus Deutschland warden? Der Council for a Democratic Germany in New York 1944–1945: Aufsätze und Dokumente* (Frankfurt am Main, 1995); Radkau, *Die deutsche Emigration*, 193–204; Liebner, *Paul Tillich*. On the role of Budzislawski in 1943, see the memorandum sent to General W. J. Donovan on 6 November 1943, in OSU, SPEC.RARE. CMS.0307: Office of Strategic Services, 1941–45, box 60, folder 1.

76. See also in this context the analysis given by Budzislawski in his memorandum on the German National Committee in Moscow, 1943, in AdK, Hermann-Scheer-Archiv, no. 1204.

77. Declaration of the Council for a Democratic Germany, April 1944, in BArch Berlin, SAPMO, NY 4217, 103, 185–89; for an early criticism of the council's nationalist conception, see the typescript "Deklaration des Kampfausschusses für ein demokratisches Deutschland [this expression refers to the council]," 3 May 1944, in BArch Berlin, SAPMO, NY 4036, 563:100–104.

78. Bertolt Brecht to Heinrich Mann, March 1944, in AdK, Bertolt-Brecht-Archiv, no. 2098/012. The OSS considered at first that the council was dominated by the Communists: see "Foreign Nationality Groups in the United States—Memorandum by the Foreign Nationalities Branch to the Director of Strategic Services, No. 187, 12 May 1944: Volksfront or Communist Front," in CIA Electronic Reading Room, FOIA no. 0 000 196 663, https://www.cia.gov/readingroom/docs/DOC_0000196663.pdf.

79. Bertolt Brecht to Karl Korsch, April 1944, in AdK, Bertolt-Brecht-Archiv, no. 1522/004.

80. Albert Norden, "Notizen über den Council for a Democratic Germany," 1962, in BArch Berlin, SAPMO, NY 4217/54, 55.

81. Memorandum against Ruth Fischer, 23 March 1944, in OSU, SPEC.RARE. CMS.0307: Office of Strategic Services, 1941–45, box 60, folder 2, 168–73, here 172.

82. Council for a Democratic Germany, draft declaration, 26 February 1945, in BArch Berlin, SAPMO, NY 4198, no. 80, 48.

83. These statements were all made in a letter from Albert Schreiner to Franz Dahlem, 18 October 1948, in BArch Berlin, SAPMO, DY 30/90300, 183–84.

84. Liebner, *Paul Tillich*, 232–33.

85. Copy of a letter from Paul Tillich to Friedrich Baerwald, postmarked 20 August 1945, in BArch Berlin, SAPMO, NY 4198, no. 80, 73–74.

86. Draft declaration by Aufhäuser and Budzislawski, undated, in BArch Berlin, SAPMO, NY 4198, no. 80, 90–92.

87. Report to the FBI, Foreign Nationalities Branch, 4 March 1942, in OSU, SPEC. RARE.CMS.0307: Office of Strategic Services, 1941–45, box 60, folder 1, 6–8.

88. Albert Schreiner, "Potsdam: Weiterexistenz und Aufgaben des Council," 20 September 1945, in BArch Berlin, SAPMO, NY 4198, no. 80, 81–85. In the GDR, too, Schreiner remained a "lonely warning voice." He was one of the few leading SED comrades to insist on recalling that the murder of the European Jews was the central Nazi crime against humanity. See on this point Mario Keßler, *Albert Schreiner: Kommunist mit Lebensbrüchen* (Berlin, 2014), 53–62, 101.

89. Hermann Budzislawski to the British Labour MP Renée Short, 13 July 1967, quoted in Joanne Sayner, *Reframing Antifascism: Memory, Genre and the Life Writings of Greta Kuckhoff* (Basingstoke, 2014), 138.

90. Hermann Budzislawski to Fritz Kortner, 18 January 1944, in AdK, Fritz-Kortner-Archiv, no. 298.

91. Minutes of a sitting of the Business Committee of the Council for a Democratic Germany, 30 April 1945, in BArch Berlin, SAPMO, NY 2198, no. 80, 52. Arnold Zweig also showed remarkably little interest in the Holocaust and its eventual consequences for his German Jewish identity, at least according to Adi Gordon, "Widersprüchliche Zugehörigkeiten: Arnold Zweig in Ostdeutschland," in *"Ich staune, dass Sie in dieser Luft atmen können": Jüdische Intellektuelle in Deutschland nach 1945*, ed. Monika Boll and Raphael Gross (Frankfurt am Main, 2013), 189–90.

92. Daniel Blatman, *Die Todesmärsche: Das letzte Kapitel des nationalsozialistischen Massenmords* (Reinbek bei Hamburg, 2011); Sven Keller, *Volksgemeinschaft am Ende: Gesellschaft und Gewalt 1944/45* (Munich, 2013).

93. See Annette Leo, "Antifaschismus," in *Erinnerungsorte der DDR*, ed. Martin Sabrow (Munich, 2009), 30–42; Karin Hartewig, *Zurückgekehrt: Die Geschichte der jüdischen Kommunisten in der DDR* (Cologne, 2000); Lutz Niethammer, *Der "gesäuberte" Antifaschismus: Die SED und die roten Kapos von Buchenwald* (Berlin, 1994).

94. State Department to Eleanor Roosevelt, 6 March 1945, in AdK, Hermann-Budzislawski-Archiv, no. 248.

95. Böker, diary, 31 March 1943.

96. Hermann Budzislawski to Joachim Radkau, 9 November 1967, in Bibliotop, Ehemaliges Redaktionsarchiv der *Weltbühne* der DDR, Budzislawski 1, ZZF I.1.186.

97. Maximilian Scheer, *Ein unruhiges Leben: Autobiographie* (Berlin, 1975), 145–46.

98. Thompson's conversation with Churchill took place on 22 April 1945. See Tippelskirch, *Dorothy Thompson*, 250.

99. Budzislawski, "Antwort an mein Pseudonym." Thompson confirmed this version of events. See Kurth, *American Cassandra*, 390; Dorothy Thompson, "The Last Time I Saw Berlin," *Saturday Review of Literature*, 15 March 1947, 9–10. I should like to thank Karina von Tippelskirch, who is currently working on a German-language biography of Thompson, for pointing out that the latter soon became aware of the numerous rapes committed by Soviet soldiers in occupied Germany.

100. Kurt Hiller to Karl Otto Paetel, 10 December 1945, in University at Albany, SUNY / M. E. Grenander Department of Special Collections & Archives (SUNY Archive), Karl Otto Paetel Papers, ger072, box 4, folder 26.

101. Albert Schreiner to Philipp Daub of the Central Committee of the SED, 9 November 1949, in BArch Berlin, SAPMO, DY 30/90300, 184.

102. Conspectus by Hermann Budzislawski of his articles for the ONA, in AdK, Hermann-Budzislawski-Archiv, no. 417. The newspaper cuttings are to be found in no. 377.

103. Donald Bell, "Passports Barriers to 'One World,'" *Denver Post*, 21 April 1947, in AdK, Hermann-Budzislawski-Archiv, no. 379; Bell, "Deadlock on the A-Bomb," *New Haven Journal-Courier*, 3 July 1946, in AdK, Hermann-Budzislawski-Archiv, no. 380.

104. Donald Bell, "Europe's Famine Goes Deeper Than Grain," *Detroit News*, 18 May 1947; Bell, "The Dream of European Unity," *New Haven Journal-Courier*, 7 May 1947; Bell, "Storm Signals Rise in Germany: Many Looking for a New Fuehrer," *Cleveland Plain Reader*, 8 April 1947; Bell, "Fascism Makes Strong Comeback," *State Journal* (Madison, WI), 9 April 1946. These cuttings are all in AdK, Hermann-Budzislawski-Archiv, nos. 379 and 380.

105. Hermann Budzislawski to Jacob Landau of the ONA, 2 November 1945, in AdK, Hermann-Budzislawski-Archiv, no. 395.

106. The quotation is from Kortner, *Aller Tage*, 275.

107. Invoice from the Lycée Français de New-York, 25 September 1945, in AdK, Hermann-Budzislawski-Archiv, no. 249.

108. OSU, Alexander Stephan Collection of FBI Files on German Intellectuals in US Exile, 1933–2003, SPEC.RARE.CMS.0307, box 35, folder 5, 9; Erna to Isidor Budzislawski, 20 May 1942, in AdK, Hermann-Budzislawski-Archiv, no. 201.

109. Manuscript of a speech by Hermann Budzislawski on his experiences in the United States, untitled, undated, in AdK, Hermann-Budzislawski-Archiv, no. 390.

110. Herman Reichenbach to Eric Werner, undated, between 1944 and 1948, in LBI, Eric Werner Collection, AR 2179, box 1, folder 10, 655–56.

Chapter 6. The War After the War

1. Hermann Budzislawski, "Die Rückwanderer," undated manuscript, in AdK, Hermann-Budzislawski-Archiv, no. 294.

2. Albert Schreiner, "Concerning Prof. Hermann Budzislawski," Leipzig, 22 February 1950, in BArch Berlin, SAPMO, NY 4198, no. 85, 99.

3. Eggebrecht and Pinkerneil, *Das Drama der Republik*, 38.

4. This is how Becher is characterized by Alfred Kantorowicz in his diary, as quoted in Wehner, *Kulturpolitik und Volksfront*, 1:406.

5. Wolfgang Schivelbusch, *Vor dem Vorhang: Das geistige Berlin 1945–1948* (Munich, 1995), 263–66.

6. Maud von Ossietzky, undated memorandum, in ZZF, NL Simone Barck, no. 3/5.

7. Franz Jack to Maud von Ossietzky, 20 May 1945, in Carl von Ossietzky University, Oldenburg, Carl von Ossietzky Archive, JB 4018-12. The name change announced by Jack finally took place in the spring of 1948, when the Schloßstraße in Berlin-Pankow became the Ossietzkystraße.

8. Ursula Madrasch-Groschopp, "Hans Leonhards Geheimnis," *Ossietzky* 4, no. 2 (2001): 55–59.

9. For further details and background material, see Wehner, *Kulturpolitik und Volksfront*, 1:381–83.

10. Copy of the inheritance certificate issued by the Local Court Berlin-Charlottenburg, Az.6 VL 84/27, 15 January 1927, in Privatarchiv Bernd F. Lunkewitz, Frankfurt am Main, Annex BK-13.

11. Peter Jacobsohn to Walther Karsch, 17 February 1948, in Privatarchiv Bernd F. Lunkewitz, Frankfurt am Main, Annex BK-20.

12. Contract establishing the firm v. Ossietzky—Verlag *Die Weltbühne*, 26 April 1947, in Bibliotop, Ehemaliges Radaktionsarchiv der *Weltbühne* der DDR, Ossietzky 1, ZZF I. 2.1. For the reestablishment of *Die Weltbühne* in the Soviet occupation zone, see Fritz Klein, "Die Neugründung der Weltbühne in der Sowjetischen Besatzungszone," in Grunewald, *Le milieu intellectual*, 559–75; Schivelbusch, *Vor dem Vorhang*, 264–73; Wehner, *Kulturpolitik und Volksfront*, 1:376–405; Sean Forner, *German Intellectuals and the Challenge of Democratic Renewal: Culture and Politics after 1945* (Cambridge, 2014), 32–34; Fair-Schulz, *Loyal Subversion*, 309–12.

13. Gabriele Müller's interview with Maud von Ossietzky and Hans Leonhard, printed in *Zeitecho*, July 1946, transcript in Bibliotop, Ehemaliges Redaktionsarchiv der *Weltbühne* der DDR, Hans Leonhard folder, personal papers.

14. Walther Karsch, "Über den Missbrauch eines Namens," *Sie: Berliner Illustrierte Zeitung*, 4 May 1947, 7. For Karsch's view at the time, see also Karsch to Peter Jacobsohn, 3 March 1947, in Privatarchiv Bernd E. Lunkewitz, Frankfurt am Main (copy).

15. Otto Stolz, ed., *Die wahre Weltbühne: Carl v. Ossietzky + Kurt Tucholsky über Kommunismus—Sowjet-Rußland-Marxismus* (West-Berlin, 1948), in Archiv für Zeitgeschichte, ETH Zürich, NL Marcel Brun, no. 255.

16. Kurt Hiller, "Aufstieg, Glanz und Verfall der Weltbühne: Schluss," *konkret*, no. 7 (1962): 20. The journal also depended on the SED financially because it had been printed since the end of the 1940s by the Berliner Verlag, which was controlled by the party. See also Frank-Burkhard Habel, "*Weltbühne*-Autoren der Weimarer Republik und ihr geistiger Einfluss auf die *Weltbühne* ab 1946," in *"Verirrte Bürger"? Kurt Tucholsky und der Weltbühne-Kreis zwischen Bürgertum und Arbeiterbewegung*, ed. Kurt Tucholsky-Gesellschaft and Ian King (Leipzig, 2016), 53.

17. Alexander Abusch, "Die Persönlichkeit Stalins," *Die Weltbühne*, 14 December 1949, 1481–1483, quoted in Klein, "Die Neugründung," 566.

18. On the power struggle between Leonhard and Harich, see Schivelbusch, *Vor dem Vorhang*, 274–81.

19. Rudolf Leonhard to Maud von Ossietzky, 21 May 1947, in ZZF, NL Simone Barck, no. 3/5 (original in AdK).

20. Agreement between Hans Leonhard and Maud von Ossietzky, 20 December 1950, in Bibliotop, Ehemaliges Redaktionsarchiv der *Weltbühne* der DDR, Ossietzky 1, ZZF II.2.15.

21. Deutsches Bundestag, 13. Wahlperiode, *Bericht der Unabhängigen Kommission zur Überprüfung des Vermögens der Parteien und Massenorganisationen der DDR über das Vermögen der Sozialistischen Einheitspartei Deutschlands (SED) jetzt: Partei des Demokratischen Sozialismus (PDS), des Freien Deutschen Gewerkschaftsbunds (FDGB), der sonstigen politischen Organisationen und Stellungnahme der Bundesregierung, 24. August 1998, Berlin 1998*, Drucksache 13/11,353, 117, https://dserver.bundestag.de/btd /13/113/1311353.pdf.

22. Simone Barck, "Die Weltbühne in der DDR: Ein Gespräch mit Ursula Madrasch-Groschopp," typescript, 26 September 2000, printed under the title "Ein altes und jederzeit junges Blatt: 'Die Weltbühne' in der DDR. Ein Gespräch mit Ursula Madrasch-Groschopp," *Deutschland Archiv* 34, no. 2 (2001): 258–68.

23. Behling, *Spur der Scheine*, 116–18; Friedrich Karl Fromm to Karl Desch, undated, and Peter Jacobsohn to Walther Karsch, 27 January 1969, both in Privatarchiv Bernd F. Lunkewitz, Frankfurt am Main. As late as 1974, Peter Theek, who had succeeded Budzislawski at *Die Weltbühne* in 1971, was still calling for regular payments to be made by the SED to Rosalie von Ossietzky-Palm, Maud's daughter: "This arrangement would certainly contribute to making the Ossietzky-Palm family more able to resist eventual attempts by Western circles to do a political deal to the disadvantage of the GDR-published *Weltbühne*." Rosalie von Ossietzky-Palm and her husband "always set great store by material interests" (Peter Theek to Heinz Geggel, head of the Agitation Section in the Central Committee of the SED, 10 April 1974, in BArch Berlin, SAPMO, DY 30/vorl. SED 18 309/1). I am grateful to Lisa Städtler, Kiel, for this reference.

24. The two partners appointed Hermann Budzislawski, who had already returned to the position of editor in chief of *Die Weltbühne* at the beginning of 1967, as sole business manager of the company. See chapter 8 for a more detailed discussion. There are copies of the partnership agreement, numbered 1475 in the 1967 register of deeds, in Privatarchiv Bernd F. Lunkewitz, Frankfurt am Main. There are further details in "Bericht der Unabhängigen Kommission," 176–79.

25. Wehner, *Kulturpolitik und Volksfront*, 1:384; Schievelbusch, *Vor dem Vorhang*, 280.

26. Lion Feuchtwanger to Hans Leonhard, transcript, quoted in Leonhard to Maud von Ossietzky, 3 December 1947, in ZZF, NL Simone Barck, no. 3/5.

27. Thomas Mann to Hans Leonhard, 29 September 1949, quoted in Klein, "Die Neugründung," 559.

28. For example, in the summer of 1947 he wrote a letter to the editor of the new periodical *Sie* (printed on 7 September 1947) contesting the assertion that Siegfried Jacobsohn and his son Peter had property rights in *Die Weltbühne*. He had, he said, acquired the journal from Edith Jacobsohn in 1934. See the copy of the letter in AdK, Hermann-Scheer-Archiv, no. 42. Budzislawski also indicated in a letter of 18 October 1947 to Walther Karsch that he had entered into contact with Peter Jacobsohn "to refresh his memory. . . . All the rights claimed by Peter Jacobsohn belong to me" (in AdK, Hermann-Budzislawski-Archiv, no. 174).

29. Communication from Jan Lowenbach of the Czech General Consulate in New York to Hermann Budzislawski, 9 October 1946, in AdK, Hermann-Budzislawski-Archiv, no. 113.

30. Berthold Viertel to Salka Viertel, 20 March 1946, in DLA, Handschriftenabteilung, no. 78 879/5.

31. Anderson, *Liebe im Exil*, 28–29.

32. Heym, *Nachruf*, 510.

33. Hermann Budzislawski later recalled in a television interview that Brecht, who thought that every situation was "transferable" to the stage, told him that he wanted to use this performance "to bring out the true facts, which I will state, and present them in the way that best serves our cause" (*Aktuelle Kamera* transmission, 10 February 1968, conversation with Hermann Budzislawski about Brecht, in DRA, no. 091732). See also James K. Lyon, *Bertolt Brecht in America* (Princeton, NJ, 1980), 323–24; Hanna Budzislawski to Berthold Viertel, 4 November 1947, in DLA, Handschriftenabteilung, no. 91.15.189/1; typescript of Hermann Budzislawski's speech on 10 February 1963 in Buckow Town Hall on the occasion of the sixty-fifth anniversary of the birth of Bertolt Brecht, in Hermann-Budzislawski-Archiv, no. 474.

34. Stephen Parker, *Bertolt Brecht: A Literary Life* (London, 2014), 501–2 (German translation: Stephen Parker, *Bertolt Brecht: Eine Biographie* [Frankfurt am Main, 2018], 773–74).

35. Hanna Budzislawski to Berthold Viertel, 4 November 1947, in DLA, Handschriftenabteilung, no. 91.15.189/1. See also Wieland Herzfelde to Ernst Bloch, 10 March 1948, in Jahn, *Ernst Bloch / Wieland Herzfelde*, 255–56.

36. Hanna Budzislawski to Berthold Viertel, 4 November 1947, in DLA, Handschriftenabteilung, no. 91.15.189/1.

37. Hermann Budzislawski to Berthold Viertel, 27 October 1947, in DLA, Handschriftenabteilung, no. 69 2232/4.

38. Willi Bredel to Hermann Budzislawski, 3 November 1947, in ZZF, NL Simone Barck, no. 3/5.

39. Hanna Budzislawski to Berthold Viertel, 20 February 1948, in DLA, Handschriftenabteilung, no. 69 2230/2. The call from Leipzig arrived on 11 February 1948. See Franz Knipping, "Der Mann, der Amerikas berühmteste Frau war: Erinnerung an den Publizisten und Politiker Hermann Budzislawski zum 100. Geburtstag am 11. Februar," *Neues Deutschland*, 10–11 February 2001, 20. On Wallace and his program, see

Thomas W. Devine, *Henry Wallace's 1948 Presidential Campaign and the Future of Postwar Liberalism* (Chapel Hill, NC, 2013); and Müller, *Krieger und Gelehrten*, 67; on Budzislawski and Wallace, see Nicholas J. Schlosser, "The Berlin Radio War: Broadcasting in Cold War Berlin and the Shaping of Political Culture in Divided Germany 1945–1961" (PhD diss., University of Maryland, 2008), 84–85; Hermann Budzislawski, "Henry Wallace—ein fortschrittlicher Amerikaner," *Neues Deutschland*, 7 October 1948, 2.

40. Hanna Budzislawski to Berthold Viertel, 16 July 1948, in DLA, Handschriftenabteilung, no. 69 2230/3. See also Rick Kuhn, *Henryk Grossman and the Recovery of Marxism* (Urbana, IL, 2007), 291n51.

41. There is a short sketch of the history of *Ost und West* in Schildt, *Medien-Intellektuelle*, 94–99.

42. Hermann Budzislawski, "Heimkehr," *Ost und West*, October 1948, 42.

43. Ibid., 43–44.

44. Quoted from Michael Wildt, "Die Angst vor dem Volk: Ernst Fraenkel in der deutschen Nachkriegsgesellschaft," in *"Ich staune, dass Sie in dieser Luft atmen können": Jüdische Intellektuelle in Deutschland nach 1945*, ed. Monika Boll and Raphael Gross (Frankfurt am Main, 2013), 317–18.

45. Carl-Jacob Danziger (Joachim Chaim Schwarz), *"Die Partei hat immer recht": Autobiographischer Roman* (Frankfurt am Main, 2015), 13.

46. Budzislawski, "Heimkehr," 44–45. A very similar view is expressed in Danziger, *"Die Partei hat immer recht,"* 49.

47. Budzislawski, "Heimkehr," 45.

48. Andrew Demshuk, *Demolition on Karl Marx Square: Cultural Barbarism and the People's State in 1968* (Oxford, 2017), 14–16.

49. Hans Mayer, interviewed by Herlinde Koelbl, in *Jüdische Portraits: Photographien und Interviews*, by Herlinde Koelbl (Frankfurt am Main, 1998), 251–59, here 254.

50. Hanna Budzislawski to Berthold Viertel, 3 October 1948, in DLA, Handschriftenabteilung, no. 69 2230/4; Albert Schreiner to Erich Zeigner, Oberbürgermeister of Leipzig, 21 August 1948, in BArch Berlin, SAPMO, NY 4198, no. 83, 61; Albert Schreiner to Herr Naumann of the Wohnungsamt, Leipzig-Gehla, 29 July 1948, in BArch Berlin, SAPMO, NY 4198, no. 84, 369.

51. The story of the house given here is based on research done by the present owner, Angela Wandelt, to whom I offer my sincere thanks for providing the relevant information. On Ries, see in particular Bernt Engelmann, *Großes Bundesverdienstkreuz mit Stern* (Göttingen, 1987), 31–33, 47–66.

52. Budzislawski to Viertel, 3 October 1948.

53. Ibid.

54. Extract from the manuscript of a speech by Hermann Budzislawski on the situation in Leipzig in 1948, untitled and undated, in AdK, Hermann-Budzislawski-Archiv, no. 390.

55. Budzislawski to Viertel, 3 October 1948. Every Thursday between November 1948 and 1952–53 Mitteldeutscher Rundfunk broadcast Hermann Budzislawski's reflections on foreign policy, some of which were also published with editorial alterations. See Willy Walther, "Hermann Budzislawski zum 65. Geburtstag," manuscript, in DRA, Pressearchiv Personalia, vol. Budi–Bülz.

56. See the details given in letters between Budzislawski and Schreiner in 1947 and 1948, in BArch Berlin, SAPMO, NY 4198, no. 70, 58–76.

57. Walter Markov, *Zwiesprache mit dem Jahrhundert*, documented by Thomas Grimm (Berlin, 1989), 184.

58. Radio broadcast, "Zu Gast bei Prof. Dr. Hermann Budzislawski," 1984, in DRA, no. 2 032 877 (15:45–17:01 mins.).

59. Heym, *Nachruf*, 609.

60. Information given to the author on 17 August 2018 by Michael Bodemann, Toronto.

61. Completion certificate made out on 1 October 1949 to Hermann Budzislawski by the Leipzig Housing Office, in LAB, C Rep. 118-01, no. 26 041.

62. Hermann Budzislawski, autobiography, 1948, in LAB, C Rep. 118-01, no. 26 041.

63. Hanna Budzislawski to Horst Baehrensprung, undated, in AdK Berlin, Hermann-Budzislawski-Archiv, no. 4.

64. Hanna Budzislawski to Friedrich Alexan, 8 November 1950, in AdK Berlin, Hermann-Budzislawski-Archiv, no. 197.

65. Hermann Budzislawski's SED questionnaire, 30 August 1950, in BArch Berlin, SAPMO, DY 30/90300, 174–75; fee statement from the *Leipziger Volkszeitung*, November 1950, in AdK, Hermann-Budzislawski-Archiv, no. 416; Michael Meyen, "Die Erfindung der Journalistik in der DDR," *Journalistik* 2, no. 1 (2019): 8.

66. Alfred Kantorowicz, "Die Rangerhöhung der Geistigen," in *Im 2. Drittel unseres Jahrhunderts: Illusionen, Irrtümer, Widersprüche, Einsichten, Voraussichten*, ed. Alfred Kantorowicz (Cologne, 1967), 117–20, here 117.

67. Quoted in Heym, *Nachruf*, 598. On the social privileges enjoyed by university teachers in the early GDR, see Ilko-Sascha Kowalczuk, *Geist im Dienste der Macht: Hochschulpolitik in der SBZ/DDR 1945 bis 1961* (Berlin, 2003), 348–80. On the material support provided to the intelligentsia in the first postwar years, see Wehner, *Kulturpolitik und Volksfront*, 2:836–56.

68. Keßler, *Westemigranten*, 308–9.

69. Johanna Budzislawski to Peter Viertel, 7 January 1979, in AdK, Hermann-Budzislawski-Archiv, no. 413.

70. Budzislawski's SED questionnaire, 30 August 1950, 174–75.

71. On the suicide of Friedrich Alexan's wife, Maria, soon after the family's return to Germany, see Irene Runge, "Dreiundsechzig," 50, in LBI, Memoir Collection (ME), no. 1514; Keßler, *Westemigranten*, 354.

72. Information given to the author by Irene Runge, Berlin, 17 August 2018.

73. On this column, which was continued after the 1970s by Ursula Winnington, see Manfred Gebhardt, *Die Nackte unterm Ladentisch: Das Magazin in der DDR* (Berlin, 2002), 137–40.

74. Axel Schildt arrived at the same conclusion for the early years of the Federal Republic. See Schildt, *Medien-Intellektuelle*, 44–46.

75. Schreiner to Zeigner, 21 August 1948, 61.

76. Manuscript autobiography of Hanna Budzislawski; Bloch, *Aus meinem Leben*, 204.

77. As also recalled in Irene Runge, "A Newcomer to the Jewish Community," in *Jews in Contemporary East Germany: The Children of Moses in the Land of Marx*, ed. Robin Ostow (Basingstoke, 1989), 44.

78. The quotations in this paragraph come from Budzislawski to Viertel, 3 October 1948.

79. For details, see Hartwig, *Zurückgekehrt*, 92–106. On the ambivalent feelings of returned Jewish emigrants, see also Andrea A. Sinn, "Returning to Stay? Jews in East and West Germany after the Holocaust," *Central European History* 53 (2020): 393–413.

80. Atina Grossman and Tamar Levinsky, "1945–1949: Way Station," in *A History of Jews in Germany Since 1945: Politics, Culture and Society*, ed. Michael Brenner (Bloomington, IN, 2018), 84.

81. Carl Zuckmayer, *A Part of Myself*, trans. Richard and Clara Winston (London, 1970), 329; in the German version, Zuckmayer, *Als wär's ein Stück von mir*, 461.

82. As quoted in Schildt, *Medien-Intellektuelle*, 140, 556.

83. Dorothy Thompson, "An meine deutschen Freunde," *Die neue Zeitung*, 19 October 1948, 3.

84. Hermann Budzislawski, "Ich war Amerikas berühmteste Frau," *Neues Deutschland*, 28 November 1948, 5.

85. Ibid.

86. Dorothy Thompson, "How I Was Duped by a Communist," *Saturday Evening Post*, 16 April 1949, in AdK, Maximilian-Scheer-Archiv, no. 42.

87. Dorothy Thompson to Ben Hibbs of the *Saturday Evening Post*, 6 January 1949, in SCRC, Dorothy Thompson Papers, box 37.

88. Dorothy Thompson, "Der mysteriöse Tod Dr. Laurence Duggan's" [*sic*], newspaper cutting, in AdK, Maximilian-Scheer-Archiv, no. 42.

89. Memorandum by Franz Dahlem, 6 December 1946, with handwritten note by Walter Ulbricht, in BArch Berlin, SAPMO, DY 30/90300, 232.

90. Jan Foitzik, "Remigranten in der Medienpolitik der sowjetischen Besatzungsmacht," in *Zwischen den Stühlen? Remigranten und Remigration in der deutschen Medienöffentlichkeit der Nachkriegszeit*, ed. Claus-Dieter Krohn and Axel Schildt (Hamburg, 2002), 107.

91. Extract from a note by Paul Walcher, 5 January 1947, and an internal SED memorandum from Paul Merker to Franz Dahlem, 13 January 1947, both in BArch Berlin, SAPMO, DY 30/90300, 227.

92. Hermann Budzislawski to Paul Merker, 16 August 1947, in BArch Berlin, SAPMO, DY 30/90300, 227.

93. Ralph Jessen, *Akademische Elite und kommunistische Diktatur: Die ostdeutsche Hochschullehrerschaft in der Ulbricht-Ära* (Göttingen, 1999), 315–16.

Chapter 7. The Invention of Socialist Journalism

1. This recruitment policy took place against a background of increasing staff shortages. The number of professors and lecturers in the universities located in the SBZ fell between the winter of 1944–45 and the summer of 1947 by approximately one-third (Jessen, *Akademische Elite*, 271).

2. Markov, *Zwiesprache*, 181.

3. Ibid., 188.

4. Hans Mayer, *Ein Deutscher auf Widerruf: Erinnerungen* (Frankfurt am Main, 1988), 2:29. See also Dietrich Staritz, "Partei, Intellektuelle, Partei-intellektuelle: Die Intellektuellen im Kalkül der frühen SED," in *Sozialismus und Kommunismus im Wan-*

del: Hermann Weber zum 65. Geburtstag, ed. Klaus Schönhoven and Dietrich Staritz (Cologne, 1993), 378–98, esp. 395.

5. Thomas Klein, *"Für die Einheit und Reinheit der Partei": Die innerparteilichen Kontrollorgane der SED in der Ära Ulbricht* (Cologne, 2002), 129–34.

6. Constantin Goschler, *Schuld und Schulden: Die Politik der Wiedergutmachung für NS-Verfolgte seit 1945* (Göttingen, 2008), 361–411; Thomas Haury, *Antisemitismus von links: Kommunistische Ideologie, Nationalismus und Antizionismus in der frühen DDR* (Hamburg, 2002), 315–24, 455.

7. Mario Keßler, "Anti-Semitism in East Germany, 1952–1953: Denial to the End," in *Unlikely History: The Changing German-Jewish Symbiosis, 1945–2000*, ed. Leslie Morris and Jack Zipes (New York, 2002), 141–44; for a full treatment, see Haury, *Antisemitismus von links*, 292–455.

8. Willi Bredel to the Minister of Education, G. Grünberg, 9 September 1947, in BArch Berlin, SAPMO, DY 30/90300, 219. For an overall picture, see Kowalczuk, *Geist im Dienste*; and Jessen, *Akademische Elite*.

9. Character sketch of Hermann Budzislawski by Paul Merker, February 1948, in BArch Berlin, SAPMO, DY 30/90300, 209; internal SED memorandum from Paul Merker to Franz Dahlem, 13 January 1947, in BArch Berlin, SAPMO, DY 30/90300, 228.

10. Statement by the S[cience] Department, 1 March 1948, in BArch Berlin, SAPMO, DY 30/90300, 207.

11. Hermann Budzislawski, "Warum feiern wir Stalin?," in AdK, Hermann-Budzislawski-Archiv, no. 414.

12. Victor Klemperer, *So sitze ich den zwischen allen Stühlen: Tagebücher 1945–1949*, ed. Walter Nowojowski in association with Christian Löser (Berlin, 1999), 1:690 (entry for 4 October 1949).

13. Ibid., 1:692 (entry for 12 October 1949).

14. Miłosz, *Verführtes Denken*, 62 (English translation: Miłosz, *The Captive Mind*, 52).

15. Budzislawski, "Warum feiern wir Stalin?"

16. Hermann Budzislawski, "Rede in den Leipziger Kammerspielen im Rahmen der Kundgebung der Kulturschaffenden für Weltfrieden und Gegen Kriegshetze vom 11. März 1949," in AdK, Hermann-Budzislawski-Archiv, no. 361.

17. At the beginning of the 1950s, Budzislawski was writing regularly for the monthly *USA in Wort und Bild*, edited by Georg Friedrich Alexan. On this, see Keßler, *Westemigranten*, 344–56.

18. Klemperer, *So sitze ich*, 2:163 (entry for 18 May 1951).

19. Manuscript of a speech by Hermann Budzislawski, incompletely preserved and without a beginning, a title, or a year, in AdK, Hermann-Budzislawski-Archiv, no. 390.

20. Ibid.

21. Ibid. For the current state of research, see Keßler, *Westemigranten*, 115–21; and James G. Ryan, *Earl Browder: The Failure of American Communism* (Tuscaloosa, AL, 1997).

22. Albert Schreiner to Philipp Daub of the SED Central Committee, 9 November 1949, in BArch Berlin, SAPMO, DY 30/90300, 184.

23. Hermann Budzislawski to Philipp Daub of the SED Central Committee, 11 November 1949, in BArch Berlin, SAPMO, DY 30/90300, 183; author's interview with Karl-Heinz Röhr and Gottfried Braun, 10 November 2020, Leipzig.

24. On the internal university context, see Arnulf Kutsch, "Kommunikation und Medienwissenschaft," in *Geschichte der Universität Leipzig 1409–2009*, vol. 4, pt. 1, ed. Ulrich von Hehl, Uwe John, and Manfred Rudersdorf (Leipzig, 2009), 755–58; Jochen Jedraszczyk, "Entideologisierung—Rekonstruktion—Re-Ideologisierung: Leipziger publizistik- und zeitungswissenschaftliche Einrichtungen 1945 bis 1952," in *Die Entdeckung de Kommunikationswissenschaft: 100 Jahre kommunikationswissenschaftliche Fachtradition in Leipzig. Von der Zeitungskunde zur Kommunikations- und Medienwissenschaft*, ed. Erik Koenen (Cologne, 2016), 155–84.

25. Hermann Budzislawski to the Party Executive of the SED, 3 May 1950, in AdK, Hermann-Budzislawski-Archiv, no. 162.

26. For the assessment of the League of Culture as "liberal-Communist," see Wehner, *Kulturpolitik und Volksfront*, 2:942.

27. Hermann Budzislawski to Philipp Daub of the SED Central Committee, 11 November 1949, in BArch Berlin, SAPMO, DY 30/90300, 183. Some of his many political speeches and addresses are preserved in AdK, Hermann-Budzislawski-Archiv, no. 361.

28. Ernst Ehrhardt to Bruno Theek, 9 June 1978, with ticket of admission enclosed, in Bibliotop, Ehemaliges Redaktionsarchiv der *Weltbühne* der DDR, Budzislawski 4, ZZF I.1.786. On Robeson, see Martin Schwander, *Paul Robeson: Eine Biographie* (Essen, 1998).

29. Memorandum from the District Leadership of the SED to the Saxon Land Leadership of the SED, 18 August 1950, in BArch Berlin, SAPMO, DY 30/90300, 177.

30. Werner Müller, Helmut Stöcker, and Renate Bischoff, "Einige Bemerkungen zur Hochschulpolitik unserer Partei vom 6. Januar 1950," in BArch Berlin, SAPMO, NY 4198, no. 83, 89–93, here 92.

31. On the notion of a *Bildungsbürger*, see Ulrich Engelhardt, *"Bildungsbürgertum": Begriffs- und Dogmengeschichte eines Etiketts* (Stuttgart, 1986).

32. This, at least, is what it says in Budzislawski's SED questionnaire of 30 August 1950, 174–75. On the SED's practice of repeatedly obtaining résumés for each person's cadre file, see Catherine Epstein, *The Last Revolutionaries: German Communists and Their Century* (Cambridge, MA, 2003), 133–34.

33. Helmut Eschwege, *Fremd unter meinesgleichen: Erinnerungen eines Dresdner Juden* (Berlin, 1991), 75–80.

34. Mario Keßler, *Die SED und die Juden—zwischen Repression und Toleranz: Politische Entwicklungen bis 1967* (Berlin, 1995), 78.

35. Hermann Budzislawski, "Verbindung von SED-Funktionären mit amerikanischen Agenten," speech delivered to the SED Betriebsgruppe of the Gewifak in Leipzig on 18 October 1950, in AdK, Hermann-Budzislawski-Archiv, no. 310.

36. Ibid.

37. See Reinhard Müller, *Menschenfalle Moskau: Exil und stalinistische Verfolgung* (Hamburg, 2001) and the currently ongoing research project "Nach Moskau: Deutsche Emigranten im sowjetischen Exil und im Kulturbetrieb der DDR," sponsored by the Fritz-Thyssen-Stiftung since 2018 and led by Christoph Garstka and Bernd Faulenbach.

38. Budzislawski, "Verbindung."

39. Ibid.

40. Hermann Budzislawski, typescript, with no title and no date, in AdK, Hermann-Budzislawski-Archiv, no. 210.

41. In this connection, see also Heym, *Nachruf*, 602, where he reports that Grotewohl in particular had a "soft spot" for artists and intellectuals.

42. Hanna Budzislawski to a Comrade Joos, 9 January 1951, in BArch Berlin, SAPMO, DY 30/90301; report dated 9 July 1955 on disputes at the Faculty of Journalism, in BStU, Außenstelle Leipzig, MfS, BV Leipzig, AP 3041/64, 23.

43. Minutes of a discussion between the SED leadership at Karl Marx University and Hermann Budzislawski, 15 January 1951, in BArch Berlin, SAPMO, DY 30/90300, 158. During that period, the Budzislawskis were prepared to bring even long-standing friends into difficulties in order to be regarded by the party as reliable, thereby saving their own skin. Thus Hanna Budzislawski claimed after the death on 24 November 1950 of their neighbor Henryk Großmann that the doctors who treated him, including Felix Boenheim, who was one of their friends, had "allowed the old man to die of hunger and thirst." As a result, the party initiated expulsion proceedings against Boenheim, although these were ultimately unsuccessful. See Thomas Michael Ruprecht, *Felix Boenheim: Arzt, Politiker, Historiker. Eine Biographie* (Hildesheim, 1992), 342.

44. SED leadership at the University of Leipzig to the Leipzig City Council, 26 April 1951, in LAB, C Rep. 118-01, no. 26 042.

45. Christian Schemmert and Daniel Siemens, "Die Leipziger Journalistenausbildung in der Ära Ulbricht," *Vierteljahrshefte für Zeitgeschichte* 61, no. 2 (2013): 210.

46. Hermann Budzislawski to Wilhelm Pieck, 15 July 1951, in AdK, Hermann-Budzislawski-Archiv, no. 167. These accusations seem to have a factual basis, as, for example, in the report of 5 July 1951 by the Volkspolizei, in BStU, MfS, BV Leipzig, AIM 263/53 "Garanti," 98.

47. Hermann Budzislawski to Wilhlem Pieck, 15 July and 8 October 1951, in AdK, Hermann-Budzislawski-Archiv, no. 167; Hermann Budzislawski to Walter Ulbricht, 21 February 1951, in AdK, Hermann-Budzislawski-Archiv, no. 168; Hermann Budzislawski to Gerhard Harig, 14 and 30 May 1951, in AdK, Hermann-Budzislawski-Archiv, no. 170.

48. Supplementary report by the Special Commission of the Central Committee on an additional investigation of Budzislawski, 3 July 1951, in BArch Berlin, SAPMO, DY 30/90300, 134.

49. Declaration of guarantee by Ernst Bloch for Johanna Budzislawski, 6 April 1951, in LAB, C Rep. 118-01, no. 26042; declarations of guarantee by Wieland Herzfelde and Ernst Bloch for Hermann Budzislawski, in LAB, C Rep. 118-01, no. 26 041, 3, 5.

50. Schemmert and Siemens, "Die Leipziger Journalistenausbildung," 215.

51. Wilhelm Pieck to Hermann Budzislawski, 26 July 1951, in AdK, Hermann-Budzislawski-Archiv, no. 167.

52. Hermann Budzislawski to Gerhard Harig, 19 September 1951, in AdK, Hermann-Budzislawski-Archiv, no. 170; memorandum from the KPKK (District Party Control Commission) to the ZPKK (Central Party Control Commission), 20 September 1951, in BArch Berlin, SAPMO, DY 30/90300, 133.

53. Knipping, "Der Mann."

54. Hermann Budzislawski to Wilhelm Pieck, 19 October 1952, in ZZF, NL Simone Barck, no. 3/5 (original in AdK, 127/4). The novel was published in the Budzislawskis' German translation in 1952 by the Verlag Volk und Welt: Frank J. Hardy, *Macht ohne Ruhm*, 2 vols. (Berlin, 1955).

55. David Brandenberger, "Stalin's Last Crime? Recent Scholarship on Postwar Soviet Antisemitism and the Doctor's Plot," *Kritika: Explorations in Russian and Eurasian History* 6, no. 1 (2005): 187–204.

56. On the Slánský trial, see Jan Gerber, *Ein Prozess in Prag: Das Volk gegen Rudolf Slánský und Genossen* (Göttingen, 2016); Wolfgang Kießling, *Partner im Narrenparadies: Der Freundeskreis um Paul Merker und Noel Field* (Berlin, 1994); Klein, *"Für die Einheit,"* 160–66. On Katz, see Anson Rabinbah, "Von Hollywood an den Galgen: Die Verfolgung und Ermordung des Otto Katz," *Zeitschrift für Ideengeschichte* 2, no. 1 (2008): 24–36; Keßler, *Westemigranten*, 51.

57. Helmut Eschwege, "Auswirkungen des Stalinismus auf die Juden der DDR von 1949 bis 1957," in *Kommunisten verfolgen Kommunisten: Stalinistischer Terror und "Säuberungen" in den kommunistischen Parteien Europas seit den dreißiger Jahren*, ed. Hermann Weber and Dietrich Staritz (Berlin, 1993), 511–17.

58. Hanna Budzislawski to Elisabeth Hauptmann, 2 March 1953, in AdK, Elisabeth-Hauptmann-Archiv, no. 210.

59. Alfred Kantorowicz, *Deutsches Tagebuch II* (West Berlin, 1979), 335, quoted in Keßler, *Westemigranten*, 380.

60. Hermann Budzislawski, "Diskussionsbeitrag: Lehren aus dem Slansky-Prozess," after 4 February 1953, in AdK, Hermann-Budzislawski-Archiv, no. 290.

61. Keßler, *Die SED und die Juden*, 103.

62. Hanna Budzislawski to Horst Baehrensprung, undated, in AdK Berlin, Hermann-Budzislawski-Archiv, no. 4.

63. Ibid.

64. Ibid.

65. For personal data on the two Eckerts, see also the information in BStU, MfS, AP 6970, vol. 82; and Horst Eckert's curriculum vitae at the end of his dissertation ("Die Beiträge der deutschen emigrierten Schriftsteller in der 'Neuen Weltbühne' von 1934–1939: Ein Beitrag zur Untersuchung der Beziehungen zwischen Volksfrontpolitik und Literatur" [PhD diss., Humboldt University, Berlin, 1962]).

66. NARA, RG 319 (U.S. Army, Military Agency Records, Counter Intelligence Corps [CIC] Investigative Records Repository), File 302122 (Report on Budzislawski, 1951); Hermann Budzislawski, short biography, 3 May 1971, in BArch Berlin, SAPMO, DY 30/90300, 36.

67. On the founding of the Faculty of Journalism, see Universitätsarchiv der Universität Leipzig (UAL), R 65, vol. 2.

68. Hermann Budzislawski, "Rede zur Verleihung der Ehrendoktorwürde am 11. Februar 1966," typescript, in AdK, Hermann-Budzislawski-Archiv, no. 297.

69. See the following autobiographies: Brigitte Klump, *Das rote Kloster: Als Zögling in der Kaderschmiede der Stasi* (1st ed., 1978; Munich, 1991); Xing-Hu Kuo, *Wodka in Sektgläsern: Cocktail meiner liebenswürdigen Stasi-Damen* (Böblingen, 1993), 20–24; Hans-Georg Kaethner, *Mit 100 DM nach Persien und lebendig zurück: Zwei Ossis in Nahost* (Munich, 2015).

70. Basil Spiru, "Vorschläge, 12. Juni 1955," in BArch Berlin, SAPMO, NY 4244/54, 64; "Auszug aus einem Strategiepapier," incomplete, in BArch Berlin, SAPMO, NY 4244/54, 118.

71. Report on the "Hirsch group," 1 June 1961, in BStU, Außenstelle Leipzig, MfS, BV Leipzig, AOP 40/64, 1:31.

72. Information report by the Leipzig State Security District Administration on the overall mood at Karl Marx University, 27 December 1956, in BStU, Außenstelle Leipzig, MfS, BV Leipzig, Leitung, 824, 42. On the dangers that might arise from the expression of dissident opinions, see Jens Blecher and Gerald Weimers, eds., *Studentischer Widerstand an den mitteldeutschen Universitäten 1945 bis 1955: Von der Universität in den GULAG. Studentenschicksale in sowjetischen Straflagern 1945–1955* (Leipzig, 2005).

73. In this connection, see also Hans Poerschke, "Anfänge marxistischer Journalistik—zwischen wissenschaftlichem Anspruch und Parteikonzept," in *Universität im Aufbruch—Leipzig 1945–1956: Beiträge des siebenten Walter-Markov-Kolloquiums*, ed. Jens Blecher and Gerald Wiemers (Leipzig, 2002), 134–39.

74. Information from BArch Berlin, SAPMO, DY 30/IV2/11/v., 1089 (Kaderakte Spiru); and Ilko-Sascha Kowalczuk, *Legitimation eines neuen Staates: Parteiarbeiter an der historischen Front. Geschichtswissenschaft in der SBZ/DDR 1945 bis 1961* (Berlin, 1997), 179–80. See the data in the catalog of professors at the University of Leipzig: https://research.uni-leipzig.de/agintern/CPL/PDF/Spiru_Basil.pdf.

75. Basil Spiru, "Notiz zum Grundlagenstudium," undated, in BArch Berlin, SAPMO, NY 4244/54, 53; Christian am Ende, "Redakteure auf dem Boden des Leninismus," *FAZ*, 24 September 1956, 2.

76. Basil Spiru, "Einige Bemerkungen zur Reorganisierung der Fakultät für Journalistik," undated, in BArch Berlin, SAPMO, NY 4244/54, 75.

77. Basil Spiru, *Giftmischer; Beiträge zur Entwicklungsgeschichte der zeitgenössischen bürgerlichen Journalistik* (Berlin, 1960), 365.

78. Quoted in Peter Theek, "Gedenkblatt für Hermann Budzislawski," *Die Weltbühne*, 26 April 1988, 539–40.

79. Hermann Budzislawski to Basil Spiru, 3 June 1955, in BArch Berlin, SAPMO, NY 4244/54, 82.

80. According to Christian Schemmert, "Beobachten und Beobachtetwerden in der Welt totaler Mitgliedschaft: Journalismusforscher im Disciplinarapparat der SED" (master's thesis, Bielefeld University, 2015), 16; Basil Spiru, "Ideologisch-politischer Zustand im 1.Studienjahr," in BArch Berlin, SAPMO, NY 4244/54, 114.

81. Victor Grossman (Stephen Wechsler), *Crossing the River: A Memoir of the American Left, the Cold War, and Life in East Germany* (Boston, 2003), 137.

82. Quoted in Meyen, "Die Erfindung," 9.

83. Klaus Höpcke, "Lehrer-Persönlichkeiten in der Fakultät für Journalistik," in Neuhaus and Seidel, *Universität im Aufbruch*, 142.

84. Röhr and Braun, interview, 10 November 2020. See also Michael Meyen and Thomas Wiedemann, "Journalism Professors in the German Democratic Republic: A Collective Biography," *International Journal of Communication* 11 (2017): Feature 1829–56.

85. "Papier der Fakultät für Journalistik," without title or year, in BArch Berlin, SAPMO, NY 4244/54, 123. "But what sort of a professor of journalism am I? I am not a journalist, I cannot write and therefore have no inclination toward scholarly activity

in the Faculty of Journalism": this is the candid admission of Heinrich Bruhn, who was the assistant dean and therefore the professor next highest in rank to Budzislawski in the faculty. Statement quoted from Basil Spiru to the Politburo of the SED Central Committee, undated, in BArch Berlin, SAPMO, NY 4244/54, 130.

86. Report on disputes at the Faculty of Journalism made by the Leipzig District Administration of the Ministry of State Security, Section V, Unit 1, on 9 July 1955, in BStU, MfS, BV Leipzig, AP 3041, 64:20–24.

87. Basil Spiru to the Politburo of the SED Central Committee, undated, in BArch Berlin, SAPMO, NY 4244/54, 130–31. See also Leipzig District Administration of the Ministry of State Security, discussion with Professor Spiru on 11 February 1957, in BStU, MfS, BV Leipzig, AP 3041, 64:12–13. In 1958 Spiru was transferred to the Faculty of Philosophy, where he became director of the Institute for the History of the European People's Democracies. Attempts to settle the internal conflicts had already failed. See, for example, "Annex to the Report to the Central Committee, Concerning Professor Spiru and Professor Budzislawski, 21 June 1955," in Sächsisches Staatsarchiv Leipzig, no. IV/7/122/019, 21:132.

88. Author's interview with Klaus Höpcke, 28 October 2019, Berlin.

89. Schemmert, "Beobachten und Beobachtetwerden," 175–76.

90. Information given to the author via email on 4 March 2020 by Alfred Eichhorn.

91. On this point, see Rudolf Reinhardt, "Auch die SED wollte ihr 'Reich,'" FAZ, 7 May 1997, 10; Siegfried Prokop, "Ernst Bloch und Wolfgang Harich im Jahre 1956," UTOPIE kreativ 184 (February 2006): 121–24.

92. Minutes of the Sittings of the Secretariat of the SED Central Committee on 16 and 17 December 1953, in BArch Berlin, SAPMO, DY 30/60465, 3; Rudolf Reinhardt, "Eine kurzlebige DDR-Wochenzeitung," FAZ, 12 June 1993, 8.

93. Reinhardt, "Auch die SED."

94. Discussion paper by Hermann Budzislawski on the newspaper project Die Republik, in AdK, Hermann-Scheer-Archiv, no. 13.

95. Ibid.

96. Ibid.

97. Council for a Democratic Germany, "Denkschrift über das Presse- und Nachrichtenwesen in Deutschland," in Was soll aus Deutschland werden? Der Council for a Democratic Germany in New York 1944–1945. Aufsätze und Dokumente, ed. Ursula Langkau-Alex and Thomas M. Ruprecht (Frankfurt am Main, 1993), 207–11.

98. "Charakteristik der Aufgaben der Wochenschrift Die Weltbühne," in ZZF, NL Simone Barck, no. 9/3.

99. Reinhardt, "Auch die SED."

100. Proposal from the Agitation and Propaganda Section to the Secretariat of the SED Central Committee, 23 October 1956, in BArch Berlin, SAPMO, DY 30/60621, 25–28.

101. Minutes of the Secretariat of the SED Central Committee, 23 October 1956, in BArch Berlin, SAPMO, DY 30/60621, 2–3.

102. Hermann Budzislawski to Rudolf Reinhardt, 7 February 1967, in Bibliotop, Ehemaliges Redaktionsarchiv der Weltbühne der DDR, Budzislawski 1, ZZF I.1.40.

103. Appraisal of Hermann Budzislawski by the Faculty of Journalism, 11 July 1963, in BArch Berlin, SAPMO, DY 30/90300, 82. On the situation in the faculty in 1958,

see "Die Erziehung und Ausbildung sozialistischer Journalisten an der Fakultät für Journalistik," submission of the Agitation and Propaganda Section to the Secretariat of the CC of the SED, 29 August 1958, in BArch Berlin, SAPMO, DY 30/IV2/9.04/21, 75–117.

104. Danziger, *"Die Partei hat immer Recht,"* 18.

105. Hermann Budzislawski, outlines of a lecture in India entitled "The Role of the GDR Press in Promoting International Understanding and Cooperation," 1961, in Privatarchiv Gottfried Braun, Leipzig.

106. Johannes H. Voigt, *Die Indienpolitik der DDR: Von den Anfängen bis zur Anerkennung (1962–1972)* (Cologne, 2008), 213.

107. Information from an appraisal of Hermann Budzislawski by the SED leadership at Karl Marx University, 4 September 1958, in BArch Berlin, SAPMO, DY 30/90300, 112; "Prof. Budzislawski bei Nehru," *Berliner Zeitung*, 29 March 1960, 5.

108. See on this point Benjamin Martin, "The Rise of the Cultural Treaty: Diplomatic Agreements and the International Politics of Culture in the Age of Three Worlds," *International History Review* 44, no. 6 (2022): 1327–46.

109. Uwe Tellkamp, *Die Schwebebahn: Dresdner Erkundungen* (Berlin, 2010), 30. Budzislawski's dissatisfaction during his period as dean is also recalled by Max Seydewitz in "Hermann Budzislawski," undated, in BArch Berlin, SgK 30, no. 0888/6, 98–105, here 104–5.

110. Hermann Budzislawski, typescript of a speech at the ceremony awarding him an honorary doctorate, in AdK, Hermann-Budzislawski-Archiv, no. 297. This was also the essential message of the festschrift published by the Faculty of Journalism in his honor: Fakultät für Journalistik der Karl-Marx-Universität, ed., *Journalismus und Gesellschaft: Hermann Budzislawski zum 65. Geburtstag* (Leipzig, 1966).

111. Hermann Budzislawski, speech at the ceremony awarding him an honorary doctorate, in AdK, Hermann-Budzislawski-Archiv, no. 297.

112. Ibid.

113. Hermann Budzislawski, *Sozialistische Journalistik: Eine wissenschaftliche Einführung* (Leipzig, 1966), 14.

114. Verena Blaum, "Budzislawski: Sozialistische Journalistik," in *Schlüsselwerke für die Kommunikationswissenschaft*, ed. Christina Holtz-Bacha and Arnulf Kutsch (Opladen, 2002), 83–85.

115. One exception was Spiru's book *Giftmischer*, which was published in 1960 by the Berlin Kongress-Verlag, with the subtitle *Beiträge zur Entwicklungsgeschichte der zeitgenössischen bürgerlichen Journalistik* (Contributions to the history of the development of contemporary bourgeois journalism).

116. Karl-Heinz Röhr, "Um journalistische Qualität geht es immer und überall," in *Biografisches Lexikon der Kommunikationswissenschaft*, ed. Michael Meyen and Thomas Wiedemann (Cologne, 2015), http://blexkom.halemverlag.de/karl-heinz-roehr/; Karl-Heinz Röhr and Willy Walther, "Hermann Budzislawski," in Fakultät für Journalistik, *Journalismus und Gesellschaft*, 9–22.

117. Budzislawski, *Sozialistische Journalistik*, 19.

118. Ibid., 21. On the importance of Socialist commitment to the party line for teaching at the Faculty of Journalism, see Helmut Warmbier, "Konzeption für die

politisch-erzieherische Arbeit im 1.Studienjahr," Leipzig, 13 November 1965, in UAL, Fak. Jour, 080, 55–57.

119. Blaum, "Budzislawski," 85.

120. "Abberufung des Genossen Budzislawski," extract from the 7 March 1962 resolutions of the Central Committee, in BArch Berlin, SAPMO, DY 30/90300, 90.

121. IM "Otto," "Zu Prof. Budzislawski," October 1965, in BStU, MfS, BV Leipzig, AIM 761/65, 80–82, here 80.

122. Ibid., 81.

123. Röhr and Braun, interview, 10 November 2020. It had been intended that the Swiss journalist and writer Jean Villain (real name Marcel Brun), a long-standing *Weltbühne* author who moved to the GDR in 1961, would become the magazine's editor in chief. He gives a detailed account of this episode in the history of the GDR media in Jean Villain, *Bitte nicht stürzen! Wie der DDR "Profil" abhanden kam und weitere Zeitungsmacher-Geschichten aus Deutsch-Fernost* (Rostock, 2004), 44–69. The Brun Archive, which is now preserved in the Archiv für Zeitgeschichte of the ETH Zürich, contains a copy of the inaugural issue of *Profil*.

124. Stephen Parker, "Fortsetzung folgt: Sinn und Form unter Wilhelm Girnius (1963–1981)," in *Zwischen "Mosaik" und "Einheit": Zeitschriften der DDR*, ed. Simone Barck, Martina Langermann, and Siegfried Lokatis (Berlin, 1999), 346.

125. On the weekend political discussions in Buckow, see Ernst Schumacher, *Mein Brecht: Erinnerungen 1943 bis 1956* (Berlin, 2006), 233–40.

Chapter 8. Belated Satisfaction

1. On the dispute over Budzislawski's retirement, see the correspondence in UAL, R 207, 8:1–7.

2. Simone Barck, "Die Weltbühne in der DDR: Ein Gespräch mit Ursula Madrasch-Groschopp," typescript, 26 September 2000, in ZZF, NL Simone Barck no. 9/13 (untitled gray folder); Ursula Madrasch-Groschopp to Rosalinde von Ossietzky-Palm, 27 February 1967, in Carl von Ossietzky University, Oldenburg, Carl von Ossietzky Archive, JB 1; Hermann Budzislawski to Ruth Seydewitz, 17 January 1967, in Bibliotop, Ehemaliges Redaktionsarchiv der *Weltbühne* der DDR, Budzislawski 1, ZZF I.1.16.

3. Hermann Budzislawski, "Rückkehr," *Die Weltbühne* 15 February 1967, 193–95.

4. Hugo Huppert to Hermann Budzislawski, 24 January 1967, in AdK, Hugo-Huppert-Archiv, no. 301.

5. Hermann Budzislawski to Hugo Huppert, 3 February 1967, 9 March 1967, and 31 August 1970, in AdK, Hugo-Huppert-Archiv, no. 301.

6. Hugo Huppert to Hermann Budzislawski, 7 February 1967, in AdK, Hugo-Huppert-Archiv, no. 301.

7. Minutes of a discussion between Budzislawski, Huppert, and Madrasch-Groschopp in Berlin, 6 April 1967, in AdK, Hugo-Huppert-Archiv, no. 301.

8. All the information in this paragraph comes from Richard Christ, *Der Tag, die Nacht, und ich dazwischen* (Rostock, 2001), 179–95.

9. In this connection, compare Monika Maron's literary portrait of an imaginary SED functionary, Herbert Beerenbaum, in her novel *Stille Zeile sechs* (Frankfurt am Main, 1991).

10. The expression "enslavement through consciousness" (*Knechtschaft durch Wissen*) comes from Miłosz, *Verführtes Denken*, 186 (English translation: Miłosz, *The Captive Mind*, 191).

11. Christ, *Der Tag*, 179–81. Similar observations were made by the journalist Brigitte Klump in her memoirs. She recalled Budzislawski's "stony face" at her interview for admission to the Faculty of Journalism but remarked that later he started to look almost "benevolent" and "fatherly" (Brigitte Klump, *Das rote Kloster: Eine deutsche Erziehung* [Hamburg, 1978], 35).

12. Written record of a conversation between Simone Barck and Ursula Madrasch-Groschopp on 21 June 1999, in Bibliotop, Ehemaliges Redaktionsarchiv der *Weltbühne* der DDR (yellow file "Die Weltbühne," no call number) .

13. Ibid.; Christ, *Der Tag*, 184.

14. Fair-Schulz, *Loyal Subversion*, 283–85, 288; "'Man brauchte nur ich zu sagen . . .': Chef-Redakteure und eine Leserin im Gespräch. Klaus Polkehn (Wochenpost), Hartmut Berlin (Eulenspiegel), Helmut Reinhardt (Die Weltbühne) und Brigitte Struzyk," in Barck, Langermann, and Lokatis, *Zwischen "Mosaik" und "Einheit,"* 117.

15. Zwerenz, *Kurt Tucholsky*, 227.

16. Erich Weinert to Hans Leonhard, 1952, quoted in Wehner, *Kulturpolitik und Volksfront*, 1:389.

17. Hermann Budzislawski to Albert Norden, 30 September 1968, in Bibliotop, Ehemaliges Redaktionsarchiv der *Weltbühne* der DDR (blue folder).

18. Hermann Budzislawski, "Henry Morgenthau heute," *Die Weltbühne*, 22 February 1967, 225–27; Budzislawski, "Oppenheimers unvollendetes Werk," *Die Weltbühne*, 28 February 1967, 257–60.

19. Hermann Budzislawski, "Krupo unter Kuratel," *Die Weltbühne*, 14 March 1967, 321–24; Budzislawski, "Volksfront im Vormarsch," *Die Weltbühne*, 28 March 1967, 385–86.

20. Heiner Winkler, "Schattenseiten des japanischen Wirtschaftswunders," *Die Weltbühne*, 2 January 1968, 15–18; Ulrich Makosch, "Amerikaner in Kambodscha," *Die Weltbühne*, 9 January 1968, 43–46; Gordon Schaffer, "Englische Zeitungswelt," *Die Weltbühne*, 16 January 1968, 79–83; Pedro Fuentes, "Völkermord im Urwald," *Die Weltbühne*, 28 May 1968, 684–88.

21. "Was geschah in der ČSSR?," *Die Weltbühne*, 27 August 1968, 1089–90.

22. Horst Schötzki, "Die nicht geheimen Geheimsender," *Die Weltbühne*, 3 September 1968, 1121–23.

23. Hermann Budzislawski to Hugo Huppert, 25 September 1968, in AdK, Hugo-Huppert-Archiv, no. 301.

24. Hugo Huppert to Hermann Budzislawski, 6 October 1969, in AdK, Hugo-Huppert-Archiv, no. 301.

25. One example is sufficient to indicate his general approach: Hermann Budzislawski, "Der kritische Augenblick," *Die Weltbühne*, 21 March 1967, 353–55.

26. These quotations all come from Hermann Budzislawski, "Wo steht die Jugend?," *Die Weltbühne*, 18 April 1967, 481–84, here 482–83. See also Henryk Keisch, "Die Voyeure der Publizistik," *Die Weltbühne*, 7 January 1969, 49–52; and Hermann Budzislawski, "Informiert oder Deformiert?," *Neues Deutschland*, 24 May 1958, 10. Budzislawski's column "Meine Meinung," which appeared every month in the periodical *Das*

Magazin between January 1966 and February 1967, took a similar line. See Keßler, *Westemigranten*, 420–22.

27. Gert Billing, "Rebellion der Studenten," *Die Weltbühne*, 26 September 1967, 1219–23; Billing, "Vor einem heißen Wintersemester?," *Die Weltbühne*, 3 October 1967, 1252–56.

28. This shortcoming already characterized *Die neue Weltbühne* in the 1940s. See Klein, "Die Neugründung," 571.

29. Elfriede Brüning, "Wer einmal aus dem Blechtopf frißt," *Die Weltbühne*, 28 May 1968, 691–94.

30. See also Lother Creutz, "Sächsiche Miniaturen," *Die Weltbühne*, 11 April 1967, 479.

31. Quoted in Andreas Hutzler, "Die Zwerchfellmauer," *Die Zeit*, 21 February 1997.

32. Klein, "Die Neugründung," 573.

33. Seydewitz, "Hermann Budzislawski," 105.

34. Sayner, *Reframing Antifascism*, 130–37; Greta Kuckhoff, "Arvid Harnack," *Die Weltbühne*, 11 November 1969, 1411–15; Kuckhoff, "Zur Kristallnacht November 1938," *Die Weltbühne*, 18 November 1969, 1449–51.

35. Simon Wiesental [*sic*], "Wer finanzierte ODESSA?," *Die Weltbühne*, 2 May 1967, 552–57.

36. On Dymschitz's life, see Anne Hartmann and Wolfram Eggeling, *Sowjetische Präsenz im kulturellen Leben der SBZ und der frühen DDR 1945–1953* (Berlin, 1998), 145–48, 552–57.

37. Hermann Budzislawski to Alexander Dimschitz [*sic*], 9 June 1967, in the Russian State Archive of Literature and Art, Moscow (RGALI), Bestand 2843, ind. 1, 856:9; Günther Weisenborn, "Ein Appell in München," *Die Weltbühne*, 5 March 1968, 292–94.

38. LAB, C Rep. 031-02-09, no. 4294 (de-Nazification file of Peter Theek, born 28 October 1924, closed until 2031). I would like to thank Bettina Theek for granting me access to important documents from this file.

39. "Wechsel bei der 'Weltbühne,'" *FAZ*, 13 November 1971, 3; Bernd-Rainer Barth, "Theek, Peter," in *Wer war wer in der DDR?*, https://www.bundesstiftung-aufarbeitung .de/de/recherche/kataloge-datenbanken/biographische-datenbanken/peter-theek.

40. Letter from Hermann Budzislawski to Peter Theek, 28 October 1974, in Privatarchiv Daniel Siemens.

41. "Vor 40 Jahren erschien Ossietzkys Weltbühne wieder in Berlin," *Die Weltbühne*, special issue (1986), in Bibliotop, Ehemaliges Redaktionsarchiv der *Weltbühne* der DDR.

42. Hermann Budzislawski, "Das streitbare Leben einer tapferen Frau," *Die Weltbühne*, 28 May 1974, 682–85.

43. Quoted from Carl Misch, "Lieber tot als Réfugié," manuscript, 12 March 1948, in SUNY Archive, Carl Misch Papers, ger067, box 1, folder 34. Masaryk died on 10 March 1948 in circumstances that have never been properly explained.

Chapter 9. In the Ambience of Power

1. This was somewhat ironic, as Bunge had previously been supported by Hermann Budzislawski in his disagreement with Helene Weigel. But she was not aware of this.

On the relationship between Bunge, Weigel, and Budzislawski, see Fair-Schulz, *Loyal Subversion*, 307–8; Sabine Kebir, *Abstieg in den Ruhm: Helene Weigel. Eine Biographie* (Berlin, 2000), 286–87.

2. Helene Weigel to the Budzislawski couple, 16 December 1960, in AdK, Helene-Weigel-Archiv, no. Ko 100; Hermann Budzislawski to Helene Weigel, 13 February 1961, in AdK, Helene-Weigel-Archiv, no. Ko 9619.

3. Hermann Budzislawski to Helene Weigel, 12 January 1961, in AdK, Helene-Weigel-Archiv, no. Ko 9620.

4. Hermann Budzislawski to the mayor of Buckow, 3 September 1970, in AdK, Hermann-Budzislawski-Archiv, no. 326.

5. The cabaret was well regarded by the SED in previous years, and it had even completed a tour through the Federal Republic. See Klaus Raddatz, memorandum to Budzislawski, 19 September 1957, in Sächsisches Staatsarchiv Leipzig, no. IV/7/122/019, 21:132.

6. Resolution by the SED leadership at Karl Marx University, 5 December 1961, on the "conclusions to be drawn" in regard to the Council of the Scoffers, in BStU, Außenstelle Leipzig, MfS, BV Leipzig, AOP 40/64, 2:69–75.

7. Supporting evidence in Schemmert and Siemens, "Die Leipziger Journalistenausbildung," 217–19. On the affair of the ban on the Council of the Scoffers, see Sylvia Klötzer, *Satire und Macht: Film, Zeitung, Kabarett in der DDR* (Cologne, 2006), 121–51; Ernst Röhl, *Der Rat der Spötter: Das Kabarett des Peter Sodann* (Cologne, 2002).

8. Memorandum on the Faculty of Journalism, 12 September 1961, in BArch Berlin, SAPMO, DY 30/IV2/9.04/558, 231–39.

9. Franz Knipping to Christian Schemmert and the author, 22 June 2013, in Privatarchiv Daniel Siemens, Newcastle upon Tyne; Knipping, "Der Mann."

10. Edith Anderson, *Der Beobachter sieht nichts: Ein Tagebuch zweier Welten* (Berlin, 1972), 11; Runge, *Dreiundsechzig*, 15; Alfred Kantorowicz, "Gebt mir Asyl," quoted in Schildt, *Medien-Intellektuelle*, 707–8.

11. Hermann Budzislawski to his daughter, Beate, 3 July 1953, in AdK, Hermann-Budzislawski-Archiv, no. 401.

12. Ibid.

13. Victor Klemperer, *The Lesser Evil: The Diaries of Victor Klemperer 1945–59*, abridged and translated from the German edition by Martin Chalmers (London, 2003), 419 (entry for 22 June 1953) (German translation: Klemperer, *So sitze ich*, 2:390).

14. The expression comes from Danziger, *"Die Partei hat immer recht,"* 115.

15. Gudrun Traumann, *Journalistik in der DDR: Sozialistische Journalistik und Journalistenausbildung an der Karl-Marx-Universität Leipzig* (Munich-Pullach, 1971), 93.

16. Fair-Schulz also makes this assessment (*Loyal Subversion*, 277).

17. This point is often overlooked. See, for example, Krauss, "Hans Habe," 264–65.

18. Report of the Commission on the Future Activities of the WFSW, in *Wissenschaftliche Welt* 21, no. 1 (1977): 23. On the early days of the World Federation, see William Styles, "The World Federation of Scientific Workers: A Case Study of a Soviet Front Organization, 1946–1964," *Intelligence and National Security* 33, no. 1 (2018): 116–29.

19. See the relevant information in the catalog of professors at Leipzig University and in LAB, C Rep. 118-01, no. 26 041; BArch Berlin, SAPMO, DY 30/90300, 7; and AdK, Hermann-Budzislawski-Archiv, no. 377.

20. Kurt Hiller, "Aufstieg, Glanz und Verfall der Weltbühne," pt. 4, *konkret*, June 1962, in LAB, E Rep. 200-63, no. 23d.

21. Radio broadcast, "Zu Gast bei Prof. Dr. Hermann Budzislawski," 19 October 1964, in DRA, no. 2 032 877 (29:22–31:30 mins.).

22. For a nuanced view of the Bitterfeld Path, see Gerd Dietrich, *Kulturgeschichte der DDR, Teil 2: Kultur in der Bildungsgesellschaft 1957–1976* (Göttingen, 2018), 847–49; and William J. Waltz, *Of Writers and Workers: The Movement of Writing Workers in East Germany* (Oxford, 2018). For the GDR mass media's tendency to take a reserved attitude toward sophisticated cultural contributions, see Classen, "Die DDR-Medien," 397.

23. Radio broadcast, "Zu Gast bei Prof. Dr. Hermann Budzislawski" (31:30–34:00 mins.).

24. Richard Stöss, "Geschichte des Rechsextremismus," 12 June 2006, https://www.bpb.de/politik/extremismus/rechtsextremismus/41907/geschichte-des-rechtsextremismus; Gideon Botsch, *Die extreme Rechte in der Bundesrepublik Deutschland 1949 bis heute* (Bonn, 2012).

25. Statement by Budzislawski at a conference organized by the PEN held on 29 September 1964 at Schloss Cecilienhof, Potsdam, on the theme "Two World Wars and German Literature," in DRA, no. 2 032 678 (from 1:32:12 mins.).

26. On this, see Franziska Kuschel and Dominik Rigoll, "Broschürenkrieg statt Bürgerkrieg: BMI und MdI im deutsch-deutschen Systemkonflikt," in *Hüter der Ordnung: Die Innenministerien in Bonn und Ost-Berlin nach dem Nationalsozialismus*, ed. Frank Bösch and Andreas Wirsching (Göttingen, 2018), 355–80.

27. Fair-Schulz, *Loyal Subversion*, 312, 333; Gordon, "Widersprüchliche Zugehörigkeiten," 198.

28. Speech by Hermann Budzislawski on 4 May 1968 at the wreath-laying ceremony for Ossietzky organized by the Peace Council of the GDR, in LAB, E Rep. 200-63, no. 23a. See also Hermann Budzislawski, "Nach dreißig Jahren," in *Die Weltbühne*, 30 April 1968, 545–47; and Budzislawski, "Wir sind zwanzig," *Die Weltbühne*, 7 October 1969, 1249–52.

29. In this connection, see also Adrian, "Epitaph für Benno Ohnesorg," *Die Weltbühne*, 13 June 1967, 747.

30. Talk by Hermann Budzislawski on the eightieth anniversary of the birth of Kurt Tucholsky, broadcast by Berliner Rundfunk on 9 January 1970, in DRA, DZ 095 346.

31. There are several examples in Joachim Walther, *Sicherungsbereich Literatur: Schriftsteller und Staatssicherheit in der Deutschen Demokratischen Republik* (Berlin, 1996).

32. Fritz Klein, who was one of the best-known historians in the GDR and who was a sympathetic observer and a long-standing contributor, summarized the dilemma faced by *Die Weltbühne* in this way in 2004: "*Weltbühne* in the GDR—a relationship full of contradictions. It is impossible to conceive of Jacobsohn, Tucholsky, and Ossietzky as participating in this politically shackled periodical. Nevertheless, it was legitimate to invoke their names when criticizing political conditions in the Federal Republic and the rest of the capitalist world, which had already been scourged by the old *Weltbühne*" ("Gedenken an Ursula Madrasch-Groschopp," *Ossietzky: Zweiwochenschrift für Politik, Kultur und Wirtschaft*, no. 4 [2004], https://www.sopos.org/aufsaetze/4035ee6947665/1.phtml.html).

33. On this, see Stefan Zahlmann, "Medien in der DDR: Medienproduktion und Medienrezeption als kulturelle Praktiken," in *Wie im Westen, nur anders*, ed. Stefan Zahlmann (Berlin, 2010), 25.

34. Detlev Brunner, "DDR 'transnational': Die 'internationale Solidarität' der DDR," in *Deutsche Zeitgeschichte—transnational*, ed. Alexander Gallus, Axel Schildt, and Detlef Siegfried (Göttingen, 2015), 64–80.

35. Assessment of Comrade Prof. Dr. Budzislawski by the Leipzig City SED leadership, 27 April 1962, in BArch Berlin, SAPMO, DY 30/90300.

36. GDR Ministry of Foreign Affairs, "Assessment of the Newly Formed Great Britain–GDR Parliamentary Group in the British House of Commons, 20 December 1965," in BArch Berlin, SAPMO, DY 30/97656.

37. GDR Ministry of Foreign Affairs, "Measures Taken by Ruling Circles in West Germany and Britain against the Growth of the British Movement for the Recognition of the GDR, 7 April 1969," in BArch Berlin, SAPMO, DY 30/97656; Stefan Berger and Norman Laporte, *Friendly Enemies: Britain and the GDR, 1949–1990* (London, 2010), 108.

38. Hermann Budzislawski, "Volkskammerbesuch in England," *Die Weltbühne*, 16 December 1969, 1569–72 (also in AdK, Hermann-Budzislawski-Archiv, no. 414).

39. Anthony Rowley, "Recognition Snag in East German Trade Discussions," *The Times* (London), 24 November 1969, 24; "East Germany May Get One Year Trade Pact," *The Times* (London), 26 November 1969, 26. On the ambivalent results of this journey, see the comprehensive account in Henning Hoff, *Großbritannien und die DDR 1955–1973: Diplomatie auf Umwegen* (Munich, 2003), 397–407.

40. Pierre Biquard, "Nachruf auf Hermann Budzislawski," *Wissenschaftliche Welt* 22, no. 2 (1978): 33; "Ein Bekenntnis zu Abrüstung und Frieden," *Neues Deutschland*, 24 November 1971, 2; Hermann Budzislawski, "Abschreckung oder Abrüstung," *Die Weltbühne*, 7 December 1971, 1537–39.

41. Memorandum by the SED's Department for University and Technical College Affairs, 29 November 1971, in BArch Berlin, SAPMO, DY 30/90300, 19.

42. Biquard, "Nachruf."

43. Decisions by the Central Committee of the SED concerning Budzislawski's journeys abroad, in BArch Berlin, SAPMO, DY 30/90300, 19.

44. Recommendation for Hermann Budzislawski's admission to membership by Rudolf Leonhard and Maximilian Scheer, undated, in AdK, Hermann-Scheer-Archiv, no. 558.

45. "Herzliche Gratulation für Nestor des Journalismus," *Neues Deutschland*, 12 February 1976, in BArch Berlin, SAPMO, DK 30/90300, 13.

46. Christoph Dieckmann, "Gysi, schuldig oder nicht?," *Die Zeit*, 29 May 2008, https://www.zeit.de/2008/23/Gysi-Portrait. On Gysi's life story, see Karin Hartewig, "A German Jewish Communist of the Second Generation: The Changing Personae of Klaus Gysi," in *Dark Time, Dire Decisions: Jews and Communism*, ed. Jonathan Fraenkel and Dan Diner (New York, 2004), 255–71.

47. Barbara Honigmann, *Georg* (Munich, 2019), 108. Another case study is Lutz Maeke, *Carl Steinhoff: Erster DDR-Innenminister. Wandlungen eines bürgerlichen Sozialisten* (Göttingen, 2020).

48. Klump, *Das rote Kloster.*

49. Anna Seghers to Hermann Budzislawski, 12 February 1976, in ZZF, NL Simone Barck, no. 3/5 (original in AdK, Hermann Budzislawski Archiv, no. 127/21); Marta Feuchtwanger to Hermann Budzislawski, 11 December 1972, in ZZF, NL Simone Barck, no. 3/5 (original in AdK, Hermann Budzislawski Archiv, no. 127/13).

50. Knipping, "Der Mann."

51. Ibid.

52. Andreas Zimmer, *Der Kulturbund in der SBZ und in der DDR: Eine ostdeutsche Kulturvereinigung im Wandel der Zeit zwischen 1945 und 1990* (Wiesbaden, 2019), 295–97.

53. Memorandum by the University and Technical College Policy Section, 19.

54. For the information on Budzislawski's stay in the Bernburg psychiatric clinic, see Andreas Juhnke, "Ein Turm in der Schlacht: Familiendrama mit Ossietzky, Brecht und Gysi in den Nebenrollen," *TransAtlantik* 12 (1990): 68–69.

55. Johanna Budzislawski to Peter Viertel, 7 January 1979, in AdK, Hermann-Budzislawski-Archiv, no. 413.

56. Hermann Budzislawski, "Varianten des Lebens," newspaper cutting from *Für Dich*, undated, in AdK, Hermann-Budzislawski-Archiv, no. 414.

57. Andreas Juhnke, "Operation Erbe," *Manager Magazin* 3 (1993): 259.

58. See the correspondence in question between Budzislawski and Kuczynski, in ZLB, NL Kuczynski (the quotation comes from Kuczynski to Budzislawski, 8 November 1967, in Kuc 2-1-W1440).

59. Honigmann, *Georg*, 44–45.

60. Hannah Arendt to Eric Werner, 27 April 1943, in LBI, Eric Werner Collection, AR 2179, box 1, folder 14, 338.

61. Hermann Eschwege (Hermann Budzislawski), "Der Weg der Juden: Ein Diskussionsartikel," *Die neue Weltbühne*, 16 March 1939, 327–31. For a Zionist critique of this view, see C[heskel] Z[wi] Klötzel, "Juden und Faschisten," *Die neue Weltbühne*, 4 May 1939, 549–52.

62. For the context, see Harry Waibel, *Die braune Saat: Antisemitismus und Neonazismus in der DDR* (Stuttgart, 2017), 82–88.

63. Heiner Winkler, "Palästina," *Die Weltbühne*, 6 June 1967, 705–10; Hermann Budzislawski, "Israel und Araber," *Die Weltbühne*, 20 June 1967, 769–72; Budzislawski, "Die Wahlen und die Wahrheit," *Die Weltbühne*, 27 June 1967, 801–5. On the openly anti-Zionist course of the SED after the Six-Day War of 1967, see Wolfgang Benz, ed., *Antisemitismus in der DDR: Manifestationen und Folgen des Feindbildes Israel* (Berlin, 2018); Geffrey Herf, *Undeclared Wars with Israel: East Germany and the West German Far Left, 1967–1989* (New York, 2016); see also the critique by Charlotte Misselwitz, "Als ob wir nichts zu lernen hätten von den linken Juden der DDR . . . : Bemerkungen zu dem Beitrag von Micha Brumlik 'Ostdeutscher Antisemitismus: Wie braun war die DDR?,'" *Deutschland Archiv*, 20 April 2020, www.bpb.de/308502.

64. Quoted from Sayner, *Reframing Antifascism*, 138.

65. "Erklärung jüdischer Bürger der DDR," *Neues Deutschland*, 9 June 1967, 2. On the context, see Esther Sattig, "Jüdisches Leben in der DDR als individuelle Erfahrung: Im Gespräch mit Salomea Genin, Irene Runge, Renate und Peter Kirchner," in Benz, *Antisemitismus in der DDR*, 165.

66. Note by the Staatssicherheit, Directorate XX/2, 29 January 1986, in BStU, MfS, BV Berlin, AIM 5998/91, pt. 2, 2:207–8.

67. Staatssicherheit, Directorate XX, Berlin Department, "Information über jugendliche Gruppierung mit faschistischen Tendenzen in Buckow, 15. Dezember 1982," in BStU, MfS, BV Berlin, AIM 5998/91, pt. 2, 1:418–19. There are many other examples of neo-Nazism and antisemitic violence in the GDR of the 1970s and 1980s in Waibel, *Die braune Saat*, 115–64.

68. SED questionnaire for members exchanging party documents submitted by Hanna Budzislawski on 1 July 1970, in BArch Berlin, SAPMO, DY 30/90301.

69. Heym, *Nachruf*, 133.

70. Honigmann, *Georg*, 53–54.

71. Hermann Budzislawski, "Warum feiern wir Stalin?," in AdK, Hermann-Budzislawski-Archiv, no. 414.

72. Hermann Budzislawski, "Lob der Weigel," typescript, in AdK, Helene-Weigel-Archiv, FH 137.

73. See the correspondence in AdK, Helene-Weigel-Archiv, no. 186, Ko 7598 and Ko 7599; there is also evidence of their readiness to give practical assistance in Klump, *Das rote Kloster*.

74. Honigmann, *Georg*, 97.

75. In AdK, Hermann-Budzislawski-Archiv, no. 413.

76. Obituary of Hermann Budzislawski by the staff of *Die Weltbühne*, printed in *Neues Deutschland*, 9 May 1978, in BArch Berlin, SAPMO, DY 30/90300, 4.

77. Program of the Memorial Service for Budzislawski, in Bibliotop, Ehemaliges Redaktionsarchiv der *Weltbühne* der DDR, Budzislawski 4, ZZF I.1.785.

78. "Hermann Budzislawski, verstorben," *BZ*, 29–30 April 1978, in LAB, C Rep. 118-01, no. 26 041.

79. Eberhard Heinrich, secretary of the Politburo Agitation Commission, emphasized exactly this point in his funeral oration for Hermann Budzislawski, delivered on 18 May 1978. There had, he said, been an inevitable development from Carl von Ossietzky's *Weltbühne*, through Budzislawski's *Neue Weltbühne*, to the GDR's *Weltbühne*. It could not appear in any other place "without contradicting the humanistic spirit and the social goals of its founders and its most important contributors" (Eberhard Heinrich, "Trauerrede auf Budzislawski," in BArch Berlin, DY 30/9947, 375–81).

80. Details in Juhnke, "Ein Turm," 70.

81. Johanna Budzislawski to Horst Eckert, 13 November 1978, in AdK, Hermann-Budzislawski-Archiv, no. 304.

82. "'Ehre Ihrem Andenken!': Notiz zum Tode Hanna Budzislawskis der SED-Kreisleitung Treptow," *Neues Deutschland*, 26 April 1979, in LAB, D Rep. 920-13, no. 48.

83. Report by Hauptmann Schiller, PdVP Berlin, 4 April 1979, in BStU, MfS HA IX/11 SV 25/79, 161–62; Juhnke, "Der Turm," 72; Juhnke, "Operation Erbe," 262; author's interview with Karl-Heinz Röhr and Gottfried Braun, 10 November 2020, Leipzig.

84. Obituary of Hanna Budzislawski in *Neues Deutschland*, 21–22 April 1979, in BArch Berlin, SAPMO, DY 30/90301. It was not until the beginning of the 1990s that her daughter, Beate Eckert, was informed of possible discrepancies between official statements and the postmortem findings. After she had spoken to the Pathology Department of the Charité, Berlin's largest university hospital, in the presence of the journalist Andreas Juhnke and inspected the relevant documents, she instructed the

attorney Ulrike Zecher to issue a criminal complaint against unknown persons on account of her mother's supposedly violent death. But the proceedings ended without any result. In 2018 I asked the Pathology Department of the Charité for its comments, but the reply was unhelpful. They do have the death certificate, but it is not accessible to researchers without the consent of either the nearest relative or the State Prosecutor's Office (information given to me on the telephone by the Berlin lawyer Ulrike Zecher on 8 January 2019 and in writing by Navena Widulin of the Berliner Charité on 15 March 2019).

85. Beate Eckert to the Politburo of the SED, 4 April 1979, in BArch Berlin, DY 30/9947, 400.

Chapter 10. What Remains?

1. Helmut Lethen, *Verhaltenslehren der Kälte: Lebensversuche zwischen den Weltkriegen* (Frankfurt am Main, 1994) (English translation: Helmut Lethen, *Cool Conduct: The Culture of Distance in Weimar Germany*, trans. Don Reneau [Berkeley, CA, 2002]).

2. Paul Betts, *Ruin and Renewal: Civilising Europe after the Second World War* (London, 2020), 381.

3. Eckert, *Die Beiträge*, 16–17.

4. Hermann Eschwege (Hermann Budzislawski), "Entgegnung," *Die neue Weltbühne*, 4 May 1939, 553–58, here 554; Kurt Tucholsky, "Heimat," in *Deutschland, Deutschland über alles* (Berlin, 1929), 226–31.

5. Wolfgang Hardtwig, "Formen der Geschichtsschreibung: Varianten des historischen Erzählens," in *Geschichte: Ein Grundkurs*, ed. Hans-Jürgen Goertz (Reinbek bei Hamburg, 1998), 178–79.

6. Ernst Toller, *Eine Jugend in Deutschland*, vol. 4 of *Gesammelte Werke* (Munich, 1978), 7. Needless to say, present-day biographers who work scientifically no longer aim at an epistemologically naive depiction of the "complete human being." They are concerned instead with investigating the relationship between biography, autobiography (of the subject of the biography), and the (objective) course of a person's life. See Volker Depkat, "The Challenges of Biography: European-American Reflections," *Bulletin of the GHI* 55 (2014): 39–48.

7. Hermann Budzislawski to Heinz Pol, 23 March 1936, in AdK, Die neue Weltbühne, box 9, preliminary signature 38, 151–52.

8. Hermann Budzislawski, "Varianten des Lebens," newspaper cutting from *Für Dich*, undated, in AdK, Hermann-Budzislawski-Archiv, no. 414.

9. Hermann Budzislawski, "Zweiter Weltkrieg: Im Konzentrationslager," typescript, part of a planned autobiography, written between 1941 and 1943, in AdK, Hermann-Budzislawski-Archiv, no. 390.

10. Ibid.

11. Hilde Walter, "Brief an eine Freundin, New York, 11. März 1941," in *Verbannung: Aufzeichnungen deutscher Schriftsteller im Exil*, ed. Egon Schwarz and Matthias Wegner (Hamburg, 1964), 94.

Epilogue

1. There is a draft will containing these provisions in AdK, Hermann-Budzislawski-Archiv, no. 326.

2. Report of a meeting with IM "Martin Kunze," 12 May 1978, in BStU, MfS, BV Berlin, AIM 5998/91, pt. 2, 1:362–63.

3. Johanna Budzislawski to Peter Viertel, 7 January 1979, in AdK, Hermann-Budzislawski-Archiv, no. 413; Johanna Budzislawski to Hertha Walcher, 13 January 1979, in BArch Berlin, SAPMO, NY 4087/77, 33.

4. Ibid.

5. Memorandum from Department XX/3 of the Ministry of State Security on Dr. Eckert, 14 April 1975, in BStU, MfS, AP 6970, 82:54.

6. Johanna Budzislawski to Peter Viertel, 7 January 1979, in AdK, Hermann-Budzislawski-Archiv, no. 413.

7. Juhnke, "Ein Turm"; Juhnke, "Operation Erbe." In 1993 the journalist Brigitte Seebacher-Brandt also published documents about the *Weltbühne* dispute: Brigitte Seebacher-Brandt, "Schwindel mit dem Etikett: Wem gehört das Erbe der Nein-sager?," *FAZ Magazin*, no. 691, 28 May 1993, 36.

8. Information given to the author on 17 February 2019 by the media historian Hans Bohrmann, Dortmund.

9. Data from a short biography of Eckert in AdK, Hermann-Budzislawski-Archiv, no. 382.

10. Extract from the Charlottenburg land register relating to Johanna Budzislawski (388:12,448) in AdK, Hermann-Budzislawski-Archiv, no. 272.

11. Statement by the Ministry of State Security on Thomas Eckert, 10 April 1987, in BStU, MfS-BdL (Büro der Leitung), no. 4022, 16–17. On the October Club, see Ulrich Mählert and Gerd-Rüdiger Stephan, *Blaue Hemden—rote Fahnen: Die Geschichte der Freien Deutschen Jugend* (Opladen, 1996), 175–78.

12. Wolf (pseudonym), Report on IM "Martin Kunze," 8 June 1979, in BStU, MfS, BV Berlin, AIM 5998/91, pt. 2, 1:399–400.

13. "Operational Information on the Person Thomas Eckert, 3 April 1987," in BStU, MfS-BdL, no. 4022, 12–13.

14. According to Juhnke, "Der Turm," 70.

15. Memorandum "On the person Eckert, Thomas," in BStU, MfS-BdL, no. 4022, 9.

16. Juhnke, "Operation Erbe," 264.

17. According to the data in the entry in the land register for Kaiserin-Augusta-Allee 87, in AdK, Hermann-Budzislawski-Archiv, no. 416.

18. Thomas Eckert to the GDR Minister of Culture, 5 October 1983, in BStU, MfS, AP 13 671, 81–82, here 82; Juhnke, "Operation Erbe," 264.

19. Hannsjörg F. Buck, "Öffentliche Finanzwirtschaft im SED-Staat und ihre Transformationsprobleme," in *Materialien der Enquete-Kommission "Überwindung der Folgen der SED-Diktatur im Prozess der deutschen Einheit,"* Deutscher Bundestag, 13. Wahlperiode (Bonn, 1998), III/2:1070–71.

20. Testimony of Gregor Gysi in 2001, quoted in Ulf Bischof, *Die Kunst und Antiquitäten GmbH im Bereich Kommerzielle Koordinierung* (Berlin, 2005), 120, 165. There are many examples in Günter Blutke, *Obskure Geschäfte mit Kunst und Antiquitäten: Ein Kriminalreport*, 2nd ed. (Berlin, 1994), 34–42; see most recently Christopher Neh-ring, "Von DDR-Millionären, Schmugglern und Raubkunst," *Gerbergasse 18: Thüringer Vierteljahrsschrift für Zeitgeschichte und Politik* 1 (2018): 34–39. On the activities of the KoKo in general, see Matthias Judt, *Der Bereich Kommerzielle Koordinierung: Das*

DDR-Wirtschaftsimperium des Alexander Schalck-Golodkowski—Mythos und Realität (Berlin, 2013), and on the KoKo's art and antiques division, see 254.

21. Thomas Eckert to the GDR Minister of Culture, 5 October 1983, 82.

22. Wolf, report on IM "Martin Kunze," 8 June 1979, in BStU, MfS, BV Berlin, AIM 5998/91, pt. 2, 1:399–400.

23. Wolf, information regarding the political attitude of the young adult Thomas Eckert, 10 April 1980, in BStU, MfS, BV Berlin, AIM 5998/91, pt. 2, 2:11.

24. Ibid. See also Blutke, *Obskure Geschäfte,*174.

25. Juhnke, "Der Turm," 71.

26. Bischof, *Die Kunst und Antiquitäten GmbH*, portrays this pattern of conduct in exemplary fashion, although without reference to the Budzislawski-Eckert case.

27. Short biography of Thomas Eckert, in AdK, Hermann-Budzislawski-Archiv, no. 382.

28. He had told the Ministry of State Security that his aspirations were no longer compatible "with what is required of him by Socialist society," and this had deprived "his life in the GDR of any further meaning." See "Operational Information on the Person Thomas Eckert, 3 April 1987," 12–13.

29. Email from Gregor Gysi to the author, 15 October 2018. Further details in Juhnke, "Ein Turm," 66–67.

30. Juhnke, "Ein Turm," 67.

31. Diary of Ministry of State Security Officer Lohr with operational entries for 1981–86, in BStU, MfS HA XX/9 1637, 127.

32. "Beweise aus der Kladde," *Der Spiegel*, 29 May 1995, 22–24. See also Joachim Nawrocki, "Unter der Last der Beweise," *Die Zeit*, 16 June 1995, https://www.zeit.de /1995/25/Unter_der_Last_der_Beweise/komplettansicht.

33. Deutscher Bundestag, 13. Wahlperiode, *Bericht des Ausschusses für Wahlprüfung, Immunität und Geschäftsordnung (1. Ausschuß) zu dem Überprüfungsverfahren des Abgeordneten Dr. Gregor Gysi gemäß § 44b Abs.2 Abgeordnetengesetz, Berlin 1998*, Drucksache 13/10,893, 50, https://dserver.bundestag.de/btd/13/108/1310893.pdf.

34. "Urteil des 7. Zivilsenats des Hamburgischen Oberlandesgerichts vom 23. März 2010," Az. 7 U 95/09.

35. "Operational Information on the Person Thomas Eckert, 3 April 1987," 12–13; "Proposal for the implementation of a measure, 9 March 1984," in BStU, MfS, AP 13 671/92, 62.

36. "Operational Information on the Person Thomas Eckert, 3 April 1987," 12–13.

37. Ibid.

38. As indicated in Seebacher-Brandt, "Schwindel mit dem Etikett."

39. Dr. Rolf Harder of the GDR Academy of Arts to Professor Kurt Hagen, member of the Politburo and Secretary of the Central Committee of the SED, 11 March 1987, in BStU, MfS-BdL, no. 4022, 6–8.

40. However, according to information received but not checked by the Ministry of State Security, Eckert had been offered a sum of 400,000 marks by Rowohlt-Verlag "for the transfer of copyright." See "Vorschlag zur Durchführung einer Maßnahme, 9. März 1984," in BStU, MfS, AP 13 671/92, 62–65, here 64.

41. Contract between Peter Jacobsohn and the Athenäum Verlag GmbH, March 1978, in Privatarchiv Bernd F. Lunkewitz, Frankfurt am Main, BK-23.

42. "Operational Information on the Person Thomas Eckert, 3 April 1987," 12–13.

43. Author's conversation with Doris Eisermann and Barbara Felsmann in Berlin, 18 December 2018.

44. "Operational Information on the Person Thomas Eckert, 3 April 1987," 12–13.

45. Transfer agreement dated 27 January 1987 but without Thomas Eckert's signature, in BStU, MfS-BdL, no. 4022, 5.

46. Günter Heyden to Kurt Hager, 6 March 1987, in BStU, MfS-BdL, no. 4022, 2–3.

47. Author's telephone interview with Deborah Vietor-Engländer, 14 December 2014.

48. Jahnke, "Ein Turm," 75; information given to the author on the telephone by Christian Booß, Berlin, 15 May 2019.

49. As early as August 1983, only a few weeks after he had moved to West Berlin, he contacted the Athenäum Verlag, asking whether they were interested in continuing their 1978 reprint of the Berlin *Weltbühne* to include the issues of *Die neue Weltbühne* between 1933 and 1939. The publishers rejected the suggestion, officially because of profitability considerations but also, as is shown by internal documents, because they feared that a copyright dispute might arise between themselves and Peter Jacobsohn, on the one side, and the Budzislawski-Eckert family, on the other. On the way *Die Weltbühne* of the Weimar period was seen in the Federal Republic at that time, see Eggebrecht and Pinkerneil, *Das Drama der Republik*, a book that was only able to appear in 1979 after Peter Jacobsohn had given his explicit consent and was not least a journalistic form of self-protection against eventual claims from the GDR by the publishers of *Die Weltbühne* founded in East Berlin in 1946 (Thomas A. Eckert to the Athenäum Verlag, 3 August 1983, and Axel Rütters, Athenäum Verlag to Thomas A. Eckert, 10 November 1983 and 3 February 1986, all in Privatarchiv Axel Rütters, Hamburg).

50. In 1992 a complete reprint of *Die neue Weltbühne* was published by K. G. Saur Verlag, Munich, with the encouragement of Thomas Eckert. He contributed a brief preface, which mainly dealt with the legal aspect and the question of the journal's ownership. The reprint, which ran to more than ten thousand pages, was priced at 2,400 marks in bookshops. Eckert did not have to advance any money, but he did not receive any share in the profits, unlike Peter Jacobsohn, who had received money from Athenäum Verlag at the end of the 1970s. The republication of anti-Fascist exile journalism was an affair of the heart for the owner of the publishing house, Klaus G. Saur, not least because it allowed him, morally at any rate, to set something against the actions of his father, who had made a career under Albert Speer as a ruthless state secretary in the Ministry of Defense and was intended by Hitler to be Speer's successor (information given by Hans Bohrmann, Dortmund, to the author via email on 17 February 2019; telephone interview with Klaus G. Saur on 19 February 2019; Thomas A. Eckert to Doris Eisermann, 5 June 1991, in Privatarchiv Doris Eisermann, Berlin).

51. Since 1990 Eckert had been in contact with Hans Bohrmann, who was at that time the director of the Institute for Newspaper Research in Dortmund. In 1993 Bohrmann declared his readiness to supervise Thomas Eckert's doctoral dissertation about his grandfather. This made Bohrmann the third supervisor of a dissertation that would never be written. The first was Elisabeth Löckenhoff, who died in 1985, and the

second was Julius H. Schoeps, who was a professor at the University of Duisburg from 1974 to 1991 and later in Potsdam.

52. Seebacher-Brandt, "Schwindel mit dem Etikett"; Beate Eckert, "Gegendarstellung," *FAZ Magazin*, 16 July 1993.

53. Thomas A. Eckert to Doris Eisermann, 2 March 1993, in Privatarchiv Doris Eisermann, Berlin.

54. Copy of Robert Marx, a lawyer in Strasbourg, to Hans Bohrmann, 22 January 1995, in the author's private possession.

55. Author's telephone interview with Barbara Honigmann, Strasbourg, 8 April 2019.

56. Dr. Verena Blaum to Christian Schemmert, 25 August 2014, in the author's private possession; Geoffrey V. Davis and Deborah Vietor-Engländer, "Thomas Eckert gestorben," *Neuer Nachrichtenbrief der Gesellschaft für Exilforschung e. V.*, no. 5, June 1995, 5, http://www.exilforschung.de/_dateien/neuer-nachrichtenbrief/NNB_05.pdf.

57. Grant of probate by the Schöneberg District Court, reference number 60 VI 90/95, 18 April 1995, in Privatarchiv Doris Eisermann, Berlin.

58. Bernd F. Lunkewitz, "In eigener Sache," *Die Weltbühne*, 8 June 1993, 708–9.

59. "Es ist Zeit, wieder frech zu werden," *Der Tagesspiegel* (Berlin), 15 March 1992; see also Bernd F. Lunkewitz, "Wer schreit denn da?," in *Die Weltbühne im Wirbel der Wende: Eine Zeitschrift im Umbruch. Oktober 1989 bis Dezember 1991*, ed. Freundeskreis der Weltbühne e. V. (Berlin, 1992), 334–35. For the names of the "well-known personalities," see the settlement ruling of the Higher Regional Court in Frankfurt am Main in the case of *Jacobsohn v. Verlag der Weltbühne*, 18 June 1993, in Privatarchiv Bernd F. Lunkewitz, Frankfurt am Main.

60. Stefan Doernberg, "Eine Nation—zwei Staaten," *Die Weltbühne*, 2 January 1990, 9–11.

61. Wolfgang Klein, "Freie Wahl? Alles klar!," *Die Weltbühne*, 20 March 1990, 353–55; Manfred Lötsch, "Querdenken als Pflicht," *Die Weltbühne*, 3 July 1990, 833–35.

62. This view in relation to the currency union of 1 July 1990 was put forward in Hans Maibaum, "Abschied ohne Würde," *Die Weltbühne*, 3 July 1990, 833–35.

63. Horst Pöttker, "Deutsche Demokatische Potential," *Die Weltbühne*, 9 October 1990, 1332–34. A critical debate on the "self-indulgent bitterness" in *Die Weltbühne* of the Wende years was initiated by the Freiburg psychoanalyst Tilmann Moser at the end of 1991, although it did not result in any decisive changes in the journal's approach. See "Permanent gepflegte Bitterkeit," *Die Weltbühne*, 26 November 1991, 1511–15.

64. Heleno Saña, "Das Elend der deutschen Intellektuellen," *Die Weltbühne*, 29 September 1992, 1217–20.

65. Telephone interview with Matthias Wedel, on 28 January 2021, Berlin.

66. Jan Ross, "Die Schwierigkeit, Nostalgie zu vermeiden," *FAZ*, 17 March 1993, 37.

67. Peter Schiffer-Jacobsohn to Hermann Budzislawski, 3 January 1936, in AdK, Die neue Weltbühne I, no. 1, 148.

68. Information from an outline of Peter Jacobsohn's life dated March 1993, in Privatarchiv Bernd F. Lunkewitz, Frankfurt am Main, BK-19; Robert Winder, *Bloody Foreigners: The Story of Immigration to Britain* (London, 2013), 311–12.

69. Draft sale and transfer agreement between Lunkewitz and Jacobsohn, in Privatarchiv Bernd F. Lunkewitz, Frankfurt am Main.

70. A point also made in "Die Weltbühne schließt," *FAZ*, 3 July 1993, 28.

71. Deutscher Bundestag, 13. Wahlperiode, *Bericht der Unabhängigen Kommission zur Überprüfung des Vermögens der Parteien und Massenorganisationen der DDR*, 178–79. Lunkewitz has been litigating for years against the Trust Agency and its legal successor, the Federal Agency for Special Assignments Related to Unification; he has put forward his own position in the book *Der Aufbau-Verlag und die kriminelle Vereinigung in der SED und der Treuhandanstalt* (Munich, 2021).

72. Bernd F. Lunkewitz, "Persönliche Erklärung des Gesellschafters der Verlag der Weltbühne GmbH," *Die Weltbühne*, 6 July 1993, 833; Lunkewitz, "In eigener Sache," 709; "Kommentar des Herausgebers Helmut Reinhardt," *Die Weltbühne*, 6 July 1993, 833.

73. I do not examine here the subsequent history of the two journals *Ossietzky* and *Das Blättchen*, founded in 1997, both of which saw and still see themselves as continuing the tradition of *Die Weltbühne*.

Bibliography

Archives

Archiv der Akademie der Künste—Literaturarchiv, Berlin (AdK)
Archiv für Zeitgeschichte, ETH Zürich
Bibliotop der Universität Leipzig (Bibliotop)
Bundesarchiv Berlin (BArch Berlin)
Carl von Ossietzky University, Oldenburg
Center for Jewish History, New York
Der Bundesbeauftragte für die Unterlagen des Staatssicherheitsdienstes der ehemaligen Deutschen Demokratischen Republik (BStU)
Deutsche Nationalbibliothek, Frankfurt am Main (DNB)
Deutsches Literaturarchiv, Marbach (DLA)
Deutsches Rundfunkarchiv, Standort Potsdam-Babelsberg (DRA)
Institut für Zeitgeschichte, Munich (IfZ)
International Institute of Social History, Amsterdam (IISH)
Landesarchiv Berlin (LAB)
Leibniz-Zentrum für Zeithistorische Forschung, Potsdam (ZZF)
Leo Baeck Institute, Center for Jewish History, New York (LBI)
National Archives and Records Administration, College Park, MD (NARA)
National Archives of India
New York Public Library (NYPL)
Ohio State University—University Libraries, Rare Books and Manuscripts Library (OSU)
Privatarchiv Gottfried Braun, Leipzig
Privatarchiv Doris Eisermann, Berlin
Privatarchiv Bernd F. Lunkewitz, Frankfurt am Main
Privatarchiv Axel Rütters, Hamburg
Privatarchiv Daniel Siemens, Newcastle upon Tyne
Privatarchiv Bettina Theek, Berlin
Russian State Archive of Literature and Art, Moscow (RGALI)
Sächsisches Staatsarchiv Leipzig
Schweizerisches Bundesarchiv, Bern (SBB)

Syracuse University Libraries, Special Collections, Research Center (SCRC)
Tschechisches Nationalarchiv Prag (TNP)
Universitätsarchiv der Eberhard Karls Universität Tübingen (UAT)
Universitätsarchiv der Universität Leipzig (UAL)
University at Albany, SUNY / M. E. Grenander Department of Special Collections &
    Archives (SUNY Archive)
Walter A. Berendsohn Forschungsstelle für deutsche Exilliteratur, Hamburg
Yivo Archives, New York
Zentral- und Landesbibliothek Berlin (ZLB)

Literature

Newspaper and journal articles from the 1920s to the 1970s are only listed here in exceptional cases, but they are always fully referenced in the notes.

Aitken, Robbie. "From Cameroon to Germany and Back via Moscow and Paris: The Political Career of Joseph Bilé (1892–1959), Performer, 'Negerarbeiter' and Comintern Activist." *Journal of Contemporary History* 43, no. 4 (2008): 597–616.
Altenhöner, Florian. *Der Mann, der den zweiten Weltkrieg begann: Alfred Naujocks, Fälscher, Mörder, Terrorist.* Münster, 2010.
Anderson, Edith. *Der Beobachter sieht nichts: Ein Tagebuch zweier Welten.* Berlin, 1972.
Anderson, Edith. *Liebe in Exil: Erinnerungen einer amerikanischen Schriftstellerin an das Berlin der Nachkriegszeit.* Berlin, 2007.
Antonello, Anna. *"Die Weltbühne" als Bühne der Welt: Politik und Literatur im Spiegel einer deutschen Zeitschrift (1918–1933).* Berlin, 2007.
Autorenkollektiv unter Leitung von Miroslav Beck und Jiři Veselý, ed. *Exil und Asyl: Antifaschistische deutsche Literatur in der Tschechoslowakei 1933–1938.* Berlin, 1981.
Bachmann, Jörg J. *Zwischen Paris und Moskau: Deutsche bürgerliche Linksintellektuelle und die stalinistische Sowjetunion 1933–1939.* Mannheim, 1993.
Balachandran, Vappala. *A Life in Shadow: The Secret Story of ACN Nambiar, a Forgotten Anti-colonial Warrior.* New Delhi, 2016.
Barck, Simone. "Ein altes und jederzeit junges Blatt: 'Die Weltbühne' in der DDR. Ein Gespräch mit Ursula Madrasch-Groschopp." *Deutschland Archiv* 34, no. 2 (2001): 258–68.
Barck, Simone. "Internationale Vereinigung Revolutionärer Schriftsteller." In *Lexikon sozialistischer Literatur: Ihre Geschichte in Deutschland bis 1945*, edited by Simone Barck et al., 223–26. Stuttgart, 1994.
Barck, Simone. "Zur Spezifik des deutschen literarischen Exils in der Sowjetunion unter kommunikationsgeschichtlichem Aspekt." In *Kommunisten verfolgen Kommunisten: Stalinistischer Terror und "Säuberungen" in den kommunistischen Parteien Europas seit den dreißiger Jahren*, edited by Hermann Weber and Dietrich Staritz, 318–26. Berlin, 1993.
Barck, Simone, Martina Langermann, and Siegfried Lokatis, eds. *Zwischen "Mosaik" und "Einheit": Zeitschriften in der DDR.* Berlin, 1999.
Barck, Simone, Silvia Schlenstedt, Tanja Bürgel, Volker Giel, Dieter Schiller, and Reinhard Hillich, eds. *Lexikon sozialistischer Literatur: Ihre Geschichte in Deutschland bis 1945.* Stuttgart, 1994.

Barth, Bernd-Rainer. "Budzislawski, Hermann." In *Wer war wer in der DDR?* https://www.bundesstiftung-aufarbeitung.de/de/recherche/kataloge-datenbanken/bio graphische-datenbanken/hermann-budzislawski.

Barth, Bernd-Rainer. "Theek, Peter." In *Wer war wer in der DDR?* https://www.bundesstiftung-aufarbeitung.de/de/recherche/kataloge-datenbanken/biographische-datenbanken/peter-theek.

Bashford, Alison, and Philippa Levine, eds. *The Oxford Handbook of the History of Eugenics.* Oxford, 2010.

Baumeister, Martin, Moritz Föllmer, and Philipp Müller, eds. *Die Kunst der Geschichte: Historiographie, Ästhetik, Erzählung.* Göttingen, 2009.

Bayerlein, Bernhard H. *"Der Verräter, Stalin, bist Du!": Vom Ende der linken Solidarität. Komintern und kommunistische Parteien im Zweiten Weltkrieg 1939–1941.* Berlin, 2008.

Bayerlein, Bernhard H. "Kein Antifaschismus ohne Antistalinismus: Willi Münzenberg, 'Die Zukunft' und die antistalinistische Wende in der deutschsprachigen Emigration 1935–1940." In *Global Spaces for Radical Transnational Solidarity: Beiträge zum Ersten Internationalen Willi-Münzenberg-Kongress 2015 in Berlin,* edited by Bernhard H. Bayerlein, Kasper Braskén, and Uwe Sonnenberg, 218–70. Berlin, 2018.

Bayerlein, Bernhard H. "Willi Münzenberg's 'Last Empire': Die Zukunft and the 'Franco-German Union,' Paris, 1938–1940; New Visions of Anti-Fascism and the Transnational Networks of the Anti-Hitler Resistance." *Moving the Social* 58 (2017): 51–80.

Bayerlein, Bernhard H., Kasper Braskén, and Uwe Sonnenberg, eds. *Global Spaces for Radical Transnational Solidarity: Beiträge zum Ersten Internationalen Willi-Münzenberg-Kongress 2015 in Berlin.* Berlin, 2018.

Becher, Peter. "Exil und Exil-Literatur in der Tschechoslowakei." In *Handbuch der deutschen Literatur Prags und der Böhmischen Länder,* edited by Peter Becher, 235–41. Stuttgart, 2017.

Becher, Peter, Steffen Höhne, Jörg Krappmann, and Manfred Weinberg, eds. *Handbuch der deutschen Literatur Prags und der Böhmischen Länder.* Stuttgart, 2017.

Behling, Klaus. *Spur der Scheine: Wie das Vermögen der SED verschwand.* Berlin, 2019.

Benz, Wolfgang, ed. *Antisemitismus in der DDR: Manifestationen und Folgen des Feindbildes Israel.* Berlin, 2018.

Berger, Stefan, and Norman Laporte. *Friendly Enemies: Britain and the GDR, 1949–1990.* London, 2010.

Betts, Paul. *Ruin and Renewal: Civilising Europe after the Second World War.* London, 2020.

Binding, Karl, and Alfred Hoche. *Die Freigabe der Vernichtung lebensunwerten Lebens. Ihr Maß und ihre Form.* Leipzig, 1920.

Biquard, Pierre. "Nachruf auf Hermann Budzislawski." *Wissenschaftliche Welt* 22, no. 2 (1978): 33.

Bischof, Ulf. *Die Kunst und Antiquitäten GmbH im Bereich Kommerzielle Koordinierung.* Berlin, 2003.

Blatman, Daniel. *Die Todesmärsche: Das letzte Kapitel des nationalsozialistischen Massenmords.* Reinbek bei Hamburg, 2001.

Blaum, Verena. "Budzislawski: Sozialistische Journalistik." In *Schlüsselwerke für die Kommunikationswissenschaft*, edited by Christina Holtz-Bacha and Arnulf Kutsch, 83–85. Opladen, 2002.

Blecher, Jens, and Gerald Wiemers, eds. *Studentischer Widerstand an den mitteldeutschen Universitäten 1945 bis 1955: Von der Universität in den GULAG. Studentenschicksale in sowjetischen Straflagern 1945–1955.* Leipzig, 2005.

Bloch, Karola. *Aus meinem Leben.* Pfullingen, 1981.

Blutke, Günter. *Obskure Geschäfte mit Kunst und Antiquitäten: Ein Kriminalreport.* 2nd ed. Berlin, 1994.

Boll, Monika, and Raphael Gross, eds. *"Ich staune, dass Sie in dieser Luft atmen können": Jüdische Intellektuelle in Deutschland nach 1945.* Frankfurt am Main, 2013.

Bösch, Frank, and Andreas Wirsching, eds. *Hüter der Ordnung: Die Innenministerien in Bonn und Ost-Berlin nach dem Nationalsozialismus.* Göttingen, 2018.

Botsch, Gideon. *Die extreme Rechte in der Bundesrepublik Deutschland, 1949 bis heute.* Bonn, 2012.

Brandenberger, David. "Stalin's Last Crime? Recent Scholarship on Postwar Soviet Antisemitism and the Doctor's Plot." *Kritika: Explorations in Russian and Eurasian History* 6, no. 1 (2005): 187–204.

Braskén, Kasper. "'Whether Black or White—United in the Fight!': Connecting the Resistance against Colonialism, Racism, and Fascism in the European Metropoles, 1926–1936." *Twentieth Century Communism: A Journal of International History* 18, no. 18 (2020): 126–49.

Braune, Andreas, and Michael Dreyer, eds. *Zusammenbruch, Aufbruch, Abbruch? Die Novemberrevolution als Ereignis und Erinnerungsort.* Stuttgart, 2018.

Brenner, Michael, ed. *A History of Jews in Germany since 1945: Politics, Culture and Society.* Bloomington, IN, 2018.

Brenner, Michael, and Gideon Reuveni, eds. *Emanzipation durch Muskelkraft: Juden und Sport in Europa.* Göttingen, 2006.

Brodersen, Momme. *Klassenbild mit Walter Benjamin: Eine Spurensuche.* Munich, 2012.

Brückenhaus, Daniel. *Policing Transnational Protest: Liberal Imperialism and the Surveillance of Anticolonialism in Europe, 1905–1945.* Oxford, 2017.

Bruhn, Heinrich. "Hermann Budzislawski: Zu seinem sechzigsten Geburtstag." *Zeitschrift für Journalistik* 2, no. 1 (1961): 1–5.

Brunner, Detlev. "DDR 'transnational': Die 'internationale Solidarität' der DDR." In *Deutsche Zeitgeschichte—transnational*, edited by Alexander Gallus, Axel Schildt, and Detlef Siegfried, 64–80. Göttingen, 2015.

Buck, Hansjörg F. "Öffentliche Finanzwirtschaft im SED-Staat und ihre Transformationsprobleme." In *Materialien der Enquete-Kommission "Überwindung der Folgen der SED-Diktatur im Prozess der deutschen Einheit."* Deutscher Bundestag, 13. Wahlperiode, III/2:975–1267. Bonn, 1998.

Budzislawski, Hermann. "Eugenik: Ein Beitrag zur Ökonomie der menschlichen Erbanlagen." PhD diss., Tübingen University, 1923.

Budzislawski, Hermann. "Heimkehr." *Ost und West* 10 (October 1948): 42–45.

Budzislawski, Hermann. *Sozialistische Journalistik: Eine wissenschaftliche Einführung.* Leipzig, 1966.

Čapková, Kateřina. "Zuflucht für Prominente: Die Tschechoslowakei und ihre Flüchtlinge aus NS-Deutschland und Österreich." *Stifter Jahrbuch*, n.s., 29 (2015): 143–60.

Christ, Richard. *Der Tag, die Nacht und ich dazwischen*. Rostock, 2001.

Classen, Christoph. "DDR-Medien im Spannungsfeld von Gesellschaft und Politik." In *Wie im Westen, nur anders: Medien in der DDR*, edited by Stefan Zahlmann, 385–407. Berlin, 2010.

Clemens, Diane. *From Isolationism to Internationalism: The Case Study of American Occupation Planning for Post-war Germany, 1945–1946*. Berkeley, CA, 1993.

Clochard, Olivier, Yvan Gastaut, and Ralph Schor. "Les camps d'étrangers depuis 1938: Continuité et adaptations. Du 'modèle' français à la construction de l'espace Schengen." *Revue Européenne des Migrations Internationales* 20, no. 2 (2004): 57–87. http://remi.revues.org/968.

Cornelißen, Christoph, and Dirk van Laak, eds. *Weimar und die Welt: Globale Verflechtungen der ersten deutschen Republik*. Göttingen, 2020.

Dahrendorf, Ralf. *Versuchungen der Unfreiheit: Die Intellektuellen in Zeiten der Prüfung*. Munich, 2006.

Danzer, Doris. *Zwischen Vertrauen und Verrat: Deutschsprachige kommunistische Intellektuelle und ihre sozialen Beziehungen (1918–1960)*. Göttingen, 2012.

Danziger, Carl-Jacob (Joachim Chaim Schwarz). *"Die Partei hat immer recht": Autobiographischer Roman*. Frankfurt am Main, 2015.

Deák, István. *Weimar Germany's Left-Wing Intellectuals: A Political History of the Weltbühne and Its Circle*. Berkeley, CA, 1968.

Demshuk, Andrew. *Demolition on Karl Marx Square: Cultural Barbarism and the People's State in 1968*. Oxford, 2017.

Depkat, Volker. "The Challenges of Biography: European-American Reflections." *Bulletin of the GHI* 55 (2014): 39–48.

Deutscher Bundestag, 13. Wahlperiode. *Bericht der Unabhängigen Kommission zur Überprüfung des Vermögens der Parteien und Massenorganisationen der DDR über das Vermögen der Sozialistischen Einheitspartei Deutschlands (SED) jetzt: Partei des Demokratischen Sozialismus (PDS), des Freien Deutschen Gewerkschaftsbunds (FDGB), der sonstigen politischen Organisationen und Stellungnahme der Bundesregierung, 24. August 1998, Berlin 1998*. Drucksache 13/11,353. https://dserver.bundestag.de/btd/13/113/1311353.pdf.

Deutscher Bundestag, 13. Wahlperiode. *Bericht des Ausschusses für Wahlprüfung, Immunität und Geschäftsordnung (1. Ausschuß) zu dem Überprüfungsverfahren des Abgeordneten Dr. Gregor Gysi gemäß § 44b Abs. 2 Abgeordnetengesetz, Berlin 1998*. Drucksache 13/10,893. https://dserver.bundestag.de/btd/13/108/1310893.pdf.

Deutscher Bundestag, 13. Wahlperiode. *Materialien der Enquete-Kommission "Überwindung der Folgen der SED-Diktatur im Prozess der deutschen Einheit."* Vol. III/2. Bonn, 1998.

Devine, Thomas W. *Henry Wallace's 1948 Presidential Campaign and the Future of Post-war Liberalism*. Chapel Hill, NC, 2013.

Dietrich, Gerd. *Kulturgeschichte der DDR, Teil 2: Kultur in der Bildungsgesellschaft 1957–1976*. Göttingen, 2018.

Dinkel, Jürgen. "Erben und vererben in der Moderne: Erkundungen eines Forschungsfeld." *Archiv für Sozialgeschichte* 56 (2016): 81–108.

Dinkel, Jürgen. "'Mecca of Oriental Patriots': Antikolonialismus in Deutschland 1900–1960." In *Weimar und die Welt: Globale Verflechtungen der ersten deutschen Republik*, edited by Christoph Cornelißen and Dirk van Laak, 53–88. Göttingen, 2020.

Düring, Marten, Ulrich Eumann, Martin Stark, and Linda von Keyserlingk, eds. *Handbuch Historische Netzwerkforschung: Grundlagen und Anwendungen*. Münster, 2016.

Durzak, Manfred. "Die Exilsituation in den USA." In *Die deutsche Exilliteratur 1933–1945*, edited by Manfred Durzak, 145–58. Stuttgart, 1973.

Durzak, Manfred, ed. *Die deutsche Exilliteratur 1933–1945*. Stuttgart, 1973.

Eberl, Immo, and Helmut Marcon. *150 Jahre Promotion an der Wirtschaftswissenschaftlichen Fakultät der Universität Tübingen: Biographien d. Doktoren u. Ehrendoktoren 1830–1980*. Im Auftrag der Wirtschaftswissenschaftlichen Fakultät der Universität Tübingen. Stuttgart, 1984.

Eckert, Horst. "Die Beiträge der deutschen emigrierten Schriftsteller in der 'Neuen Weltbühne' von 1934–1939: Ein Beitrag zur Untersuchung der Beziehungen zwischen Volksfrontpolitik und Literatur." PhD diss., Humboldt University, Berlin, 1962.

Eggebrecht, Axel, and Dietrich Pinkernell. *Das Drama der Republik: Zum Neudruck der Weltbühne*. Frankfurt am Main, 1979.

Ehmer, Hermann. "Löwenstein, Hubertus." In *Neue Deutsche Biographie*, 15:100–101. Berlin, 1987.

Ehrlich, Lothar, and Gunther Mai, eds. *Weimarer Klassik in der Ära Ulbricht*. Cologne, 2000.

Engelhardt, Ulrich. *"Bildungsbürgertum": Begriffs- und Dogmengeschichte eines Etiketts*. Stuttgart, 1986.

Engelmann, Bernt. *Großes Bundesverdienstkreuz mit Stern*. Göttingen, 1987.

Enseling, Alfons. *Die Weltbühne: Organ der intellektuellen Linken*. Münster, 1962.

Epstein, Catherine. *The Last Revolutionaries: German Communists and Their Century*. Cambridge, MA, 2003.

Epstein, Catherine. "'The Production of Official Memory' in East Germany: Old Communists and the Dilemmas of Memoir-Writing." *Central European History* 32, no. 2 (1999): 181–201.

Erben, Dietrich, and Tobias Zervosen, eds. *Das eigene Leben als ästhetische Fiktion: Autobiographie und Professionsgeschichte*. Bielefeld, 2018.

Erpenbeck, Fritz. *Emigranten*. Berlin, 1954.

Eschwege, Helmut. "Auswirkungen des Stalinismus auf die Juden der DDR von 1945 bis 1957." In *Kommunisten verfolgen Kommunisten: Stalinistischer Terror und "Säuberungen" in den kommunistischen Parteien Europas seit den dreißiger Jahren*, edited by Hermann Weber and Dietrich Staritz, 507–21. Berlin, 1993.

Eschwege, Helmut. *Fremd unter meinesgleichen: Erinnerungen eines Dresdner Juden*. Berlin, 1991.

Fair-Schulz, Axel. *Loyal Subversion: East Germany and Its Bildungsbürgerlich Marxist Intellectuals*. Berlin, 2009.

Fakultät für Journalistik der Karl-Marx-Universität, ed. *Journalismus und Gesellschaft: Hermann Budzislawski zum 65. Geburtstag*. Leipzig, 1966.

Fittko, Lisa. *Solidarität unerwünscht: Meine Flucht durch Europa. Erinnerungen 1933–1940.* Munich, 1992.

Flake, Otto. *Das Ende der Revolution.* Berlin, 1920.

Foitzik, Jan. "Remigranten in der Medienpolitik der sowjetischen Besatzungsmacht." In *Zwischen den Stühlen? Remigranten und Remigration in der deutschen Medienöffentlichkeit der Nachkriegszeit,* edited by Claus-Dieter Krohn and Axel Schildt, 93–113. Hamburg, 2002.

Forner, Sean. *German Intellectuals and the Challenge of Democratic Renewal: Culture and Politics after 1945.* Cambridge, 2014.

Forschungsgruppe Deutsche Exil-Literatur in der CSR. "Zur Frage der deutschen antifaschistischen Emigration in der CSR 1933–1939." *Philologica Pragensia* 18, no. 1 (1975): 4–24.

Fraenkel, Jonathan, and Dan Diner, eds. *Dark Times, Dire Decisions: Jews and Communism.* New York, 2004.

Franke, Julia. "De véritable 'boches': Französische und emigrierte deutsche Juden im Paris der dreißiger Jahre." In *Jüdische Emigration zwischen Assimilation und Verfolgung: Akkulturation und jüdischer Identität,* edited by Claus-Dieter Krohn, Erwin Rotermund, Luz Winckler, Irmtrud Wojak, and Wulf Koepke, 80–105. Munich, 2001.

Freundeskreis der Weltbühne e. V., ed. *Die Weltbühne im Wirbel der Wende: Eine Zeitschrift im Umbruch. Oktober 1989 bis Dezember 1991.* Berlin, 1992.

Freyberg, Jutta von. *Sozialdemokraten und Kommunisten: Die Revolutionären Sozialisten Deutschlands vor dem Problem der Aktionseinheit 1934–1937.* Cologne, 1973.

Friedlander, Judith. *Vilna on the Seine: Jewish Intellectuals in France since 1968.* New Haven, CT, 1990.

Friedrichs, Anne. "Placing Migration in Perspective: Neue Wege einer relationalen Geschichtsschreibung." *Geschichte und Gesellschaft* 44, no. 2 (2018): 167–95.

Fritzsche, Peter. "Vagabond in the Fugitive City: Hans Ostwald, Imperial Berlin and the Grossstadt-Dokumente." *Journal of Contemporary History* 29, no. 3 (1994): 385–402.

Gailus, Manfred, and Daniel Siemens, eds. *"Hass und Begeisterung bilden Spalier": Horst Wessels politische Autobiographie.* Berlin, 2011.

Gallus, Alexander. *Heimat "Weltbühne": Eine Intellektuellengeschichte im 20. Jahrhundert.* Göttingen, 2012.

Gallus, Alexander, Axel Schildt, and Detlef Siegfried, eds. *Deutsche Zeitgeschichte—transnational.* Göttingen, 2015.

Gaupp, Robert Eugen. *Unfruchtbarmachung geistig und sittlich Kranker und Minderwertiger: Erweitertes Referat, erstattet auf der Jahresversammlung des Deutschen Vereins für Psychiatrie am 2. September 1925 in Kassel.* Berlin, 1925.

Gebhardt, Manfred. *Die Nackte unterm Ladentisch: Das Magazin in der DDR.* Berlin, 2002.

Gerber, Jan. *Ein Prozess in Prag: Das Volk gegen Rudolf Slánský und Genossen.* Göttingen, 2016.

Gieseke, Jens. "Soziale Ungleichheit im Staatssozialismus: Eine Skizze." *Zeithistorische Forschungen / Studies in Contemporary History* 10, no. 2 (2013): 173–98.

Glade, Henry. "Carl Zuckmayer." In *Deutschsprachige Exilliteratur seit 1933,* edited by John M. Spalek and Joseph Strelka, 2:1043–56. Bern, 1989.

Goebbels, Joseph. *Die Tagebücher von Joseph Goebbels*. Issued under the authority of the Institut für Zeitgeschichte and with the assistance of the Russian State Archive Service. Edited by Elke Fröhlich. Pt. 1, *Aufzeichnungen 1923–1941*, vol. 6, *August 1938 to June 1939*. Munich, 1998.

Goertz, Hans-Jürgen, ed. *Geschichte: Ein Grundkurs*. Reinbek bei Hamburg, 1998.

Gordon, Adi. "Widersprüchliche Zugehörigkeiten: Arnold Zweig in Ostdeutschland." In *"Ich staune, dass Sie in dieser Luft atmen können": Jüdische Intellektuelle in Deutschland nach 1945*, edited by Monika Boll and Raphael Gross, 171–204. Frankfurt am Main, 2013.

Goschler, Constantin. *Schuld und Schulden: Die Politik der Wiedergutmachung für NS-Verfolgte seit 1945*. Göttingen, 2008.

Großbölting, Thomas. *SED-Diktatur und Gesellschaft: Bürgertum, Bürgerlichkeit und Entbürgerlichung in Magdeburg und Halle*. Halle an der Saale, 2001.

Grossman, Atina, and Tamar Levinsky. "1945–1949: Way Station." In *A History of Jews in Germany Since 1945: Politics, Culture and Society*, edited by Michael Brenner, 55–84. Bloomington, IN, 2018.

Grossman, Victor (Stephen Wechsler). *Crossing the River: A Memoir of the American Left, the Cold War, and Life in East Germany*. Boston, 2003.

Grunewald, Manfred, ed. *Le milieu intellectual de gauche en Allemagne, sa presse et ses réseaux (1890–1960) / Das linke Intellektuellenmilieu in Deutschland, seine Presse und seine Netzwerke (1890–1960)*. Bern, 2002.

Grüttner, Michael. *Studenten im Dritten Reich*. Paderborn, 1995.

Günther, Georg, and Reiner Nägele, eds. *Musik in Baden-Württemberg: Jahrbuch 1998*. Vol. 5. Stuttgart, 1998.

Habel, Frank-Burkhard. "*Weltbühne*-Autoren der Weimarer Republik und ihr geistiger Einfluss auf die *Weltbühne* ab 1946." In *"Verirrte Bürger"? Kurt Tucholsky und der Weltbühne-Kreis zwischen Bürgertum und Arbeiterbewegung*, edited by Kurt Tucholsky-Gesellschaft and Ian King, 48–67. Leipzig, 2016.

Haffner, Sebastian. *Defying Hitler: A Memoir*. Translated by Oliver Pretzel. London, 2003.

Haffner, Sebastian. *Geschichte eines Deutschen: Die Erinnerungen 1914–1933*. Stuttgart, 2000.

Harders, Levke. "Migration und Biographie: Mobile Leben beschreiben." *Österreichische Zeitschrift für Geschichtswissenschaften* 29, no. 3 (2018): 17–36.

Hardtwig, Wolfgang. "Formen der Geschichtsschreibung: Varianten des historischen Erzählens." In *Geschichte: Ein Grundkurs*, edited by Hans-Jürgen Goertz, 169–88. Reinbek bei Hamburg, 1998.

Hardy, Frank J. *Macht ohne Ruhm*. 2 vols. Berlin, 1955.

Hartewig, Karin. "A German Jewish Communist of the Second Generation: The Changing Personae of Klaus Gysi." In *Dark Times, Dire Decisions: Jews and Communism*, edited by Jonathan Fraenkel and Dan Diner, 255–71. New York, 2004.

Hartewig, Karin. *Zurückgekehrt: Die Geschichte der jüdischen Kommunisten in der DDR*. Cologne, 2000.

Hartmann, Anne, and Wolfram Eggeling. *Sowjetische Präsenz im kulturellen Leben der SBZ und der frühen DDR 1945–1953*. Berlin, 1998.

Haubl, Rolf. "Autobiographisches Erzählen: Sprechen und Schreiben." In *Das eigene Leben als ästhetische Fiktion: Autobiographie und Professionsgeschichte*, edited by Dietrich Erben and Tobias Zervosen, 333–46. Bielefeld, 2018.

Haury, Thomas. *Antisemitismus von links: Kommunistische Ideologie, Nationalismus und Antizionismus in der frühen DDR*. Hamburg, 2002.

Heintz, Georg. *Deutsches Exil 1933–1945*. Vol. 1, *Index der "Neuen Weltbühne" von 1933–39*. Wiesbaden, 1982.

Herf, Geffrey. *Undeclared Wars with Israel: East Germany and the West German Far Left, 1967–1989*. New York, 2016.

Heym, Stefan. *Nachruf*. Munich, 2018.

Hiller, Kurt. *Rote Ritter: Erlebnisse mit deutschen Kommunisten*. Afterword by Eugen M. Brehm. Berlin, 1980.

Höpcke, Klaus. "Lehrer-Persönlichkeiten an der Fakultät für Journalistik." In *Universität im Aufbruch—Leipzig 1945–1956: Beiträge des siebenten Walter-Markov-Kolloquiums*, edited by Manfred Neuhaus and and Helmut Seidel, 140–44. Leipzig, 2002.

Hoff, Henning. *Großbritannien und die DDR 1955–1973: Diplomatie auf Umwegen*. Munich, 2003.

Holtz-Bacha, Christina, and Arnulf Kutsch, eds. *Schlüsselwerke für die Kommunikationswissenschaft*. Opladen, 2002.

Honigmann, Barbara. *Georg*. Munich, 2019.

Horn, Gerd-Rainer. *European Socialists Respond to Fascism: Ideology, Activism and Contingency in the 1930s*. New York, 1996.

Hosfeld, Rolf. *Tucholsky: Ein deutsches Leben*. Munich, 2012.

Huß-Michel, Angela. *Literarische und politische Zeitschriften des Exils 1933–1945*. Stuttgart, 1987.

Jacoby, Henry. *Davongekommen: 10 Jahre Exil 1936–1946. Prag, Paris, Montauban, New York, Washington. Erlebnisse und Begegnungen*. Frankfurt am Main, 1982.

Jacoby, Henry. *Von des Kaisers Schule zu Hitlers Zuchthaus: Erlebnisse und Begegnungen. Geschichte einer Jugend links-außen in der Weimarer Republik*. Frankfurt am Main, 1980.

Jahn, Jürgen, ed. *Ernst Bloch / Wieland Herzfelde, "Wir haben das Leben wieder vor uns": Briefwechsel 1938–1949*. Frankfurt am Main, 2001.

Jarmatz, Klaus, Simone Barck, and Peter Diesel. *Exil in der UdSSR*. Leipzig, 1979.

Jedraszczyk, Jochen. "Entideologisierung—Rekonstruktion—Re-Ideologisierung: Leipziger publizistik- und zeitungswissenschaftliche Einrichtungen 1945 bis 1952." In *Die Entdeckung der Kommunikationswissenschaft: 100 Jahre kommunikationswissenschaftliche Fachtradition in Leipzig. Von der Zeitungskunde zur Kommunikations- und Medienwissenschaft*, edited by Erik Koenen, 155–84. Cologne, 2016.

Jessen, Ralph. *Akademische Elite und kommunistische Diktatur: Die ostdeutsche Hochschullehrerschaft in der Ulbricht-Ära*. Göttingen, 1999.

Jessen, Ralph. "'Bildungsbürger,' 'Experten,' 'Intelligenz': Kontinuität und Wandel der ostdeutschen Bildungsschichten in der Ulbricht-Ära." In *Weimarer Klassik in der Ära Ulbricht*, edited by Lothar Ehrlich and Gunther Mai, 113–34. Cologne, 2000.

Judt, Matthias. *Der Bereich Kommerzielle Koordinierung: Das DDR-Wirtschaftsimperium des Alexander Schalck-Golodkowski—Mythos und Realität*. Berlin, 2013.

Juhnke, Andreas. "Ein Turm in der Schlacht um die Weltbühne: Familiendrama mit Ossietzky, Brecht und Gysi in den Nebenrollen." *TransAtlantik* 12 (1990): 65–75.

Juhnke, Andreas. "Operation Erbe." *Manager Magazin* 3 (1993): 256–70.

Kaethner, Hans-Georg. *Mit 100 DM nach Persien und lebendig zurück: Zwei Ossis in Nahost*. Munich, 2015.

Kantorowicz, Alfred. *Deutsches Tagebuch II*. West-Berlin, 1979.

Kantorowicz, Alfred. *Im 2. Drittel unseres Jahrhunderts: Illusionen, Irrtümer, Widersprüche, Einsichten, Voraussichten*. Cologne, 1967.

Kantorowicz, Alfred. *Nachtbücher: Aufzeichnungen im französischen Exil 1935 bis 1939*. Edited by Ursula Büttner and Angelika Voß. Hamburg, 1995.

Kaplan, Marion. "Festrede." In *50 Jahre—50 Quellen: Festschrift zum Jubiläum des Instituts für die Geschichte der deutschen Juden*, edited by Institut für die Geschichte der deutschen Juden, 16–25. Hamburg, 2016.

Kater, Michael H. *Studentenschaft und Rechtsradikalismus in Deutschland 1918–1933: Eine sozialgeschichtliche Studie zur Bildungskrise in der Weimarer Republik*. Hamburg, 1975.

Kebir, Sabine. *Abstieg in den Ruhm: Helene Weigel. Eine Biographie*. Berlin, 2000.

Keller, Sven. *Volksgemeinschaft am Ende: Gesellschaft und Gewalt 1944/45*. Munich, 2013.

Keßler, Mario. *Albert Schreiner: Kommunist mit Lebensbrüchen*. Berlin, 2004.

Keßler, Mario. "Anti-Semitism in East Germany, 1952–1953: Denial to the End." In *Unlikely History: The Changing German-Jewish Symbiosis, 1945–2000*, edited by Leslie Morris and Jack Zipes, 141–54. New York, 2002.

Keßler, Mario. *Die SED und die Juden—zwischen Repression und Toleranz: Politische Entwicklungen bis 1967*. Berlin, 1995.

Keßler, Mario. *Ruth Fischer: Ein Leben mit und gegen Kommunisten (1895–1961)*. Cologne, 2013.

Keßler, Mario. *Westemigranten: Deutsche Kommunisten zwischen USA-Exil und DDR*. Cologne, 2018.

Keun, Irmgard. *Gilgi, eine von uns*. Berlin, 1931.

Kiesel, Helmuth. "Die literarische Verarbeitung der Novemberrevolution in der Weimarer Republik." In *Zusammenbruch, Aufbruch, Abbruch? Die Novemberrevolution als Ereignis und Erinnerungsort*, edited by Andreas Braune and Michael Dreyer, 249–69. Stuttgart, 2018.

Kießling, Wolfgang. *Partner im Narrenparadies: Der Freundeskreis um Paul Merker und Noel Field*. Berlin, 1994.

Kirschnick, Sylke. "Republikanismus aus Alternativlosigkeit: Zum Demokratiedenken Gabriele Tergits." In *Vernunftrepublikanismus in der Weimarer Republik: Politik, Literatur, Wissenschaft*, edited by Matthias Weipert and Andreas Wirsching, 311–21. Stuttgart, 2008.

Klein, Anne. *Flüchtlingspolitik und Flüchtlingshilfe 1940–1942: Varian Fry und die Komitees zur Rettung politisch Verfolgter in New York und Marseille*. Berlin, 2007.

Klein, Fritz. "Die Neugründung der Weltbühne in der Sowjetischen Besatzungszone." In *Le milieu intellectual de gauche en Allemagne, sa presse et ses réseaux (1890–1960) / Das linke Intellektuellenmilieu in Deutschland, seine Presse und seine Netzwerke (1890–1960)*, edited by Manfred Grunewald, 559–75. Bern, 2002.

Klein, Thomas. *"Für die Einheit und Reinheit der Partei": Die innerparteilichen Kontrollorgane der SED in der Ära Ulbricht*. Cologne, 2002.

Klemperer, Victor. *LTI—Lingua Tertii Imperii: Notizbuch eines Philologen*. Berlin, 1947.

Klemperer, Victor. *So sitze ich den zwischen allen Stühlen: Tagebücher 1945–1949.* 2 vols. Edited by Walter Nowojowski in association with Christian Löser. Berlin, 1999.

Klemperer, Victor. *The Lesser Evil: The Diaries of Victor Klemperer 1945–59.* Abridged and translated from the German edition by Martin Chalmers. London, 2003.

Klötzer, Sylvia. *Satire und Macht: Film, Zeitung, Kabarett in der DDR.* Cologne, 2006.

Klump, Brigitte. *Das rote Kloster: Als Zögling in der Kaderschmiede des Stasi.* 1st ed., 1978; Munich, 1991.

Klump, Brigitte. *Das rote Kloster: Eine deutsche Erziehung.* Hamburg, 1978.

Knipping, Franz. "Der Mann, der Amerikas berühmteste Frau war: Erinnerung an den Publizisten und Politiker Hermann Budzislawski zum 100. Geburtstag am 11. Februar." *Neues Deutschland,* 10–11 February 2001, 20.

Koebner, Thomas, ed. *Weimars Ende.* Frankfurt am Main, 1982.

Koelbl, Herlinde. *Jüdische Portraits: Photographien und Interviews.* Frankfurt am Main, 1998.

Koenen, Erik, ed. *Die Entdeckung der Kommunikationswissenschaft: 100 Jahre Kommunikationswissenschaftliche Fachtradition in Leipzig. Von der Zeitungskunde zur Kommunikations- und Medienwissenschaft.* Cologne, 2016.

Konrád, György, and Iván Szelényi. *Die Intelligenz auf dem Weg zur Klassenmacht.* Frankfurt am Main, 1978.

Konrád, György, and Iván Szelényi. *The Intellectuals on the Road to Class Power.* Translated by Andrew Arato and Richard E. Allen. New York, 1979.

Kortner, Fritz. *Aller Tage Abend.* Munich, 1976.

Koselleck, Reinhart. "Erinnerungsschleusen und Erfahrungsschichten: Der Einfluß der beiden Weltkriege auf das soziale Bewußtsein." In *Zeitschichten: Studien zur Historik,* 265–84. Frankfurt am Main, 2003.

Koselleck, Reinhart. *Sediments of Time: On Possible Histories.* Translated and edited by Sean Franzel and Stefan-Ludwig Hoffmann. Stanford, CA, 2018.

Koselleck, Reinhart. "Sluices of Memory and Sediments of Experience: The Influence of the Two World Wars on Social Consciousness." In *Sediments of Time: On Possible Histories,* translated and edited by Sean Franzel and Stefan-Ludwig Hoffmann, 207–24. Stanford, CA, 2018.

Koselleck, Reinhart. *Zeitschichten: Studien zur Historik.* Frankfurt am Main, 2003.

Kowalczuk, Ilko-Sascha. *Geist im Dienste der Macht: Hochschulpolitik in der SBZ/DDR 1945 bis 1961.* Berlin, 2003.

Kowalczuk, Ilko-Sascha. *Legitimation eines neuen Staates: Parteiarbeiter an der historischen Front. Geschichtswissenschaft in der SBZ/DDR 1945 bis 1961.* Berlin, 1997.

Kracauer, Siegfried. *Die Angestellten: Aus dem neuesten Deutschland.* Frankfurt am Main, 1930.

Krauss, Marita. "Hans Habe, Ernst Friedländer, Hermann Budzislawski—drei Schicksale." In *Zwischen den Stühlen? Remigranten und Remigration in der deutschen Medienöffentlichkeit der Nachkriegszeit,* edited by Claus-Dieter Krohn and Axel Schildt, 245–66. Hamburg, 2002.

Krohn, Claus-Dieter, Erwin Rotermund, Lutz Winckler, Irmtrud Wojak, and Wulf Koepke, eds. *Jüdische Emigration zwischen Assimilation und Verfolgung, Akkulturation und jüdischer Identität.* Munich, 2001.

Krohn, Claus-Dieter, and Axel Schildt, eds. *Zwischen den Stühlen? Remigranten und Remigration in der deutschen Medienöffentlichkeit der Nachkriegszeit*. Hamburg, 2002.

Krüger, Horst. "Berlin als Treffpunkt von Antikolonialisten und Antiimperialisten in der Zeit der Weimarer Republik." *Bulletin des Arbeitskreises "Zweiter Weltkrieg"* 3–4 (1987): 94–105.

Kuchenbecker, Antje. *Zionismus ohne Zion: Birobidžan. Idee und Geschichte eines jüdischen Staates in Sowjet-Fernost*. Berlin, 2000.

Kuck, Nathanael. "Anti-colonialism in a Post-imperial Environment: The Case of Berlin, 1914–33." *Journal of Contemporary History* 49, no. 1 (2014): 134–59.

Kuhn, Rick. *Hendryk Grossman and the Recovery of Marxism*. Urbana, IL, 2007.

Kuo, Xing-Hu. *Wodka in Sektgläsern: Cocktail meiner liebenswürdigen Stasi-Damen*. Böblingen, 1993.

Kurth, Peter. *American Cassandra: The Life of Dorothy Thompson*. Boston, 1990.

Kurt Tucholsky-Gesellschaft and Ian King, eds. *"Verirrte Bürger"? Kurt Tucholsky und der Weltbühne-Kreis zwischen Bürgertum und Arbeiterbewegung*. Leipzig, 2016.

Kuschel, Franziska, and Dominik Rigoll. "Broschürenkrieg statt Bürgerkrieg: BMI and MdI im deutsch-deutschen Systemkonflikt." In *Hüter der Ordnung: Die Innenministerien in Bonn und Ost-Berlin nach dem Nationalsozialismus*, edited by Frank Bösch and Andreas Wirsching, 355–80. Göttingen, 2018.

Kutsch, Arnulf. "Kommunikation und Medienwissenschaft." In *Geschichte der Universität Leipzig 1409–2009*, vol. 4, pt. 1, edited by Ulrich von Hehl, Uwe John, and Manfred Rudersdorf, 741–59. Leipzig, 2009.

Langkau-Alex, Ursula, and Thomas M. Ruprecht, eds. *Was soll aus Deutschland werden? Der Council for a Democratic Germany in New York, 1944–1945: Aufsätze und Dokumente*. Frankfurt am Main, 1995.

La Roche, Emanuel. *Im Dorf vor der Stadt: Die Baugenossenschaft Neubühl, 1929–2000*. Zürich, 2019.

Laudani, Raffaele, ed. *Im Kampf gegen Nazideutschland: Die Berichte der Frankfurter Schule für den amerikanischen Geheimdienst 1943–1949*. Frankfurt am Main, 2016.

Leins, Claudia. "Robert Eugen Gaupp: Leben und Werk." PhD diss., University of Tübingen, 1991.

Lenger, Friedrich. "Netzwerkanalyse und Biographieforschung—einige Überlegungen." *Bios* 18 (2005): 180–85.

Leo, Annette. "Antifaschismus." In *Erinnerungsorte der DDR*, edited by Martin Sabrow, 30–42. Munich, 2009.

Lethen, Helmut. *Cool Conduct: The Culture of Distance in Weimar Germany*. Translated by Don Reneau. Berkeley, CA, 2002.

Lethen, Helmut. *Verhaltensweisen der Kälte: Lebensversuche zwischen den Weltkriegen*. Frankfurt am Main, 1994.

Liebner, Petra. *Paul Tillich und der Council for a Democratic Germany (1933–1945)*. Frankfurt am Main, 2001.

Linse, Ulrich. *Die entschiedene Jugend 1919–1921: Deutschlands erste revolutionäre Schüler- und Studentenbewegung*. Frankfurt am Main, 1981.

Linse, Ulrich. *Die Kommune der deutschen Jugendbewegung: Ein Versuch zur Überwindung des Klassenkampfes aus dem Geiste der bürgerlichen Utopie. Die kommunistische Siedlung Blankenburg bei Donauwörth 1919/20*. Munich, 1973.

Lipphardt, Veronika. *Biologie der Juden: Jüdische Wissenschaftler über "Rasse" und Vererbung 1900–1935.* Göttingen, 2008.

Loeb, Moritz A. *Berliner Konfektion.* Berlin, 1904.

Loeb, Moritz A. *Um die Zukunft der Berliner Jüdischen Gemeinde.* Berlin, 1930.

Lulay, Birgit. *Eugenik Sozialismus: Biowissenschaftliche Diskurse in den sozialistischen Bewegungen Deutschlands und Großbritanniens um 1900.* Stuttgart, 2021.

Lunkewitz, Bernd F. *Der Aufbau-Verlag und die kriminelle Vereinigung in der SED und der Treuhandanstalt.* Munich, 2021.

Lunkewitz, Bernd F. "Wer schreit denn da?" In *Die Weltbühne im Wirbel der Wende: Eine Zeischrift im Umbruch. Oktober 1989 bis Dezember 1991,* edited by Freundeskreis der Weltbühne e. V., 334–35. Berlin, 1992.

Lyon, James K. *Bertolt Brecht in America.* Princeton, NJ, 1980.

Maas, Liselotte. *Handbuch der deutschen Exilpresse 1933–1945.* Vol. 4, *Die Zeitungen des deutschen Exils in Europa von 1933 bis 1939 in Einzeldarstellungen.* Munich, 1990.

MacKinnon, Janice R., and Stephen R. MacKinnon. *Agnes Smedley: The Life and Times of an American Radical.* Berkeley, CA, 1988.

Madrasch-Groschopp, Ursula. *Die Weltbühne: Porträt einer Zeitschrift.* Augsburg, 1999.

Madrasch-Groschopp, Ursula. "Hans Leonhards Geheimnis." *Ossietzky* 4, no. 2 (2001): 55–59.

Maeke, Lutz. *Carl Steinhoff: Erster DDR-Innenminister. Wandlungen eines bürgerlichen Sozialisten.* Göttingen, 2020.

Mahl, Thomas E. *Desperate Deception: British Covert Operations in the United States, 1939–44.* Washington, DC, 1998.

Mählert, Ulrich, and Gerd-Rüdiger Stephan. *Blaue Hemden—rote Fahnen: Die Geschichte der Freien Deutschen Jugend.* Opladen, 1996.

"'Man brauchte nur ich zu sagen . . .': Chef-Redakteure und eine Leserin im Gespräch. Klaus Polkehn (Wochenpost), Hartmut Berlin (Eulenspiegel), Helmut Reinhardt (Die Weltbühne) und Brigitte Struzyk." In *Zwischen "Mosaik" und "Einheit": Zeitschriften in der DDR,* edited by Simone Barck, Martina Langermann, and Siegfried Lokatis, 116–28. Berlin, 1999.

Manjapra, Kris. *The Age of Entanglement: German and Indian Intellectuals across Empire.* Cambridge, MA, 2016.

Mann, Thomas. *Tagebücher 1940–1943.* Edited by Peter de Mendelssohn. Frankfurt am Main, 1982.

Marchand, Thierry, and Gérard Bourdin. *Exils normands: Les "ressortissants ennemis" internes dans les centres de rassemblement des étrangers de Normandie (1933–1960).* Lisieux, 2014.

Markov, Walter. *Zwiesprache mit dem Jahrhundert.* Documented by Thomas Grimm. Berlin, 1989.

Maron, Monika. *Stille Zeile sechs.* Frankfurt am Main, 1991.

Martin, Benjamin. "The Rise of the Cultural Treaty: Diplomatic Agreements and the International Politics of Culture in the Age of Three Worlds." *International History Review* 44, no. 6 (2022): 1327–46.

Marx, Henry. "Arbeitsverwaltung und Organisation der Kriegswirtschaft." In *Das Reichsarbeitsministerium im Nationalsozialismus: Verwaltung—Politik—Verbrechen,* edited by Alexander Nützenadel, 282–312. Göttingen, 2017.

Maurer Zenck, Claudia, and Peter Petersen, eds. *Lexikon verfolgter Musiker und Musikerinnen der NS-Zeit.* Hamburg, 2010.

Mayer, Hans. *Ein Deutscher auf Widerruf: Erinnerungen.* Vol. 2. Frankfurt am Main, 1988.

Meyen, Michael. "Die Erfindung der Journalistik in der DDR." *Journalistik* 2, no. 1 (2019): 3–32.

Meyen, Michael, and Thomas Wiedemann, eds. *Biographisches Lexikon der Kommunikationswissenschaft.* Cologne, 2017.

Meyen, Michael, and Thomas Wiedemann. "Journalism Professors in the German Democratic Republic: A Collective Biography." *International Journal of Communication* 11 (2017): Feature 1829–56.Meyer, Christian. *Die dunkle Seite der Jugendbewegung: Vom Wandervogel zur Hitlerjugend.* Tübingen, 2013.

Miłosz, Czesław. *The Captive Mind.* Translated by Jane Zielonko. London, 1985.

Miłosz, Czesław. *Verführtes Denken.* Foreword by Karl Jaspers. Cologne, 1955.

Misselwitz, Charlotte. "Als ob wir nichts zu lernen hätten von den linken Juden der DDR . . . : Bemerkungen zu dem Beitrag von Micha Brumlik 'Ostdeutscher Antisemitismus. Wie braun war die DDR?'" *Deutschland Archiv,* 29 April 2020. www.bpb.de/308502.

Mittenzwei, Werner. *Die Intellektuellen: Literatur und Politik in Ostdeutschland von 1945–2000.* Leipzig, 2001.

Mocek, Reinhard. *Biologie und soziale Befreiung: Zur Geschichte des Biologismus und der Rassenhygiene in der Arbeiterbewegung.* Frankfurt am Main, 2002.

Morgenstern, Andreas. "Hier ruft die Schwarze Front! Der Weg des Rundfunkpioniers Rudolf Formis." *Rundfunk und Geschichte* 42, no. 3–4 (2016): 15–23.

Morris, Leslie, and Jack Zipes, eds. *Unlikely History: The Changing German-Jewish Symbiosis, 1945–2000.* New York, 2002.

Mottier, Véronique. "Eugenics and the State: Policy-Making in Comparative Perspective." In *The Oxford Handbook of the History of Eugenics,* edited by Alison Bashford and Philippa Levine, 134–53. Oxford, 2010.

Müller, Reinhard. *Menschenfalle Moskau: Exil und stalinistische Verfolgung.* Hamburg, 2001.

Müller, Tim B. *Krieger und Gelehrte: Herbert Marcuse und die Denksysteme im Kalten Krieg.* Hamburg, 2010.

Münzner, Daniel. *Kurt Hiller: Der Intellektuelle als Außenseiter.* Göttingen, 2015.

Nannini, Clémence. "L'internement des indésirables pendant la seconde guerre mondiale: Aspects du phénomène dans les Basses-Alpes. Mémoire de 4ème année." Master's thesis, Université de Lyon–Université Lumière Lyon 2, Lyon, 2017.

Natonek, Hans. *In Search of Myself.* New York, 1943.

Nehring, Christopher. "Von DDR-Millionären, Schmugglern und Raubkunst." *Gerbergasse 18: Thüringer Vierteljahrsschrift für Zeitgeschichte und Politik* 1 (2018): 34–39.

Neubauer, John, and Borbála Zsuzsanna Török, eds. *The Exile and Return of Writers from East-Central Europe: A Compendium.* New York, 2009.

Neuhaus, Manfred, and Helmut Seidel, eds. *Universität im Aufbruch—Leipzig 1945–1956: Beiträge des siebenten Walter-Markov-Kolloquium.* Leipzig, 2002.

Niethammer, Lutz. *Der "gesäuberte" Antifaschismus: Die SED und die roten Kapos von Buchenwald.* Berlin, 1994.

Nützenadel, Alexander, ed. *Das Reichsarbeitsministerium im Nationalsozialismus: Verwaltung—Politik—Verbrechen.* Göttingen, 2017.

Ó Dochartaigh, Pól, and Alexander Stephan, eds. *Refuge and Reality: Feuchtwanger and the European Émigrés in California.* New York, 2005.

Ostow, Robin. "Being Jewish in the Other Germany: An Interview with Thomas Eckert." *New German Critique* 38 (1986): 73–87.

Ostow, Robin, ed. *Jews in Contemporary East Germany: The Children of Moses in the Land of Marx.* Basingstoke, 1989.

Oswalt, Stefanie. *Siegfried Jacobsohn: Ein Leben für die Weltbühne. Eine Berliner Biographie.* 2nd ed. Gerlingen, 2002.

Otto, Martin. "Carl Sartorius." In *Neue Deutsche Biographie*, 22:440–41. Berlin, 2005.

Paetel, Karl O. "Eine Grenze. Eine Grenze?" In *Verbannung: Aufzeichnungen deutscher Schriftsteller im Exil*, edited by Egon Schwarz and Matthias Wegner, 108–15. Hamburg, 1964.

Palmier, Jean-Michel. *Weimar in Exile: The Antifascist Emigration in Europe and America.* New York, 2017.

Parker, Stephen. *Bertolt Brecht: A Literary Life.* London, 2014.

Parker, Stephen. *Bertolt Brecht: Eine Biographie.* Frankfurt am Main, 2018.

Parker, Stephen. "Fortsetzung folgt: Sinn und Form unter Wilhelm Girnius (1963–1981)." In *Zwischen "Mosaik" und "Einheit": Zeitschriften in der DDR*, edited by Simone Barck, Martina Langermann, and Siegfried Lokatis, 346–59. Berlin, 1999.

Pasdzierny, Matthias. "Ernst Engel." In *Lexikon verfolgter Musiker und Musikerinnen der NS-Zeit*, edited by Claudia Maurer Zenck and Peter Petersen. Hamburg, 2010. https://www.lexm.uni-hamburg.de/object/lexm_lexmperson_00001808.

Paul, Diane B. *The Politics of Heredity: Essays on Eugenics, Biomedicine, and the Nature-Nurture Debate.* Albany, NY, 1998.

Peters, Susanne. *William S. Schlamm: Ideologischer Grenzgänger im 20. Jahrhundert.* Berlin, 2013.

Peterson, Walter F. *The Berlin Liberal Press in Exile: A History of the Pariser Tagblatt—Pariser Tageszeitung 1933–1940.* Tübingen, 1987.

Petersson, Fredrik. "Imperialism and the Communist International." *Journal of Labor and Society* 20, no. 1 (2017): 23–42.

Pieper, Josef. *Noch wusste es niemand: Autobiographische Aufzeichnungen 1904–1945.* Munich, 1976.

Pike, David. *German Writers in Soviet Exile, 1933–1945.* Chapel Hill, NC, 1982.

Poerschke, Hans. "Anfänge marxistischer Journalistik—zwischen wissenschaftlichem Anspruch und Parteikonzept." In *Universität im Aufbruch—Leipzig 1945–1956: Beiträge des siebenten Walter-Markov-Kolloquiums*, edited by Manfred Neuhaus and Helmut Seidel, 134–39. Leipzig, 2002.

Prager, Katharina. "Amerika ist trotz allem großartig—die transkulturellen Leben und autobiographischen Praktiken der Familie Viertel." *Österreichische Zeitschrift für Geschichtswissenschaften* 29, no. 3 (2018): 37–57.

Price, Ruth. *The Lives of Agnes Smedley.* Oxford, 2005.

Prokop, Siegfried. "Ernst Bloch und Wolfgang Harich im Jahre 1956." *UTOPIE kreativ* 184 (February 2006): 121–24.

Quetting, Michael. *Journalistin und Organisatorin, Friedensaktivistin und Nazigegnerin, die Nobelpreismacherin Milly Zirker 1888–1971.* Sankt Ingbert, 2007.

Rabinbach, Anton. "Staging Antifascism: *The Brown Book of the Reichstag Fire and Hitler Terror.*" *New German Critique* 35, no. 1 (2008): 97–126.

Rabinbach, Anton. "Von Hollywood an den Galgen: Die Verfolgung und Ermordung des Otto Katz." *Zeitschrift für Ideengeschichte* 2, no. 1 (2008): 24–36.

Radkau, Joachim. *Die deutsche Emigration in den USA: Ihr Einfluß auf die amerikanische Europapolitik 1933–1945.* Gütersloh, 1971.

Radkau, Joachim. "Die *Weltbühne* als falscher Prophet? Prognostische Versuche gegenüber dem Nationalsozialismus." In *Weimars Ende*, edited by Thomas Koebner, 57–79. Frankfurt am Main, 1982.

Ragg, Albrecht. "The German Socialist Emigration in the United States, 1933 to 1945." PhD diss., Loyola University, Chicago, 1973.

Regler, Gustav. *Das Ohr des Malchus: Eine Lebensgeschichte.* Frankfurt am Main, 1975.

Regler, Gustav. *The Owl of Minerva: The Autobiography of Gustav Regler.* Translated by Norman Denny. London, 1959.

"Reichenbach, Bernhard." In *Biographisches Handbuch der deutschsprachigen Emigration nach 1933–1945.* Vol. 1, *Politik, Wirtschaft, Öffentliches Leben*, edited by Werner Röder and Herbert A. Strauss, 591. Munich, 1999.

Röder, Werner, and Herbert A. Strauss, eds. *International Biographical Dictionary of Central European Emigrés 1933–1945.* Vol. 2/1. Munich, 1983.

Röhl, Ernst. *Der Rat der Spötter: Das Kabarett des Peter Sodann.* Cologne, 2002.

Rohlén-Wohlgemuth, Hilde. "Die Familie Alexander Levy in Eschwege." *Eschweger Geschichtsblätter* 5 (1994): 51–54.

Röhr, Karl-Heinz. "Um journalistische Qualität geht es immer und überall." In *Biografisches Lexikon der Kommunikationswissenschaft*, edited by Michael Meyen and Thomas Wiedemann. Cologne, 2015. http://blexkom.halemverlag.de/karl-heinz-roehr/.

Röhr, Karl-Heinz, and Willy Walther. "Hermann Budzislawski." In *Journalismus und Gesellschaft: Festschrift. Hermann Budzislawski zum 65. Geburtstag*, edited by Fakultät für Journalistik der Karl-Marx-Universität Leipzig, 9–22. Leipzig, 1966.

Runge, Irene. "A Newcomer to the Jewish Community." In *Jews in Contemporary East Germany: The Children of Moses in the Land of Marx*, edited by Robin Ostow, 43–52. Basingstoke, 1989.

Ruprecht, Thomas Michael. *Felix Boenheim: Arzt, Politiker, Historiker. Eine Biographie.* Hildesheim, 1992.

Ryan, James G. *Earl Browder: The Failure of American Communism.* Tuscaloosa, AL, 1997.

Sabrow, Martin, ed. *Erinnerungsorte der DDR.* Munich, 2009.

Sabrow, Martin. "Memoiren der Macht: Gedachte Geschichte der Autobiographik kommunistischer Parteifunktionäre." In *Geschichte denken: Perspektiven auf die Geschichtsschreibung heute*, edited by Michael Wildt, 186–207. Göttingen, 2014.

Sahl, Hans. "Memoiren eines Moralisten." In *Memoiren eines Moralisten—das Exil im Exil*, 7–227. Munich, 2008.

Sahl, Hans. *Memoiren eines Moralisten—das Exil im Exil.* Munich, 2008.

Sanders, Marion K. *Dorothy Thompson: A Legend in Her Time.* Boston, 1973.

Sattig, Esther. "Jüdisches Leben in der DDR als individuelle Erfahrung: Im Gespräch mit Salomea Genin, Irene Runge, Renate und Peter Kirchner." In *Antisemitismus in der DDR: Manifestationen und Folgen des Feindbildes Israel*, edited by Wolfgang Benz, 158–84. Berlin, 2018.

Sauerteig, Lutz. "Von Hodann zu Amendt: Vorstellungen von sexueller 'Liberalisierung,' kindlicher Sexualität und Geschlechterverhältnissen in der Sexualerziehung um 1900 und um 1968." In *Lebensreform um 1900 und Alternativmilieu um 1980: Kontinuitäten und Brüche im Milieu der gesellschaftlichen Selbstreflexion im frühen und späten 20. Jahrhundert*, edited by Detlef Siegfried and David Templin, 213–51. Göttingen, 2019.

Saurer, Martin. "Liesl Frank, Charlotte Dieterle and the European Film Fund." PhD diss., University of Warwick, 2010.

Sayner, Joanne. *Reframing Antifascism: Memory, Genre and the Life Writings of Greta Kuckhoff.* Basingstoke, 2014.

Schaad, Martin. *Die fabelhaften Bekenntnisse des Genossen Alfred Kurella.* Hamburg, 2014.

Scheer, Maximilian. *Ein unruhiges Leben: Autobiographie.* Berlin, 1975.

Schemmert, Christian. "Beobachten und Beobachtetwerden in der Welt totaler Mitgliedschaft: Journalismusforscher im Disziplinarapparat der SED." Master's thesis, Bielefeld University, 2015.

Schemmert, Christian, and Daniel Siemens. "Die Leipziger Journalistenausbildung in der Ära Ulbricht." *Vierteljahrshefte für Zeitgeschichte* 61, no. 2 (2013): 201–37.

Schildt, Axel. *Medien-Intellektuelle in der Bundesrepublik.* Edited by Gabriele Kandzora and Detlef Siegfried. Göttingen, 2020.

Schiller, Dieter. *Der Traum von Hitlers Sturz: Studien zur deutschen Exilliteratur 1933–1945.* Frankfurt am Main, 2010.

Schiller, Dieter. "Die 'Weltbühne' im Prager Exil." In *Der Traum von Hitlers Sturz: Studien zur deutschen Exilliteratur 1933–1945*, 271–83. Frankfurt am Main, 2010.

Schiller, Dieter. "'Wir konnten nicht mit dem K-Unglück rechnen . . .': Der Verlag 10. Mai in Paris 1938/39." In *Der Traum von Hitlers Sturz: Studien zur deutschen Exilliteratur 1933–1945*, 181–98. Frankfurt am Main, 2010.

Schivelbusch, Wolfgang. *Vor dem Vorhang: Das geistige Berlin 1945–1948.* Munich, 1995.

Schlosser, Nicholas J. "The Berlin Radio War: Broadcasting in Cold War Berlin and the Shaping of Political Culture in Divided Germany, 1945–1961." PhD diss., University of Maryland, 2008.

Schmidt, Siegfried. "Hermann Budzislawski und die Leipziger Journalistik." In *Biografisches Lexikon der Kommunikationswissenschaft*, edited by Michael Meyen and Thomas Wiedemann. Cologne, 2017. http://blexkom.halemverlag.de/schmidt-budzislawski/.

Schönhoven, Klaus, and Dietrich Staritz, eds. *Sozialismus und Kommunismus im Wandel: Hermann Weber zum 65. Geburtstag.* Cologne, 1993.

Schuetze-Coburn, Marje. "Feuchtwanger's Relocation to Southern California: Frustration & Successes." In *Refuge and Reality: Feuchtwanger and the European Émigrés in California*, edited by Pól Ó Dochartaigh and Alexander Stephan, 101–8. New York, 2005.

Schumacher, Ernst. *Mein Brecht: Erinnerungen 1943 bis 1956.* Berlin, 2006.

Schwander, Martin. *Paul Robeson: Eine Biographie*. Essen, 1998.

Schwarz, Egon, and Matthias Wegner, eds. *Verbannung: Aufzeichnungen deutscher Schriftsteller im Exil*. Hamburg, 1964.

Schwartz, Michael. *Sozialistische Eugenik: Eugenische Sozialtechnologien in Diskurs und Politik der deutschen Sozialdemokratie 1890–1933*. Münster, 1992.

Seebacher-Brandt, Brigitte. "Schwindel mit dem Etikett: Wem gehört das Erbe der Neinsager?" *FAZ Magazin*, no. 691, 28 May 1993, 36.

Siati, Giuseppe de, and Thies Ziemke, eds. *Prag-Moskau: Briefe von und an Wieland Herzfelde 1933–1938*. Kiel, 1991.

Siegfried, Detlef, and David Templin, eds. *Lebensreform um 1900 und Alternativmilieu um 1980: Kontinuitäten und Brüche im Milieu der gesellschaftlichen Selbstreflexion im frühen und späten 20. Jahrhundert*. Göttingen, 2019.

Siemens, Daniel. "Elusive Security in the GDR: Remigrants from the West at the Faculty of Journalism in Leipzig, 1945–1961." *Central Europe* 11, no. 1 (2013): 23–45.

Siemens, Daniel. "Konzepte des nationaljüdischen Körpers in der frühen Weimarer Republic." *Zeitschrift für Geschichtswissenschaft* 56 (2008): 30–54.

Siemens, Daniel. "Kühle Romantiker: Zum Geschichtsverständnis der 'jungen Generation' in der Weimarer Republik." In *Die Kunst der Geschichte: Historiographie, Ästhetik, Erzählung*, edited by Martin Baumeister, Moritz Föllmer, and Philipp Müller, 189–214. Göttingen, 2009.

Siemens, Daniel. *Metropole und Verbrechen: Die Gerichtsreportage in Berlin, Paris und Chicago 1919–1933*. Stuttgart, 2007.

Sinn, Andrea A. "Returning to Stay? Jews in East and West Germany after the Holocaust." *Central European History* 53 (2020): 393–413.

Später, Jörg. *Siegfried Kracauer: Eine Biographie*. Frankfurt am Main, 2016.

Spiru, Basil. *Giftmischer: Beiträge zur Entwicklungsgeschichte der zeitgenössischen bürgerlichen Journalistik*. Berlin, 1960.

Staritz, Dietrich. "Partei, Intellektuelle, Parteiintellektuelle: Die Intellektuellen im Kalkül der frühen SED." In *Sozialismus und Kommunismus im Wandel: Hermann Weber zum 65. Geburtstag*, edited by Klaus Schönhoven and Dietrich Staritz, 378–98. Cologne, 1993.

Stock, Ernst, and Karl Walcher. *Jacob Walcher (1887–1970): Gewerkschafter und Revolutionär zwischen Berlin, Paris und New York*. Berlin, 1998.

Stolz, Otto, ed. *Die wahre Weltbühne: Carl v. Ossietzky + Kurt Tucholsky über Kommunismus—Sowjet-Rußland-Marxismus*. West-Berlin, 1948.

Stöss, Richard. "Geschichte des Rechtsextremismus." 12 June 2006. https://www.bpb.de/politik/extremismus/rechtsextremismus/41907/geschichte-des-rechtsextremismus.

Studer, Brigitte. *Reisende der Weltrevolution: Eine Globalgeschichte der Kommunistischen Internationale*. Berlin, 2020.

Styles, William. "The World Federation of Scientific Workers: A Case Study of a Soviet Front Organization, 1946–1964." *Intelligence and National Security* 33, no. 1 (2018): 116–29.

Tellkamp, Uwe. *Die Schwebebahn: Dresdner Erkundungen*. Berlin, 2010.

Teuber, Toralf. *Ein Stratege im Exil: Hermann Budzislawski und die "Neue Weltbühne."* Frankfurt am Main, 2004.

Thompson, Dorothy. *"I Saw Hitler!"* New York, 1932.

Thompson, Dorothy. *Listen, Hans.* Boston, 1942.

Tiemann, Dieter. "Kurt Tucholsky und *Die Weltbühne.*" In *Le milieu intellectual de gauche en Allemagne, sa presse et ses réseaux (1890–1960) / Das linke Intellektuellenmilieu in Deutschland, seine Presse und seine Netzwerke (1890–1960),* edited by Manfred Grunewald, 269–85. Bern, 2002.

Tippelskirch, Karina von. "Central Europe in Vermont: German Exile Writers and the American Journalist Dorothy Thompson." In *Networks of Refugees from Nazi-Germany: Continuities, Reorientation, and Collaboration in Exile,* edited by Helga Schreckenberger, 142–60. Leiden, 2016.

Tippelskirch, Karina von. *Dorothy Thompson and German Writers in Defense of Democracy.* New York, 2018.

Toller, Ernst. *Eine Jugend in Deutschland.* Vol. 4 of *Gesammelte Werke.* Munich, 1978.

Trapp, Frithjof. "Konfliktlinien im linksintellektuellen Milieu: Die Ossietzky-Kampagne des frühen Vorkriegsexils." In *Le milieu intellectual de gauche en Allemagne, sa presse et ses réseaux (1890–1960) / Das linke Intellektuellenmilieu in Deutschland, seine Presse und seine Netzwerke (1890–1960),* edited by Michael Grunewald, 479–98. Bern, 2002.

Traumann, Gudrun. *Journalistik in der DDR: Sozialistische Journalistik und Journalistenausbildung an der Karl-Marx-Universität Leipzig.* Munich-Pullach, 1971.

Traussnig, Florian. *Geistiger Widerstand von außen: Österreicher in US-Propagandainstitutionen im Zweiten Weltkrieg.* Vienna, 2017.

Tucholsky, Kurt. *Ausgewählte Briefe 1913–1935.* Edited by Mary Gerold-Tucholsky and Fritz J. Raddatz. Reinbek bei Hamburg, 1962.

Tucholsky, Kurt. *Deutschland, Deutschland über alles.* Berlin, 1929.

Ulbrich, Claudia, Hans Medick, and Angelika Schaser, eds. *Selbstzeugnis und Person: Transkulturelle Perspektiven.* Cologne, 2012.

Ulbrich, Claudia, Hans Medick, and Angelika Schaser. "Selbstzeugnis und Person: Transkulturelle Perspektiven." In *Selbstzeugnis und Person: Transkulturelle Perspektiven,* edited by Claudia Ulbrich, Hans Medick, and Angelika Schaser, 1–19. Cologne, 2012.

Veselá-Ducháčková, Gabriela. "Hermann Budzislawski." In *Exil und Asyl: Antifaschistische deutsche Literatur in der Tschechoslowakei 1933–1938,* edited by Autorenkollektiv unter Leitung von Miroslav Beck und Jiři Vesely, 157–64. Berlin, 1981.

Victor, Walther. *Kehre über die Berge: Eine Autobiographie.* Berlin, 1982.

Viertel, Salka. *Das unbelehrbare Herz.* Hamburg, 1970.

Villain, Jean (Marcel Brun). *Bitte nicht stürzen! Wie der DDR "Profil" abhanden kam und weitere Zeitungsmacher-Geschichten aus Deutsch-Fernost.* Rostock, 2004.

Voigt, Johannes H. *Die Indienpolitik der DDR: Von den Anfängen bis zur Anerkennung (1952–1972).* Cologne, 2008.

Voigts, Manfred. *Oskar Goldberg: Der mythische Experimentalwissenschaftler—ein verdrängtes Kapitel jüdischer Geschichte.* Berlin, 1992.

Waibel, Harry. *Die braune Saat: Antisemitismus und Neonazismus in der DDR.* Stuttgart, 2017.

Walter, Hans-Albert. *Deutsche Exilliteratur 1933–1950.* Vol. 3, *Internierung, Flucht und Lebensbedingungen im Zweiten Weltkrieg.* Stuttgart, 1988.

Walter, Hans-Albert. *Deutsche Exilliteratur 1933–1950.* Vol. 4, *Exilpresse.* Stuttgart, 1978.

Walter, Hans-Albert. *Gib dem Herrn die Hand, er ist ein Flüchtling.* Düsseldorf, 2016.

Walter, Helmut. "Beckerath, Herbert von." In *Biographisches Handbuch der deutschsprachigen wirtschaftswissenschaftlichen Emigration nach 1933*, vol. 1, *Adler–Lehmann*, edited by Harald Hagemann and Claus-Dieter Krohn, 34–36. Munich, 1999.

Walter, Hilde. "Brief an eine Freundin, New York, 11. März 1941." In *Verbannung: Aufzeichnungen deutscher Schriftsteller im Exil*, edited by Egon Schwarz and Matthias Wegner, 92–96. Hamburg, 1964.

Walther, Joachim. *Sicherungsbereich Literatur: Schriftsteller und Staatssicherheit in der Deutschen Demokratischen Republik.* Berlin, 1996.

Walther, Willy. "Hermann Budzislawski." In *Namhafte Hochschullehrer der Karl-Marx-Universität Leipzig*, 1:62–71. Leipzig, 1982.

Waltz, William J. *Of Writers and Workers: The Movement of Writing Workers in East Germany.* Oxford, 2018.

Weber, Hermann. "Rosenfeld, Kurt." In *Neue Deutsche Biographie*, 22:66–67. Berlin, 2005.

Weber, Hermann, and Dietrich Staritz, eds. *Kommunisten verfolgen Kommunisten: Stalinistischer Terror und "Säuberungen" in den kommunistischen Parteien Europas seit den dreißiger Jahren.* Berlin, 1993.

Weber, Horst, and Stefan Drees. *Quellen zur Geschichte emigrierter Musiker 1933–1950 / Sources Relating to the History of Émigré Musicians 1933–1950.* Vol. 2. Munich, 2005.

Wegewitz, Markus. "Kultivierter Antifaschismus: Nicolaas Rost und der lange Kampf gegen den Nationalsozialismus 1919–1967." PhD diss., Friedrich Schiller University, Jena, 2021.

Wehner, Jens. *Kulturpolitik und Volksfront: Ein Beitrag zur Geschichte der Sowjetischen Besatzungszone Deutschlands 1945–1949.* 2 vols. Frankfurt am Main, 1992.

Weinberg, Robert. *Stalin's Forgotten Zion: Birobidzhan and the Making of a Soviet Jewish Homeland; An Illustrated History, 1928–1996.* Berkeley, CA, 1998.

Weipert, Matthias, and Andreas Wirsching, eds. *Vernunftrepublikanismus in der Weimarer Politik: Politik, Literatur, Wissenschaft.* Stuttgart, 2008.

Werner, Michael, and Bénédicte Zimmermann. "Vergleich, Transfer, Verflechtung: Der Ansatz der Histoire croisée und die Herausforderung des Transnationalen." *Geschichte und Gesellschaft* 28 (2002): 607–36.

Wilbrandt, Robert. *Karl Marx: Versuch einer Einführung.* Leipzig, 1918.

Wilbrandt, Robert. *Sind die Sozialisten sozialistisch genug?* Berlin, 1919.

Wilbrandt, Robert. *Sozialismus.* Jena, 1919.

Wildt, Michael. "Die Angst vor dem Volk: Ernst Fraenkel in der deutschen Nachkriegsgesellschaft." In *"Ich staune, dass Sie in dieser Luft atmen können": Jüdische Intellektuelle in Deutschland nach 1945*, edited by Monika Boll and Raphael Gross, 317–44. Frankfurt am Main, 2013.

Wildt, Michael, ed. *Geschichte denken: Perspektiven auf die Geschichtsschreibung heute.* Göttingen, 2014.

Willer, Stefan. "Kulturelles Erbe: Tradieren und Konservieren in der Moderne." In *Erbe: Übertragungskonzepte zwischen Natur und Kultur*, edited by Stefan Willer, Sigrid Weigel, and Bernhard Jussen, 160–201. Berlin, 2013.

Willer, Stefan, Sigrid Weigel, and Bernhard Jussen, eds. *Erbe: Übertragungskonzepte zwischen Natur und Kultur.* Berlin, 2013.

Winder, Robert. *Bloody Foreigners: The Story of Immigration to Britain.* London, 2013.

Wolf, Christa. *The Quest for Christa T.* Translated by Christopher Middleton. New York, 1979.

Wolff, Frank. "Die unsichtbare Ruine des Kalten Kriegs: Die 'Mauer in den Köpfen' 30 Jahre nach dem Mauerfall." *Geschichte der Gegenwart*, 15 September 2019. https://geschichtedergegenwart.ch/die-unsichtbare-ruine-des-kalten-kriegs-die-mauer-in-den-koepfen-30-jahre-nach-dem-mauerfall/.

Zahlmann, Stefan. "Medien in der DDR: Medienproduktion und Medienrezeption als kulturelle Praktiken." In *Wie im Westen, nur anders: Medien in der DDR*, edited by Stefan Zahlmann, 9–33. Berlin, 2010.

Zahlmann, Stefan, ed. *Wie im Westen, nur anders: Medien in der DDR.* Berlin, 2010.

Zierlewagen, Marc. "Sondheimer, Albert." In *Frankfurter Personenlexikon.* https://frankfurter-personenlexikon.de/node/3822.

Zimmer, Andreas. *Der Kulturbund in der SBZ und in der DDR: Eine ostdeutsche Kulturbewegung im Wandel der Zeit zwischen 1945 und 1990.* Wiesbaden, 2019.

Zuckmayer, Carl. *A Part of Myself.* Translated by Richard Winston and Clara Winston. London, 1970.

Zuckmayer, Carl. *Als wär's ein Stück von mir: Horen der Freundschaft.* Frankfurt am Main, 1967.

Zwerenz, Gerhard. *Kurt Tucholsky: Biographie eines guten Deutschen.* Gütersloh, 1979.

Interviews with Contemporary Witnesses

Deborah Vietor-Engländer, 14 December 2014 (by telephone)

Irene Runge, 17 August 2018 (by telephone)

Doris Eisermann and Barbara Felsmann, 18 December 2018 (in Berlin, in person)

Klaus G. Saur, 19 February 2019 (by telephone)

Barbara Honigmann, 8 April 2019 (by telephone)

Christian Booß, Berlin, 15 May 2019 (by telephone)

Klaus Höpcke, 28 October 2019 (in Berlin, in person)

Karl-Heinz Röhr and Gottfried Braun, 10 November 2020 (in Leipzig, in person)

Matthias Biskupek, 27 January 2021 (by telephone)

Matthias Wedel, 28 January 2021 (by telephone)

I also interviewed members of the Eckert family, but they prefer not to be mentioned by name in this book.

Index

Abusch, Alexander, 89, 93

Ackermann, Anton, 74

aid organizations: American Guild for German Cultural Freedom, 88, 95, 102–3, 105–6; American Rescue Committee, 97–98, 102; Emergency Committee in Aid of Displaced Foreign Scholars, 107; French League for the Defense of Human and Citizens' Rights, 87; Hebrew Immigrant Aid Society, 103; HICEM (acronym covering three Jewish migration associations), 102–3, 170; Jewish Labor Committee, 97; Joint Distribution Committee, 128; League for Human Rights, 71, 92; National Refugee Council (USA), 110

Akademie der Künste (Academy of the Arts), Berlin, 8, 235

Alexan, Georg Friedrich (Georg Kupfermann), 138, 148–49

Alexandrovsky, Sergei, 80

Alliez (Major), 89

Anderson, Edith, 210

anti-colonialism and anti-Imperialism, 31–33, 38, 169–70, 178–79

anti-fascism, 5–6, 8, 45, 47–50, 53, 63, 65, 70, 74, 84, 88, 93, 112–14, 127–28, 137, 142, 148, 168, 180, 197, 206, 211, 215, 219, 224, 241

antisemitism, 25, 51–52, 89, 107, 150, 159, 170, 213, 216–17

Apfel, Alfred, 42, 92–93

Arendt, Hannah, 65, 215

Arid, Albert, 45

Artists' Colony Berlin-Wilmersdorf, 38, 44–45

Aryanization, 143–44

Ascoli, Max, 114

associations, leagues and voluntary organizations: Action Committee of German Oppositionists, Paris, 65, 83, 85; Anti-Fascist Defense League, 45; League Against Colonial Oppression, 31; League Against Imperialism, 32; League for the Defense of the Negro Race, 38; Wandervogel movement, 19, 35; Workers' International Relief (IAH), 45; World Federation of Scientific Workers, 181; World Peace Council, 181, 204

Atlantic Charter, 112–13

Aufhäuser, Siegfried, 70, 74, 124, 126–27

Aufricht, Ernst Josef, 108

autobiography, 21, 30, 40, 44, 108, 115, 224; memory and, 16, 217; narratives and genre of, 5, 213, 225; publishing plans for an, 107, 119, 217, 225

George L. Mosse Series in the History of European Culture,
Sexuality, and Ideas

Steven E. Aschheim, Annette Becker, Skye Doney,
and David J. Sorkin
Series Editors

Of God and Gods: Egypt, Israel, and the Rise of Monotheism
Jan Assmann

*Messengers of Disaster: Raphael Lemkin, Jan Karski, and
Twentieth-Century Genocides*
Annette Becker; translated by Käthe Roth

*Respectability and Violence: Military Values, Masculine Honor, and
Italy's Road to Mass Death*
Lorenzo Benadusi; translated by Zakiya Hanafi

The Enemy of the New Man: Homosexuality in Fascist Italy
Lorenzo Benadusi; translated by Suzanne Dingee and Jennifer Pudney

*The Holocaust and the West German Historians: Historical Interpretation and
Autobiographical Memory*
Nicolas Berg; translated and edited by Joel Golb

Surreal Geographies: A New History of Holocaust Consciousness
Kathryn L. Brackney

Collected Memories: Holocaust History and Postwar Testimony
Christopher R. Browning

Contemporary Europe in the Historical Imagination
Edited by Darcy Buerkle and Skye Doney

Cataclysms: A History of the Twentieth Century from Europe's Edge
Dan Diner; translated by William Templer with Joel Golb

Fascination with the Persecutor: George L. Mosse and the Catastrophe of Modern Man
EMILIO GENTILE; TRANSLATED BY JOHN AND ANNE C. TEDESCHI

La Grande Italia: The Myth of the Nation in the Twentieth Century
EMILIO GENTILE; TRANSLATED BY SUZANNE DINGEE AND JENNIFER PUDNEY

The Invisible Jewish Budapest: Metropolitan Culture at the Fin de Siècle
MARY GLUCK

Carl Schmitt and the Jews: The "Jewish Question," the Holocaust, and German Legal Theory
RAPHAEL GROSS; TRANSLATED BY JOEL GOLB

Unlearning Eugenics: Sexuality, Reproduction, and Disability in Post-Nazi Europe
DAGMAR HERZOG

Reason After Its Eclipse: On Late Critical Theory
MARTIN JAY

Rescue and Remembrance: Imagining the German Collective After Nazism
KOBI KABALEK

Some Measure of Justice: The Holocaust Era Restitution Campaign of the 1990s
MICHAEL R. MARRUS

The Best Weapon for Peace: Maria Montessori, Education, and Children's Rights
ERICA MORETTI

Confronting History: A Memoir
GEORGE L. MOSSE

Nazi Culture: Intellectual, Cultural, and Social Life in the Third Reich
GEORGE L. MOSSE

Last Days of Theresienstadt
EVA NOACK-MOSSE; TRANSLATED BY SKYE DONEY AND BIRUTĖ CIPLIJAUSKAITĖ

What History Tells: George L. Mosse and the Culture of Modern Europe
EDITED BY STANLEY G. PAYNE, DAVID J. SORKIN, AND JOHN S. TORTORICE